T

2

2

1

MACMILLAN MODERN NOVELISTS

General Editor: Norman Page

MACMILLAN MODERN NOVELISTS

Published titles

ALBERT CAMUS   Philip Thody
JOSEPH CONRAD   Owen Knowles
FYODOR DOSTOEVSKY   Peter Conradi
WILLIAM FAULKNER   David Dowling
E. M. FORSTER   Norman Page
WILLIAM GOLDING   James Gindin
GRAHAM GREENE   Neil McEwan
HENRY JAMES   Alan Bellringer
DORIS LESSING   Ruth Whittaker
MARCEL PROUST   Philip Thody
BARBARA PYM   Michael Cotsell
SIX WOMEN NOVELISTS   Merryn Williams
JOHN UPDIKE   Judie Newman
EVELYN WAUGH   Jacqueline McDonnell
H. G. WELLS   Michael Draper

Forthcoming titles

F. SCOTT FITZGERALD   John S. Whitley
GUSTAVE FLAUBERT   David Roe
JOHN FOWLES   Simon Gatrell
JAMES JOYCE   Richard Brown
D. H. LAWRENCE   G. M. Hyde
MALCOLM LOWRY   Tony Bareham
GEORGE ORWELL   Valerie Meyers
MURIEL SPARK   Norman Page
GERTRUDE STEIN   Shirley Neuman
VIRGINIA WOOLF   Edward Bishop

MACMILLAN MODERN NOVELISTS
WILLIAM FAULKNER

David Dowling

MACMILLAN

First published 1989

Published by
MACMILLAN EDUCATION LTD
Houndmills, Basingstoke, Hampshire RG21 2XS
and London
Companies and representatives
throughout the world

Typeset by Wessex Typesetters
(Division of The Eastern Press Ltd)
Frome, Somerset

Printed in China

Dowling, David, 1950-
William Faulkner.—(Macmillan modern
novelists).
1. Fiction in English. American writers.
Faulkner, William. Critical studies
I. Title
813'.52
ISBN 0-333-42855-2
ISBN 0-333-42856-0 Pbk

Contents

Acknowledgments

The author and publishers thank the following for permission
to use copyright material: 'The History of Yoknapatawpha
County' from *Crowell's Handbook of Faulkner*: A Complete Guide
to the Books of William Faulkner by Dorothy Tuck copyright
© 1964 by Harper and Row, Publishers, Inc. Reprinted by
permission of Harper and Row, Publishers, Inc and Chatto and
Windus Ltd/The Hogarth Press. Farrar, Strauss & Giroux for
the genealogical tables from Edmund Volpe's *A Reader's Guide to
William Faulkner*. etc. . . .

'You seem to be spending too much time thinking about Bill Faulkner.'
C. Israel, 'Encounter with William Faulkner',
Dialogue 2, 2 (1969) 113.

General Editor's Preface

The death of the novel has often been announced, and part of the secret of its obstinate vitality must be its capacity for growth, adaptation, self-renewal and even self-transformation; like some vigorous organism in a speeded-up Darwinian ecosystem, it adapts itself quickly to a changing world. War and revolution, economic crisis and social change, radically new ideologies such as Marxism and Freudianism, have made this century unprecedented in human history in the speed and extent of change, but the novel has shown an extraordinary capacity to find new forms and techniques and to accommodate new ideas and conceptions of human nature and human experience, and even to take up new positions on the nature of fiction itself.

In the generations immediately preceding and following 1914, the novel underwent a radical redefinition of its nature and possibilities. The present series of monographs is devoted to the novelists who created the modern novel and to those who, in their turn, either continued and extended, or reacted against and rejected, the traditions established during that period of intense exploration and experiment. It includes a number of those who lived and wrote in the nineteenth century but whose innovative contribution to the art of fiction makes it impossible to ignore them in any account of the origins of the modern novel; it also includes the so-called 'modernists' and those who in the mid- and late-twentieth century have emerged as outstanding practitioners of this genre. The scope is, inevitably, international; not only, in the migratory and exile-haunted world of our century, do writers refuse to heed national frontiers – 'English' literature lays claim to Conrad the Pole, Henry James the American, and Joyce the Irishman – but geniuses such as Flaubert, Dostoevski and Kafka have had an influence on the fiction of many nations.

Each volume in the series is intended to provide an introduction to the fiction of the writer concerned, both for those approaching him or her for the first time and for those who are already familiar with some parts of the achievement in question and now wish to place it in the context of the total *oeuvre*. Although essential information relating to the writer's life and times is given, usually in an opening chapter, the approach is primarily critical and the emphasis is not upon 'background' or generalisations but upon close examination of important texts. Where an author is notably prolific, major texts have been selected for detailed attention but an attempt has also been made to convey, more summarily, a sense of the nature and quality of the author's work as a whole. Those who want to read further will find suggestions in the select bibliography included in each volume. Many novelists are, of course, not only novelists but also poets, essayists, biographers, dramatists, travel writers and so forth; many have practised shorter forms of fiction; and many have written letters or kept diaries that constitute a significant part of their literary output. A brief study cannot hope to deal with all these in detail, but where the shorter fiction and the non-fictional writings, public and private, have an important relationship to the novels, some space has been devoted to them.

NORMAN PAGE

Chronology

1825	William Clark Falkner ('The Old Colonel') born in Knox County, Tennessee.
1842	He arrives in Mississippi.
1846–7	He serves in the Mexican War.
1848	John Wesley Thompson Falkner ('The Young Colonel') born.
1849	W. C. Falkner kills Robert Hindman, is tried and acquitted.
1851	W. C. Falkner kills E. W. Morris, is tried and acquitted.
1861	Mississippi secedes; W. C. Falkner and the Magnolia Rifles enter the Civil War.
1862	Replaced as regiment commander, W. C. Falkner returns to Mississippi.
1863	He forms the Partisan Rangers and reenters the war.
1870	J. W. T. Falkner's son Murry Cuthbert is born.
1871–2	W. C. Falkner, Richard Thurmond and others organise a company to build a railroad.
1881–4	W. C. Falkner writes *The White Rose of Memphis*, tours Europe, writes *Rapid Ramblings in Europe*.
1885	J. W. T. Falkner moves his family to Oxford Mississippi.
1889	After being elected to the state legislature W. C. Falkner is shot by Thurmond.
1896	Murry Falkner marries Maud Butler and they settle in New Albany.
1897	William Cuthbert Falkner is born 25 September.
1898	Murry Falkner is appointed treasurer of the railroad and the family moves to Ripley.
1899	Murry C. Falkner Jr is born.
1901	John Wesley Thompson Falkner III is born.

1914   W. F. quits school after several years of increasing resistance; friendship with Phil Stone.
1915   W. F. quits eleventh grade.
1916   W. F. works briefly in his grandfather's bank but gravitates to student activities at the University of Mississippi.
1918   Estelle Oldham engaged; W. F. tries to elist, is rejected, changes name to Faulkner and enlists in the RAF (Canada); WWI ends while he is still in training; he returns to Oxford.
1919   First published poem 'L'Après-Midi d'un Faune' in *New Republic*; W. F. enrols at university, publishes poems and drawings.
1920   Resigns from university but writes *The Marionettes* for student drama group.
1922   Serves as scoutmaster and postmaster.
1924   *The Marble Faun* (Boston: Four Seas).
1925   In New Orleans Faulkner writes for the *Times-Picayune*; travels in Europe, returns to Oxford.
1926   *Soldiers' Pay* (New York: Horace Liveright).
1927   *Mosquitoes* (New York: Boni and Liveright); Liveright rejects *Flags in the Dust*.
1928   *The Sound and the Fury* written.
1929   *Sartoris* (New York: Harcourt Brace & Co.); marries Estelle Franklin; *The Sound and the Fury* (New York: Jonathan Cape and Harrison Smith).
1930   Buys antebellum house 'Rowan Oak'; *As I Lay Dying* (New York: Jonathan Cape and Harrison Smith).
1931   Alabama Faulkner is born and dies; *Sanctuary* (New York: Jonathan Cape and Harrison Smith); *These Thirteen* (short stories) (New York: Jonathan Cape and Harrison Smith).
1932   Works in Hollywood; Murry Falkner dies; *Light in August* (New York: Harrison Smith and Robert Haas).
1933   *A Green Bough* (New York: Harrison Smith and Robert Haas); Jill Faulkner born; W. F. buys an aeroplane.
1934   W. F. begins *Absalom, Absalom!*; writes several stories that become *The Unvanquished*; *Doctor Martino and Other Stories* (14 stories) (New York: Harrison Smith and Robert Haas).

1935	*Pylon* (New York: Harrison Smith and Robert Haas); Dean Faulkner dies in an air crash.
1936	*Absalom, Absalom!* (New York: Random House).
1938	*The Unvanquished* (New York: Random House).
1939	*The Wild Palms* (New Yok: Random House).
1940	Mammy Caroline Barr dies; *The Hamlet* (New York: Random House).
1942	*Go Down, Moses* (New York: Random House).
1943	W. F. begins *A Fable*.
1946	*The Portable Faulkner*, ed. Malcolm Cowley.
1948	*Intruder in the Dust* (New York: Random House).
1949	*Knight's Gambit* (six stories) (New York: Random House).
1950	W. F. wins the Nobel Prize; *Collected Stories* (forty-two stories) (New York: Random House).
1951	*Notes on a Horsethief* (later in *A Fable*) (Greenville, Miss.: Levee Press); *Requiem for a Nun* (New York: Random House).
1954	*A Fable* (New York: Random House).
1955	*Big Woods* (New York: Random House).
1957	Writer-in-residence at University of Virginia; *The Town* (New York: Random House).
1959	*The Mansion* (New York: Random House).
1960	Maud Butler Falkner dies.
1962	*The Reivers* (New York: Random House); W. F. dies 6 July.

1

Introduction

CRITICAL ISSUES

Faulkner's definition of the critic: 'He's a good deal like the minister – you don't need to listen to him unless you need him.'[1]

'To read Faulkner is to invite a mixed and troubling pleasure. He is an ingenuous man, of strong feelings, a dedicated sincerity and poor equipment: a maimed genius. By no means the least of his handicaps – and from the point of view of mere pleasure as a Common Reader it is one of his greatest – is the fact that he cannot write plain English; not because he is untutored but because his psyche is completely out of his control. . . . This creates a strong and often wholly justifiable temptation in the reader to cease to pay attention; thereby, it may be, losing some of his best things when, quite without warning, the divine current is switched on again. The attentive listener nudges one awake with, 'That was *good!*', one pricks up one's ears; by the time one has caught his drift once more the divine current has probably been switched off again.'[2]

Sean O'Faolain

'How is one to understand Faulkner the mythmaker: as dramatist, as historian, as novelist, as moralist, or metaphysician? Clearly, the form of the works as a whole does not support any single formal thesis, except possibly that of the poetic. For Faulkner is a poet, in the only real sense of that word. He deals with ambiguity of all kinds, forces ambiguity, compounds and diffuses it, leaving all paths which might conceivably lead to an already discovered destination. Poetry is the known language of

1

myth; it is synthetic, but not merely synthetic – it is dialectic. The problem is enhanced in Faulkner's work by his attempt to recreate dramatically as well as epically the conscience of his race; there is a fusion of forms. His is the first major attempt since Melville to place America in the great tradition of human-descent, to relieve us of the terrible oppression of isolation, and at the same time to show us the mirror of the future wherein this mythical tradition meets its test, its Golgotha. The form consequently is fluid, overlapping, never coming to rest, creating its own antitheses and syntheses.'[3]

J. B. Meriwether

'Because it is himself that the Southerner is writing about, not about his environment: who has, figuratively speaking, taken the artist in him in one hand and his milieu in the other and thrust the one into the other like a clawing and spitting cat into a croker sack. ... We seem to try in the simple furious breathing (or writing) span of the individual to draw a savage indictment of the contemporary scene or to escape from it into a make-believe region of swords and magnolias and mockingbirds which perhaps never existed anywhere. Both of the courses are rooted in sentiment; perhaps the ones who write savagely and bitterly of the incest in clayfloored cabins are the most sentimental.'[4]

W. Faulkner

'The European reader finds something uniquely American in Faulkner, and obviously no European could have written his books; the few European commentators that I have read seem to me to glorify Faulkner in a provincial American (or Southern) vacuum. I believe that as his personality fades from view he will be recognised as one of the last great craftsmen of the art of fiction which Ford Madox Ford called the Impressionist Novel. From Stendhal through Flaubert and Joyce there is a direct line to Faulkner, and it is not a mere question of influence. Faulkner's great subject, as it was Flaubert's and Proust's, is passive suffering, the victim being destroyed either by society or by dark forces within himself. Faulkner is one of the great exemplars of the international school of fiction which for more than a century has reversed the Aristotelian doctrine that tragedy is an action, not a quality.

William Faulkner's time and place made it possible for him to extend this European tradition beyond any boundaries that were visible to novelists of New England, the Middle West, or the Far West. The Greco-Trojan myth (Northerners as the upstart Greeks, Southerners as the older, more civilized Trojans) presented Faulkner, before he had written a line, with a large semi-historical background against which even his ignorant characters, like Lena Grove or Dewey Dell Bundren, as well as the more civilized Compsons and Sartorises, could be projected in more than human dimensions.'[5]

Allen Tate

'Faulkner was essentially a boyish mind for all his complexity, a mind humorous in the broad country fashion, and given to lazy improvisations . . . a greatness moving in a void . . . his inability to choose between Dostoevsky and Hollywood Boulevard . . . his every character and observation are lost in the spool of his rhetoric . . . Faulkner's style is a discursive fog.'[6]

Alfred Kazin

'For each new reader, each new critic who takes up Faulkner's task of wondering, musing, and mulling, and each new interpretation that proves less than definitive is in some sense a contribution to the saga as well as a tribute to its founder.'[7]

Olga Vickery

There are obvious objections to this undertaking. For one thing, do we need another book on Faulkner? 'In the light of thirty years of intense examination by literally hundreds of critics, one might reasonably wonder if anything else remains to be said about the fiction of William Faulkner.'[8] For another, isn't his presentation of women and blacks objectionable? Leslie Fiedler says, 'In the work of Faulkner, the fear of the castrating woman and the dis-ease with sexuality present in the novels of his contemporaries, Fitzgerald and Hemingway, attain their fullest and shrillest expression.'[9] And Gail Mortimer concludes, 'Most of Faulkner's fictive women tend to be parodies: sexually intense physical presences, dessicating spinsters, faded housewives, or venerated old ladies . . . he can conceive of strength only in

masculine terms.'[10] Of the blacks, a recent critic concludes,
'The more Faulkner probes the myth [of the South], the more
central it becomes, while the more he confronts its visceral,
elemental issue – the hallucinatory figure of "the Negro" – the
more he recoils into a form of outrage that is ambivalent in the
extreme.'[11]

The charge of sexism will probably stick, not because his
creations do not serve the purpose and mood of his fictions, but
because a 'normal', intelligent woman is hard to find anywhere
in Faulkner. As he himself admitted in a letter of 1926 to Anita
Loos, 'I am still rather Victorian in my prejudices regarding
the intelligence of women, despite Elinor Wylie and Willa
Cather and all the balance of them.'[12] The question of racism is
more complex. Faulkner's own utterances seem to me to show a
sophisticated grasp of social complexities and an understanding
that the problem is fundamentally one of sign systems, for
example:

> It is possible that the white race and the Negro race can
> never really like and trust the other; this for the reason that
> the white man can never really know the Negro, because the
> white man has forced the Negro to be always a Negro rather
> than another human being in their dealing, and therefore the
> Negro cannot afford, does not dare, to be open with the white
> man and let the white man know what he, the Negro, thinks.
> But I do know that we in the South, having grown up with
> and lived among Negroes for generations, are capable in
> individual cases of liking and trusting individual Negroes,
> which the North can never do because the Northerner only
> fears him.[13]

James Snead's recent study *Figures of Division* (Methuen, 1986)
begins by saying that 'the futility of applying strictly binary
categories to human affairs is the main lesson of Faulkner's
novels.' (ix)

Quite apart from the semiotic exploration and challenge of the
texts involved, most of Faulkner's portrayals are justifiable in
context. To condemn him for not having intellectual women or
successful blacks is to demand that Yoknapatawpha be a replete
and exemplary universe, and it is neither. It is a society which *does*
have slaves and repress its women. Faulkner is fascinated by such

a clearly flawed society, and much of his fiction deals with how new members of that society are persuaded to accept its conditions. His portrayal of children – Sarty Snopes, Quentin Compson, Vardaman Bundren, Chick Mallison – deserves more recognition. Looking back at his career and society in 1956, Faulkner said in puzzlement: 'There's no problem among the children, they play together and sleep together and eat together. It's only when they get old and inherit that Southern economy which depends on a system of peonage do they accept a distinction between the black man and the white man.'[14]

But we must beware of too much emphasis on sociology. In 1963 Van Wyck Brooks observed that most Faulkner critics were 'serious moralists'[15] and the worse for it. This study builds on the recent work of critics like Irwin, Kawin and Matthews, and attempts to show how Faulkner explores the interplay between society and the individual, history and now, in terms of the language we think, speak, and tell stories in. Readers unfamiliar with Faulkner's 'world' are pointed to the excellent general studies listed in the Bibliography; for this study, I assume the reader has at hand simply a copy of Faulkner's text and the readiness to read closely.

READING FAULKNER

'When I had finished [*A Fable*] I was still awhirl in pools of words and feelings which affected me like powerful music where the meaning is seldom questioned . . . [After rereading] slowly emerging into the clear fountain-light where the characters, the scenes, the meanings appeared starkly outlined, solid, real, good. This was William Faulkner's world, and I had found it to keep.'[16]

Music, and then a world – the reading experience of Faulkner, if Janet Frame is right, is a complex and exhilarating business not to be polished off at one sitting. The writing, at least in the opinion of another Southern writer Flannery O'Connor, is also a complex affair: 'Probably the real reason I don't read him is because he makes me feel that with my one-cylinder syntax I should quit writing and raise chickens altogether.'[17] We might crudely divide Frame's perception of texture and text as that curious amalgam of poetry and prose which makes his fiction so 'difficult'. The poetry may lyrically describe the evolution of Yoknapatawpha County, Mississippi, or the spirals and peregrinations of consciousness as it reflects upon itself; the prose may describe the Jefferson mob as it goes about an efficient lynching, or those blunt moments of self-awareness and decision-making which come upon Faulkner's characters, as upon us all, unawares. In other words, the distinction is not so much between outer and inner, between the narrative and the philosophical gloss which many critics have discerned (usually favouring the former and deploring the latter) as between two styles of writing, both of which are essential to the 'mental' *and* 'physical' worlds of his fiction.

The American South seems to exist conceptually only as a space between opposites: ante-bellum and post-War, North/South, black/white, country/city. So the idea of binaries, doublings and repetition recurs in Faulkner criticism, particularly in the last decade. Whether in psychological terms as father fights son or sibling,[18] or stylistic terms in a fondness for presenting oxymorons and 'choosing not to choose' between them,[19] Faulkner seems to inhabit a world of unresolved tensions. But it is, for Faulker, not simply a matter of charting the outlines of this grand chess-game; there is ambivalence even in regard to the boundaries themselves, a desire both to maintain them and to collapse them into a harmonious 'grey' which beckons as an end to writing and intolerable 'différance' (the French critic Jacques Derrida's portmanteau word to suggest that the 'distinguishing' function of verbal signs also involves an endless incompletion or deferral of 'complete' meaning): 'His preoccupation with boundaries is also a preoccupation with their loss, collapse, or blurring.'[20]

Once we have this 'key' of opposites, we can begin to understand Faulkner better. On the one hand he was the inheritor of a Calvinist tradition which saw the world in 'black and white terms' ('black' and 'white' are, of course, literally appropriate terms to use of Faulkner, not only because of his concern with relations between white and black people, but also because of his ambivalent views about black words on white pages). Women are saints or instruments of the devil, and the world is a moral gymnasium, a continual test of courage and endurance. But Faulkner also admired writers and artists who blurred those oppositions, who luxuriated in the fleeting, the sensuous, the undifferentiated. As we shall see when looking at his early influences, if was as if humanist and even 'decadent' values had to fight for a position in his mind over an immoveable substratum of Protestant gloom and rigour. Jean-Paul Sartre, one of the French critics (Malraux and Camus were others) who promoted Faulkner in Europe when he was being neglected in his own country during the forties, sensed exactly this: 'Faulkner's despair seems to me to precede his metaphysics.'[21] This despair gives to Faulkner's public pronouncements that quality of 'strain' reminiscent of Victorian commentators like Tennyson and Arnold whose private poetry played out their anxieties and sensuality. Consider, for example:

> I think that man's free will functions against a Greek background of fate, that he has the free will to choose and the courage, the fortitude to die for his choice, is my conception of man, is why I believe that man will endure. That fate – sometimes fate lets him alone.[22]

But that despair also makes his stories and novels ruthless dissections of human beings alone and in society. By contextualising his characters in the most literal sense, Faulkner helps the reader learn by the experience of reading how far we are all victims of our time, place and inheritance. Reading Faulkner, we read the least recognised aspects of ourselves. While Faulkner's experimentation in form and style makes him a major precursor of current postmodernist writers, the range of his achievement and his commitment to human beings as social animals place him firmly in the great tradition.

FAULKNER'S LIFE

On reading other authors: 'Madam, did you ever hear of a whore sleepin' with a man for fun?'

On drinking: 'There's a lot of nourishment in an acre of corn.'

On biography: 'It is my ambition to be ... abolished and voided from history ... "He made the books and he died." '[23]

Despite his desire for anonymity, and the focus of this study on
language and technique, a glance at Faulkner's biography will
lead us into the world of his fiction because, as biographer
David Minter observed, for Faulkner life was inseparable from
situation: 'Every exploration of family becomes an exploration
of region, and every exploration of either becomes an exploration
of self.'[24]

In 1842 a seventeen-year-old penniless runaway arrived from
Tennessee in the hill country of northern Mississippi, east of
the delta and about fifty miles northeast of Oxford. William
Clark Falkner (1825–89), Faulkner's great grandfather, soon
made his mark. He captured a wanted murderer then sold
copies of his life to the crowd awaiting the execution. In 1849
while reading law, Falkner stabbed to death a man who pulled
a gun on him, was acquitted, shot one of the victim's protesting
friends, was again acquitted and escaped the gun of the first
victim's father. But the greatest stories he bequeathed to the
Faulkner family arose out of the Civil War, when as a colonel
he led his own 2nd Mississippi Infantry regiment, the 'Magnolia
Rifles', in the first battle of Manassas. After his deposition in
the military election of 1862 (which says something about his
ability to relate to his men), he returned home and raised the
1st Mississippi Partisan Rangers; but the pattern of his life had
been established: 'he seemed always to be struggling up to
some grand eminence, then getting shot down.'[25]

After the war the 'Old Colonel' did better: he built a railroad
through the hill country of Mississippi, ran a law practice,
owned a large plantation and a saw mill, was elected to the
state legislature, and wrote a serialised novel *The White Rose of
Memphis* (1881) which went to thirty-five printings. He met a
predictably violent end when a defeated candidate in the state
election, his former partner Thurmond, shot him in the streets
of Ripley in 1889.

He left an ambiguous but inescapable example to his great
grandson, born eight years later on 25 September 1897. His
marble effigy stood in Tippa county, but the Old Colonel's
name was changed by the time it reached Faulkner; the
additional 'u' Faulkner attributes to repeated mispronunciation,
but 'Maybe . . . I secretly was ambitious and did not want to
ride on grandfather's coat-tails, and so accepted the 'u', was

glad of such an easy way to strike out for myself.'[26] The
ancestral hand was, in fact, laid upon the writer by his
grandfather, the 'Young Colonel' J. W. T. Faulkner (1848–1922),
who sold the Gulf and Chicago Railroad in 1902 and devoted
himself to an extensive criminal law practice and the Mississippi
Senate. It was he who named his grandson after the Old
Colonel. In his white suit and cigar, the Young Colonel was the
original of the Southern magnate of 'The Dukes of Hazard' and
(as Faulkner would say) a thousand avatars; he once threw a
brick from his car through the window of the First National
Bank in Oxford, saying, 'My Buick, my brick, my bank.'[27]

Faulkner's father Murry could not fill the family boots so
well, although he shared the men's penchant for guns. In 1891
he had a fight with a jealous neighbour, was shot in the back
and mouth and survived. His father misfired six times when
attempting to defend his son, but it was a reluctant gesture,
since he believed Murry had it coming to him: 'I would have
had to do it myself anyway,' he is reported to have said.[28]
(Relations between fathers and sons in the Fa(u)lkner clan
seem to have been uniformly strained.) Murry moved to Oxford,
the county seat with a population of 1800, to be near the 'Big
Place' of his father, and his disappointed career as business
manager of the fledgling University of Mississippi was enlivened
only by dreams of becoming a rancher, and by hunting trips to
a two-roomed cabin near the Tallahatchie River. He died in
1932.

Young Faulkner grew up in an atmosphere of story which
made the past constantly more vivid than the present. He
listened and listened: to his maternal grandmother Leila Butler
('Damuddy'), a fierce spirit who considered her daughter had
married beneath her and wrote letters to 'Miss Maud Butler in
the care of Mr Murry Faulkner'; to Caroline Barr ('Mammy
Callie') the black nanny to whom Faulkner dedicated *Go Down,
Moses* and who was steeped in family history and ghost stories
of the Tallahatchie bottom; to his father's friends on hunting
trips; to gossip around the courthouse; and to his grandfather's
stories of the Old Colonel as he sat on the verandah of the Big
Place. Faulkner's mother contributed to his 'manly' upbringing:
a sign above the stove read, 'Don't Complain Don't Explain',
and she made him wear a corset to school for two years to

improve his posture. J. W. T. told the boy, 'You've got a back just like the Old Colonel but you've got to be a better man than he was.'[29]

Although he disliked school, Faulkner early on decided that he would take on his great grandfather in the arena of literature. In Grade 3 he told his teacher he wanted to be a writer, 'like my great-granddaddy'.[30] His own early life progressed inauspiciously, a failure after such high expectations which perhaps contributed to his later reticence and privacy. In 1917 his first love Estelle Oldham married someone else, and the following year he managed to get into the RAF (by claiming to have been born in Finchley in 1898), but only got as far as Toronto before the Armistice. From 1922–4 he was postmaster at the University of Mississippi and unsuccessful student and scoutmaster. He dressed like a dandy, was known on campus as 'Count No Count', and contributed poetry and playlets to university groups. Only with the fortunate advice and encouragement of mentors like Phil Stone the lawyer, and Sherwood Anderson the short story writer, did Faulkner's career as a writer begin to take shape.

The legend to which Faulkner's fiction contributed, his version of his family's and society's history was a late chapter in the 'History of Yoknapatawpha'. Dorothy Tuck's excellent reconstruction of Faulkner's version from his fiction (see *Appendix*) may be supplemented by Malcolm Cowley's:

> The Deep South was settled partly by aristocrats like the Sartoris clan and partly by new men like Colonel Sutpen. Both types of planters were determined to establish a lasting social order on the land they had seized from the Indians (that is, to leave sons behind them). They had the virtue of living single-mindedly by a fixed code; but there was also an inherent guilt in their 'design', their way of life, that put a curse on the land and brought about the Civil War. After the War was lost, partly as a result of their own mad heroism . . . they tried to restore 'the design' by other methods. But they no longer had the strength to achieve more than a partial success, even after they had freed their land from the carpetbaggers who followed the Northern armies. As time passed, moreover, the men of the old order found they had Southern enemies too: they had to fight against a new

exploiting class descended from the landless whites of slavery days. In this struggle between the clan of Sartoris and the unscrupulous tribe of Snopes, the Sartorises were defeated in advance by a traditional code that prevented them from using the weapons of the enemy.[31]

This legend, with the antebellum South as an Eden and the War as the Fall into time and commerce, was sustained by literature and taletelling. One critic describes how in the 1830s, 'the narratives of the frontier circle, as they draw around their evening fire, often turn upon the exploits of the old race of men, the heroes of the past days, who wore hunting shirts, and settled the country.'[32] Southern writers like Sidney Lanier reinforced the myth of a gallant, aristocratic South of the eighteenth century, self-contained and ruled by a few hundred families. After the Civil War the tradition of Southern humour became popular, with the influence of Sir Walter Scott replaced by that of Mark Twain and George Harris's plainspeaking *Sut Lovingood: Yarns Spun by a Nat'ral Born Durn'd Fool* (1867). The consequence for Faulkner's fiction was that he inherited a stylised, high romantic or Gothic sensibility, along with a more demotic, yarn-spilling humour, which led Malcolm Cowley to conclude, 'If you imagine Huckleberry Finn living in the House of Usher and telling uproarious tales while the walls crumble about him, that will give you the double quality of Faulkner's work at its best.'[33]

Arising as it does out of a family and social ethos saturated with versions of the past, Faulkner's fiction everywhere intertwines and combats history. The Civil War itself created rather than destroyed the myth of a lost Golden Age, through what Robert Penn Warren called the 'powerful, painful, grinding process by which an ideal emerges out of history'.[34] The more sinister facts of the antebellum South, the anomalies of the War itself (Abraham Lincoln, for example, informing a black leader at the White House in 1862 that 'It is better for us both to be separated'),[35] were ironed out in Biblical, apocalyptic interpretations. For the Union the Civil War was the good North versus the barbarian South; the South, in defeat and as the post-war years lengthened into an intolerable wasteland of guilt and occupation, restated the romantic view of the Edenic antebellum plantations.

Such a powerful mythological pattern, reinforced in Faulkner's own family, would be difficult to overthrow. To a Japanese audience Faulkner put the matter simply: 'One hundred years ago there were two cultures, two economies in my country, the United States, and ninety-five years ago we fought a war over it and my side were whipped';[36] but simultaneously, like Quentin Compson, he declared his allegiance: 'I will still defend it even if I hate it.'[37]

Yet there is a danger in letting the South bulk too large in understanding Faulkner's work.[38] Critics are fond of quoting Faulkner on the moment when he realised that his 'own little postage stamp of native soil was worth writing about', but they ignore what he went on to say: '. . . by sublimating the actual into the apocryphal I would have complete liberty to use whatever talent I might have to its absolute top'.[39] The novelty of Faulkner's postage stamp, particularly to a non-American reader, and the persistence and powerful presentation of the dominant myths of his fictional world, may make the reader forget how 'apocryphal' (i.e. unauthorised) and objectionable were many of Faulkner's stories to a society unusually pre-occupied with fabricating and maintaining a reputable past. A neighbour of Faulkner in Oxford is quoted as saying, 'Some of Faulkner's writings are about as popular in his home country as a dead skunk would be in a sleeping bag';[40] and when Faulkner received the Nobel Prize in 1950, a *New York Times* editorial protested, 'Incest and rape may be common pastimes in Faulkner's "Jefferson Mississippi", but they are not elsewhere in the United States.'[41] There is in non-American readers an even stronger tendency to accept Faulkner's material as 'fact' because in America anything can happen: 'Europeans have unfortunately tended to read Faulkner's Gothic and symbolic distortions of life in Mississippi as literal sociological reporting.'[42] The truth is, of course, that Faulkner's Yoknapatawpha is an imaginative construct, one more version of a history already seen as a grand fabrication. In the end, there is not much separating the stories of Sutpen and Snopes.

If Faulkner subscribed to the myth of fallen Eden at all, it was in connection with the land and the native Indians. Faulkner would discriminate between the landscape he loved to hunt in, and the man-made ugliness he hated. In 1925 he wrote, 'The beauty – spiritual and physical – of the South lies in the fact that God has done so much for it and man so little.'[43]

The revival of Faulkner's reputation in the 40s and 50s in the English-speaking world tended to emphasise his regionalism, whereas the French had long recognised his stylistic genius as well. Malcolm Cowley's introduction to his landmark *Portable Faulkner* (1946) stressed the importance of Yoknapatawpha, setting for twelve books and at least thirty stories. All Faulkner's writing, he said, was 'blocks of marble from the same quarry . . . planks from a still-living tree'. Faulkner was being used, in part, as a flagship for the critical enterprise of Cowley, Warren, Tate, O'Donnell and others to establish a 'Southern renaissance' which was rooted in place and community, conservative and anti-intellectual. Only recently has that emphasis on content and region given way to more sophisticated textual criticism. Allen Tate's 1963 analysis quoted in the *Introduction* marks this transition.

In this study I hope to suggest that it is in the textual interplay with the reader that Faulkner's themes are generated; but this is simply to bring us back to Southern history and to know it for the first time. Born into a world where legend intertwined with reality, devoted to turning that world into art (the apocryphal), Faulkner would find in the very process of textualising the chaos of experience, not only metaphors for the Southern experience but the experience itself. And, of course, because we all inherit a told world, if not so spectacularly as Faulkner and his people, we readers recognise in his tensions between living and telling the dynamics of our own consciousness.

FAULKNER'S STYLE

'First, we have the Non-Stop or Life Sentence. The first two and a half pages of *Absalom, Absalom!* consist of seven sentences. . . . To penetrate Mr Faulkner's sentences is like hacking your way through a jungle. The path closes up at once behind you, and in no time at all you find yourself entangled in a luxuriant mass of modifiers, qualifications, relative clauses, parenthetical phrases, interjected matter, recapitulations, and other indications of a Great Style. All of Mr Faulkner's shuddery inventions pale in horrendousness before the mere notion of parsing him.

After the Life Sentence comes the Far Fetch or Hypertrope.

Very few things in the book remain themselves. Each one reminds Mr Faulkner of something else. . . .

Then we have what may be called Anti-Narrative, a set of complex devices used to keep the story from being told. . . . as a technician he has Joyce and Proust punch-drunk.'[44]

Long sentences, difficult comparisons and formal complexities: not the stylistic formula for popular success, if you judge the common reader, as does Mr Fadiman in the above abrasive comments, as wanting a straightforward narrative in the 'plain style'. The issue of Faulkner's style has in recent years, with more sophisticated notions of 'speech act' and 'reader response', become a central critical focus, but opponents are probably no more persuaded now than in earlier years that Faulkner means something by his style. Exasperated critics still react with fury and despair, with 'an explosion of adjectives, both laudatory and derogatory: *ambiguous, over-elaborate, surrealistic, romantic, precious, lyrical, incantatory, turgid, baroque, archaic, compulsive, hypnotic, lush, bizarre, picturesque, garrulous, eccentric.*'[45] If only, they say, Faulkner would write simply, then we might want to learn about the fascinating world of the American South which he wants to present to us.

For the irascible Wyndham Lewis, Faulkner's poetic use of language was a dismal failure:

But there is a lot of *poetry* in Faulkner. It is not at all good. And it has in the end a rather comic way of occurring at a point where, apparently, he considers that the *atmosphere* has run out, or is getting thin, by the passage of time become exhausted and requiring renewal, like the water in a zoological-garden tank for specimens of fish. So he pumps in this necessary medium, for anything from half a dozen to two dozen lines, according to the needs of the case. . . .

His characters demand, in order to endure for more than ten pages apparently, an opaque atmosphere of whip-poor-wills, cicadas, lilac, 'seeping' moonlight, water-oaks and jasmine . . .[46]

Faulkner himself encouraged this sense of stylistic failure by adopting the pose of the untutored genius at the mercy of his pen, each work a proximate attempt. 'I have written too fast, too much', he said in 1941. 'I decided what seems to me now a long time ago that something worth saying knew better than I did how it needed to be said, and that it was better said poorly even than not said. And besides, there would always be a next time, since there is only one truth and endurance and pity and courage.'[47] In 1953 he declared, 'What an amazing gift I had: uneducated in every formal sense, without even very literate, let alone literary, companions, yet to have made the things I made, I don't know where it came from.'[48] Such humility, as we know from his wide reading early in his career, was part the pose of the country bumpkin and part a Romantic belief in the inspirational wind. There is probably some truth in his 'untutoredness', as he confessed when discussing Conrad's English: 'I never went to school enough to save myself the shortcuts of learning English'.[49] But there was also a clearly articulated rationale for the infamous Faulknerian sentence. First, belying the insouciance of that first quotation, there was a personal sense of urgency, 'the compulsion to say everything in one sentence because you may not live long enough to have two sentences';[50] this gives the reader that unmistakable sense of being in the presence of a mind that is indefatigable, sometimes feverish, in its attempt to unearth the truth. Second, there was the psychological reason:

> A character in a story at any moment of action is not just himself as he is then, he is all that made him, and the long sentence is an attempt to get his past and possibly his future into the instant in which he does something. . . .[51]

Third, there was the artistic reason, to make his works not, as Malcolm Cowley put it, hewn from a single plank, but integral works of art: 'I was still trying to reduce my own individual experience of the world into one compact thing which could be picked up and held in the hands at one time.'[52] Critics have amplified both these last points, and I will deal with them in order.

The sense of Faulkner's characters, especially his *speakers*, as mired in the past, was well expressed by the French novelist Camus in 1957 concerning *Requiem for a Nun*: 'une spirale, interminablement dévidée, de mots et de phrases conduit celui qui parle aux abîmes des souffrances ensevelis dans le passé'.[53]

This spool of words supplied the apt title for D. M. Kartiganer's stylistic study of Faulkner, *The Fragile Thread*, 'by which the little surface corners and edges of men's secret and solitary lives may be joined for an instant now and then . . .'.[54] The connection may be made by unearthing a personal past or making contact with the community – its cultural past and its present network. In the most obvious example, words are what Ratliff, Stevens and Mallison use to bind the town of Jefferson together against the silent enemy Snopes. The conflict in the town is thus internalised into the very texture of the novel that is describing it, with the unarticulated action of the Snopeses contrasting with the thought and feeling of their opponents: as one critic put it, 'Rather than turning the plot into a melodramatic struggle between heroes and villains, Faulkner chose to give his narrators the weapon of words, allowing them to write talk and text in such a way as to work against, or formally slow the otherwise inexorable movement of plot.'[55]

At a more personal level, in the family sagas of Sartoris, Sutpen and Compson, complicated language is used by fathers and sons as they attempt to reinforce or break out of the snares of heredity. Here the shapes of language itself are something inherited by the son, and talk is therefore turned upon itself in complicated patterns of repetition and cancellings, as J. T. Irwin discusses in his book *Doubling and Incest: Repetition and Revenge* (1975). One of the most powerful effects of Faulkner's interior monologues is the sense of a failure to unite with anything or to fully articulate a predicament. One of his most common syntactical patterns is a series of negatives resolving, or rather collapsing, in a bland assertion, for example, 'When he saw us he did not stop. He didn't hurry, either. He just turned and went back . . .' ('Mistral', *Collected Stories* 867). There is often the sense of a sinking through layers of consciousness to a bedrock of instinct or belief which will never become apparent to the protagonist because it cannot be articulated but which, it is implied, governs his or her behaviour, as in this sequence from 'The Bear': 'He had not expected it. He had not even feared that . . . He did not even tell himself that . . . He believed that . . .' (*Go Down, Moses*, 137). Faulkner's clearest statement of this psychological truth comes in *Light in August*: 'Memory believes before knowing remembers.' (111) Remembrance or articulation is subordinate to 'belief'. The verbal texture of Faulkner's novels is often 'incantatory, hypnotic, garrulous . . .' precisely *because* it is the conscious medium of his characters. Action or plot happens on a different plane and is usually motivated not by this muddled consciousness but by external or subconscious forces. Faulkner himself described the typical modern character immersed in forces and facts but not in control of them, in a memorable image: 'to exist alone inside a vacuum of facts which he did not choose and cannot cope with and cannot escape from like a fly inside an inverted tumbler.'[56] So strong is Faulkner's sense of an inarticulable context in the midst of endless articulation that it has led one critic, Walter Slatoff, to write a study of Faulkner's style called *Quest for Failure*.

There is, then, a productive and often calculated quality of 'failure' in Faulkner's prose, whose characteristic turn Slatoff identifies as the oxymoron: 'Without contraries there is no progression.' At the very heart of a Faulknerian sentence there is a tension between freedom and necessity, the open future or interior and the dictating past or exterior. Irving Howe, describing the prose style of Sherwood Anderson, could have been talking of Faulkner when he identified these two tones: 'a tension between its underlying loose oral cadences and the stiffened superimposed beat of a prose almost Biblical in its regularity.' The result is 'a hushed bardic chant, low-toned and elegaically awkward, deeply related to native speech rhythm yet very much the result of literary cultivation.'[57]

Is there then any possibility of completion or aesthetic satisfaction at the end of a Faulkner novel? One response is to see all the novels as emptying into each other in a vast, incomplete *comédie humaine* betraying an overall tone of authorial despair, as when Alfred Kazin discerns often a kind of void at the center of the rhetorical storms.[58] But recently critics have found through a study of language and application of contemporary literary theory a method of supporting Faulkner's own intention to make objects one can hold in one's hands. Faulkner's 'abîmes' or gaps may be profitably seen as intentional, as Jean-Paul Sartre intimated when he perceived a 'trick' in Faulkner's style, the trick of keeping secrets, of telling just a little.[59] Why not tell it all? Because Faulkner knew that you could never tell it all, that there was no 'metaphysical presence' (to use the language of deconstruction) despite the myth of the South, but only texts upon texts. The play that

goes on as a reader reads a Faulkner novel mirrors the play of
the characters' consciousnesses between past and present,
private and public stories. The central drama of his novels is
the struggle of the text itself 'for a comprehensible design'.[60]
The possibility of achieving the formal perfection of Keats's
Grecian urn is balanced or cancelled by the appeal of the
unfinished present, so the endings of his novels often have that
curious sense of being halfway between achieved desire and
patent pretence. What Conrad Aiken in 1939 called Faulkner's
'parrotlike mechanical mytacism (for it is really like a stammer)
with which he will go on endlessly repeating such favorites as
"myriad, sourceless, impalpable . . ."'[61] vouchsafes the mystery
and incompletion of consciousness against the often violent,
strongly plotted narratives with their spectacular dénouements
which form not the urn but the inverted tumbler. This very
tension, as I have said, echoes the psychological reality of
Faulkner's characters, attracted to an uncritical dream of
antebellum (or pre-pubescent) Eden; and as R. M. Weaver
says of the typical Southerner, 'analysis is destructive of the
kind of reality which he most wishes to preserve'.[62]

Earlier I explained how Faulkner's thinkers or talkers are
often opposed to undesirable doers. The relationship between
text and world, that is, the place of language, may profitably be
seen as the central battlefield in Faulkner's fiction, as crucial to
man's survival and endurance as the battlefield at Antietam.
J. T. Matthews concludes that Faulkner's major fiction 'elevates
fabrication over representation';[63] but the crucial point is that
the distinction itself becomes meaningless, the choice being
only between better and worse kinds of 'fabrication'. Still,
Matthews usefully introduces such current critical terms as
textuality and the play of language into Faulkner criticism,
with extremely fruitful results. Alerted to the importance of
types of discourse, the reader will find numerous appearances of
documents, letters, inscriptions and the like in Faulkner's
fiction; the judgment tends to be against those rigid encodings
of the past such as gravestone inscriptions, and for the openness
of redefinition, conversation and taletelling.

It is in considering 'tellers and listeners', in Barbara Hardy's
useful phrase, that we can most clearly appreciate Faulkner's
central concern with the reading experience itself. In 1977 Hugh

Kenner observed Faulkner's 'trick of playing verbal affinities across syntactic ones, so that we barely trouble to follow the syntax';[64] later he refined this idea, finding a play between the ostensible spoken and written word within Faulkner's novels. What the reader must do is (as by now you would expect) become oxymoronic, both listening and reading at the same time. Listening involves joining the community on the steps of the general store and listening to Ratliff or some other taleteller embroider an established field of information already familiar to us; we don't mind hearing stories twice, we don't mind details being slightly changed, and we don't particularly want the story to end. At the same time, reading involves responding to the printed word, taking notes, following syntax and the directions of parentheses and italics, ellipses and chapter divisions, what Kenner calls 'hundreds of running feet of lazily coiled rusty rhetoric and thickets of unregarded narrative gestures'.[65] A simple example of these ideas is a passage from *Requiem for a Nun*:

> a man ... who would not only never need nor intend to forgive anyone anything, he would never even realise that anyone expected him to forgive anyone anything; who wouldn't even bother to forgive her if it ever dawned on him that he had the opportunity, but instead would simply black her eyes ... (152)

Here, the effort to *read* the description of the man's imaginative limitations and potential requires great attention to the logic of double negatives, comparatives and profuse verbs, while the *listener* grabs the answering 'but instead' which is a simple, colloquial affirmation by means of action. A Faulkner reader constantly pivots between reading and listening, between the simplicity yet solitude of 'fact' and the complexity yet communality of rumour and opinion.

My approach to Faulkner in this book is to foreground the aspect of Faulkner's language play, which takes us more surely than the American South, symbolism, Gothicism or psychology, to the heart of Faulkner's genius. We will see how the larger units of story and novel capitalise on this dialectic of dead shape and living profusion when we look at individual texts.

Here I would like to analyse three different passages, including a 'pumped-up' poetic one, to show how Faulkner is in complete control of the narrative situation.

J. E. Bunselmeyer has distinguished two broad styles in Faulkner, the comic and the contemplative.[66] I will not consider Faulkner's last novel *The Reivers* (1962) in my later discussion, because I think it a slight work, little more than the 'reminiscence' of the subtitle. But it is useful here as an example of the sustained comic style, even in the first few chapters which establish the framework of inherited stories, always a fraught subject in Faulkner. Consider the passage:

> The decree, as old as the stable itself, was that the only pistol connected with it would be the one which stayed in the bottom right-hand drawer of the desk in the office, and the mutual gentlemen's assumption was that no one on the staff of the establishment even owned a firearm from the time he came on duty until he went back home, let alone brought one to work with him. Yet – and John had explained it to all of us and had our confederated sympathy and understanding, a unified and impregnable front to the world and even to Father himself if that unimaginable crisis had ever arisen, which it would not have except for Boon Hogganbeck – telling us (John) how he had earned the price of the pistol by doing outside work on his own time, on time apart from helping his father on the farm, time which was his own to spend eating or sleeping, until on his twenty-first birthday he had paid the final coin into his father's hand and received the pistol; telling us how the pistol was the living symbol of his manhood, the ineffaceable proof that he was now twenty-one and a man; that he never intended to, declined even to imagine the circumstance in which he would ever, pull its trigger against a human being, yet he must have it with him; he would no more have left the pistol at home when he came away than he would have left his manhood in a distant closet or drawer when he came to work; he told us (and we believed him) that if the moment ever came when he would have to choose between leaving the pistol at home, or not coming to work himself, there would have been but one possible choice for him. (10)

We begin with an ancient decree, a sourceless legend which binds the living. The second sentence begins the complications, conveyed through syntax as much as anything. The parenthesis establishes the community of 'gentlemen' defined by a common 'story' and by their opposition to 'Father'; it also slips from the distant past, when John explained to us, to the putative future of the story, when we will learn what Boon actually did. The verb 'telling us' seems to combine with 'yet' as part of a subordinate phrase, but a glance ahead at the end of the sentence and paragraph shows that we never reach a main verb. In that case the main sentence begins with 'and John' and the 'yet' is left unrelated, a dangling qualification to John's rules which subverts the following description of John's pacific precautions. The subordinate phrase is about 'telling' and 'told', and 'we' become the implicated listeners as we sense the ponderous logic and insistence of John's speech. However, most of the reported speech is free, using balanced phrasing and words and imagery which we could not exactly imagine coming from John's lips. The effect of the legalistic rephrasing is to emphasise the townspeople's attempts to codify a behaviour everywhere undermined by the rough justice of the gun. The clear ironic implication is that the gun/penis is vital to John's self-conception.

Sometimes in Faulkner, instead of this kind of right-branching qualification or reiteration, we find folk wisdom presented aphoristically in balanced sentences whose logic is sometimes a complex affair of antonyms and double negatives. Mark Twain's famous story about a frog has Smiley say, 'Maybe you understand frogs and maybe you don't understand 'em; maybe you've had experience, and maybe you ain't only a amature, as it were. Anyways, I've got *my* opinion, and I'll resk forty dollars that he can outjump any frog in Calaveras County.' When Faulkner's characters are in difficulty, these 'maybe's' present an impossible range of alternatives usually shortcircuited by some instinctive action; but when they are at their leisure, they skewer a human truth in a word (e.g. 'amature') or redefinition of a word. In *The Reivers*, the narrator expounds on the nature of the child:

There is no crime which a boy of eleven had not envisaged long ago. His only innocence is, he may not yet be old

enough to desire the fruits of it, which is not innocence but
appetite; his ignorance is, he does not know how to commit
it, which is not ignorance but size. (46)

The passage is typical in its attribution of layers of consciousness
and 'knowing' even to children, and the aphoristic form inverts
logic so that the reader must work to untangle the new
definitions. The logic of each half requires the words 'lack of'
before 'appetite' and 'size'; because the reader is forced to
supply the logic, s/he also considers the possibility that growing
up is simply a deterministic affair of acquiring 'adult' sins. And
this, the question of whether children learn because of or
despite the example of their elders, is the theme of many
Faulkner novels, though not worked out in *The Reivers*.

My final example comes from *Absalom, Absalom!*, Rosa
Coldfield's central, italicised monologue in Chapter 5. It is an
excellent example, like most of the novel, of what Wright
Morris identifies as the 'pollen-laden ambience' of Faulkner's
prose[67] with its sexual freight, its 'sense of incipient
accouchement'. Here Rosa tells of Sutpen's end:

> *I never owned him; certainly not in that sewer sense which you would
> mean by that and maybe think (but you are wrong) I mean. That did
> not matter. That was not even the nub of the insult. I mean that he was
> not owned by anyone or anything in this world, had never been, would
> never be, not even by Ellen, not even by Jones' granddaughter. Because
> he was not articulated in this world. He was a walking shadow. He
> was the light-blinded bat-like image of his own torment cast by the
> fierce demoniac lantern up from beneath earth's crust and hence in
> retrograde, reverse; from abysmal and chaotic dark to eternal and
> abysmal dark completing his descending (do you mark the gradation?)
> ellipsis, clinging, trying to cling with vain unsubstantial hands to what
> he hoped would hold him, save him, arrest him – Ellen (do you mark
> them?), myself, then last of all that fatherless daughter of Wash Jones'
> only child who, so I heard once, died in a Memphis brothel – to find
> severence (even if not rest and peace) at last in the stroke of a rusty
> scythe. I was told, informed of that too, though not by Jones this time
> but by someone else kind enough to turn aside and tell me he was dead.
> 'Dead?' I cried. 'Dead? You? You lie; you're not dead; heaven cannot,
> and hell dare not have you!'* (171–2)

In the first sentence, Rosa protests too much by even raising the idea of sexual possession and then denying it. Her sense of insult one must deduce by an absent logic, and has to do with Rosa's conception that the sexual relationship *must* involve ownership, something that she could never achieve over Sutpen; for Rosa, the fraught notion of sexuality involves power alone. The rest of her speech, indeed, demonstrates Sutpen's fascination to her precisely because he is owned by no one, not even God. Like Lucifer he challenges her Southern religiosity, and Rosa's imagery is torn between triumphant damnation and the tragic setting of a bright sun, a Faustian over-reacher. If he is a bat he is also Dracula; if he is not 'articulated' he is also the unutterable 'Word' itself. The balanced epithets 'abysmal . . . chaotic . . . eternal . . abysmal' also suggest his godhead as he traverses Creation from Chaos to eternity. One can sense Rosa's conflict in the image of 'vain unsubstantial hands': the epithets fight against each other, the one asserting the fact of Sutpen, the other denying it. By etherealising Sutpen, of course, Rosa removes his threatening sexuality. She sees his proposal to her as a demand for companionship rather than for the breeder of a male heir, and turns the women into rescuers. Notice how she avoids contemplating Milly Jones altogether, substituting her daughter and deleting Sutpen's sexual involvement in the word 'fatherless'. Rosa lines herself up as one of 'them' further to avoid contemplating the sexual challenge. The women become the figures of power, marks of gradation in Sutpen's degradation; the two parentheses indicate both her unease with the image and her hysterical relishing of Sutpen's descent. His death, Rosa pretends to treat with casual disdain ('someone else' told her) whereas his 'severence' is actually seen as severence from the women rather than life, suggesting an image of castration. Rosa's glee at that conclusion is in conflict with her lust for Sutpen, indicated by her Brontean conclusion; she cannot regard him as dead, addressing him in the second person in what might be a curse but is also an adoration of the superman.

The power of this passage is achieved not only by the complex logic and tension of the imagery, but also by the rhythm of the sentences which proceed from abrupt dismissal to a gathering wave of emotion which both tells a story and betrays the speaker's emotional climax ('hold him, save him, arrest him'). Faulkner's poetic, contemplative style catches the quality of consciousness so that the reader may eventually pass beyond the 'meanings' of the words and phrases to appreciate the shape of a mind. It is paradoxical that Faulkner's most wordy prose often acts as a kind of orchestration which takes the reader beyond literacy. As Faulkner once said:

> I must try to express clumsily in words what the pure music would have done better. That is, music would express better and simpler, but I prefer to use words as I prefer to read rather than listen. I prefer silence to sound, and the image produced by words occurs in silence. That is, the thunder and the music of the prose takes place in silence.[68]

There is a way, then, of turning to profitable account every one of Alfred Kazin's adjectives when he describes Faulkner's as 'perhaps the most elaborate, intermittently incoherent and ungrammatical, thunderous, polyphonic rhetoric in all American writing'.[69] One more point should be made, of course, in a consideration of Faulkner's style, and that is the sheer verve, freedom and inventiveness with which he mines the riches of the English language. As early as 1922 he had declared the British use of it as 'a Sunday night affair of bread and milk'; the American language was, he said, 'a rainbow'.[70]

2

Early Work

POETRY

In 1937 Graham Greene wrote, 'All Mr. Faulkner's narrators speak the same bastard poetic prose.'[71] Faulkner himself regarded prose as the resort of the failed poet, and in the early 1920s put his energies into a poetry heavily influenced by Housman, Swinburne, Eliot, Verlaine and the Symbolists. Those apprentice works reveal not only the sources of Faulkner's often ornate, poetic prose style but also the thematic oppositions which preoccupied him throughout his fiction. John Pikoulis contrasts in Faulkner the poet with his love of ambiguity and 'being', and the novelist with his drive towards narrative and resolution,[72] but it is the very tension between these roles that makes him such a remarkable novelist.

The Marionettes, Faulkner's university playlet of 1920, draws on Verlaine's *Fantoches* as well as the *commedia del arte* figure of Pierrot, whose repressed sexual desire for Marietta splits him into two aspects: a lecherous Jurgen-figure and an impotent but beautiful faun. This 'marble faun' of Faulkner's next publication is like the lovers on Keats's Grecian urn, symbol of stylised sexuality offering cold immortality rather than life and loss. According to one critic, the faun's predicament embodies polarities and oppositions to be found again in all of Faulkner's later writings: stasis versus motion, consciousness versus experience, dream versus reality, self versus world.[73] In the dream play, Pierrot struggles with the problem without resolving it as the hero does in Cabell's popular novel of the time, *Jurgen*: 'Love alone can lend young people rapture, however transiently, in a world wherein the result of every human endeavour is transient, and the end of all is death.' (Ch. 8) The original

25

Pierrot is, in Brewer's pithy definition, 'a man in growth and a child in mind and manners'. Captivated by the ethereal Columbine (who, like him, is invisible to mortals), Pierrot cannot abandon the Swinburnian world of dreamy idealism for the gratifications of lusty, amoral Harlequin; yet the imperative to life and action means that he cannot enjoy the bliss of mere dreaming.

Pierrot's melancholy is even more apparent in a poem of 1921 which has him contemplating the corpse of Columbine and beyond her his dead reflection in a mirror. In her skirts he reads 'The symbol of his own life: a broken gesture in tinsel.'[74] Clearly Faulkner was attracted to the cynicism of Housman's *Shropshire Lad* whose poem 'The True Love', for example, features a young lover already dead, throat cut, and 'The still air of the speechless night,/When lovers crown their vows' (LIII). Life promises articulation into language, pain, suffering, aging and conscription. The burden of the past and demands of society, a strong theme in Housman, would become a central theme of Faulkner's later fiction ('When shall I be dead and rid/Of the wrong my father did?' [XXVIII]), but for the moment Faulkner was examining the mysteries of sexuality, and finding that fulfilment and consciousness were only reminders of mortality. As Housman advises, 'Think no more; 'tis only thinking/Lays lads underground' (XLIX). Faulkner's adolescent despair culminates in the collection of poems *Vision in Spring* (1921) which one critic claims is 'the pivotal work in Faulkner's self-apprenticeship':[75]

> But you are young, Pierrot; you do not know
> That we are souls prisoned between a night and a night;
> That we are voiceless pilgrims here alone
> Who were once as arrogant in youth as you are,
> But now with our spent dreams are overblown. (16)

The Marble Faun (1924) and *A Green Bough* (1933) continue the poet's critique of the emotions:

> Man comes, man goes, and leaves behind
> The bleaching bones that bore his lust;
> The palfrey of his loves and hates
> Is stabled at the last in dust.

He cozened it and it did bear
Him to wishing's utmost rim;
But now, when wishing's gained, he finds
It was the stead that cozened him. (*Green Bough*, 24)

Everywhere is the tension between life's allure to the 'marble-bound' and art's allure to the poet, weary of life and bullets through the heart. Increasingly one sees the debt to early T. S. Eliot above all other poets, in such lines as, 'I should have been a priest in floorless halls/Wearing his eyes thin on a faded manuscript'.

That last couplet, however, does suggest a more hopeful resolution of the poet's dilemma, one implicit in the very creation of the poetry all along. Many of these poems were addressed to Faulkner's lovers – Estelle Franklin, Helen Baird, Meta Wilde, Joan Williams – but were in themselves a 'safe' emotional activity for a man who found women both attractive and threatening. Faulkner's imitations of the Symbolists were a way of stylising and prolonging his own emotions, strategies which many of his later fictional heroes also contrive. Hugh Kenner describes how the typical Symbolist work 'prolongs what it cannot find a way to state with concision'.[76] According to Kenner, Symbolist poets are haunted by Time which will erode the longed for, 'polyvalent word'. The refusal to resolve issues or clarify images is a way of cheating Time in the work, even while the work laments the ravages of Time. Thus the night is not really 'speechless', the pilgrims not really 'voiceless' while the text continues to utter. In 1921 Faulkner reviewed Conrad Aiken's symphonic poem sequences praising his 'polyphonic effects' and arguing that 'aesthetics is as much a science as chemistry'.[77] Like the elegant black and white line drawings which Faulkner used to illustrate *The Marionettes*, like Pierrot before the mirror, like the puppet itself, Faulkner's poems attempt to hold reality in a solution of aesthetic effects. This ideal becomes the discursive subject of a 1925 poem, 'Bill':

Son of earth was he, and first and last
His heart's whole dream was his, had he been wise,
With space and light to feed it through his eyes,
But with the gift of tongues he was accursed.

Soon he had reft the starlight from the stars
And wind from trees he took, of love and death
He proudly made a sterile shibboleth,
'Till deafened, he forgot what silence was.

Then he found that silence held a Name,
That starlight held a face for him to see,
Found wind once more in grass and leaf, and She
Like silver ceaseless wings that breathe and stir
More grave and true than music, or a flame
Of starlight, and he's quiet, being with her. (112)

Torn from solipsism by a fall into literature, the artist
struggles among signs and signifieds but his creations are
'sterile' until he finds a new kind of 'silence', a new way of
naming perceptions and motion. This 'She' (the syntax suggests)
is found in the ecstasy of aesthetic contemplation whose
movement is soothing rather than arousing. Thus the 'she's' of
earlier poems, the real recipients of the love poems or the
avatars of Columbine, are replaced by the 'She' of art which
offers the artist silence and quietude. Seen in this way, it was a
natural evolution for Faulkner to move from poetry to prose,
where the all-important creative activity itself can be extended
in time; as Kenner says, 'The Symbolist's ideal timelessness
becomes the taleteller's ideal leisure.'[78]

In 'Mayday' (1925), a medieval romance, Faulkner dramatises
a Mississippi custom that on May Day you will see in a stream
the girl you will marry. Galwyn dreams of a beautiful woman
in a stream, and the alternative to this hypnotic merging with
'Little Sister Death' (the Franciscan expression popular with
Faulkner) is the repetitious unreality of ordinary existence. Yet
woman is also the *femme fatale* in many of Faulkner's early
poems and stories, including 'The Kid Learns', a 1925 New
Orleans story. In 'Mayday', 'She is like a little statue of ivory
and silver for which blood has been spilt . . . Her breasts are
like ivory crusted jewels for which men have died, for which
armies have slain one another and brother has has [sic]
murdered brother.' (43–5) The typographical error in this line
foreshadows the intense preoccupation in the later fiction with
incest and the protection of the little sister. There begins to

emerge an opposition between the frozen ideal and the turmoil of yearning, just as there is in Keats's 'Ode on a Grecian Urn' – a favourite poem of Faulkner. One of his earliest prose pieces 'The Hill' (1922) describes a man on a journey frozen into a dream while 'time and life terrifically passed him and left him behind'.[79] The 'marble-bound' faun must be rejected in favour of the flux, that stream of consciousness dramatised in the characters of his novels and described in an early poem where consciousness is seen to 'whirl to infinite fragments, like brittle sparks,/Vortex together again, and whirl again' (*Green Bough*, 13).

Perhaps the best statement of Faulkner's developing aesthetic is not a poem but a story of 1922–5 called 'Nympholepsy', which followed the weary pilgrimage of a nameless labourer after a day of hard work. He looks forward to 'perhaps a girl like defunctive music, moist with heat, in blue gingham'[80] – certainly not a Columbine. His 'swinish instincts' propel him after a glimpsed girlish figure through a twilight pastoral scene, but silence makes him fearful. He blunders into a river where 'he saw death like a woman shining and drowned and waiting'; still he is pursuing the vision 'like a ship on a silver sea'. Woman as death is also woman as 'incontrovertible consummation', the sexual object he has only been able to touch briefly. But, nearing the town, the man forgets the vision and imagines once more 'a girl like defunctive music' – 'Behind him labor, before him labor; about all the old despairs of time and breath.'

In Faulkner's early work, then, Woman beckons to consummation or death – both, for the young poet in his decadent romanticism, make perfect music. So Pierrot serenades his Marietta:

Then we shall be one in the silence, Love! the pool and the
    flame,
Till I am dead, or you have become a flame. (*The Marionettes*,
    20)

Life may be a chasing after shadows (or as Galwyn puts it, 'Man is a buzzing fly beneath the inverted glass tumbler of his illusions'), but there is energy and delight in it: '"It occurs to

me," young Sir Galwyn continued profoundly, "that it is not
the thing itself that man wants, so much as the wanting of it."'
(*Mayday*, 71, 80)

THE NOVELS

SOLDIERS' PAY

In 1922 while reviewing the playwright Eugene O'Neill,
Faulkner wrote, 'Nowhere today, saving in parts of Ireland, is
the English language spoken with the same earthy strength as it
is in the United States; though we are, as a nation, still
inarticulate.'[81] In his first novel *Soldiers' Pay* (1926) he revelled
in the idiom of the returning World War I soldier Gilligan, and
even drew on the Irish plays of Synge (*The Playboy of the Western
World*) and O'Casey (*The Silver Tassie*) for his plot. But as
Kreiswirth says, the novel is 'an elaborate verbal hybrid':[82]
Faulkner was trying his hand at a comedy of manners, a
Huxleyan debate, a Lawrentian analysis of sexual relations,
and in the middle of it all was perfecting his own sense of style
and structure. Words like 'reft, reave, withal' vie with lyrical
descriptions of sultry Southern afternoons, while the young
novelist finds his way through a restrictive plot of a disabled
warrior's return home to the themes and forms of his maturity.

Shell-shocked Donald Mahon, clutching his copy of *A
Shropshire Lad*, is a grotesque embodiment of the preoccupation
with arrested perfection in Faulkner's early work. For Margaret,
who eventually marries him, he is a safe alternative to the pain
of her soldier husband, 'dear dead Dick'. For young Emmy he
is a mockery of her previous passion with him, as for the
flapper Cecily he is the mockery of future passion because of his
deformities. His father the rector, timeless in his rose garden,
refuses to see time's ravages on his son. Januarius Jones is the
satyr in the garden, a character probably inspired by Cabell's
Jurgen (1919). Faulkner's declared themes of sex and death are
crudely epitomised in the climax when Jones seduces Emmy
while the funeral of Donald is in progress.

More interesting than the juvenile lusts of Jones are the
attitudes of the men to Margaret. Young Julian Lowe writes
her love letters, relishing notional sex as an alternative to his
frustrated desire to become an icon in death like Donald; it is

not so much that 'they stopped the war on him' as that he wants to arrest himself in some romantic attitude. Gilligan pursues Margaret forlornly, frustrated by her remoteness. Indeed Margaret, Faulkner's first novelistic woman, is introduced as a stylised character out of Aubrey Beardsley. As a critic observes, she suggests the calm of the Grecian urn 'but without the compensatory idea that the arrested state defies the evanescence of time and life'.[83]

Even Cecily, for all her edgy flirtatiousness, is a symbol of remote stillness for her rejected lovers. George feels himself to be 'an awkward, ugly gesture in unquicked clay' (145) as he sits on a stone monument and gazes at her, while Jones is 'a fat Mirandola in a chaste Platonic nympholepsy, a religio-sentimental orgy in grey tweed, shaping an insincere, fleeting articulation of damp clay to an old imperishable desire, building himself a papier-mâché Virgin' (226). That mention of 'nympholepsy' reminds us of Faulkner's story (p. 29), and the end of *Soldiers' Pay* generalises the sense of sexual yearning in the same cadences as the ending of that story, as the rector listens to the sounds of a negro service: the beautiful, soaring singing 'fading away along the mooned land inevitable with to-morrow and sweat, with sex and death and damnation . . .' (326). What Donald represents – life-in-death, a not quite achieved heroism – is matched by what the women represent – sex-in-innocence, a not quite achieved consummation. Everywhere there is yearning for resolution, a retreat from life's paradoxes, and failure.

The novel contains clues to the future literary experimenting of Faulkner, his impatience with formal grammar and syntax to capture the flux as well as the arrested moment. He uses Joycean devices such as the onomatopoeia of a cracked record interspersed with stream-of-consciousness (272), sections for each hour of the day (235) or for each voice as in a play (149, 264–6). He uses parentheses to carry a consciousness on through another scene, whether it be the barely audible comments of the townsfolk (107) or an extrasensory exchange between Gilligan and Donald (105). He presents a stylised party scene as if it were a transcription into prose of the black and white 'Jazz Age' illustrations he executed for student magazines. And of course he hones the familiar style of mingling motion with stasis: on the train 'the towns like bubbles of ghostly sound

beaded on a steel wire' (19), and in the streets the monotonous
wagons with their burdens – 'a pagan catafalque under the
afternoon. Rigid, as though carved in Egypt ten thousand years
ago. Slow dust rising veiled their passing, like Time . . .' (148–
9). Faulkner is less sure in handling larger sections of the novel.
Apparently he moved them around a good deal; this restlessness
shows particularly after Chapter 5. Here Faulkner seems to
break out from the confines of the country house he has set up,
seeking the larger canvas. He introduces other war widows,
other war heroes, as if Rector Mahon's family of two could not
provide him with the kind of intra-familial passions which
would suffice later on; indeed his interest is strongly drawn by
Cecily's family and the incestuous attentions of her father,
prototype for Mr Compson.

It is a novel about past and future and the domination of
icons. As the soldiers travel home they are 'caught both in the
magic of change' (17), but few of the characters can face the
responsibility of letting others change. The Romans had an
expression for soldiers, 'stipendium merere', deserving pay, but
Faulkner's characters are looking for a pay-*off*, a way to avoid
the present rather than to prepare for the future. Returning
from the battle of sex and death to the real world of compromise
is difficult for them. Jones, near the beginning, observes to the
rector how the church spire seen against moving clouds gives
the 'perfect illusion of slow falling' (50). This will be the
characteristic psychological condition of Faulkner's later heroes
and heroines, a limbo between action and reflection, but in this
first novel his unsteady grasp of plot invention and stylistic
innovation meant that he found his métier only fitfully.

MOSQUITOES

Mosquitoes (1927), Faulkner's second novel, is a pot-pourri of
styles and ideas uneasy in its rigid framework of prologue, four
days on a boat, and epilogue. Virginia Woolf's early novel *The
Voyage Out* also focuses on a witty group of people on a boat,
but it moves to a feverish climax while Faulkner's buzzes about
as aimlessly as a mosquito. The epigraph suggests that this
may have been the novelist's intention, to show how middle-
aged ideas of love and beauty 'become contemptuous through
ubiquity and sheer repetition', but Faulkner is not at home
with a Huxleyan comedy of ideas either in wit or originality.

The result is 'a weird compound of old and new'[84] where social comedy vies with a Lawrentian search for sexual fulfilment.

The contrast is evident at the outset. Talliaferro is a derivative Prufrockian character who languishes in his bath and worries about his balding pate. The 'cruellest months' of spring are gone but he still desires, though with 'no particular object at all' (27); he shamelessly pursues anything in skirts, hoping that 'something I can say' will successfully seduce. The sculptor Gordon, on the other hand, senses in the young Patricia something 'sexless, yet somehow vaguely troubling' (26) as she admires his torso of an adolescent girl. The prose breaks into a stream of consciousness:

> what will you say to her bitter and new as a sunburned flame bitter and new those two little silken snails somewhere under her dress horned pinkly yet reluctant o israfel ay wax your wings with the thin odourless moisture of her thighs strangle your heart with hair a fool fool cursed and forgotten of god (45)

Unarticulated publically, Gordon's passion for the young girl's beauty is a pulse at the heart of the novel. When Patricia apparently elopes, Gordon also mysteriously disappears for a time, and while he measures her head for sculpting he recalls a story about a king who desired beauty and mourned when he discovered that it was in the past, in youthful love – 'But that was long ago and she is dead.' (227) Instead of making love to her he spanks her, an extreme attempt to possess her inviolate, the equivalent of locking her up in a book (224), as he says.

Situated between these two characters is the writer Dawson Fairchild, modelled on Faulkner's mentor Sherwood Anderson. His task is to get beyond Talliaferro's pragmatism with words, to write without trying to impress a girl and yet to sculpt something as pure and durable as Gordon's marble. The task is difficult because 'Love itself is stone blind' and love expressed in literature tends to be, according to Fairchild, hermaphroditic, perverse. The Semitic man Wiseman seems to speak for Faulkner when he suggests that the writer should write instinctively, like Balzac, about the life around him. By ignoring self he will express self, for 'a book is the writer's secret life, the dark twin of a man: you can't reconcile them' (209). The best writing, Fairchild agrees, is 'a kind of singing rhythm in the world that you get into without knowing it, like a swimmer gets into a current' (207). Unfortunately Faulkner only talks *about* this kind of writing in the novel, except in that stream of consciousness passage of Gordon's, and again at the end when he imitates Joyce's 'Night-town' section of *Ulysses*, which seems not so much a revelation (Fairchild is left vomiting on a street corner) as a rejection once and for all of the mannered prose of his first two novels.

Instead of writing a comedy of manners, then, we see that in this novel Faulkner was hammering out his aesthetic theory. The carved torso, even the swimming Jenny, her body 'an ecstasy in golden marble', are icons for the literary work of art itself: as the two girls caress each other below deck, the gentlemen artists discuss art above. Faulkner has not got beyond the conception of female beauty in his early poetry as something threatening and kin to Little Sister Death (Fairchild calls women 'Merely articulated genital organs' [201]), but he is beginning to explore the power of language and storytelling. Perhaps beauty can be 'locked up in a book' without lessening it. The appropriately named Wiseman asserts, 'The Thing is merely a symbol for the Word' (111). The current can go in the opposite direction, not things as signs but signs as things. The ideal may not be physical consummation but the work of art which does not 'reduce' the thing to a sign, but which, as a sign, has its own correlative beauty.

However, at the same time as the novelist's task to reify the world in language is outlined, there is a constant undercurrent in the novel of cynicism and despair – here are the real mosquitoes. Wiseman calls Fairchild an emotional eunuch and warns against the 'morphine' of language; even the narrator sighs, 'Talk, talk, talk: the utter and heartbreaking stupidity of words. It seemed endless, as though it might go on forever. Ideas, for ever. Ideas, thoughts, became mere sounds to be bandied about until they were dead.' (156) Novels do not come out of it very well. 'Faulkner' even appears in the novel as the crazy man who once admired Jenny's body but who confesses to being a liar by profession (123). There is no doubt that Faulkner is using Fairchild in this novel as a doppelgänger, a means of working through to a relationship between life and art which will be mutually creative rather than debilitating.

Fairchild is a dismal adult, but Faulkner has matured and found a balance between life (Talliaferro) and art (Gordon). While the fictional novelist recalls the time he spied upon girls in an outhouse, Faulkner will take Quentin looking at his sister's muddy drawers as the dramatic centre of the well-wrought urn of *The Sound and the Fury*, spun out of his unconscious perhaps but shaped by the Gordon, the sculptor in him.

Bleikasten is right to observe that in *Mosquitoes*, 'as in *Soldiers' Pay*, the ballet of desire is little more than the empty flutter of prurient marionettes',[85] but although it is a failure as a novel, it is a crucial document in Faulkner's aesthetic progress. The Talliaferros and Fairchilds are objectified and put behind him and he is freed into a new kind of articulacy. If the novel is, as Millgate describes it, 'a kind of ragbag into which he could gather up all the usable odds-and-ends of his brief literary past',[86] then there is also an urgent sorting out going on. Seeing the novel in this way we may not be so surprised as others have been at the subsequent flowering.

SARTORIS

Sartoris (1929), said Faulkner in an interview, 'has the germ of my apocrypha in it'.[87] It, or rather its expanded original *Flags in the Dust*, rejected by Liveright in 1927 and finally published in 1974, marks Faulkner's breakthrough into the Promised Land of Yoknapatawpha County. In this novel, too, Faulkner created the originals of Gavin Stevens in Horace, Ratliff in Suratt, the first Snopes, and the groundwork for *Sanctuary*, *The Unvanquished* and several flying stories. In writing it he 'discovered that writing was a mighty fine thing – you could make people stand on their hind legs and cast a shadow.' He explained in a *Paris Review* interview that 'my own little postage stamp of native soil was worth writing about . . . by sublimating the actual into the apocryphal I would have complete liberty to use whatever talent I might have to its absolute top'. The critic Albert Guerard even goes so far as to identify the precise moment of breakthrough – when Faulkner was writing the apostrophe to the mule.[88]

Sartoris may mark a stylistic flowering, but the plot is an amalgam of the two previous novels. Instead of Mahon we have Bayard Sartoris as the returned soldier, and instead of the artists of *Mosquitoes* buzzing about those adolescent torsoes, we

have Horace Benbow with his glass vases and sister Narcissa.
The abridgement diminished Horace's role severely so that the
intended balance is less obvious, but in the Sartoris family
legends Faulkner discovered the perfect 'objective correlative'
for his concern with time, death and a patterned object of desire.
For Bayard is trapped like a fly in the bottle of his family's
expectations as surely as Faulkner's previous male characters,
and here Horace, are trapped into infatuation with the urn-like
female, the unravish'd bride of quietness. The exemplary
pattern of male daring and foolhardy action is, in fact, a
dangerously seductive lure to quietness and peace, a surrender
to the pattern of the past and to death itself which becomes as
powerful as sexual desire to Bayard and his subsequent avatars.
(André Bleikasten has pointed out that Bayard and Horace are
merged into Quentin Compson in Faulkner's next novel, where
incestuous desire comes from an unwillingness to face the
openness of the future or sexual maturity.)

The world of Bayard Sartoris's Jefferson is a world of change.
Like E. M. Forster in *Howards End*, Faulkner fills his landscape
with the new technology of locomotion, not just the Colonel's
trains but those machines 'a gentleman of his day would have
scorned and which any pauper could own' (*Flags* . . . 102).
Change prompts a yearning for the past – according to John
Matthews 'the rites of mourning inhabit every recess of this
novel'[89] – particularly when that past is imaged as an Eden
from which all have fallen. Johnny falling from his aeroplane,
Bayard falling from the horse, the possum falling from the tree
to be devoured by the dogs, Snopes falling from Narcissa's
window into the flowerbox, Horace falling in love, Bayard
falling from the road, from the air: Faulkner fills *Sartoris* with
fallings. They stand not for escape but for a mere dependence
upon things higher, prior.

The great tragedy is that these governing actions and ideas
may be, like Faulkner's entire oeuvre, 'apocryphal', of doubtful
authenticity. What reifies them is words. A comparison with
the earlier versions shows how Faulkner was becoming
increasingly aware of the power of language to build a world.
Flags in the Dust begins *in mediam fabulam*, with old Falls telling
the story of how the Colonel outwitted the Yankees. In *Sartoris*
that story is relegated to the end of the chapter, and we begin
instead with two old men and the ghost of a third. It is an

appropriate beginning to Faulkner's lifelong saga, bringing 'the spirit of the dead man into that room where the dead man's son sat and where the two of them, pauper and banker, would sit for a half an hour in the company of him who had passed beyond death and then returned.' (1) Falls presents Old Bayard with the Colonel's pipe, tempting him to take into his mouth the fatal communion wafer, the breath of the word of the past, to mouth it ghostly into the present air. But it is Aunt Jenny (Virginia du *Pré*) the virgin who *preys* on the Sartoris male line and tells the story – 'and her voice was proud and still as banners in the dust' (19). Old Falls does tell stories of the real Civil War, but he keeps these tales, like his tobacco, safely tied up under wraps. They are told *against* the mythmaking, reminding us of leaders who left the battlefield to plant their corn, who stole horses and let prisoners get away. The War, too, has unleashed Caspey's tongue, and his comments too work against Virginia's mythmaking and in agreement with the captured Yankee major who saw that the War meant the end of the old order – 'No gentleman has any business in this war.' (16)

Nevertheless for young Bayard the family history is too strong, a nightmare from which he cannot awake. Narcissa lulls him asleep with some cheap romance, but he wakes again from the more terrifying fiction within which he lives: a hall of mirrors doubling and redoubling, where the first Bayard pairs with young Johnny, old John with grandson Bayard – except that Bayard is not glorious. The Great War repeats the Civil War as an arena where legends are forged. Like his great-grandfather, Bayard has the temerity to survive the war, but he has rejected the legend which alone can be 'reconstructed' in the post-bellum world and provide a framework for future life. His sense of failure turns to guilt, and he imagines, 'You killed Johnny' (311). He seeks 'comprehension not vindication' (323) but his grandfather will not help him to that knowing cynicism which sustained him and his father. Old John had said:

In the nineteenth century genealogy is poppycock. Particularly in America, where only what a man takes and keeps has any significance and where all of us have a common ancestry and the only house from which we can claim descent with any

assurance is the Old Bailey. Yet the man who professes to
care nothing about his forebears is only a little less vain than
the man who bases all his actions on blood precedent. And I
reckon a Sartoris can have a little vanity and poppycock, if
he wants it. (92)

For Old Bayard his family history is one illusion mimicking
another, yet he survives by consciously casting himself in the
last mythic role of overseer of doom to the house: 'I reckon Old
Marster is keeping me for a reliable witness to the extinction of
it.' (104) Believing and not believing, he inscribes the latest
names and dates in the great family Bible in the attic just as he
had rewritten the history on his father's tombstone, and so seals
Bayard's doom.

For a saga so concerned with fathers, sons and brothers, this
novel is remarkable for the way Faulkner has isolated Bayard,
refusing to use the techniques of conventional fiction. We rarely
enter the hero's mind, not even during his curious courtship
and marriage to Narcissa. He is like a clapperless bell. Indeed
there is bell imagery throughout the novel, particularly with
Horace seeking in his sister then in his Bell(e) the meaning of
peace 'within the cool bell of silence' (176). In *Flags in the Dust*
Narcissa is seen at the end as a lily after Bayard's storming:
'the lily had forgotten it as its fury died away into fading
vibrations of old terrors and dreads, and the stalk recovered
and the bell itself was untarnished save by the friction of its
own petals' (*Flags* . . . 368). The closest Bayard comes to such
peaceful reverberation is on the hunt where the dogs' voices
sound 'like touched bells or strings' (332); but even there they
serve only to remind Jackson and Stuart what a fine hunter
Bayard's brother Johnny was. Old Bayard is at home in his
'citadel of silence' but young Bayard searches for the resonant
gesture or word. We see him doing reckless things in an effort to
realise himself: parodying romantic, gentlemanly gestures with
his drunken black combo serenading the girls of the town;
wandering the countryside over Christmas in search of family,
father, brothers, redemption; courting death in car and plane. To
underline his hopeless entrapment in an empty ideal, Faulkner
gives him a wife and son only to rob him of them in the very year
when his brother was reasserting the power of the male Sartoris
myth over him. Bayard cannot even burn his brother's

possessions without the backward glance which betrays all. Bayard, in effect, is trapped between the silences of death and a predetermined, overdetermined life as a Sartoris.

Within these reverberations Faulkner found the perfect location for his meditation on Southern history, dramatising the art versus life debate of *Mosquitoes* in the past versus present debate of great families. *Sartoris* displays a new confidence in the power of language to celebrate as well as to interrogate itself. Here, then, we first sense the Faulkner 'style'. As in *Mosquitoes*, there is much that is against words in *Sartoris*. Aunt Jenny believes 'it was the name' (371) which doomed the Bayards, and Narcissa 'mans her walls with invincible garrisons' (356) under the lexical threat. At times the language of the novel seems to disappear into its own cancellations, as when Belle reaches out to Horace with that 'hopeful unillusion that fools itself' (195), or when Bayard describes the war with the young men as 'fallen angels, beyond heaven or hell and partaking of both: doomed immortality and immortal doom' (126). In the earlier version especially, Faulkner portrays Horace as being seduced by words rather than Belle's reality for, as he says to his sister, 'I have always been ordered by words.' (340) And we see the sweaty, Uriah-like Snopes haunting Narcissa with his fevered words which are all the more odious and threatening because they are substitutes for deeds. Above all there is the deathly spell cast by Aunt Jenny's words and those genealogies in the Bible or the cemetery.

Nevertheless *Sartoris* also flowers like the wisteria with beautiful, evocative language, 'taking on a mellow splendour like wine' (9). The novel is filled with the rich sounds of the Southern night, an atmosphere which extends to Aunt Jenny's evocation of the battlefields: 'Thus they sat in the poignance of spring and youth's immemorial sadness, forgetting travail and glory, remembering instead other Virginian evenings with fiddles among the myriad candles and slender grave measures picked out with light laughter and lighter feet . . .' (11–12). Language gives a texture to the present by evoking the past as well as other senses, as in the above example, or in briefer refrains like 'There was a bed of salvia where a Yankee patrol had halted on a day long ago' (6); or the silver spoons 'worn now almost to paper thinness where fingers in their generations had held them; silver which Simon's grandfather Joby had

buried on a time . . .' (39). It is language which enables
Faulkner to set up motifs like the bells, or like 'wings': aeroplane
wings, Horace's 'flaming verbal wings' (172), unwinged peace
(175), Narcissa's hair in wings, actors in the wings. Language is
seductive because it gives access to beauty, whether in Johnny's
laughing at the word 'death' and in Aunt Jenny's recreation
of the famous incident with the anchovies, or Faulkner's
revelation of a girl beyond the veil of the garden 'with a bronze
swirling of hair and a small, supple body in a constant epicene
unrepose . . .' (55). In the conflict between silence and speech,
Horace's glass and the bell beating within it, Faulkner brings
out the irony in Keats's 'Ode on a Grecian Urn', a poem which
until this point in Faulkner's development had been a source of
imagery but not dialectic:

> Thou still unravish'd bride of quietness!
> Thou foster-child of Silence and slow Time,
> Sylvan historian, who canst thus express
> A flowery tale more sweetly than our rhyme . . .

Of course it *is* the rhyme we remember, not its referent the urn,
if there ever was one. So on the marvellous last page of *Sartoris*
Faulkner throws an urn even while he deconstructs it, lavishing
his language on a debilitating legend, setting the scene for a
tranquil resolution even as he plants the seeds of endless discord
beyond the pages of the novel and down the Sartoris line:

> The music went on in the dusk softly; the dusk was peopled
> with ghosts of glamorous and old disastrous things. And if
> they were just glamorous enough, there was sure to be a
> Sartoris in them, and then they were sure to be disastrous.
> Pawns. But the Player, and the game He plays . . . He must
> have a name for His pawns, though. But perhaps Sartoris is
> the game itself – a game outmoded and played with pawns
> shaped too late and to an old dead pattern, and of which the
> Player Himself is a little wearied. For there is death in the
> sound of it, and a glamorous fatality, like silver pennons
> downrushing at sunset, or a dying fall of horns along the
> road to Roncevaux. (380)

This passage is wedged between Aunt Jenny's question to

Narcissa, 'Do you think you can change one of 'em with a name?' Having accepted a determinism created by language, she cannot see language conquering language. Narcissa, however, like the children at the end of *Wuthering Heights*, sees beyond the inscribed language of Aunt Jenny and the Sartoris sarcophagus, to her own dream poem of peace. She will have none of Aunt Jenny's confusing the 'unborn with the dead' (358); despite her name, she will break apart the narcissistic, fatal oxymorons of doom/immortal and glamorous/disastrous; she will even break Faulkner's well-wrought urn, which has her called 'Narcissa', casts spells as powerful as the one quoted above, and contrives to introduce even into the rustic McCallum family a dog called 'General' and his mutant puppies. She will quit the language game of Sartoris.

With *Sartoris* Faulkner indeed possessed his most fruitful terrain, 'doubtful authenticity' itself. In all three novels of his apprenticeship, however, he had not discovered his most fruitful relationships, the articulated connections between sibling and sibling, and sibling and father. Because of the separating out of the Horace/Narcissa plot and then its subsequent truncation from *Flags in the Dust*, Faulkner was still, it seemed, keeping young girls at a distance from his main themes. Bayard's relationship with his brother remains hidden in the clouds above France, and he has no father. It was in his next novel, *The Sound and the Fury*, that Faulkner made the family central and at the same time reshaped the urn itself into four sections crucial to the whole design rather than perfunctory as in the remnants of *Sartoris*. *Sartoris* is an impressive antechamber to the mansion of Faulkner's *anni mirabiles*.

THE SOUND AND THE FURY

In April 1925 Faulkner published a sketch in a New Orleans newspaper called 'The Kingdom of God' which featured a howling idiot holding a broken narcissus. In 1928, disappointed by the rejection of *Flags in the Dust*, he returned to that image; through its pathos, nostalgia and impotence he was at last able fully to possess his Yoknapatawpha County. It was not just 'the picture of the little girl's muddy drawers'[90] which was the germ of the novel, but brother Benjy's hopeless love of his sister's innocence. His whole condition, in a sense, is Benjy's stunned reaction to that loss, and Faulkner's perfect image for the post-

bellum South. As he made clear in his 1946 appendix to the
novel, Faulkner was fascinated by Benjy's life-in-death, the
vibrancy with which he lives lost moments, like a sleepwalker.
Even when gelded in 1913, or committed in 1933, he 'lost
nothing then either because, as with his sister, he remembered
not the pasture but only its loss, and firelight was still the same
bright shape of sleep'.[91]

Earlier, in 1933, Faulkner wrote an introduction to *The Sound
and the Fury* in which he described the novel as his 'turning
point', where he learnt how to escape and to indict simultaneously. If in earlier novels he was too bound up in the
conflict between escapers and indicters, here the conflict would
be managed and objectified through formal invention. Indeed
the ostensible focus of the Compson family saga, Caddy, would
be absent, 'un-penetrated', even while the novel is 'about' her
fall and penetration. Replacing the girl as the well-wrought urn
would be the book itself, and the opening line of Dilsey's fourth
section is the signal that Faulkner has successfully climbed out
of the vase, that claustrophobic mouse-wheel where three
brothers chase their sister. 'I had made myself a vase,' says
Faulkner:[92]

> ... One day it suddenly seemed as if a door had clapped
> silently and forever to between me and all publishers'
> addresses and booklists and I said to myself, Now I can
> write. Now I can just write. Whereupon I, who had three
> brothers and no sister and was destined to lose my first
> daughter in infancy, began to write about a little girl. ...
>
> The story is all there, in the first section as Benjy told it. I
> did not try deliberately to make it obscure; when I realised
> that the story might be printed, I took three more sections,
> all longer than Benjy's, to try to clarify it. ... And I have
> learned but one thing since about writing. That is, that the
> emotion definite and physical and yet nebulous to describe
> which the writing of Benjy's section of *The Sound of the Fury*
> gave me – that ecstasy, that eager and joyous faith and
> anticipation of surprise which the yet unmarred sheets
> beneath my hand held inviolate and unfailing – will not
> return.[93]

What delighted Faulkner about Benjy was that the character

allowed him freedom to indulge 'his most persistent stylistic trait – composition by analogy . . . as though a whirlwind of rhetorical implications had grown from each seeded image'.[94] This centrifugal stream of consciousness paradoxically anchored on a few central images or primal experiences was to prove Faulkner's métier. In the case of Benjy the stream is pure, uninterrupted even by dialogue, which is recorded but not reacted to. Instead of interruptions we find a train of association, indicated in the text by italics (when Faulkner's editor Ben Wasson introduced gaps to indicate shifts of scene and deleted the italics, Faulkner was adamant that the section be 'a continuous whole'[95]).

Benjy's monologue is uttered in 1928 when he is 33 years old, but concerns chiefly the years 1898–1912. It begins with the golfers 'hitting', and ends with a recollection of sleep with Caddy, and the dark going in 'smooth, bright shapes' (73). The punning connection is of course 'Caddy/caddie', but the symbolic connection is that Benjy's mind makes an endless series of 'hits' of smooth and bright memories in an attempt to reach, to fill, that hole or gap in his centre which is the loss of his sister; Benjy's mind is like a pinball machine with the ball – consciousness, desire – never falling into its cup to finish the game. It ranges over the significant events of his life dictated by a logic of contiguity of sound or sense only, registering everything except his own 'white noise' of bellowing or whimpering. While it records rhetorical speeches, its own language is simple, non-metaphoric, and flattens out every utterance to a 'said'. This 'tale told by an idiot full of sound and fury signifying nothing' signifies nothing to the idiot, not even the sound and fury which the other family members clearly have to put up with from Benjy. But this is not to say that Benjy finds nothing significant; the one thing with meaning in his life is his sister's child-life, the *idée fixe* for which time and sense have stopped: the first words Benjy hears in the novel are 'Here caddie', and the last gesture of the novel, Benjy's contented gazing at the passing scene on the familiar route to the cemetery, enacts those words as, in Bleikasten's term, 'the concealed utterance of desire': [96] 'Here is Caddy.'

In every way Benjy is a substitute for the real thing. His name is changed from Maury so that he becomes the Biblical Benjamin, replacement for the notional perfect son sold into slavery. His namesake Uncle Maury does 'utter his desire', with Benjy as go-between, but with disastrous results; so does Benjy, chasing after the schoolgirls and being gelded as punishment. Indeed Benjy's whole life is predicated on absence of the real thing, whether intelligence or sexual or spiritual fulfilment. Luster discovers that he bellows when objects are removed from his presence. He regards Caddy's wedding as a funeral, knowing intuitively Yeats's truth that 'Love has pitched her palace in the place of excrement': sexual fulfilment masquerading as a plenitude is for him a fall from grace, an evacuation, an emptying, a loss of presence. Language itself is a sign of that loss: Dilsey and Roskus argue that Benjy knows 'lot more than folks think' (29) about words, but what he knows is that words are a sign for an absent presence. Caddy tries to be wordless, part of Benjy's pastoral world (the setting for most of Benjy's section is a garden) – 'Caddy took the kitchen soap and washed her mouth at the sink, hard. Caddy smelled like trees' (46) – but it doesn't work. She has climbed the tree of knowledge too, has looked in the window and seen death. She has accepted the destructive fire of passion and change for the momentary warmth it gives; her daughter's boyfriend offers to teach Benjy the trick of keeping a lighted match in your mouth. But Benjy has stopped short of language or full articulation. Fire remains a harmful mystery to him. He has prioritised sight and sound over feeling, knowing instinctively that that is the best way to keep the pain of loss at bay. Avoiding absence, Benjy lives in a kaleidoscopic world of uninterpreted impressions, filled not with adult commitments, pains and desires but with the bright shapes of semi-articulated desire. The whole section masterfully takes us into this sensory world, but nowhere more remarkably than in the scene where Benjy accosts the schoolgirl:

> I was trying to say, and I caught her, trying to say, and she screamed and I was trying to say and trying and the bright shapes began to stop and I tried to get out. I tried to get it off my face, but the bright shapes were going again. They were going up the hill to where it fell away and I tried to cry. But when I breathed in, I couldn't breathe out again to cry, and I tried to keep from falling off the hill and I fell off the hill into the bright, whirling shapes. (51)

Faulkner captures all the pain of autism here, with Benjy trying to break through self (face) and private language (bright shapes) to authentic relationship, or even authentic expression (crying); but, caught forever on an in-breath, held in fearful suspension from commitment to life, he falls, not like Caddy into experience, but back into the pinball machine of his game of words, which are but signs of absence.

If Benjy's section is the first movement of Faulkner's symphony sounding the themes and fitfully developing them, then Quentin's section is the slow dance. He is described in Faulkner's Appendix:

> Who loved not his sister's body but some concept of Compson honour precariously and (he knew well) only temporarily supported by the minute fragile membrane of her maidenhead as a miniature replica of all the whole vast globy earth may be poised on the nose of a trained seal. Who loved not the idea of the incest which he would not commit, but some presbyterian concept of its eternal punishment. . . . But who loved death above all, who loved only death . . .[97]

Quentin's speech appears normal but he is as insulated from the present as his brother Benjy, particularly during the recollection of two primal scenes: his fight with Caddy's boyfriend and the events of that day; and his interview with his father. In the latter he reduces himself to silent insignificance – 'and I temporary'. The section begins with dawn and his falling 'in time again', and ends with his preparations to exit from time forever. The shadow (first noun of his section) which haunts him is his own mortality, which he identifies with his sister's pre-sexual being. He is 'but a walking shadow' for whom, in a terrifyingly complete inverse logic, life is death, Caddy's sexual flowering a fall into decay, and time an outrage to be stopped at all costs, either by smashing a watch or taking one's own life. He even wishes he could have been his own father's father, or Dalton Ames's mother, to put a stop to the absurd cycle of procreation.

However, Faulkner carefully indicates that Quentin is closer to normalcy than these feverish moments might suggest. At breakfast he forgets about time and then has to excuse himself for his lapse; he is aware of his own neurosis, and spends much of the day doing normal things. Even though he greets the little girl at the bakery with 'Hello sister', he treats her with genuine kindness. He might have been sustained by the kind of aristocratic 'morality' which he sees in Gerald and his mother, as he rows down the river and she travels in grand isolation but parallel to him. But Mrs Compson has abdicated, offering no resistance to Mr Compson's misogyny which, in combination with Quentin's genuine love for his sister, becomes an intolerable contradiction: women, the one possible escape from Mr Compson's bleak, nihilistic world, are bitches.

One senses Mr Compson's doom (as Faulkner would call it) throughout the section, primarily as an epistemological scepticism. Because of time, the 'minute clicking of little wheels' (75), and because words live in time, meaning constantly decays. Meaning, the modern semioticians tell us, is founded on difference from other signs. Mr Compson denies difference: 'virginity', 'death', 'time' gain no meaning even from their opposites 'unvirgin', 'life', or 'eternity'. His nostalgia for erudition only increases his bitterness: '*Father said it used to be a gentleman was known by his books; nowadays he is known by the ones he has not returned*' (79). His vision of the world is one of increasing entropy, a decay to sameness and silence. Women exacerbate matters by insisting on a moral dimension but enacting only one side, the evil:

> Father and I protect women from one another from themselves our women *Women are like that they don't acquire knowledge of people we are for that they are just born with a practical fertility of suspicion that makes a crop every so often and usually right they have an affinity for evil . . . fertilizing the mind for it . . .* (94–5)

The pain for the reader lies in seeing that father and son are alike in being disappointed idealists who allow women no space to be between saint and sinner. Quentin is caught in the cul-de-sac of his parents' marriage but hasn't his father's resilience or awareness of rhetoric. For him, words are absolutes: 'sister' must not become 'mother', or if it does, the rest of language folds into its opposites like a stack of cards collapsing. It is Caddy caught in time whom Quentin abhors. He is not nostalgic in any simple sense for the 'was' of childhood, but is in revolt at the way meaning can change in cycles, daughter implying mother; hence 'Again. Sadder than was. Again. Saddest of all. Again.' (94)

In a way, Quentin's mother is the more fatal influence, and here we see how Faulkner's family-based saga plays out the macrocosmic drama of the South. The Compson family had connections with Colonel Sartoris, and even though Mr Compson teaches that 'all men are just accumulations dolls stuffed with sawdust' (174) there is the memory of a time when people rose above themselves to honour and glory and a meaningful death. So Quentin used to think of death 'as a man something like Grandfather a friend of his', and 'Grandfather was always right' (175). Mrs Compson, however, cannot play the complicated games of elevation and sublimation which are the subject of so many of Faulkner's novels about the myth of the South. She married above herself but cannot understand her husband's scepticism as anything other than thorough-going, concluding, '*Then we were all poisoned.*' (100) It is this epistemological and historical extremism which Quentin inherits. From her he learns about the unseen evil which is impossible to fight. She it is who, like Rachel in her dying moments, names Benjy as 'child of bad omen' – it was the father Jacob who changed it again to Benjy the 'child of good omen' (see *Genesis* 34:18–19). She it is who wails, 'she (Caddy) doesn't tell things she is secretive you don't know her I know things . . . she not only drags your name in the dirt but corrupts the very air your children breathe . . .' (102). At first Quentin thinks it is just a matter of private and public, of telling or not telling family secrets, but when combined with his father's scepticism, his mother's extremism is fatal.

We can see the extent of Quentin's transformation by contrasting two scenes, the one in which he shoots Herbert's voice through the floor before he can 'tell', and the one where his father tells him that all words belong to a fallen world: 'It's nature is hurting you not Caddy and I said That's just words and he said So is virginity and I said you don't know. You can't know and he said Yes.' (115)

What happens in Quentin's furious adolescence, then, is a result of his father's and mother's influence upon his language. According to Mr Compson, opposites become conflated, chiefly in his idea of women:

> With all that inside of them shapes an outward suavity
> waiting for a touch to. Liquid putrefaction like drowned
> things floating like pale rubber flabbily filled getting the
> odour of honeysuckle all mixed up. (127)

So when Quentin plays out symbolically ambivalent scenes like
the muddying of Caddy, he at once acknowledges and protests
against her sexuality; in the climactic scene with the pocket knife
('do you want me to/yes push it/touch your hand to it' [151]),
which is simultaneously rejection by murder and possession by
rape, Quentin seeks to reify his sister but only as an entity
inviolable to anyone else. Only in extremely fraught, contrived
actions like these can such ambivalence be sustained. In words,
these ambivalences fall apart into Mrs Compson's absolutes
which blight her children: 'there's a curse on us its not our fault
is it our fault' (157), Quentin asks Caddy. This is most obvious
in Quentin's present existence at Harvard, where the watch is
destroyed and then rescued, water is at first cleansing (the boys
bathing) and then destructive (their splashes ruin the bread),
the little girl is innocently guided but society imposes a guilt,
and, most traumatically, the aristocrat Gerald talks about the
bitchery of women, 'without anything else they can do except
lie on their backs.' (165) It is this last polarity which reminds
Quentin of his mother (aristocratic yearning) and father (women
and the 'sorry ends thereof') and sends him into his most
violent fight. Eventually Quentin sees himself

> lying neither asleep nor awake looking down a long corridor
> of grey half-light where all stable things had become shadowy
> paradoxical all I had done shadows all I had felt suffered
> taking visible form antic and perverse mocking without
> relevance inherent themselves with the denial of the
> significance they should have affirmed thinking I was I was
> not who was not was not who. (169)

The awkward prose shows Quentin oscillating between opposites
(asleep/awake, paradox, denial) and a general murkiness (grey,
shadowy, without relevance), just as we see him during this one
day oscillating between present and past, a sense brilliantly
captured by Faulkner in a pun – '*I see saw did I see not good-bye*'
(171). At this point, halfway through the novel, the reader also

senses a balance between the two brothers, between Benjy's heart and Quentin's head, between Benjy's bellowing and Quentin's quiet reflection, between Benjy's fire and Quentin's water. We see that in a way they were paired with the wrong parent: Benjy, demanding nothing from life, is rejected by his mother ('Dilsey said it was because Mother was too proud for him' [169]), while Mr Compson is the last person Quentin should be going to with his anxieties about morality and the expected behaviour of an aristocratic sister. They are paired also in their fixation upon their sister, the sole source of meaning in both their lives. Because Benjy's watch has broken, he can endure; but Quentin must break his himself because he cannot endure.

In many respects Quentin is an artist, the artist of Faulkner's youth who, unlike Horace Benbow, is not content to substitute glass vases for innocent girls. His aim had been to 'isolate [Caddy] out of the loud world' into silence, to remove her from narrative altogether, to maintain her as a lyric poem to patch over the empty world left to him by his parents. He even suggests a fiction of incest to rewrite the world, at least to *contain* the fall within the family. By the time we read this new story, however, Quentin's section has carefully modulated from a cool narrative to italics, lack of punctuation and a chaotic timeframe where past overlays present. An astute reader, noting the eighteen-year flashback from Benjy's scene, will understand that even Quentin's final rewriting, his own suicide by drowning, has redeemed nothing. The only person to visit his grave and that of Caddy is his brother who does not even accept the story that Caddy has fallen.

To move forward to a day before Benjy's section, then, suggests an explanation, a joining. Instead, we are given a third response to the Compson world which is also acutely self-conscious and limited. Jason has been seen as one of Faulkner's nastiest characters, and he certainly reveals his conceit, hypocrisy and lust for power here. *Wuthering Heights*, a novel recalled by the scenes of intense fraternal love in Quentin's section, has Heathcliff persecuting the new generation of an equally incestuous family, and like him, Jason fights to maintain power and deny a slow regeneration. He is as obsessed by Caddy as are his two brothers, but she signifies for him a loss of social prestige and wealth rather than innocence or meaning.

Her marriage to Herbert is identified in Jason's mind with the fall of the family and his disinheritance, and young Quentin is a living reminder of her sin. 'Once a bitch always a bitch,' Jason begins his section, parroting his mother's morality. He is more aware than brother Quentin was that his father left him nothing, not even language (he replies sarcastically 'That's so' when Mrs Compson reminds him he has his father's first name); now his life is dedicated to the bitter absolutism of his mother's language:

> Me, without any hat, in the middle of the afternoon, having to chase up and down back alleys because of my mother's good name. Like I say you can't do anything with a woman like that, if she's got it in her. If it's in her blood, you can't do anything with her. (232)

But like his mother, Jason has become manipulative and hypocritical. He secretly despises his mother and all Southern belles with pretensions to breeding, preferring instead his Memphis mistress Lorraine. For all his concern for the family tradition, he would prefer to remain the childless 'sweet daddy' of her love letters. While preaching right conduct to his niece, he is busy swindling her of her mother's maintenance money, an action which itself encourages Quentin to depend on other men.

Jason allows nothing to pierce this hermetic circle of 'doublethink'. For him the devil is without rather than within, whether in Jews, eastern bankers, niggers, circus folk or those people he hates most, hypocrites. (One of Faulkner's cleverest authorial ironies occurs in Jason's line, 'if there's one thing gets under my skin, it's a damn hypocrite.' [228]) His typical statements are impervious to attack because they half-acknowledge the truth, from his indictments of his townsfolk – 'It's a good thing the Lord did something for this country; the folks that live on it never have' – to his rhetorical flourishes which always conceal a barb: 'I have as much pride about my kinfolks as anybody even if I don't always know where they came from. . . . Let her out all day and all night with everything in town that wears pants, what do I care.' At this point in the novel, it is even refreshing to find someone at last pointing the finger at Mrs Compson's failings, and even his most objectionable acts of torture – allowing Caddy a glimpse of her daughter, burning the circus tickets before Luster's eyes – are balanced by the rarely glimpsed despair which afflicts Jason just as it did his brother Quentin:

'Whatever I do, it's your fault,' she says. 'If I'm bad, it's because I had to be. You made me. I wish I was dead. I wish we were all dead.' Then she ran. We heard her run up the stairs. Then a door slammed.
'That's the first sensible thing she ever said,' I says. (260)

Nevertheless, the imperviousness of Jason's fury is finally what makes the reader recoil from what Faulkner called his 'viciousness'. If Benjy's section is characterised by the undiscriminating marker of 's/he said', and Quentin's by a transcendence of personality into timeless dialect in 'and i . . . and he', then Jason's 'I says' is not only the storyteller in command of his selected material, but the belligerent asserter whose mind will never change. While appearing to be the sole support of the Compsons, Jason efficiently ends the line by alienating Quentin, remaining childless, selling the house and betraying the family honour: 'When a Compson turns Snopes, then the family has indeed run out, and the end of an order has come.'[98]

In his Appendix, Faulkner argued that Jason was terrified of Dilsey and negroes generally. The last movement of the book is Dilsey's, of whom Faulkner wrote simply, 'They endured.' It comes on Easter Sunday, completing the historical and symbolic chronology of the sections (Benjy 1898–1912, Friday; Quentin 1898–1910, Thursday; Jason 1928, Saturday), and the progressive movement outward to detached narration and upward from submerged consciousness. It was Faulkner's way, he said, of reluctantly 'getting out of the book'[99] and it gives the reader a distance from which to see the Compson story in its tragic pattern. As one critic put it, 'She recovers for us the spirit of tragedy which the patter of cynicism has often made seem lost.'[100] At first she reminds us of the physical world with her own draped body like a monumental Greek figure and with the whole exhausting business of feeding and tending the family. But her strength comes from the spiritual world, not the sealed dialectic of the Compsons but the invigorating, spacious world

of negro Christianity. Her broad vision encompasses the
contingent circumstances of the family unit in an apocalyptic
pattern – 'I've seed de first an' de last.' Unlike Jason, who sees
himself unfairly pitted against Omnipotence, or Quentin whose
enemy is time, Dilsey subsumes tomorrow and tomorrow in a
simple lament which promises a solution: 'Dis long time, O
Jesus.' Her chorus is impersonal, unarticulated, trusting. Early
in Benjy's section we saw her rejecting names in favour of the
'Book' – *'They'll read it for me. All I got to do is say Ise here.'* (56)
Now, in the church service, Dilsey returns to that world:

> And the congregation seemed to watch with its own eyes
> while the voice consumed him, until he was nothing and they
> were nothing and there was not even a voice but instead their
> hearts were speaking to one another in chanting measures
> beyond the need for words . . . (295)

The tragedy of the Compsons is that they are slaves to each
other and to the past (Faulkner said they were 'still living in
the attitudes of 1859 or '60'[101]). While their story is told over
Easter, they all remain crucified, alive or dead, on the cross of
idealism. Paradoxically it is the black servants who are free,
partly because they are free from language. As I have argued,
the Compson parents offer two untenable theories of language,
two extremes of meaningless flux and frozen meaning. Quentin's
problem is that he wants to believe what he says, Jason's that
he does believe what he says, and Benjy's that he says nothing.
     Faulkner invented a final scene which brilliantly encapsulates
these themes. Luster cheerfully drives Benjy to the cemetery:
'Ain't de same boneyard y'all headed fer. Hum up, elefump.'
(320) Already the Compsons are mocked by time: death takes
all, and the 'battered and lopsided surrey' in which they drive
is an anachronism, even if the car gives Compsons like Jason a
headache. Benjy clutches his splinted narcissus, signifying the
propped up kingdom of Compson introversion. In an attempt
to demonstrate Compson 'quality' around the monument to the
long gone grandfathers, Luster exposes the Compson lunacy:
the family is stuck in time, in an 'ordered place' (the last words
of the novel) which signifies nothing but the mindless journey
to the grave. When Jason yells at Luster, 'Get the hell on home
with him' (321) he is voicing just one of the many puns with

which this highly textured novel is laced. The Compson mythology cannot find a home between the ideal and the absurd, so the children must live in hell, and tell their idiotic stories there. It must be noted, finally, that Dilsey does not 'tell' her story at all; in this novel, only the three Compson boys are locked in language. By making his novel the very urn that holds, even creates, the ideas of beauty and nobility, by removing the object of regard – Grandfather Compson, Caddy – and leaving a monument and a punning sound, Faulkner hit upon the technique for his major novels. The forces that generate all that sound and fury are enacted, held in suspension, and so made to signify.

3

The Thirties

AS I LAY DYING

As I Lay Dying (1930) continues the themes of *The Sound and the Fury*: the family, language, madness. Indeed in 1946 Random House published the two novels back to back. But in the new novel there is no fourth section to confirm our detached perspective on events and family members; paradoxically, the fragmented, multi-faceted form is more consistently enigmatic than the earlier novel: 'It is the novel's very control, its internal truth to itself, that has led to the huge collection of fragmentary and conflicting critical commentary.'[102] It was written, according to Faulkner, around December 1929 in a space of 47 days while he was working nightshift as a stoker in the powerplant of the University of Mississippi. Even though there is evidence of some revision, the text in what one critic called its 'nakedness of form'[103] certainly reads as Faulkner's *tour de force*. Again Faulkner focuses on a single family, but taking the place of Caddy as focus for the children is the mother Addie Bundren, signifying the other of that pair of concepts in Faulkner's world, sex and death. It is as if we learn here about those Compson children peering in the windows at Damuddy's deathbed, rather than up at Caddy's muddy drawers. The children have counterparts: Jason and Jewel, Quentin and Darl, Benjy and Vardaman, Caddy and Dewey Dell. But instead of three monologues we have fifteen, some of which belong to characters outside the family – not servants, for we have moved (as Faulkner cuttingly said) from princes to peasants,[104] but neighbours and townsfolk. Some of these monologues are for the purpose of getting the story told without an omniscient narrator, but Faulker is also considering the family in a wider social context, just as a public burial is a communal as well as a familial rite.

However, the family, especially Darl with 19 of the 59 sections, dominates the telling.

Early on, Anse Bundren meditates on the significance of roads:

> When he aims for something to be always a-moving, He makes it longways, like a road or a horse or a wagon, but when He aims for something to stay put, He makes it up-and-down ways, like a tree or a man. (30)

Anse attributes all his worries to his family's living near the road and being lured into living longways 'like a snake' rather than up and down. By the end of the novel when we learn of his wife's adultery with the minister Whitfield we may sympathise with Anse's view: the 'upright' visitor come in off the road is a snake in the grass indeed. Anse also helps explicate the curious title of the book, an allusion to *The Odyssey* Book XI where Agamemnon recalls his murder and his wife's refusal to 'shut my eyes with her hands or to close my mouth'. Here, while the crime is the same (Addie has killed Anse metaphorically as husband), it is the wife who dies, yet she is given a monologue near the end of the novel. Addie also uses imagery of a vertical-horizontal axis:

> And so when Cora Tull would tell me I was not a true mother, I would think how words go straight up in a thin line, quick and harmless, and how terribly doing goes along the earth, clinging to it, so that after a while the two lines are too far apart for the same person to straddle from one to the other; and that sin and love and fear are just sounds that people who never sinned nor loved nor feared have for what they never had and cannot have until they forget the words. (162)

For Anse, the horizontal is the instrument and a person's rightful stature is vertical; for his wife, the horizontal is life fully lived, and the vertical is a Tower of Babel of meaningless language, language as a substitute for authentic living. Out of this dialectic between life and language the novel is composed, the activating question being whether consciousness can exist without language, or can be fulfilling with it.

The title addresses this interrogation of the nature of the
'sound and the fury' of language in several ways. The preposition
'as' throws us into time and consciousness; the 'I' is the vertical,
Anse's tree, but the character referred to spends the whole of
the novel's time horizontal, either in bed or in the coffin. What
is more, she is being moved along a road, which for Addie is
lifegiving but which in Anse's view can only bring problems.
The verb 'lay' may be read as present (='lie') or past tense,
and the whole novel oscillates between 'said' and 'say' as if
unsure whether consciousness is constituted in language by a
story, in the past tense, or by present witnessing. (When
characters are emotionally involved in what they relate, they
tend to use the present tense rather than the past, which
indicates detachment.) For Addie the past is only words but
conversely, for Anse, the past and Addie's adventures 'on the
road' are what brought us here – the past explains the present.
Lastly the participle 'dying' is a semantic sleight of hand which
turns an absurd absolute into a continuing action. What is
more, it is logically impossible for it to be preceded by a first
person past tense, as in this title; dying is not something one
gets better from. One is forced to assume that the 'I' is
addressing us from beyond the grave, or, when one encounters
the treatment of religion in figures like Cora Tull and Whitfield,
that the 'I' is a fictive construct, suggesting the well documented
experience of dying people when their whole life flashes before
them. But Addie dies early on, so where else can we locate this
titular 'I'? In a sense, Addie doesn't die; her memory lingers on
to dominate her family's thoughts, not just because they are
fulfilling her request for a burial in Jefferson. She dominates the
book precisely because of her epistemological scepticism
articulated in her section but experienced by all her family,
through love, genes, or upbringing. She dominates the book not
as a fact but as a condition, as an anguished, unanswered
question about the relationship of language and consciousness,
society and personal fulfilment. The title *As I Lay Dying* is a
subordinate clause inviting the proposition that something
happened: what happens is the novel, the consciousnesses of a
group of characters as they try to find some balance, some
equation, some meaning between vertical and horizontal, self
and world, reflection and action, noise and communication.
    When Peabody says that death is 'merely a function of the

mind – and that of the minds of the ones who suffer the bereavement' (38), he restates the tension of that marvellous title in another way. For Peabody the mind is a 'merely'; it functions best 'when it all runs along the same' (64), as Tull puts it, and people like Darl have problems because 'he just thinks by himself too much'. He admires someone like Jewel who in the opening scene walks right through the cotton house rather than around it. Darl, however, takes the mind's functions seriously. Not only does he use a lot of words, and vividly, but he also perceives things without words, like Dewey Dell's secret:

> He said he knew without the words, like he told me that ma is going to die without words, and I knew he knew because if he had said he knew with the words I would not have believed that he had been there and saw us. (23)

According to Addie, Darl was a sign that words were trickery, a second child breaking the circle and opening up the endless contingency of procreation. His birth prompted Addie to strike the bargain with Anse about her burial, so that she could symbolically bow to her father's philosophy that 'the reason for living was to get ready to stay dead a long time' (157). This philosophy, which smacks of Mr Compson's intellectual nihilism, takes a pair of opposite concepts (life/death) and lays them out in a line with a causal connection (it even lays out death in time, like the title). It is as much a trick of words as is Addie's disillusionment with love and marriage, and suggests that the polarities of vertical and horizontal, words and meaning, are even more insecure than we thought; indeed they are interchangeable. This is what we see in the texture of Darl's prose: it is at once rhetorical, significant ('It takes two people to make you, and one people to die. That's how the world is going to end' [34]), and trivial, a screen behind which the important perceptions and actions take place. In other words, the language itself reads like a *tour de force*, a brittle covering for something else.

The same comments apply to the other monologues, but Darl is the key. Ironically Cora judges that Darl stands at his mother's door with 'his heart too full for words' (21) when actually his heart is too full *of* words. He constantly defines himself through the syntax of simple phrases: 'I cannot love my

mother because I have no mother. . . . I don't know what I am.
I don't know if I am or not . . .' and, when Vardaman says
'But you *are*' he replies, 'I know it. . . . That's why I am not *is*.
Are is too many for one woman to foal.' (91) Only his mother's
love would cast the magic spell to authenticate his being, to
collapse the distinction between talking and being, to allow him
to be both upright and meaningful. As we see him his only
choices are the 'frozen attitudes, dead gestures of dolls' (194):
an upright talker of no-wind, no-sound, or a horizontal, eloquent
dead man. His words, especially near the end, are full of images
of empty and filled vessels, but the only vessel he is allowed to
fill is his mother's coffin, dead beside her. Neither his jealous
tricks against the favoured younger brother Jewel, nor his
apocalyptic attempt to break the spell and burst into meaning
by burning the body, can win Addie's love now. At the end he
is left in a cage in Jackson, a mad space the only space left for
him, but in this death the consciousness *is* still living, in fact
detached into a third person. Finally we see that the novel's
title could well apply to Darl himself.

All the characters are located in time and space in these
terms of vertical and horizontal. Indeed Anse even sees his son
Darl in these terms; he was all right until the land, which fills
his eyes, was laid longways instead of 'up-and-down' (31).
Dewey Dell's pregnancy results from her reaching the end of
the picking row and then lying horizontal with Lafe. Cash
makes his mother's coffin on the bevel because as he explains
in his neat list of instructions, '13. It makes a neater job' (75),
reconciling the two directions in a 45 degree angle. Vardaman's
loyalties are with the vertical, illustrated when he bores holes
into the coffin. He wants his mother to be an 'I', alive in death.
As he cannot comprehend her actual death, so he cannot
comprehend that she was once alive, or wished to be, in the
horizontal sense of active engagement with experience. The
most obvious dramatisation of vertical/horizontal is water, rain
and flood. When it first begins to rain, Darl envies the identity
of the vertical raindrops on the roof: 'How often have I lain
beneath rain on a strange roof, thinking of home.' (74) But the
vertical does not promise security, as Cash found when he fell
and broke his leg. What it does augur is the swollen rivers in
which Vardaman's fish might swim, God's benediction at once
cleansing, liberating, and destructive, as it washes away the

corn and cotton seed and frustrates the Bundren's route to Jefferson. In this way Faulkner makes ambiguous the Bundren parents' moralisings on the proper element and orientation of the human: in nature, vertical and horizontal are intimately linked as cause and effect. The women provide a related image of horizontal life when they reverse Addie's body in the coffin so that her wedding gown will spread: seen from above (and Faulkner assists us with a diagram) Addie has been upended, just as for those few moments of her life she upended conventional expectations about women's role in marriage. Ironically, it is the God-fearing women who have provided the appropriate metaphor for Addie's flouting of conventions; now she travels down the road head first rather than feet first, a motion suggesting a live fish. Vardaman matures during the novel, until at the river he regards his mother as a fish given her freedom. However, Addie's spirituals have not got her very far along that road; they have been as circular as Vardaman's toy train on its track. Faulkner seizes his opportunities to remind us of this kind of circular motion in the environment, even to the paradox of the mules' ears 'motionless in tall and soaring circles' (93). This motion is extended when the wagon passes the turn-off to New Hope Church: 'beyond it the red road lies like a spoke of which Addie Bundren is the rim' (96). If Addie travelled in her life, it was a circular motion, centrifugally spiralling away from convention but hopelessly tied to it like a model plane on a wire – her partner in sin is none other than the minister of that church.

Faulkner further complicates the spatial dimension with a series of puns on 'Bundren-burden-bound-bored'. Vardaman bores the holes, but Tull rings the changes on that sound:

> If it's a judgment, it ain't right. Because the Lord's got more to do than that. He's bound to have. Because the only burden Anse Bundren's ever had is himself. And when folks talks him low, I think to myself he ain't that less of a man or he couldn't a bore himself this long. (66)

Addie is a 'burden' to her family because they are 'bound' to her as a sheaf of 'I's'; but each member must also 'bear' himself or herself along the 'road of life', and forbear the others. Cora Tull sings, 'I am bounding toward my God and my reward'

(84), her leaps halfway between horizontal living and the vertical ascension to which she aspires. She tells her childless husband, 'I have bore you what the Lord God sent me' (66); she has born him nothing, but has 'bored' him and the neighbours with her words of religiosity. The climactic episode of crossing the river which comes at the centre of the novel shows the Bundren family 'bound' together in the face of a common enemy. The narrative itself drives into and across the river, and the whole section, from the first removal of the coffin, is given a distinct beginning and end by Cash's two short monologues:

> It won't balance. If they want it to tote and ride on a balance, they will have – . . . (87)

> It wasn't on a balance. I told them that if they wanted it to tote and ride on a balance, they would have to – (153)

Yet the balance has been righted, the burden delivered, the bound across the river made.

At this point in the novel Faulkner makes his most daring move, presenting a trio of voices – Cora, Addie, Whitfield – in a formal, linguistic, and theological display of the themes. Addie's voice comes from beyond the grave. It is a shock to the reader, as if Caddy were given voice. One might imagine that Addie is in that limbo-stage described by her father as 'getting ready to stay dead a long time' (157); but in terms of the novel she is a confirmation and completion of the title, her voice bodying forth the illogic but artistic mastery and imaginative truth at the heart of it. Addie is afflicted by contingency, her mortality, and the insufficiency of words to bind on any sort of permanence. At first she makes the children 'aware of me' by cruel beatings, then when she gives birth to Cash she feels that one's children are one's scourges, locking a mother into the necessary patterns of child-rearing. Language had nothing to do with it; language was 'just a shape to fill a lack' (160). Indeed, Addie's epistemological scepticism extends to the shape itself: she forgets the name of Anse's 'jar', and her own earlier name of 'virgin'. With her second son she even forgets herself as a violated circle, because she is living in a world based not on either/or but on endless multiplicity, endless difference, endless traces. Addie's monologue is, in fact, a remarkable dramatisation of the principles of deconstructive criticism. Addie is aware of our longing for a transcendent antecedent, the 'Word', but knows it is illusory. Recognising the ad hoc nature of language, but unable to face the consequences of her scepticism and 'play', she resorts to instinctual knowings:

> But then I realized that I had been tricked by words older than Anse or love, and that the same word had tricked Anse too, and that my revenge would be that he would never know I was taking revenge. And when Darl was born I asked Anse to promise to take me back to Jefferson when I died, because I knew that father had been right, even when he couldn't have known he was right any more than I could have known I was wrong. (161)

It is as if Addie is playing with two packs of cards, twisting and shifting between a through-going deconstruction and a fierce assertion of her self. This drives her into logical contradictions like the notion, here, of a revenge which is not recognised as such, or of Addie knowing she is right when she could not recognise any evidence to the contrary. Her anguish is more existential than deconstructive. This is shown in her judgment of religious fanatics like Cora as sayers rather than doers, her decision to reflect back to Anse what he wants to see rather than a 'not-Anse' (a situation of Sartrean bad faith), and her attempt to serve her blood by having an affair with Whitfield. Yet Addie's whole life, and her final speech, are evidence of someone who holds values passionately. Words may be 'the gaps in people's lacks' (163), orphans of prior deeds, but Addie herself uses gaps to hide her affair. She says that she 'did not lie' to Anse, 'just refused' him, that she 'tried to deceive no one . . . merely took the precautions that he thought necessary' (163); and she says that her extraordinary parcelling out of subsequent children was all part of cleaning up the house in preparation for death. But the account is too pat, too riven with tensions. The conjunction of 'lay/lie' in Addie's account of her relationship with Anse, like the 'Bundren' cluster which I analysed above, is just one indication of the power of language. For Addie, 'lying' with someone is 'lying', contravening the social code, and she 'lies' when she says that she did not care. The rest of her life is an attempt to balance the books, if you take away the inherited despair which begins to look more and more maudlin. Even the title of the novel tempts the tongue to the word 'lying' and the implication that this very speech is a piece of highly crafted rhetoric. Proof of that is the fact that this woman who has such contempt for words speaks nine pages of them from beyond the grave.

There are three further ways in which Addie's speech can be reintegrated into the text and play of meanings of the novel. First, there is the linguistic point that you can only bemoan an absence if you have surrounded it, defined it by presence. Addie does this when she describes 'the shape of a   ' (161), and John Matthews clarifies the point: 'The "pure" space of silence is in fact already a syntactical unit, part of the system of articulated differences that constitutes writing. In this more complicated way Addie's virginity (like Caddy's) is not the "hypothetically pure" language . . . but a voiceless yet already written language.'[105]

Second, Addie's speech is embedded between those of Cora and Whitfield. Each of these ends by praying for Addie, but each is 'moralizing and empty rhetoric'.[106] They are of a different order, however. Cora is ignorant of the truth, while Whitfield manipulates it; Cora Tull 'toils' in the field, while the minister's 'wit' puts the field to profitable use. Joseph Gold sees an ancestor in the Rev. George Whitfield, an eighteenth-century evangelist of whom Fielding's Parson Adams said, 'When he began to call nonsense and enthusiasm to his aid, and set up the detestable doctrine of faith against good works, I was his friend no longer . . .'.[107] For Whitfield, sin vanishes when Addie dies and he sees no need to make amends to Anse. He 'framed the words' (167) which he would use, but the message remains as empty as Addie's idea of language itself – not absent, but a culpable lack. We have, then, a trinity of religious thinkers, one ignorant of language, one a manipulator of it, and each framing Addie, crucified on her father's cross of cynicism, ignorant of her own manipulation of language, caught between two worlds of religious fervour and intellectual relativism.

Third, Addie's speech is cradled, like her coffin, between the family members she loved or created. She may be dead, but her influence lives on and her children must bear the burden of her **semantic** muddles and spiritual despair. Her speech is also located between the flood and the fire, the first a culmination of Addie's cold revenge, where the whole family labours to fulfil her request, and the second a dramatisation of that other side of her which Darl has inherited, her capacity for spontaneous, passionate action.

Vardaman recalls how Darl told him their mother was in her coffin asking God to help her hide away from the sight of man and 'lay down her life' (200). Darl intuits that Addie's greatest burden was her fecund body, a burden Dewey Dell is discovering for a new generation. Perhaps Addie's extremity arose from the contradiction of bearing new life while preparing for death. Certainly the common focus of mortality and fecundity is what the female form had meant for Faulkner and his avatars in his fiction so far. The Christians of Yoknapatawpha have solved the contradiction by the myth of immortality; for Moseley the druggist, life is hard because then people have a reason 'to be good and die' (191). For an atheist like Addie, 'laying' down for sex is seen, in bleaker moments, as dying. For her second son Darl, the one who convinced her conceptually that her circle was shattered and her life was indeed contingent and doomed, the intellectual conflict is more subtle. For Darl, being an inexperienced male, the emotional life is more demanding than the physical. The rest of his siblings muddle through the absurdities of physicality – Dewey Dell with her pregnancy, Cash the carpenter with his twice broken leg, Jewel with his horses as physical substitutes for his mother – but Darl operates within the shifting, rarified atmosphere of emotional allegiances. Like Hamlet, his burden is consciousness, not the body; in one section he says:

> How do our lives ravel out into the no-wind, no-sound, the weary gestures wearily recapitulant: echoes of old compulsions with no-hand on no-strings: in sunset we fall into furious attitudes, dead gestures of dolls. (194)

> It would be nice if you could just ravel out into time. (196)

Darl cannot escape the vertical 'I' of self-consciousness, but he also uses language far more adeptly and awarely than his mother to articulate his condition. He explores all the resources of vocabulary, typography (as when his jealous observations of

Jewel appear in italics) and narrative – he knows what is happening, almost extra-sensorily, because he tells stories. He is in fact at ease with time: he knows the secrets of the two Bundren women, accepts their mortality and tries to put an end to the unnatural attenuation of the moment of Addie's death through action, by creating a funeral pyre. The result, for him, is the asylum in Jackson. Rejected and betrayed by his family, Darl's world collapses into a universal 'yes' just as his mother's had been circumscribed into a 'no'. We are reminded of the motif of the circle as Darl departs on a train like the model one of Vardaman which goes round and round.

The family, on the other hand, ravel out into time, even though Cash and Dewey Dell bear the scars. Even Cash welcomes the 'graphophone', another circular instrument but one which broadcasts melodies. In Faulkner's daringly comic ending, at least Anse thinks that the family has not come full circle but started on a new road: 'Meet Mrs Bundren.' By that act of naming the past is expunged and the family reconstituted; at the same time Addie's revenge is nullified. The journey, for Anse, has resulted in a physical and spiritual rebirth and the only victims of the mother's dying wishes are her children: Darl committed, Vardaman toy-less, Dewey Dell twice abused, Cash a cripple and Jewel horse-less. We saw how Addie was in fact subtle with words, not as subtle as her husband or lover but able to shore up her sense of self. Only Darl is unable to weave actions and words together as camouflage for each other. His action of burning the coffin, perhaps the one genuine act of respect for the dead in the whole novel, is open and therefore capable of misreading. No wonder his final speculation rejects logic and ruefully acknowledges the supremacy of animal desire:

> A nickel has a woman on one side and a buffalo on the other; two faces and no back. I don't know what that is. Darl had a little spy-glass he got in France at the war. In it it had a woman and a pig with two backs and no face. I know what that is. (241)

One critic has rightly said that Darl is destroyed by his attempt to 'straddle language and being',[108] but I do not believe that Addie is as innocent as he makes her out to be. There is a conflict, as another critic suggests, between pride and nakedness in the novel,[109] in the sense that what the reader reads are monologues which the family members would never reveal to each other, even while they reach out to each other frankly for support. The prose, abjuring the mimesis which made *The Sound and the Fury* such a *tour de force*, suggests (like Virginia Woolf's *The Waves*) the shared preoccupations of the family at a lower level of consciousness. But only young Vardaman comes close to saying what he thinks, and even he is quickly learning subterfuge and repression. Faulkner's preoccupations here may seem similar to his previous novels, particularly *The Sound and the Fury* with Addie replacing Caddy: female sexuality, innocence and experience, the past seeping into the present. But here we can see his interest in the medium of language growing, how it both dictates and mocks our thoughts, how the larger discourses – religion, morality, history – impinge on the group, and how the individual voice operates within that group. *As I Lay Dying* is remarkable for not employing a narrator; Addie fails to fulfil the promised role of the title, and Darl begins to 'tell' himself in the third person only when he has gone crazy. The *reader* must constitute the coffin, the action, the drama, 'out there' beyond and between the consciousnesses, with only the family's unreliable texts as guide. In this way the reader fills in the jar, the frame, and becomes aware of the complex grid references which Faulkner can generate between the horizontal of text and the vertical of reader-constituted life.

SANCTUARY

Sanctuary (1931) was, according to its author, 'a cheap idea, because it was deliberately conceived to make money'.[110] A comparison with earlier versions suggests that Faulkner made it tighter, more violent and more dramatic before publication, but critics are uncertain whether the sensationalism can be justified. For some it is the 'twentieth century initiator of . . . the contemporary American Gothic';[111] for Malraux it was somewhere between a detective story without detectives, and a Greek tragedy;[112] Leslie Fiedler expressed the critical unease succinctly:

> *Sanctuary* is, on the one hand, the darkest of all Faulkner's books, a brutal protest to the quality of American life written in the pit of the Great Depression; but on the other hand, it

is the dirtiest of all the dirty jokes exchanged among men
only at the expense of the abdicating Anglo-Saxon virgin.[113]

Even more than *As I Lay Dying*, it is an unmediated novel;
there are no clues, even agonising ones such as Quentin would
give, to the perspective one should have on the outrageous
events. The reader, as one critic neatly puts it, 'is in free
fall'.[114] A reader becoming used to Faulkner's characteristic
preoccupation with interpretation and revision might be forgiven
for thinking the novel is closer to Mickey Spillane than Greek
tragedy. In Faulkner's development, I think the novel does
mark a final, violent abandonment of his obsessive motif of
woman as virginal urn, but it enacts a conception of her at the
opposite pole, as wide-open whore. Still, Faulkner does
effectively explore what can happen in a world where fellow-
feeling is totally suppressed in favour of greed and gratification;
or, more exactly, where language is suppressed in favour of
physical needs and reflexes. The brutality is as much a part of the
tone as of the narrative, since it denies the reader empathy. What
Clifton Fadiman called Faulkner's 'coiled and deadly prose'[115]
discloses with snakelike imperturbability a dehumanised world.
Reacting, the reader must assume the role of chorus, adding in
protest the missing dimension. (It is no coincidence that the
novel's 'sequel' *Requiem for a Nun* [1951] should be cast as a
playscript.) But of course, that dimension is missing from many
of the characters of *Sanctuary* – that ability to empathise beyond
oneself, to temper appetite with humane concern, to understand
the otherness of others, hence their sanctity or 'sanctuary' to
themselves. Even Gowan and Temple are not immune from
this charge of trespass, of willful intrusion: Gowan crashes his
car while trying to reach the remote Goodwin house, and once
there, Temple unaccountably rushes straight into the house.
What Faulkner has done here is to explore his theme of
innocence and experience through motifs of territory, showing
how the quest for experience may involve invasion, and that,
conversely, a reaction to invasion, upsetting the equilibrium of
isolated selves, is counter-invasion.

Self-consciousness, as in all Faulkner's work, is not necessarily
a passport to moral rectitude and respect for the other; nor are
his villains moronic or 'evil'. There is in Popeye's gang a kind
of honesty, most apparent in the speeches of behaviour of the

woman, who explains exactly how she feels about the 'rich bitch' Temple even as she warns and helps her. She comes from a background which plays out its feelings, as when her father shot dead her suitor. She tells Temple exactly what will happen if she stays. Even Popeye presents himself frankly, almost iconographically as the black-suited gangster with the slouch hat and cigarette in one corner of his mouth. He is a walking cliché, dangerous but recognisable. There are no contradictions in him, as there are in the drunken Gowan slobbering about Virginian gentlemen. Neither his appearance ('that vicious depthless quality of stamped tin' [1]) nor his eyes ('two knobs of soft black rubber' [2]) allow an observer to generate the complex mirror-imagery of self-reflexion of which Benbow is so fond. He is simply there, and Benbow has trespassed. Like Temple, Benbow makes no attempt to leave the forbidden place, for reasons that have to do with his own divided sense of self, imaged on the first page in the 'broken and myriad reflection of his own drinking' (1). Later, in a key passage Horace explains what he thinks of mirrors:

> There was a mirror behind her [Little Belle] and another behind me, and she was watching herself in the one behind me, forgetting about the other one in which I could see her face, see her watching the back of my head with pure dissimulation. That's why nature is 'she' and Progress is 'he'; nature made the grape arbor, but Progress invented the mirror. (9)

Here Horace prides himself on being male, progressive, self-aware, yet compared to the low-life in *Sanctuary* he is extremely self-deluded and unknowing. For example, despite his broadmindedness he attributes his step-daughter's loves to the seasons, rather than acknowledging a separate space, self-consciousness or 'sanctuary' in women.

Before we give too much to Popeye and his gang, however, we must emphasise that they are limited to stimulus and response. They assume that if a girl comes to stay the night in your house and stands by a bed wearing a coat and little beneath it, then she is asking to be seduced. Only Horace's civilised environment keeps him from the same attitude towards women. But the difference between Popeye and Horace, as traced in the novel, is that the latter has the opportunity to grow, to 'progress', through the acquisition and use of language. In that emblematic opening scene Popeye has a gun in his pocket, Horace a book. For Popeye the gun or phallus is an instrument of self-defence and retaliation; for Horace the book is a potent instrument to disclose the world. Because he knows the names of birds, he is not frightened of them, as Popeye is. When he realises that his life consists not only of fetching shrimp for his wife but of being a 'shrimp', he leaves on the strength of that subliminal pun. Later when he finally 'reads' the photograph of his stepdaughter it is 'propped against a book' (113) and he recognises the face behind the surface, 'older in sin than he would ever be', gazing beyond his own shoulder. What Horace recognises is the independence of Little Belle from him and the danger of seeing the world as a surface only, because this may mean seeing it as a reflection of a projected self.

Before considering the emotional climax of the novel, which comes two-thirds through the book, we should observe Temple's development. Unlike Horace, Temple is deprived of language except the language of the body. Even at the dances, her 'waist shaped slender and urgent in the interval, her feet filling the rhythmic gap with music' (18); even in her flights around the Goodwin house 'she faced Popeye with a grimace of taut, toothed coquetry' (31). She is the true narcissist, enthralled by her own body and its potency. Surprised in her ablutions and at the last moment of possible escape when she could simply run off into the trees, she turns back to the house, or rather watches herself do so (61). At the moment of violation, then, her cry is, 'Something is happening to me . . . I told you all the time!' (68) But she hasn't 'told'; her tongue has been tied by the fact that her body has become the object of the male gaze. In effect, her body has told 'you' (the unspecified male audience) that something *should* happen to her; and now, in a form, it is.

During the horrific flight of Chapter XVIII, then, Temple appears as a soundless, open mouth, as in Munch's famous painting 'The Scream'. Incapable of ex-pressing, she im-presses only, a fact that Popeye manipulates unerringly when he quells her by showing her her face in the car mirror. Now completely divorced from the natural temporal rhythms of courtship and motherhood, Temple is presented to us at Miss Reba's merely

as a mechanical doll, her feet clattering like the metallic claws
of the pink and blue puppies. The clock has stopped, time is
'moribund', she has been 'fixed' so that her blood will not flow.
A violated temple, she has become a sanctuary to any man who
comes to her; appropriately with this bitter redefinition, the
chapter ends in a cacophony of unintelligible noises:

> . . . she heard him begin to make a whimpering sound. . . .
> His hand clamped over her mouth. . . . she saw him . . .
> making a high whinnying sound like a horse. Beyond the
> wall Miss Reba filled the hall, the house, with a harsh
> choking uproar of obscene cursing. (108)

The 'comic relief' interlude with the town and country
Snopeses only intensifies my feeling that *Sanctuary* is, beyond its
sensationalism, a study of language. Here we see how language
can either sustain a kind of innocence, as with the Snopes boys
staying in a boardinghouse rather than a 'brothel', or perpetuate
subterfuge as with Clarence. When Temple recounts Popeye's
first molestation, she too reveals how she thought of using
language ('I'd say . . . I'd say . . .'); this amounts to a subterfuge
pretending innocence, pretending to accept that she is victim or
body only. Horace's subsequent vision of two lovers in an alley,
the woman swooning and the man 'speaking in a low tone
unprintable epithet after epithet' (152), confirms his view of a
world of evil, where people are isolated in spirit but invaded in
body, where the only intercourse is sexual. Then Faulkner gives
us that amazing scene where Horace vomits over the photograph
of Little Belle, over the fact of sexuality itself. The passage
modulates into a vision of Temple herself, rushing towards the
stars bound naked on a flat car, while the only noise is 'the
faint, furious uproar of the shucks' (153). In its opposing
movements, downward from the cross and shooting upward
like a rocket, the passage symbolises the two warring conceptions
of sex as fall or consummation. The power and integrity of the
scene comes from the fact that while Faulkner has dramatised
the horror of nonverbal behaviour earlier, he also shows its
fascination to the literate Horace, even, perhaps especially,
after he has recognised the female's (Temple's, Little Belle's)
otherness.

That chapter ending, with its uprush of imagery and energy

is repeated three more times as the novel ends. At the end of
Chapter XXIV the abducted Temple glimpses Popeye from the
car, his star-like match 'sucked with the profile into darkness
by the rush of their passing' (166). When Horace stumbles
upon Goodwin's lynchers at the end of Chapter XXIX, he
experiences the fire as 'a voice of fury like in a dream, roaring
silently out of a peaceful void' (204). And at the very end
Temple, in the Luxembourg Gardens, lets her imagination
dissolve out 'into the sky lying prone and vanquished in the
embrace of the season of rain and death' (219). The ambiguous
effect in all of these endings is of a dream-like escape from self
and responsibility, balanced by a more sinister sense of
penetration or violation of that space or sanctuary. In each case
silence reigns, or at least the non-verbal 'white noise' of the
shucks (the novel is full of clickings, hissings and sighs).
Meaning is conferred only by the narrator's voice, and even
then, it is the reader who must build out of these enigmatic but
highly charged endings a meaningful shape. I have mentioned
the idea that the reader of *Sanctuary* is in a free fall, and that
mood illustrates the unreflective world of both the gangsters
and Temple. Temple says little that is not curt command, and
Faulkner deliberately avoids any sustained interior monologue,
emphasising instead the sequences when she is alone in a room
and 'finds herself' doing things. But these characters are 'flat'
also in the sense that they do things one after another without
an articulated connection; we rarely have a feeling of inner
calculation or conflict, that is, consciousness. What Faulkner
achieves through *his* language, reinforced by Horace's more
articulate conflict, is a demonstration of how the urge to sex
and the urge to death become indistinguishable in a nonverbal
environment. Popeye plugs Red in the head, Temple in the
genitals – it is the same thing. Temple, originally seeking Red
as an escape, caresses Popeye at the dance hall whispering
'Give it to me, Daddy' (162), not knowing herself whether she
is groping for his penis or his gun, or for her death or his. A
moment later she is groping for Red, 'her mouth gaped and
ugly like that of a dying fish as she writhed her loins against
him' (164). Finally, Popeye kills his own sex substitute, Red,
while Temple condemns Goodwin to death in her one verbal
enactment of Popeye's physical control over her. In a loveless
world, sex *is* death.

Nor is there any relief for the reader in the larger social world, where words seem to breed only mass bigotries and miscarriages of justice. In the silent world of *Sanctuary*, the maiden in distress is not tied to the tracks awaiting a gallant rescue, but willingly spreads her body on the train itself, and the feverish pace of the novel contributes to that sense of a world of automatons bound on collision courses by their own clockwork, since clock-time has stopped. The only progress possible is towards death, the orgasmic immolation or holocaust of fire as seen in Temple's body, the mob's killing of Goodwin, or Popeye's mother's revenge.

By accepting fully the dreary implications of the novel's worldview, I think we can avoid the contortions of critic George Toles, whose excellent summary of the linguistic surface of the novel as 'layers of ugly, disjointed tropes'[116] leads him to argue that the characters actually reject its 'leering, sadistic grip' just as they reject their roles as stock characters of pulp fiction. This reading presumes that without imputing a moral dimension the characters are left in an unarticulated void. Yet there *is* a central theme to the novel which is desire, unspoken and unspeakable because it is bodily. Faulkner strips away the theoretical clothing he gave desire in his first novels, and the substitution of family he gave it in *The Sound and the Fury* and *As I Lay Dying*, and fully evokes it through his language and its gaps. Those chapter endings are surely not 'futile closures'[117] but dramatisations of the limits of desire, as they portray people's notions of 'sanctuary', the private spaces which must not be violated. For the townsfolk the prison confers no sanctuary on Goodwin. The sanctuary of their own secret selves has been violated by this public enactment of deflowering the virgin and the fire is a substitute for their own lust. Horace, particularly through his relation with Goodwin's woman, has learnt that he must let the women he knows control their own sanctuaries, that he will find no place for himself where he desires: God may be a woman, always and already violated, and now taking the pragmatic steps, as Horace's wife does, of locking the front door. Temple, rescued by her 'sugar-daddy' the judge from the court where she has perjured herself, seems no longer capable of evaluating the world at all, has no inner-outer sense on which to build the very ideas of desire and 'sanctuary'.

The history of Popeye, expanded from earlier drafts of the novel, lends support at the end to this deterministic interpretation. Stronger even than desire, past experience dominates behaviour and mocks idealist distinctions between self and other, sanctuary and danger. As one critic puts it, 'Son of a syphilitic strikebreaker who deserts his family; grandson of a pyromaniac; given to cutting up small animals with scissors; and venomously allergic to alcohol, Popeye is rather a compendium of naturalistic doom.'[118] The philosopher Benbow and the virgin Temple are starting to look like leftovers from Faulkner's earlier phase; his attention is turning to the broader contexts of family and society, and the linguistic world his characters inhabit. The complex interaction of personal moment and public history formed the basis for the remaining novels, including the semi-dramatised sequel *Requiem for a Nun*.

REQUIEM FOR A NUN

What prompted Faulkner to return to Temple Drake after twenty years and continue her story in *Requiem for a Nun* (1951)? The answer can be found in the curious form of the text, hardly a novel and hardly a play; one critic called it 'a vacuous charade'[119] while John Lehmann in *The Listener* called it 'a wonderful example of Faulkner's power of dramatic suspense. . . . Faulkner is a great poet and tragedian.'[120] Certainly the word 'requiem' suggests meditation rather than drama, but the word 'nun' applied to the 'nigger dope-fiend' Nancy requires an explanation, and it is the slow meditation on who she is, and how she could be *named* in that way, which constitutes the drama. In *Sanctuary* we saw the juxtaposition of wordless crime and wordy justice; we also had Gowan's tortuous letter to Narcissa, pleading his valour despite his desertion of Temple by twisting suppression, or not-naming, into love: 'But if my heart were as blank as this page, this would not be necessary at all.' (86) There is no place for such nostalgia for the pre-verbal in this novel. Faulkner underlines the significance of naming by prefacing each of the three 'acts' with a *tour de force*, a history of the South as the acquisition of speech and writing, symbolised in establishing the buildings of justice in the wilderness. His subtitles – A Name for the City, Beginning was the Word, Nor Even Yet Quite Relinquish – suggest a development from sign to rhetorical assertion to dialectical qualification, as language becomes more sophisticated and impossible to live outside of. The question a reader asks throughout the 'play' is: how did the South 'get' to this point? Is the South epitomised in this 'case'? Is Stevens correct when he tells Temple, 'The past is never dead. It's not even past' (85)?

The first prologue recounts the fall of Jefferson into print. The massive lock which had been attached to the mail bag – not even to lock it, but more, as it were, to lock it away in favour of the spoken word – precipitates a complicated deal, itself based on the existence of written government statutes and finally resolved by another act of naming (of the town), which results in the previously ignored documents of the settlement being formally preserved and therefore imbued with significance through time:

> a meagre, fading, dog eared, uncorrelated, at times illiterate sheaf of land grants and patents and transfers and deeds, and tax- and militia-rolls, and bills of sale for slaves, and counting-house lists of spurious currency and exchange rates, and liens and mortgages, and listed rewards for escaped or stolen Negroes and other livestock, and diary-like annotations of births and marriages and deaths and public hangings and land-auctions, accumulating slowly . . . (9)

The townsfolk are perfectly happy with the pre-literate flux; Ratcliffe's name evolves as it is used by those who 'had dispensed with the eye in the transmission of words' (20), it is difficult to distinguish police officer from criminal, and at one point they are happy to give the town two names. The grinding haul into literacy is comic and pathetic. At this stage the townspeople can be caught out by the written word, as Ratliff is when he suggests, 'Put it on the Book' (25); but they are happy with naming the town Jefferson, since it is something they can see and can share in 'one compound dream-state' (35). But as soon as their lives are quantified, time and money become a puzzle and a burden, each word, each fifteen dollars owed, sounding like the town clock to the resident pigeons, 'which even after a hundred years, they still seem unable to get used to, bursting in one swirling explosion out of the belfry as though the hour, instead of merely adding one puny infinitesimal more to the long weary increment since Genesis, had shattered the

virgin pristine air with the first loud ding-dong of time and
doom' (49). Faulkner's brilliant prose mirrors the message; the
whole section is in one long sentence, a roller-coaster precipitated
by its first words 'The courthouse'. We are given history as a
fall into time and memory, that fall memorialised in the prose
of the second prologue, again one long sentence, but presented
as one extended name or definition of 'JACKSON'. That we
are dealing with the monumental Word here is cleverly indicated
in the first paragraph which refers to 'a capital, the Capital of a
Commonwealth' (91): the capital city capitalises itself on the
page, growing before our very eyes from small 'c' to big 'C' to
two 'C's'. Faulkner describes geological ages as successive
imprints upon 'the broad blank mid-continental page' (92).
Places are named, becoming 'points' for men to rally to (97).
But already Faulkner introduces the problems of a wordy
society, where 'men's mouths were full of law and order, all
men's mouths were round with the sound of money' (96) – here
we have, if not an echo of Temple's scream, at least a sense
of blockage and obfuscation. Constitutions are drawn up and
behaviour becomes the servant of definitions hinged upon
propositional logic: for example 'the principle that honour must
be defended whether it was or not since, defended, it was,
whether or not' (98).

By the third prologue the pace of history has increased,
thanks to the written word. The prose spills and tumbles as
Faulkner in one glorious sweep describes the evolution of the
modern United States out of the Civil War. The 'prints' of
moccasins are erased in favour of legal documents and
architectural plans; the Indian Queen's signature ('X') unleashes
the flood of westward expansion. But in the midst of this flood
we are asked to follow one 'story', 'the incident, ephemeral of
an afternoon in late May, unrecorded by the town and the
county because they had little time too' (208), of a girl in the
old jail who glimpses a soldier out in the street during a battle,
and later marries him. Her scratching on the glass – '*Listen,
stranger; this was myself: this was I*' (231) – is the human *was*
which the narrator endorses, standing for 'youth and dream'
rather than 'fact and probability' (230). The jail itself had been
ripped open, one wall destroyed and its significance as a
reminder of the past overwhelmed by Jefferson's developers.
What Faulkner does by removing the fourth wall of the

theatrical set is remind us that stories are what matters, but also that we must revivify them in our own imaginations from the scratchings on the glass which are the playtext of *Requiem for a Nun*.

In this self-reflexive fashion, then, the text knits together prologues and play; the reader can redeem the fall into print by reconstructing (and that word has its ironic historical overtones) Temple Drake's reality. Moreover, this reconstruction is part of the very play itself. Temple's task is to turn the law's printed story – Nancy's guilt – into a profitable experience by talking, not to finish the plot (she hopes to be rid of the 'metaphor' of her own guilt [105]) but to open up new experience. Talk is what has been denied Temple, from her first associations with Popeye; here we see her going not to her husband but to her uncle Gavin Stevens, and arguing that if people only had someone to listen to them, there would be no crime (141). Her tragedy is that she has been surrounded by people who do not listen; rather, they use her as a character in their own preplanned fictions. Popeye is likened by Stevens to the Sultan Schariah who wanted each sexual experience to climax in death – that is why he had Red killed; Stevens himself echoes Horace Benbow when he warns against 'haggling with putrefaction' (117); and Nancy forces an end to Temple's story by smothering her baby instead of 'sending her the word' (239). That is, Temple is surrounded by extremists of one sort or another, who believe in the law – of the gun, of justice, of God. Temple, though, is trying something different, trying to get away from fact to truth. She realises that to do this, 'I've got to say it all' (116) and that 'it wasn't even the letters. It was me.' (169) Other characters lock her into history: Stevens talks about the past as a language, but a language 'set' into a promissory note with a catch in it (144–5); Gowan has trapped Temple in an endless round of gratitude despite the fact that he, if anyone, caused her fall to begin with. Yet during the play we see Temple accepting the past and, what is more difficult, taking it into the future with her, keeping it pliable and alive. She sees that her aim is not to save Nancy but to live more aware, and indeed her behaviour with Red's brother shows that she is one of the few characters to have acted true to themselves throughout.

It may seem that I am being too ingenious in defending

Temple, but unless we understand her bravery and intelligence the text will seem enigmatic to us. Critics have seen Faulkner as endorsing Nancy thoroughly: '. . . in the explicitly affirmative pose he adopted more and more in his later work, [he] uses Nancy's primitive faith to show that human life can be endowed with meaning'.[121] But there is an absolutism in Nancy's pronouncements and her taking authority into her own hands, which is surely worrisome. Faulkner is careful to remind us near the end of the last act that Nancy lost the child she was carrying when someone kicked her (245) – motivation enough for envy of the rich white woman no better than herself who has two healthy children.

The play, then, is a sophisticated enactment of the prologues' idea of the proliferating written word. Temple recognises her 'letters' as irrelevant to her emotional trajectory and tries to be true to her dream of a sexually fulfilling partnership. Nancy upholds the 'Word' of God, arguing that women know what a person 'is' even if men listen to what that person says (240). She resigns herself to the highest level of justice (in her eyes) while Temple remains on earth wrestling with the ravelled ends of unfinished stories, recognising not justice but the necessity of taking responsibility for one's actions. For her it means suffering. Gavin Stevens sneeringly describes it as 'an orgasm of abjectness and moderation' (129) but Temple does learn to say it all, even to Nancy, and to accept the existential uncertainties at the end of the play. Even in her misery she will not 'yet quite relinquish' a sustaining belief in those rare past moments of love, as the girl in the jail scratched her name and dared to reach for pleasure. In the end we may ask who is the true nun dedicated to life's possibilities, Nancy or Temple?

LIGHT IN AUGUST

Light in August (1932) is Faulkner's first novel to address directly the issue of slavery and racism. The working title for the novel was 'Dark House', suggesting not only those morbid sanctuaries of Hightower and Joanna Burden and the communal problems of different habitations ('My Father's mansion has many rooms') but also, to extend the image, the portrayal of the black hero Joe Christmas from the exterior as a puzzling but unavoidable presence. Here Faulkner considers the issue of black identity as one of language or naming. The black American writer Ralph

Ellison explains how writing about the American Negro also involves writing about oneself and the fundamental questions of existence:

> Let Tar Baby, that enigmatic figure from Negro folklore, stand for the world. He leans, black and gleaming, against the wall of life utterly non-committal under our scrutiny, our questioning, starkly unmoving before our naive attempts at intimidation. Then we touch him playfully and before we can say *Sonny Liston!* we find ourselves stuck. Our playful investigations become a labour, a fearful struggle, an *agon*. Slowly we perceive that our task is to learn the proper way of freeing ourselves, to develop, in other words, technique. Sensing this, we give him our sharpest attention, we question him carefully, we struggle with more subtlety; while he, in his silent way, holds on, demanding that we perceive the necessity of calling him by his true name as the price of our freedom. It is unfortunate that he has so many, many 'true names' – all spelling chaos; and in order to discover even one of these we must first come into the possession of our own names. For it is through our names that we first place ourselves in the world.[122]

When Ellison considers Faulkner he acknowledges that the 'namer' was 'seeking out the nature of man' by writing about the Negro, was 'more willing perhaps than any other artist to start with the stereotype, accept it as true, and then seek out the human truth which it hides.'[123]

Light in August demonstrates that the real hindrance to emancipation is a mutual fiction which requires Joe's acceptance of society's label. Agonisingly we follow his apparent determination to remain a victim, despite the fact that his blood, if it mattered at all, is probably part-Mexican. For the society of Jefferson Joe functions as a sign in a fossilised system of meaning whose authority is historical; all the characters in the novel are shaped by their pasts, although only the principal characters are aware of it and fight against it. The human truth which the present labelling hides is existence in time with the concomitant threat of change, but in Joe's case the past, or his childhood, only offers him more signs, moreover signs which contradict themselves. To the end of his life he is barred from possessing his own name. Alfred Kazin correctly identifies Joe as 'an abstraction seeking to become a human being. . . . the most solitary character in American fiction.'[124] Faulkner himself recalled, 'That to me was the tragic, central idea of the story – that he didn't know what he was.'[125]

We must be careful, however, not to make Joe into an empty cipher. Because he is not part of society he can see it objectively as an outsider, and on the evidence of his childhood it is understandable that he should judge it as wanting. It is this very judgment, this sense of disappointment, which antagonises the people of Jefferson. When he first appears in the town and in the novel, at the mill, he is an elusive contradiction – 'He looked like a tramp, yet not like a tramp either.' (27) The men take his distance as scorn, and threaten to 'run him through the planer . . . maybe that will take that look off his face' (28). It is ironic that the townsfolk should want to erase someone who does not know who he is, but this is because he seems to be significant by his enigmatic separateness and potentiality. This polarised ambiguity is sensed by the men in his very name, either grabbed out of the air *or*, in its initials, sign of messianic doom.

The long sweep of flashback from Chapters 6–12 allows us to fill in to some degree Joe's silhouette. His primal scene with the dietitian at the orphanage hopelessly entangles several sign systems in his mind: the white of her room and toothpaste is desirable but furtive, while his own guilt is black (the first time he hears the word is when the guilty dietitian hisses at him 'you little nigger bastard' [114]); grown-ups or authority figures punish, but in puzzling ways (instead of a smack, Joe receives the bribe of money); and sexuality, or rather feminine sensuality, is both attractive and dangerous (by association it causes him to vomit and eventually to be sent away from the orphanage). Once more we see Faulkner grounding his themes in personal history, particularly in sexual relationships and the male's early struggles with the notion of the virgin/whore. It is not surprising that Joe's subsequent adolescence is confused: he beats the black girl instead of making love to her, and roams America playing black stud to white women and white seducer to black girls. For Joe, sexual relationships are power relationships because he sees himself always on a chessboard facing a piece of the opposite colour. Not only are sexual relationships 'coloured'; for Joe the simplest act of giving or receiving food becomes fraught with menace and challenges his fragile identity. These complexities are reinforced by the behaviour of his various guardians: the men are brutal Calvinists trying to beat religion into him, the women secretly offering sustenance. The fog of social and spiritual contradictions into which young Joe is thrust is epitomised in the scene when McEachern catches up with him at the dance hall. It is the confrontation of youth and age, Joe's rite of passage, one of many moments when he resolves contradiction by physical violence; yet Faulkner contrives to present the scene as confused, tentative, and only dimly perceived. The point of view is not even Joe's but McEachern's:

> Perhaps it did not seem to him that he had been moving fast nor that his voice was loud. Very likely he seemed to himself to be standing just and rocklike and with neither haste nor anger. ... Perhaps they were not even his hands which struck at the face of the youth whom he had nurtured and sheltered and clothed from a child, and perhaps when the face ducked the blow and came up again it was not the face of that child. But he could not have been surprised at that, since it was not that child's face which he was concerned with: it was the face of Satan, which he knew as well. And when, staring at the face, he walked steadily toward it with his hands still raised, very likely he walked toward it in the furious and dreamlike exaltation of a martyr who has already been absolved, into the descending chair which Joe swung at his head, and into nothingness. Perhaps the nothingness astonished him a little, but not much, and not for long. (191–2)

McEachern does not see Joe as a person but as an incarnation of the Devil. Contrasting with the certainty of the fanatic is the uncertainty of the narrator. Here is the dominant voice of the novel with its litany of uncertain 'perhapses' resolved by, or rather resorting desperately to, an action: 'Anyway ...' Joe's blank face is a palimpsest for whatever his antagonist wishes to see there, even though he is made to play a part in a passion play which is given no justification by the text (McEachern finds nothingness rather than congratulating angels).

As readers we must be alert when any of the book's many narrators becomes declarative. Just as none of the Compson boys achieves the detachment of Dilsey, so none of *Light in August*'s many 'narrators' finds peace in explanation. Even Gavin Stevens, making his first appearance in a Faulkner novel, can only explain in the conventional terms of his time and place. For him, it *is* a matter of blood:

> Because the black blood drove him first to the negro cabin. And then the white blood drove him out of there, as it was the black blood which snatched up the pistol and the white blood which would not let him fire it. And it was the white blood which sent him to the minister . . . (424)

In a sense, of course, Stevens is correct in his analysis: *Light in August* is a story of bad blood, determinist, Darwinian – Joe is a sport. But he has been made by human beings, not genes. Faulkner subtly tempts the reader into using Joe as a symbol but we must resist, even when the imposed scheme comes not from a ranting preacher or rationalising lawyer, but from the artistic texture of the book itself. I have in mind the marvellous sequence at the end of Chapter 5, leading up to the murder and just before the long digression into Joe's past. Here Joe traverses Jefferson uneasily, and Faulkner presents the town as a Dantean icon, the black pit of the slave section Freedman Town embedded like 'the original quarry, abyss itself' (108) within the sparkling rim of lights of the white suburbs. The whole section uses imagery of black and white, and Joe is alienated from both races. He wears a white shirt and black pants. But the reader must see all this as an overlaid, reductive system which offers a false, polarised choice between black and white. To accept this patterning is to step from the difficult halflight of a late August day into the fatal simplicities of the Jefferson men.

Like a fly drawn into a web, then, Joe penetrates the dark forest to the Burden mansion, where his spiritual and psychological confusion is completed. He cannot play Joanna's impossible games, cannot be both seducer and salvation, servant and confessor. A victim of her own tortured genealogy, Joanna demands that Joe be both Christ and cross, cursed and chosen (240), burden and boon. Even her sexual games share that contradiction of black and white, motion and stasis which Faulkner maintains throughout this long novel: Joe finds her

> in the wild throes of nymphomania, her body gleaming in the slow shifting from one to another of such formally erotic attitudes and gestures as a Beardsley of the time of Petronius might have drawn. She would be wild then, in the close, breathing halfdark without walls, with her wild hair, each strand of which would seem to come alive like octopus tentacles, and her wild hands and her breathing: "Negro! Negro! Negro!" (245)

Like Medusa, Joanna would have Joe her thing, now stud, now student, yet it is only *after* her appalling ultimatum fails and the gun misfires that Joe reacts with violence. In the end, Joe's faltering progress as victor/victim resolves into the simplicity of one more game, Percy Grimm's deadly game of chess. Percy the proto-Fascist, as Faulkner later called him, is one of many Faulkner characters who favours the imperatives of the hunt to the vacillations of peaceful reflection, yet in accordance with the polarised, mirror-image technique of the novel, even he is seen as a servant: 'Above the blunt, cold rake of the automatic his face had that serene, unearthly luminousness of angels in church windows. He was moving again almost before he had stopped, with that lean, swift, blind obedience to whatever Player moved him on the Board.' (437) As throughout the novel, violence gives way to ambiguity about the meaning of that action, even Joe's murder and castration. The 'pent black blood' (440) which pours from Joe's loins is a trap for the unlearning reader to copy Steven's theorising and deduce that Joe did, after all, have Negro in him. But while Faulkner litters the novel with imagery of Joe stepping into black men's shoes and feeling the blackness rise up his body it is imagery only, part of a shifting sign system which the narrators and people of Jefferson lay over Joe, the human being whose rich blood is as black as anyone's.

After Joe's death, as at the end of *Sanctuary*, Faulkner employs the image of the rising rocket, again with contradictory connotations of outrage and serenity. We are told that Joe's example, or rather the sign of Joe, will remain in the memory of Jefferson, but 'not fading and not particularly threatful', only a potential agent for change. Faulkner is too wary of the power of the past – indeed *Light in August* insists on that fact on every page – to promise amelioration. Instead we are left, at the end of this horrendous chapter, with the sound of the police siren passing beyond the realm of hearing. The scream of protest becomes mute.

The novel is remarkable for its interweaving several stories and narrators. The three mains strands culminate in the three final chapters. Both Lena and Joe make demands upon Hightower, but only for Lena is he a sanctuary. This is because the Reverend Hightower is trapped in the head where Joe is trapped in the body. His obsession is a version of old Sartoris's foolhardy and gallant cavalry raid. Inheritor of impossible contradictions, chiefly a Calvinist abolitionist father who nevertheless fought with the Confederate Army, Hightower cannot live in the present and cannot confront the black fact. He alienates his wife and drives her eventually to suicide, loses his congregation and retreats to brood at his window, dreaming of a release from consciousness in the glorious abandonment of action. His apotheosis follows Joe's; the man of religion and intellect is as cornered as Joe is by his society's crude laws. He envisages an apocalyptic wheel symbolising the tide of history and time, offering him the excuse of inevitability and powerlessness. On that wheel he sees the faces of all the people he has known, including the matched pair of Joe and Grimm, which 'seem to strive (but not of themselves striving or desiring it: he knows that, but because of the motion and desire of the wheel itself) in turn to free themselves one from the other, then fade and blend again' (466). The wedges blur into motion again as ratiocination capitulates to futile action, ironically invested by Faulkner with all the power of his rhetoric. It is the completion of a masterful chapter poised between blockage and dissolution, endless repetition and a kind of closure (critics debate whether Hightower dies at this point or not):

> Like a long sighing of wind in trees it begins, then they sweep into sight, borne now upon a cloud of phantom dust. They rush past, forwardleaning in the saddles, with brandished arms, beneath whipping ribbons from slanted and eager lances; with tumult and soundless yelling they sweep past like a tide whose crest is jagged with the wild heads of horses

and the brandished arms of men like the crater of the world in explosion. They rush past, are gone; the dust swirls skyward sucking, fades away into the night which has fully come. Yet, leaning forward in the window, his bandaged head huge and without depth upon the twin blobs of his hands upon the ledge, it seems to him that he still hears them: the wild bugles and the clashing sabres and the dying thunder of hooves. (466–7)

The third plot is given the third and final ending to the novel; it also began the novel. Lena Grove, ancient symbol of fertility and patience, travels in and out of Jefferson uttering only, 'My, my. A body does get around.' (26,480) It is an utterance which punningly describes the essence of the novel. The reader has come 'a-round' full circle through death and despair to Lena, her new baby and the comic pastoral of her final scene with the decent Byron Bunch. At the beginning of the novel Lena's body is indeed round, since she is well pregnant with Lucas's baby. Although her end supplies a formal completion and turns from things dying to things newborn, it is not quite the frozen composure of the lovers on Keats's (round) Grecian urn (which is specifically alluded to twice in the novel). Lena arrived with a past, and leaves with a future. But her trajectory through the novel is like an arrow through a rotten apple, and she carries a minimal kind of hope away with her. She also carries Byron Bunch, one of the few decent men in the town.

For the first time since *The Sound and the Fury* Faulkner gives scope to the interior monologue and to a variety of narrators. Space and time are continually foregrounded as the parameters of *Light in August*, not simply in the chases and the way the outsiders circle around the various dark houses of Jefferson, but in the reading experience itself. Lena is the most commonsensical of thinkers, as she places herself within the logic of space and time and imagines her boyfriend Lucas also placing himself by means of space and the numbers one, two and three (father, mother, baby):

Thinking, 'And if he is going all the way to Jefferson, I will be riding within the hearing of Lucas Burch before his seeing. He will hear the wagon, but he wont know. So there will be

one within his hearing before his seeing. And then he will see
me and he will be excited. And so there will be two within
his seeing before his remembering.' (6)

While Lena knows exactly where she is and where she is
going, the other major characters – Joe, Joanna and Hightower –
slip and slide in time, barely connecting with the present.
Faulkner suggests the domination by memory and the
subconscious by using italics to suggest a different layer of
thought, more powerful but unarticulated to the thinker.
'Memory believes before knowing remembers', the first sentence
of Chapter 6 (111), could stand as an epigraph to *Light in
August*. Faulkner's characters may anguish and go through the
motions of independent thought ('knowing' or 'remembering'),
but generally they are portrayed as acting in accordance with
deeply submerged imperatives inherited through childhood
incidents or from the tribe and the tribe's ancestors ('memory'
and 'belief'). In Faulkner's world even learning from history
will not necessarily exempt one from repeating it, as the
example of Hightower shows. Consciousness is so difficult,
hedged around with 'perhaps' and 'seems' and 'maybe'; action
is a seductive release. As the Compson family were obsessed by
a moment in their past, so the people of Jefferson are obsessed
by the Civil War when they fell from Eden and the fabric of
their lives was rent. Joe is a sign of their guilt and defeat but
they are chained to him as sign, because to ignore his blood
would be to deny the antebellum social system and the reasons
for the War. The odds against 'free' thought or action are
therefore huge; the past seems to seep into every corner of the
novel's present, an idea dramatised in the organisation of the
novel which presents effects before causes, action before
reflection. In particular, the Calvinist fathers who litter the
book seem to have a preternatural ability to seek out evil and to
perpetuate it. Joe's grandfather Doc Hines, foaming his pieties
and inciting the crowd to lynch his own grandson, is one of
Faulkner's most terrible creations.

Nevertheless the attempt must be made to articulate the past
and the roots of social attitudes, to expose the inbuilt sign
systems (black/white, male/female) with their violent crudities,
and to create a better world for Lena's baby than was offered to
Millie's. *Light in August* is one of Faulkner's most sophisticated

novels because it enacts the very extremes it exposes. Hightower and Stevens belong to that line of articulate paralytics stretching from Talliaferro and Quentin through Benbow to the tellers of *Absalom, Absalom!* When Hightower left the church upon news of his wife's suicide,

> He was keeping his face concealed from the [camera] in front, and next day when the picture came out in the paper it had been taken from the side, with the minister in the middle of step, holding the hymn book before his face. And behind the book, his lips were drawn back as though he were smiling. But his teeth were tight together and his face looked like the face of Satan in the old prints. (63)

What happens to the spiritual leader in the South is a grotesque Jekyll/Hyde personality split. Here the inner man gleefully regards the destruction of his family and church; and Faulkner reminds us of yet another doubling, as Lucifer was once the brightest of angels. In scenes like these Faulkner vividly dramatises the torments of Southern thinkers and reformers, but the rest of the novel deals with the inarticulate who are governed by the very symbols which are the devices of literature. Their single dimension is the dimension of Hightower's upheld hymnary, its symbols twisted but simple and murderous in intent. As the townspeople gather at the scene of Joanna's murder, they instantly believe 'aloud that it was an anonymous negro crime committed not by a negro but by Negro' (271); equipped with a paucity of expression, they begin their rollercoaster ride of prejudice, and Faulkner brilliantly highlights the problem of signs in the following paragraph:

> Then there was nothing for them to look at except the place where the body had lain and the fire. And soon nobody could remember exactly where the sheet had rested, what earth it had covered, and so then there was only the fire to look at. So they looked at the fire, with that same dull and static amaze which they had brought down from the old fetid caves where knowing began. . . . [The firemen] came too and were shown several different places where the sheet had lain, and some of them with pistols already in their pockets began to canvass about for someone to crucify. (272)

The slide from reality to legend is effortlessly accomplished.

Between these two groups, the articulate and the inarticulate, rebounds the novel's central character, someone who scarcely seems present in language at all, either to himself or to the reader; he is trapped in his body and awaits a 'spell', a widening of the vocabulary which may free him. In the meantime he is an absence, a wall waiting to be filled with the town's graffitti and the reader's ineffectual sympathy. Only the example of Lena's fortitude will move us beyond the 'gale' of history and the 'burden' of bigotry to listen for Joe's real name: ' "Now I got to get up again," she said aloud.' (410)

PYLON

The opening of Shushan Airport in New Orleans in 1934 was the basis for Faulkner's novel *Pylon* (1935). Faulkner had bought his own plane in 1933 and had, of course, received some training as a pilot in Canada during the First World War. Eight months after the publication of *Pylon*, Faulkner's brother Dean would be killed in Faulkner's own plane while barnstorming.

Like the blacks, Faulkner's flying daredevils were outsiders, but unlike them, they had no history or religion. As the author later said, '. . . they were outside the range of God . . . they had escaped the compulsion of accepting a past and a future . . . they had no past. They were as ephemeral as the butterfly . . .'.[126] While Faulkner's thematic focus here is yet again the mysterious woman and the heroic young man, the characters are sketchy and his energies seem more devoted to formal experimentation, to seeing what happens to the spoken and printed word in a modern technological society. It is no coincidence that his filtering subject is a newspaper reporter whose assignment is to comprehend and explicate the recent and transitory sport of the aerial circus. Albert Guerard may complain that Faulkner's 'imaginative presentness' is his trouble here, 'as always',[127] but then Faulkner clearly feels the modern age is itself in trouble by its 'presentness'.

The newspaper is Faulkner's symbol of the transitory in modern life, the failure to contextualise events. He reproduces headlines in a Joycean or Cubist fashion to show their triviality and irrelevance; even the editor, looking at tomorrow's galley, sees 'nothing new' but 'that cross-section out of time space as though of a light ray caught by a speed lens for a second's fraction between infinity and furious and trivial dust' (55). The headlines, 'that cryptic staccato cross-section of an instant crystallized' (62), miss the substance, the truth, the 'very insoluble enigma of human folly and blundering'. That day's newspaper is seen a third and final time in the clutches of the drunken reporter, 'the dead instant's fruit of forty tons of machinery and an entire nation's antic delusion' (81). Hagood the editor encourages the reporter into what would now be called the 'New Journalism', complaining that 'you listen and see in one language and then do what you call writing in another' (32). But although the reporter's telephone calls to the editor are an avalanche of emotional impressions, the story he finally submits in the last lines of the novel is dry and distanced; the emotion is appended 'savagely in pencil': *I guess this is what you want, you bastard . . .*' (230). The reporter is barred from compelling journalism because of his own desire for anonymity; his name is a secret and his mother an embarrassment – even his apartment looks like a stage set. This sounds like the perfect credentials for the reporter as impartial witness, yet without a sense of identity, a connection with society and a history, he has no framework for telling his stories.

The motley group of flicrs, being outsiders, offer the most likely possibility of genuine talk; indeed by the end of the novel, by means of drunken brawls and his generosity, the reporter has established a relationship with them all. But they are no more articulate than the impersonal, ignored announcer's voice over the loudspeakers which epitomises the official, sanctioned voice of New Valois. When Schumann and the reporter talk, although bonded by love for the same woman, 'it was as though the silence were the dialogue and the actual speech the soliloquy, the marshalling of thought' (125). This modern city of inarticulate lost souls would remind us of T. S. Eliot even if the allusions (as in the chapter heading 'The Love-song of J. A. Prufrock') were not ubiquitous. But unlike Prufrock, who in some sense speaks for himself ('you and I'), the characters of *Pylon* are remote even from themselves. It is the narrator who articulates their 'Yair's' (for 'yes') and overlays the narrative with sequences of Cubist word-painting such as:

the garblement which was the city: the scabby hop poles

which elevated the ragged palm-crests like the monstrous
broom-sage out of an old country thought, the spent stage of
last night's clatterfalque Nile barge supine now beneath
today's white wings treadings, the hydrant gouts gutter
plaited with the trodden tinsel-dung of stars . . . (152)

. . . lost lost lost all ultimate blue of latitude and horizon; the
hot rain gutterful plaiting the eaten heads of shrimp; the ten
thousand inescapable mornings wherein ten thousand
swinging airplanes stippleprop the soft scrofulous soaring of
sweating brick and ten thousand pairs of splayed brown
hired Leonora feet tiger-barred by jaloused armistice with
the invincible sun: the thin black coffee, the myriad fish
stewed in a myriad oil – to-morrow and to-morrow and tomorrow . . . (207)

Certain verbal combinations recur in the novel, like 'gutter'
and 'plait', and the neologism 'garblement' and pun
on 'catafalque' in the extract above highlight Faulkner's
preoccupation with meaningless noise. He evokes a high-tech
world of gloss, a surface of signs without depth, like
contemporary photorealist paintings of American jukeboxes or
deserted streets. This overlay is like gold in a mediaeval
manuscript, an over-rich adornment which makes the text itself
exemplify the theme of glossy, brittle and impenetrable surfaces.
    The fatal 'presentness' of New Valois society is also evoked in
a series of images to do with flashing instants. Like the
newspaper headlines, the reporter himself seems to exist only
tenuously, for the moment, as he crosses the busy streets 'like
one of those apocryphal night-time bat creatures whose nest or
home no man ever saw, which are seen only in mid-swoop,
caught for a second in a light beam between nothing and
nowhere' (57). At the end of the novel, in the long, bleak coda
by the lake during the search for the pilot's body, the reporter
looks at the distant beacon:

Steady and unflagging the long single spoke of the beacon
swept its arc across the lake and vanished into the full
broadside of the yellow eye and, already outshooting, swept
on again, leaving that slow terrific vacuum in mind or sense

which should have been filled with the flick and swish which never came. (185)

Unlike Prufrock, who lacks the courage to force the moment to its climax, the reporter knows what he wants and tries to get it. Flying itself is, for him, a sexual orgasm ('he says it's like flying in and out of a – organization maybe' [71]), and he joins the fliers because he recognises that they are living the moment. He even makes his intentions plain to Laverne, the eternal female descending, as it were, in her parachute with skirts billowing. But he is frustrated by the lack of a code or system which would anchor the fliers to society and time: the boy doesn't know who his 'old man' is, Laverne seems to have at least two co-equal lovers, they all seem to have neither past nor future. They often seem a different species altogether, wedded to their machines, made of valves and rods. And yet they are also living fully, authentically, in the 'now'; this is what attracts the reporter.

One can sense here Faulkner's ambivalence about the modern age. The freedom of flight, regardless of conventions of time and place, is seductive, yet the newspaper and the whole vapid milieu of the city Mardi Gras suggest that there is little separating the open tarmac and the waste land. That ambivalence informs the plot itself, which has the reporter becoming a part of the actual aeroplane fuselage in an attempt to impress Laverne. In fact, he is abetting Roger's extremely conventional motivation to win enough money to support Laverne's second child. The ambivalence is also in the writing, alternately flat and flowery, faithful to the monosyllabic dialogue of the characters as well as ebulliently allusive to Shakespeare, Keats and Eliot.

For the reporter, resolution of polarities will come only when the word is married to the flesh. What he wants is to 'be the name, my name, you see' (128), for Laverne. The street he lives in has its name in chipped mosaic, '*The Drowned*' (65), but he wants a world where the soul can fly, where there is no division between fact and feeling, city and soul. The reporter is working on a Sunday feature 'about how the loves of Antony and Cleopatra had been prophesied all the time in Egyptian architecture only they never knew what it meant; maybe they had to wait on the Roman papers.' (148–9) The idea, like the idea of Cleopatra's catafalque, is splendid, but by the time people knew about glory it has been reduced to the 'papers'. At the beginning of the novel we are told that New Valois's airport 'seemed to float lightly like the apocryphal turreted and battlemented cities in the coloured Sunday sections . . .'. (14) Similarly, the word 'pylon' originally referred to the gateway to an Egyptian temple; the spectators and media try to maintain the impression of the airport as a shrine to daredevil supermen, but for the fliers a pylon is merely a useful marker for an air race, and the feats are simply a job. For the reporter the pylons are certainly not the gateway to sexual bliss, but by the end of the novel he has learned a great deal about how to express the power of the imagination. After his vigil by the lake, he returns and writes his own version of what has happened and what will happen. The story of gallant contest, faithful friends and the reporter recalled lovingly in a future time by Laverne and her son, is contradicted by the narrative itself, yet within that narrative we see an opposite movement: Dr Shumann burns the boy's money, then, translating his appearance into the required sign, makes his own 'happy ending' by adopting him as their grandson. Faulkner, in other words, is culminating his disquisition on language in the modern world with a postmodernist technique of alternative endings. He suggests that the issue is not whether we have the resource of courage to live richly, but whether we have the courage to commit ourselves to our best 'reading' of the signs. By involving himself so intimately in the fates of all the fliers, the reporter has shown that he has that courage; whether we read him as he would wish is up to our generosity.

ABSALOM, ABSALOM!

Many critics regard *Absalom, Absalom!* (1936) as Faulkner's greatest novel. For Albert Guerard it is 'the culminating novel of Conradian impressionism',[128] while Michael Millgate is impressed by 'those audacious ambiguities, juxtapositions and effects of delayed revelation which give the novel its extraordinary qualities of moral complexity and narrative suspense.'[129] In the novel Faulkner returns to the great Southern dynasties of Sartoris and Compson, this time creating a new one in the Sutpens. But if the theme is the burden of the past which afflicted Bayard Sartoris, the form is that of *The Sound and the Fury* where intense family feeling and conflict are what shatter the psyche's effort to knit together the past. The complicating factor is the matter of *Light in August*, with its racism and epistemological doubt. Sutpen's One Hundred may seem a long way from Feinman's airport, or Gavin Stevens' rooms for that matter, but once more we must listen to people as they try to accommodate themselves to the past in order to humanise the present. Here, the hermeneutic problem is the obverse of *Pylon*, where the reporter seemed to succeed in investing a scattered present with the meaningful continuity of story; here there is *only* story, the characters involved seeming to exist so much in language rather than a physical setting that the novel becomes one of 'self-incarceration'.[130] Not that the characters are divorced from their environment; one of the novel's most original implications is that public history as much as family history is a matter of stories to which society gives its assent. The story of Sutpen becomes the story of the South, and the task of present-day inhabitants is to 'reconstruct', not the courthouses and mansions but a tolerable legend. As one critic puts it, the attempt by the youngest men Shreve and Quentin 'to understand the fable is also an attempt to control or even negate the power of the culture that produced it'.[131] Thomas Sutpen is not only the brother-in-law of the woman who tells Quentin the story, but also figures as a larger-than-life symbol of the Southern inheritance.

By foregrounding the actual process of story-telling or myth-making, Faulkner suggests analogies, perhaps equations, between biological and narrative patterning; as Sutpen attempted to father a world, so Quentin attempts to tell a tale. Both have an ideal of what their creation should look like – a progression of gallant white knights/pages untarnished by elements beyond the 'family'. The complicating irony is that Charles Bon the halfbrother is not 'pure' white. The gaps in the Sutpen saga which Quentin tries to fill are like the black letters he must search for to fill the white page – as mysterious, as unvirginal, as necessary for human truth as the impulse which took Sutpen to a coloured lover in the first place. We have met tellers and listeners in many previous novels – Aunt Jenny, Horace Benbow, Gavin Stevens – but in *Absalom, Absalom!* the *reader* is forced through the same frustrations and uncertainties, so that process rather than product is what finally matters, the reading experience rather than narrative dénouement. We find ourselves in an unstratified verbal world of metonymy rather than metaphor, denied even a sequential order, for, as one critic put it, 'Faulkner tries to undermine the reader's spatiality, his power to re-read, put down the book . . .'.[132] Chapters end not by summing up but by opening out into new material, compelling the reader to launch into the next breathless swoop. The reading experience of this novel has been well summed up by two critics, Conrad Aiken and Ilse Lind:

> . . . the form is really circular – there is no beginning and no ending properly speaking, and therefore no *logical* point of entrance: we must just submit, and follow the circling of the author's interest, which turns a light inward towards the centre, but every moment from a new angle, a new point of view. The story unfolds, therefore, now in one colour of light, now in another, with references backward and forward: those that refer forward being necessarily, for the moment, blind. What is complete in Mr. Faulkner's pattern, *a priori*, must nevertheless remain incomplete for us until the very last stone is in place; what is 'real' therefore, at one stage of the unfolding, or from one point of view, turns out to be 'unreal' from another; and we find that one among other things with which we are engaged is the fascinating sport of trying to separate truth from legend, watching the growth of legend from truth, and finally reaching the conclusion that the distinction is itself false.[133]

> As the legend grows through the narrators' successive contributions, [the reader's] capacity to estimate the various degrees of distortion increases. However, such is the ordering of the narrative that the magnification of events occurs always in advance of an understanding of the distortions which cause it. The reader is consequently affected sensibly before he can react intellectually. He knows that the narrators' conjectures are often in point of literal fact impossible, but he is forced to give them provisional credence; in so doing, he is taken in despite his reservations. Thus it is that the incredible tragedy of Sutpen's ambition and fall is brought into being.[134]

Perhaps because they came from a culture whose history was generally agreed upon and seldom revised, British critics did not take kindly to this kind of mystification. Walter Allen referred to the 'nimiety of lunatics' in the novel,[135] while Maurice Richardson described the novel as being written 'partly in a leisurely repetitive rocking-chair style, midway between an old Southern folk epic and Miss Stein's continuous present, and partly in [Faulkner's] most intensive turgid manner, the manner of the mammoth sentences'.[136] But to appreciate the novel one need only assent to that commonplace of current critical thinking, that 'reality' is a verbal construct. In *Absalom, Absalom!* is foregrounded the truth of many other Faulkner novels, that story-telling is world-making.

The first sentence of the novel sounds the themes. It looks forward to the setting of Thomas Pynchon's influential short story 'Entropy', where the hero attempts to create a hermetically sealed environment immune to change and the erosion of meaning. Rosa Coldfield (herself sending readers back to Miss Haversham) has stopped time in her father's room. The room is emblematic of the words to be uttered in it. It is 'called the office because her father had called it that'. The atmosphere is 'dead . . . airless' just as the language and the wisdom are dead, inherited, received; and Rosa is about to attempt to pass it on in the same airtight package to young Quentin. 'Someone's' old belief that 'dark' means 'cool' is falsified by the heat present in the room, yet past time – 'two o'clock . . . September . . . forty-three summers' – dominates. In attempting to deny the natural cycle of the sun, tradition has exacerbated its effects; this ironic rebounding is to be a recurrent idea in the novel. The atmosphere of that office is also sullied by 'dust motes' which Quentin thinks of as traces of the old paint, the old surfaces of things, now mysteriously blown into the room despite the airtight seal. As it is for Pynchon's characters, the world of Faulkner's thinkers is not divisible into the neat bars of black and white logic, but is seaped into by outside forces, by weather, and by the past itself as it crumbles and mutates into present lives.

Throughout the novel we are aware of wordsmiths trying to articulate the preverbal world of Sutpen, particularly Rosa. She regards Sutpen's black workers as creatures without language who speak 'not needing words probably, in that tongue in

which they slept in the mud of that swamp and brought here
out of whatever dark swamp he had found them in and
brought them here' (24). Sutpen himself she regards as someone
needing the Coldfield name but himself a walking lie. Her
respectable society shares a limited language as it shares a
world of customs and morality: 'the people we lived among
knew that we knew and we knew they knew we knew and we
knew that they would have believed us about whom and where
he came from even if we had lied . . .' (17). But Sutpen is
beyond this knowledge, just as Clytie on the stairs is *'listening to
or for something which I myself could not hear and was not intended to
hear'* (138). It would be easy to say that this preverbal world is
chaotic and meaningless, but Rosa's great monologue in Chapter
5, the centre of the novel, suggests that things are more
complicated. There she describes *'that deep existence which we lead,
to which the movement of limbs is but a clumsy and belated accompaniment
like so many unnecessary instruments played crudely and amateurishly out
of time to the tune itself'* (137). Rosa's obsession with Sutpen is as
much the result of fascination for origins and originals as of
hatred. She may pen her thousand odes to Southern soldiers,
*'embalming blotting from the breathable air the poisonous secret effluvium
of lusting and hating and killing'* (169) but it is Sutpen himself, not
her self-imprisoned father, who embodies those chivalrous
ideals. Rosa describes him as a man of few words but a single
purpose, a challenge to her neat view of world history as
articulate, civilised order evolving from pre-literate chaos. In
fact Sutpen spiritually seduces Rosa because he has the appeal
of the word with God, a fusion of word and act (even if the
word 'Coldfield' was acquired yesterday) which appeals to all
educated people with nostalgia for a time when people were
fully 'present' in their words. When Rosa is in his house, it
seems to her that it was *'the house itself that said the words'* (138).
This suppressed invalidation of Rosa's values makes us view
her speech with increasing irony. The spinster with her legs
dangling from the chair, trying to cut herself off from the
outside world in an airless environment of black and white,
cannot stop talking. She is certainly aware of her feverish
preoccupation with words; she knows that she spent her youth
listening at doors instead of living, but having only language to
live in, she has polarised experience and cut herself off from her

'natural' progression. Sex, for example, is for Rosa either death
or the chance to become a male:

> But it was no summer of a virgin's itching discontent; no
> summer's caesarean lack which should have torn me, dead
> flesh or even embryo, from the living: or else, by friction's
> ravishing of the male-furrowed meat, also weaponed and
> panoplied as a man instead of hollow woman. (145)

Not surprisingly, then, she 'talks up' Bon into the ideal
lover, not only never consummated but never seen: '*I became all
polymath love's androgynous advocate.*' (146) The father, however, is
impossible: Sutpen, returned from the War, is both ideal and
real – a forgotten, carved inscription and brutal limbs – and he
challenges Rosa to remain hollow, speaking woman, or become
silent man. Seeing life in these polarised terms, Rosa of course
refuses, but her appeal to Quentin is for moral approval, while
her real anguish is 'why' she got herself into that predicament,
why she should be outraged, why she should refuse:

> *I will tell you what he did and let you be the judge. (Or try to tell you,
> because there are some things for which three words are three too many,
> and three thousand words that many words too less, and this is one of
> them. It can be told; I could take that many sentences, repeat the bold
> blank naked and outrageous words just as he spoke them, and bequeath
> you only that same aghast and outraged unbelief I knew when I
> comprehended what he meant; or take three thousand sentences and
> leave you only that Why? Why? and Why? that I have asked and
> listened to for almost fifty years.) But I will let you be the judge and
> let you tell me if I was not right.* (167)

We see Rosa, then, torn between putting her faith in the
community of discourse, and the brute physical. While Bon
appeals to her as the conventional romantic hero, with '*something
anyway of the old lost enchantment of the heart*' (150), his father is
even more appealing because in a sense he represents a rare
amalgam of those two values: he may brawl with his black
workers, but he builds a conventional plantation dynasty out of
nothing. In fact Sutpen's mulatto progeny signify perfectly the
accomplishment of this fusion. Rosa sees Clytie as wild, untamed,

while ' *'Sutpen' is the silent unsleeping viciousness of the tamer's lash*' (156). Indeed, Rosa's attraction to Bon, we later learn, is part of the same impulse to see in black-white the resolution of her dilemma.

Mr Compson, who shares the first half's telling with Rosa, balances her with his male preoccupations of honour, homosexual love and father-son conflict. As in *The Sound and the Fury* and like his avatar, Addie's father in *As I Lay Dying*, Mr Compson inclines to the fatalistic which is often based on ignorance or repression of the facts. He would prefer Clytie were called Cassandra (62) to reinforce a sense of fate, but Clytemnestra would seem equally appropriate to a family where a black, Wash Jones, would finally wreak vengeance upon the master of the house. Compson would prefer to think of Rosa as 'incapable of either discrimination or opinion or incredulity' (66), rather than countenance that she, a woman, might have quite as profound and plausible ideas as he does about the fall of Sutpen and the South. He dwells on his image of Rosa sewing for Judith's trousseau, ignorant of her sexual awareness and desire for Bon, in the same way as his description of young girls suggests a repressed fascination and fear of womanhood (67). Compson projects his own sense of superior, fin de siècle civilisation onto Bon, admiring his 'fatalistic and impenetrable imperturbability' (94). He has just enough facts to fit the story into his system of preferred human truths – that Bon seduced Henry, that Henry manipulated his sister Judith through incestuous identification, that Henry hated his father, 'the father who is the natural enemy of any son' (104). Compson's evidence is slim, but with the confidence of a bad psychoanalyst he finds this the more compelling. He judges Henry's desires, for instance, then admits that if it went on, it went on 'not in Henry's mind but in his soul' (96); and in the following sentence once can see the conjuror slyly at work: 'And this: the fact that even an undefined and never-spoken engagement survived, speaking well for the postulation that they did love one another . . .' (104) – here, the only speaker, verbaliser, is Compson the taleteller. However, he does in one crucial passage admit doubts, gaps in the story which he feels justified in filling with the assumptions of Freudian psychology, and which for the reader will only be filled by continued reading:

They are there, yet something is missing; they are like a

chemical formula exhumed along with the letters from that forgotten chest, carefully, the paper old and faded and falling to pieces, the writing faded, almost indecipherable, yet meaningful, familiar in shape and sense, the name and presence of volatile and sentient forces; you bring them together in the proportions called for, but nothing happens; you re-read, tedious and intent, poring, making sure that you have forgotten nothing, made no miscalculation; you bring them together again and again nothing happens; just the words, the symbols, the shapes themselves, shadowy inscrutable and serene, against the turgid background of a horrible and bloody mischancing of human affairs. (101)

This could stand as a description of the reading process in *Absalom, Absalom!* where what the deconstructionists would call the old metaphysics of 'presence and name' are undermined, freed into the play of relativity and changing significance. Here Compson's doubts are momentarily given expression, just as Sutpen's natural instincts, given momentary expression, are seen to have undermined his whole structuralist programme.

The relationship between writing and speech, the stature of documents, headstones and confessions, are at the heart of the debate in the novel. At times the principal characters seem to deride language: Sutpen comes into contact with the Coldfields only because he needs their names on a wedding licence (16); Rosa self-consciously eulogises the Confederate dead in her odes; and Compson suggests that Judith reads among the lettering of Sutpen's headstone in the hall 'more of maiden hope and virgin expectation than she ever told Quentin about' (190). Yet for all three, words can also have a magical power: Sutpen forces his schoolteacher to admit that what he read out of his book about the West Indies was true enough to form the basis of his grand design; Rosa believes there is a 'fatality and curse' upon her family; and Compson argues that Henry 'put the spell on' Judith (107). Judith and Ellen have contrasting attitudes to language: the mother is fatalistic, seeing in Bon a completion of her life, her family already a fading photograph 'like painted portraits hung in a vacuum' (75), while her daughter Judith is a relativist aware that meaning is created and lost by people. Her letter to old Mrs Compson eloquently **expresses** her wish to leave some mark on the wall of history not

by inscribing a message but by passing something on, to 'be
remembered even if only from passing from one hand to
another, one mind to another, and it would be at least a
scratch, something . . .' (127).

It is Mr Compson who identifies in the conflict of Henry and
Charles the philosophical issue exemplified in the above
attitudes (even though he attributes the conflict to invented, or
only partially correct, motives). The sophisticated European
Bon is at home with 'différance' (not for nothing is he French)
and the play of signs. Photographs do not seal one's doom, as
they do for Ellen and Rosa; they are constantly being 'developed'
and overlaid one upon the other, 'fixed' only when the viewer –
in this case the superstitious, simpleminded Calvinist Henry –
gives assent. In a remarkable passage Compson describes
Charles working on Henry like a photographer, in a 'dialogue
without words, speech, which would fix and then remove
without obliterating one line of the picture, this background,
leaving the background, the plate prepared innocent again . . .
the plate unaware of what the complete picture would show . . .'
(111). A little later Compson dramatises the conflict when the two
men argue about Charles's marriage to the octoroon. Compson
has Charles mocking Henry's morality of 'archaic and forgotten
symbols' (118) while Henry argues for absolute morality:

> Suppose I assume an obligation to a man who cannot speak
> my language, the obligation stated to him in his own and I
> agree to it: am I any the less obligated because I did not
> happen to know the tongue in which he accepted me in good
> faith? No: the more, the more. (118)

For Charles, manipulating language gives power; for Henry,
abandoning the rules means anarchy.

Between these two poles Faulkner's debate with history plays
itself out, particularly in the person of Quentin, 'weak from the
fever yet free of the disease and not even aware that the freedom
was that of impotence' (12). In this early statement we can
decode the disease which is the legend of Southern gallantry,
the fever which is the multiplying versions of it, and the
impotence which comes with freedom. The disease is the 'ur-
legend' or, in the case of this novel, Sutpen's 'design', the
central story which, once disclosed, lies as the main strand in

the texture of the novel. Even for Sutpen himself it is already a story belonging to the tribe rather than to himself; as he tells old Compson of his childhood during the hunt for the architect 'he was not bragging about something he had done; he was just telling a story about something a man named Sutpen had experienced, which would still have been the same story if the man had had no name at all' (247). The fever is in the obsessive retellings and exegesis carried on in the post-Civil War world by people like Rosa and Quentin. Lastly, the word 'impotent' echoes throughout the book: from Sutpen himself worried over his impotence (160) and so propositioning Rosa; to Rosa herself impotent (151, 170) with rage since Sutpen's proposal and death; to Henry and Charles 'impotent even with talk' (114) according to Compson. What the second half of the novel does is explore this idea of impotence against the idea of a rigid, life-denying Southern morality.

For Wash as for Rosa, Sutpen is the archetypal Southern overlord, quintessence of power. Yet, as we learn of the fate of his grand design during Chapter 7, we see that the potency is impotent before chance and time. Mr Compson refers to '*that old impotent logic and morality . . . the old morality which had never yet failed to fail him*' (279–80). He is describing the motivation which leads Sutpen to insult Rosa by suggesting a trial coupling, a final, desperate salvo in an attempt to sire a suitable heir. But he goes on to suggest that as Sutpen's physical potency wanes, his imaginative power increases, and Rosa's refusal is seen as part of the old morality – family honour, retribution – which must now simply be bypassed, '*was just a delusion and did not actually exist*'. At this crucial point in the narrative Shreve interrupts Quentin with 'Let me play a while now,' and starts describing Wash. Earlier Shreve shrewdly (the words suggestive of each other) reduces this Byzantine Southern tale to this judgment on Sutpen: 'He chose lechery. So do I.' (275) Now, once again, Shreve is hot on the trail of the dénouement, sensing in the constant presence of Wash a final, racial débâcle. But Quentin does not let him take over, interrupting him 'without comma or colon or paragraph' (280). In his description of Wash, Quentin displays some of Shreve's 'playfulness', but it is circumscribed by an obsessive urge to tell which comes from that Southern awareness of the extremes of behaviour to which its morality can lead.

Wash himself can 'play'; when Sutpen is away he becomes an honorary white, and he and Clytie replay Sutpen's primal scene at the front door. But his rejection has quite a different outcome: where Sutpen had erected a life's design based on stereotype and stratification, Wash both knows that he could enter the house (that is, that Sutpen's racism is a complicated matter) and decides not to, for personal reasons – '*because I aint going to force Mister Tom to have to cuss a nigger or take a cussing from his wife on my account*' (282). Wash has a profundity and humility entirely lacking in his master. His catchphrase – 'they kilt us but they aint whupped us yit' – points away from the physical to the spiritual, and he admires Sutpen as a brave individual. He is galvanised into action not because Sutpen has got his daughter pregnant, but because he puts his horse before Millie. In response to Sutpen's verbal, then physical 'whupping', Wash in defence of his and his daughter's dignity wields the scythe of Time on Sutpen; then, with the integrity of a Greek tragic hero, he takes the lives of his own family.

Wash, then, suggests the kind of 'playful' mind which can go along with the Southern rules yet find space for human dignity within them. In contrast Sutpen is, like Conrad's Kurtz, an amoral force. He is even ready to abandon the 'old morality' which contrived to set son against son, in order to father a halfcaste son on Milly at the end. His one allegiance is to his male line, in effect to himself, and in this narcissistic world even the last spluttering of imaginative potency cannot comprehend the feelings of the one friend he might ever have had, his servant Wash. His end is, finally, appropriate: dedicated to the defeat of time and change by amassing wealth and power in one place, he is cut down by the symbol of Time when he rejects his own offspring because, being a girl, the baby would in time go out of his control. Wash, willing even to endow Sutpen with the supernatural power he actually wants, not to *be* right but to 'make hit right' (284), simply cannot endure the wrongness of rejecting life.

In these ways Faulkner broadens his theme of racism until it encompasses the vanity of human wishes. Sutpen is no machiavellian devil; his very simplicity is his tragedy. He is correct when he tells old Compson that his 'trouble was innocence' (220). From his first experience as victim of a social code he dedicates his life not to dismantling that code (which included slavery) but to achieving a safe niche within it. Pursuing this chimera of power he disregards the potency of his own loins and of the chance which brings Bon back into his family. In the end we see Sutpen impotent within the 'mind-forg'd manacles' of that code. At the same time what we experience as readers are the efforts of other Southerners to decode themselves, to break the grip of the code over them by exorcising the ghost of Sutpen, that shape which the man himself could never fully embody.

Quentin comes closer than Rosa or his father to seeing, at least intellectually (the question of whether one should enter as evidence his subsequent behaviour, as documented in *The Sound and the Fury*, is moot), the danger of replacing that code either with Gothic fantasies or psychoanalytic explanations which are equally effective manacles. But Quentin's problem is dramatised throughout the novel in the relationship between himself and Shreve. In the last chapters the parallels with Henry and Bon are made explicit, 'four of them and then just two – Charles-Shreve and Quentin-Henry' (334). The first couple are 'alien' liberals, while the second couple are caught in the mire of family and the South. Quentin makes another grouping when he declares, '*Maybe Father and I are both Shreve*' (262), suggesting Shreve's fascination for psychological extrapolation which he shares with Mr Compson, as well as sympathy with Quentin, as a young man trying to find an identity (Canadians are notoriously preoccupied with the question 'Who am I?'). Indeed, Shreve's earlier flippancy ('better than Ben Hur' [217]) changes to feverish involvement near the end of the story when the focus is on the half-brothers. At times Quentin and Shreve are seen as interchangeable, especially as speaker and listener of the tale; at others theirs is almost a flirtatious relationship of 'a youth and a very young girl' (299). What is going on in that cold New England dormitory room is the freighted subtext of the entire novel as Shreve is at once attracted and repelled by Quentin and the values of his Southern subjects.

Shreve is outraged by the mechanics of sex and is in search of values. He reveals his own ambiguous attitudes towards social structures and freedom when he describes with fascination Charles Bon's youth, '*with so few fathers*' (308) and too much freedom; further on, Shreve bitterly characterises the institution of marriage and the sexual act itself in images of incarceration:

... thank God you can flee, can escape from that massy five-
foot-thick maggot-cheesy solidarity which overlays the earth,
in which men and women in couples are ranked and racked
like ninepins; thanks to whatever Gods for that masculine
hipless tapering peg which fits light and glib to move where
the cartridge-chambered hips of women hold them fast ...
(312)

But instead of dwelling on the sense of 'sin' (324) which he
finds so dominant and ludicrous in the Southern Calvinist
mind, Shreve teases out from Quentin's story the hidden core:
'And now we're going to talk about love.' (316) For Shreve,
love is what existed between Charles, Henry and Judith: a
transcendent, sexless, Platonic love which could not survive
under the barrage of social pressures and even of language
itself. You could not 'tell' this love, only the violent deeds
which gave it away. At times that kind of love exists also in the
room, when Shreve and Quentin, teller and listener, 'overpass'
the narrative into an imaginative kinship, in 'some happy
marriage of speaking and hearing wherein each before the
demand, the requirement, forgave condoned and forgot the
faulting of the other ... in order to overpass to love, where
there might be paradox and inconsistency but nothing fault nor
false' (316). In the ideal situation of love, the position of the
speaker or listener 'needs neither detailing nor recapitulation'
(315), as the lawyer's letter of introduction to Sutpen puts it.
Text falls away as emotional fusion is finally achieved. All the
young men of the novel seek this lotusland of kindred spirits
where the gulf between action and meaning, reality and
interpretation, dissolves. But such a state is almost impossible to
achieve. Impatiently Shreve dreams not of promiscuity but of
sinful coupling (324) where at least some kind of meaningful
action might be achieved. Here he is the mirror image of
Charles, who lacks the validation of a father (as Shreve lacks a
country) and seeks restlessly for a meaning to be imposed upon
his actions, badgering Henry even on the battlefield to judge
him or in some similar way give him 'permission' to act (345,
349). Eventually, of course, the love between the brothers is
disastrous, since Sutpen has engineered it so that his Southern
world of meaning will be imposed, at whatever cost; Henry
capitulates to this more easily achieved kind of meaning and

sees Charles not as his brother, lover almost, but as *'the nigger that's going to sleep with your sister'* (358). Shreve recognises the ultimate paradox of the story, that Henry's law while violent is based on a passion more warm and loving than the cool liberalism of Charles or himself, the northern avatar.

Shreve's brutal, bullying conclusion to the novel emphasises that paradox. From one perspective the Gothic excesses of the dénouement remind one of the last act of a bad revenge play; Shreve sarcastically totes up the score as blacks try to 'get rid of' whites and clear the ledger. The reader may look forward with Shreve to the day when all human beings are 'grey' like Jim Bond and race will no longer be a component of meaning. But what bonds, what values, will survive to that new 'grey' age? Perhaps a better world would be the kind which Mr Compson looks forward to in his letter, where Rosa Coldfield's ghosts are *'actual people'* to be really loved or hated, where 'credibility' becomes 'certainty', where the white page is covered with black names, where the story goes on. Faulkner finds exactly the right pivotal conclusion in Quentin's cry of despair and triumph, *'I dont hate it'*. The alternative to hate is love, presumably, the elusive centre of the novel murkily embodied if not stated in the actions of fathers, sons, daughters, siblings, friends and lovers. But Quentin's cry points rather to the excluded middle, neither hate nor love but a precarious safety of noncommittal.

Quentin, of course, is searching the character of Henry for his motivation for murder. As the narrative spools out he is presented with three possible crimes: bigamy, incest and miscegenation. On the one hand, the last of these would seem to Quentin the least offensive to himself; the other two are at once more trivial, and closer to Quentin's own obsessions with his sister Caddy. But miscegenation is also the most arbitrary of crimes, a social fabrication without foundation in the conventions of romantic love (contra bigamy) or biological expedience (contra incest). The reason which Quentin drives towards is the reason which robs Henry of independence from his father's world and law, even while Sutpen himself is exempt. Shreve too, of course, has recognised the value of the South, how its structures and proscriptions at least provide a framework of meaning for human action, particularly for the sexual impulse, no matter how flawed and retributive. But for Quentin the pressure of paradox, now seen clearly from the geographic distance of Cambridge, is becoming intolerable, and will be held back by the tricks of language only for so long.

Utterance itself is problematic, because we must to some extent use and endorse the language of the tribe even as we seek to analyse it and move it in the direction of something else. In a world without history Sutpen's design was enough, but for the present narrators story and language have designs upon them even as they speak. Words will not resolve the conflict they have started; the inscriptions on the tombstones or the trivial conversation between Henry and Quentin demonstrate that. Declarations or questions and answers, like Sutpen's design of revenge, must be abandoned in favour of an unending play of language. J. T. Irwin in his book *Doubling and Incest/Repetition and Revenge* (1975) shows how Faulkner's characters repeatedly play out irresolvable conflicts between father and son. John Matthews supports this view with a deconstructive approach to the novel, showing how Mr Compson and Quentin are telling their own stories through Sutpen's, and how Rosa's story is in many ways a grotesque version of Quentin's (substitute Charles Bon for Caddy). Both critics agree that a resolution or suspension of the arguments can be found only in the texts themselves: between the white space of limitless freedom and the codified meanings of words as declared by Sutpen's 'dictionary' (his symbolic presence), the field of play is the endlessly creative and qualifying word itself.

The idea is obvious in the density of the text itself. One critic has shown in graph form how the metaphorical intensity rises to a crescendo in Chapter 7 when Sutpen's early life is related (or fabricated),[137] as if the tellers are trying to free Sutpen from one dominant, declarative embodiment. The first half of the novel concerns Rosa and Mr Compson, the older generation, as they try to cope with their own psychological reactions to the Sutpen saga; the second half of the novel concentrates on Quentin and Shreve, the younger generation, as they set about rewriting and reorganising the past into a plausible, tolerable version. To the last word, the text itself is a place of intense but exhilarating freedom, while the icy winds of systems and inherited guilts blow outside. *Absalom, Absalom!*, the title, alludes to David's lament to his son Absalom, after he has killed his older brother Amnon for his incest with Tamar. Fathers should die before their sons, complains David. But fathers do not, because they are encoded in the language the sons must use; the only escape is into what one critic aptly called 'the flux of fiction'[138] – into that churning water the reader of this, more than any other of Faulkner's novels, must also be prepared to jump.

Henry's murder took place three weeks after the assassination of Abraham Lincoln, and a month after the end of the Civil War. Faulkner's novel came out in the same year as Mitchell's *Gone With the Wind*. While one work of art tells us that something has ended, the other insists on the complexities of history and demonstrates just how difficult any but the most sentimental version of the past is to construct.

THE WILD PALMS

The Wild Palms (1939) is about survival. Taking a break from the increasing density of his Yoknapatawpha world, Faulkner ranged all over the United States and Mississippi as he again addressed the question of the nature of the sexual impulse and man's notion of woman. In his story 'The Wild Palms' he would portray doomed lovers, the hapless Wilbourne caught in Charlotte's romantic dream where 'love and suffering are the same thing' (43). Metaphorically, the two lovers are 'swept away' by their own antagonism and suspicion of everyday reality, thrown into each other's arms and fatally reinforcing their solipsistic view of a fragile love setting them against the world and time. This story on its own would be powerful enough, but Faulkner's love of dialectic and of formal experimentation led him to introduce another story by way of musical counterpoint, a separate story entirely but presented in alternating chapters (later editions have separated the stories completely and diminished this contrapuntal effect). In 'Old Man' the objective correlative of the flood of passion is reified, as it were, in the 1927 Mississippi River flood. The nameless prisoner and the woman are literally swept away but – and this is the crucial point – remain thoroughly 'grounded' in their attitudes towards fate and towards each other.

While the relationship in neither story is fully satisfactory, the space between them resonates with possibilities of how to live; as Stein advises in Conrad's *Lord Jim*, the secret of survival is to submit to the destructive element, 'and with the exertions

of your hands and feet in the water make the deep, deep sea
keep you up'. Somewhere in the gap between the two stories, or
more particularly the attitudes of the two male heroes Harry
and the convict towards women and children, is the point of
balance where emotional and physical floods are well managed.
There stand the wild palms, bending with the wind but not
falling.

The title story occupies two thirds of the book and, while
largely a flashback from the opening scene, moves steadily
downwards to Charlotte's death and Harry's conviction. In
contrast, the convict's story is geographically circular and comic
from the outset, since the tone of storytelling ('Once . . . there
were two convicts . . .') and the cynical vigour of the convict's
language suggest fairly certainly that this hero did survive – the
interest is in plot, in just how he outwitted the 'Old Man'.
Faulkner also arranges the blocks of narrative so that the reader
senses not only the parallel situations of being 'swept away' but
also the gradual prominence of the quiet convict. The sections
of his story gradually increase in length until the penultimate
fourth sections of each story are almost equal. Section 3 of 'Old
Man' ends with the birth of the baby, while the fourth section
of 'The Wild Palms' has Wilbourne aborting the Buchners'
foetus and attempting to abort Charlotte. The lovers' bungling
need contrasts with the convict's 'husbanding' of life and careful
return of the woman to where he found her, while Wilbourne's
support (from Rittenmeyer, his lover's husband) contrasts with
the legalistic cover-up by the prison warden in the final section
of 'Old Man'. The convict who has no friends is a gentleman;
Wilbourne, who has selfless friends and gets all the breaks,
seems ungrateful and churlishly fatalistic. There are more
detailed counterpoints as well: Charlotte's bleeding and the
convict's bleeding nose, the caring doctor on the barge and the
bungling Wilbourne, the convict's sophisticated respect for
lying 'like a fine and fatal blade' and Wilbourne the abortionist's
pretence of naiveté; and, most obviously, the parallel situations
of the two heroes, thrown from a monastic existence into close
relationship with a woman, finding transient peace in a retreat
(the Utah mine, the Cajun settlement), and ending up in the
same prison. These complex connections of similarity and
contrast force the reader to cross and recross the no man's land
between each story, to decide whether these are simply two

views of women and men together, or whether Faulkner is generating some hypothesis between these two unlikely poles.

Wilbourne believes that his love is special, a departure from the normal flow of humanity: '*You are born in anonymous lockstep with the teeming anonymous myriads of your time and generation; you get out of step, falter once, and you are trampled to death*' (48). He believes that Charlotte, like all women, is trying to domesticate this rare love, make it a place where they can go on living, and while he recognises the good sense of this and understands his own fear ('*Maybe I'm not embracing her but clinging to her because there is something in me that won't admit it can't swim . . .*' [77]), he cannot quite forsake his conventional thinking, shaped by the sentimental love stories he writes so well. Much of the psychological interest of the novel lies in Wilbourne's efforts to escape the clichés of sentimental fiction. While Charlotte the realist keeps her passion and her body alive, Wilbourne oscillates ineffectually between two floods, passion and convention. As he explains it to McCord, we see that it is he who does not want to grow up or, as he puts it, to fall through the timeless moment of orgasm into time and responsibility: 'You know: *I was not*. Then *I am*, and time begins, retroactive, is was and will be. Then *I was* and so I am not and so time never existed. It was like the instant of virginity, it was the instant of virginity . . .' (126-7). So it is Wilbourne who cannot accept the child who is the result of their love, and marks the lovers' reentry into time. Charlotte, for all her tough talking, is the more open to persuasion and change. She recognises that the flaw is 'something in the man and the woman that dies' (201), that is not courageous enough to carry through the love into time. The penultimate irony is that Wilbourne cannot even preserve his beloved in the very act of preserving her; the ultimate irony is that, at the end, he chooses to remain alive to remember her: '*between grief and nothing I will take grief*' (300). This recognition of the importance of time, reality, meat (the flesh) comes too late for poor Charlotte.

The convict, too, uses the word 'meat' as he contemplates the woman he has rescued: '*And this is what I get. This, out of all the female meat that walks, is what I have to be caught in a runaway boat with.*' (138) His frustration, of course, arises from her condition of pregnancy, a sign that she has already fallen into someone else's time, as it were. But it is not until the last page of the novel that we learn why the convict has withdrawn himself from the flood of passion. That first attempted robbery was on behalf of a girl, the present Mrs Vernon Waldrip. The convict has learnt that love can take a man into a different kind of timelessness, the timelessness of prison. He has surrendered to a fatalistic misogyny, to a belief in 'the old primal faithless Manipulator of all the lust and folly and injustice' (227); yet there is still an instinct which makes him a fighter, which helps him to save himself and the woman from the flood. Nevertheless, Faulkner resists an easy plot resolution. Our expectation of an upbeat ending, a reward for the convict and a balance for the dreary wasteland of 'The Wild Palms', is frustrated as the convict readily accepts another ten years away from 'women'.

If we ask ourselves why Wilbourne doesn't simply go out and get a job to support his family, or why the convict doesn't make an approach to the mother he has saved, we come close to the heart of this curious novel. It is a book about idealism. That is the reason for the working title 'If I forget thee, Jerusalem,'[139] referring to Psalm 137 and the song of the exiles. Instead of the waters of Babylon we have Old Man Mississippi. The convict is a victim of his memories, rejecting society because his girl and his robbery did not match the fictions of his *Detectives' Gazette*; likewise Wilbourne is too pure in his idealism – he cannot 'sing' at all for fear of breaking his ideal. There is something dangerous, Faulkner suggests, in all idealism which does not allow the dreamer to balance in the flood, to surrender and resist in equal measure, knowing when to give and when to stand firm. Is there a rapprochement possible, a meeting in no man's land where the instinctive courage of the convict and the absolute dreams of Wilbourne might be reconciled? This is the question which the novel leaves us with, the more powerful for having to be inferred by the reader from the dual structure. But embedded in the section concerning the convict's stay with the Cajuns there is a passage in parentheses which emanates from neither the woman nor the convict but the narrator himself, and which points to this central concern with love and idealism:

> the old married: you have seen them, the electroplate reproductions, the thousand identical coupled faces with only a collarless stud or a fichu out of Louisa Alcott to denote the

sex, looking in pairs like the winning braces of dogs after a
field trial, out from among the packed columns of disaster
and alarm and baseless assurance and hope and incredible
insensitivity and insulation from tomorrow, propped by a
thousand morning sugar bowls or coffee urns; or singly,
rocking in porches or sitting in the sun beneath the tobacco-
stained porticoes of a thousand county court-houses, as
though with the death of the other having inherited a sort of
rejuvenescence, immortality; relict, they take a new lease on
breath and seem to live forever, as though that flesh which
the old ceremony or ritual had morally purified and made
legally one had actually become so with long tedious habit
and he or she who entered the ground first took all of it with
him or her, leaving only the old permanent enduring bone,
free and trammelless . . . (233)

We are still not very far from the issues of Faulkner's early
poetry and prose. Again we have the 'meat', time and love;
woman as Lilith and woman as Eve; man as thinker and man
as actor; an abhorrence of respectability and a yearning for
immortality. For all Faulkner's fascination with the pressures
exerted by family, these are the issues which continued to grip
his imagination. Millgate suggests that there is an unarticulated
urgency in these novels set beyond Yoknapatawpha (such as
The Wild Palms, Pylon and *Mosquitoes*) which perhaps comes from
deep personal involvement.[140] I have argued that Faulkner does
communicate the issues and conflicts clearly through his formal
devices of split narrative and language play, but it is certainly
true that he is more articulate when the voice he uses comes
more naturally to him. The Snopes Trilogy would allow him to
luxuriate in those voices whose rhythms he knew so well, and to
embed these lifelong concerns with the ideal and the real
(especially concerning men's conceptions of women) in a dense
social fabric. In *The Wild Palms* Faulkner draws together his two
worlds, the intense psychological impotence and blockage of the
Sartoris-Compson-Sutpen vein, and the laconic, shrewd integrity
of the smalltown folk of Yoknapatawpha. Intense idealism with
intense sexuality becomes viciously self-protective and life-
denying, while taciturn realism may permit an unsuspected
reverence for life to flourish.

4

The Late Work

THE SNOPES TRILOGY

THE HAMLET

The Hamlet (1940) is the first manifestation in novel form of a project which was to stretch over 33 years, from 'Father Abraham' around 1926 to the third novel in the 'Snopes Trilogy', *The Mansion* (1959) (the middle novel was *The Town* [1957]). In 1945 Faulkner wrote to Malcolm Cowley that *The Hamlet* was 'incepted' as a novel, but it represents a skilful melding and reworking of several earlier short stories, including 'The Hound' (1930, basis for the story of Mink and Houston), 'Spotted Horses' (1931), 'Lizards in Jamshyd's Court' (1932), 'Fool About a Horse' (1936), and 'Barn Burning' (1938). John Pikoulis describes in detail how these stories have been reworked from 'narrative samplers'[141] into a fictional history of the community of Frenchman's Bend. He suggests a tension between the variety of tales of a static community (reminiscent, perhaps, of Anderson's *Winesburg, Ohio*) and recurring themes of economy overruling passion, which suggest the inevitable demise of the pastoral world. Certainly the key protagonists reflect this demise: Ratliff, the businessman who prefers to gossip on the steps of the general store, beaten by Flem Snopes, the dedicated moneymaker who is virtually silent throughout the trilogy. In subsequent volumes Faulkner adjusts his narrative method to suggest a formal counter, as it were, to Flem's progress. Warren Beck describes it well:

> The omniscience of *The Hamlet* richly furnishes the stage and gives the narrative its tremendous impetus; the first person reports which make up *The Town* turn illuminative speculation

upon emergent facts of character and action; *The Mansion* emphasises theme and resolution by apposing the two methods.[142]

In *The Hamlet* Faulkner focuses not on the impotent ricochet between present and past as in previous Yoknapatawpha novels, but on inexorable progress as the new men, the Snopeses, establish and extend their empire. The quartet of sections – Flem, Eula, The Long Summer and The Peasants – is skilfully interwoven, sharing central protagonists like Ratliff, Snopes or Varner, as well as the stories which grow out of each other like ripples in a pool. For example, the retarded Isaac (Ike) Snopes through whom Ratliff foils Flem in the first story is a main focus of the third story, while the other focus there, the Mink-Houston feud, is also mentioned at the end of the first story. The story of the teacher Lebove might seem an exercise in mock-romance, but he is later used by Ratliff as (he thinks) a trump-card in getting Flem to sell the Frenchman's Place, and the teacher's departure opens the way for another Snopes, I. O., to ease his way into the community. Despite these careful joints, however, Faulkner leaves his narrative airy enough for us to feel the town as a real community with edges and corners which are beyond our knowledge. While Ratliff's storytelling ability and his determination to take on Snopes suggest that he represents the best the town has to offer, we do not forget that those nameless groups around Varner's store or watching Ike or the horse auction have their own stories, too.

Ratliff is introduced as 'bland affable ready ... pleasant, affable, courteous, anecdotal and impenetrable' (12). He epitomises all that Faulkner recognises as good in the town: thrift, shrewdness, communality, effacing generosity, loyalty and humility – and also all that is bad: a fascination with intrigue and the baroque, a love of gossip and the tall story which lead him at times to act more like Brer Fox than Brer Rabbit. What finally endears him to us is his effacing irony when he declares his impartiality ('I never made them Snopeses and I never made the folks that can't wait to bare their backsides to them' [290]) or his own fallibility – 'I used to think I was smart, but now I don't know.' (320) Ratliff also appeals as a kind of middle way, since he is possessed neither by love of money nor love of women (he enjoys a 'hearty celibacy', we are told). In contrast, the other central characters pursue their lusts with an excess which is mirrored in the kind of prose Faulkner uses.

The most obvious example is the portrayal of Eula Varner, 'an eleven-year-old girl who, even while sitting with veiled eyes against the sun like a cat on the schoolhouse steps at recess and eating a cold potato, postulated that ungirdled quality of the very goddesses in his [the teacher Labove's] Homer and Thucydides: of being at once corrupt and immaculate, at once virgins and the mothers of warriors and grown men' (105–6). Faulkner creates a scene of Dionysiac excess where the bovine goddess, Venus herself, arouses the boys of the town to Attic contests for hopeless possession. But lurking in the exuberant prose are more ominous signs: Ratliff sees in Eula's face 'only another mortal natural enemy of the masculine race' (139) because, like the convict's woman in *The Wild Palms*, she is only 'meat' (Ratliff uses the word): dumb and illiterate. Upon this inappropriate vehicle the men of the town have loaded their literate imaginings – 'a word, a single will to believe, born of envy and old deathless regret . . . the word, the dream and wish of all male under sun capable of harm . . . the word, with its implications of lost triumphs and defeats of unimaginable splendour . . .' (138). The point is, the men of Frenchman's Bend are ready to give their souls to a dumb creature. How much more profitable it is for Flem Snopes to take her, for in taking 'Hell' he is adding to his property. Faulkner makes this clear in the remarkable, italicised parable which ends Book 2 and into which the description of Eula modulates. The equation here between sexual attraction and damnation is dramatised by several other male characters in the novel, too. In his doomed assault on Eula, Labove 'continued to hack in almost an orgasm of joy at the dangling nerves and tendons of the gangrened member long after the first bungling blow' (112); Houston falls victim to Lucy Pate while at school – 'It was as though she had merely elected him out of all the teeming earth . . .' (185); Mink, approaching the prostitute whom he marries, 'was resigned to the jealousy and cognisant of his fate' (213).

It is wrong, I think, to label this overwhelming theme as misogynist. Faulkner's point is that the men *perceive* themselves as fated to be seduced. After this initial folly, they transfer their sense of victimisation from women to economics, with what tragic results the Mink-Houston débâcle exemplifies. Only Flem is able to take a woman and remain invincible (at least in this novel), particularly because he has no 'words', no imaginings: Eula is simply one more possession, indistinguishable from his other holdings.

Balancing this bleak view of sexuality, of course, is the pastoral idyll of Ike Snopes and his cow. Rejecting commerce (Houston's coin), Ike and the cow walk into a Constable landscape suffused with diurnal rhythms of dawn and starlight, conveyed in some of Faulkner's most luxuriant, soaring prose:

> Then the sun itself: within the half-mile it overtakes him. The silent copper roar fires the drenched grass and flings long before him his shadow prone for the vain eluding treading; the earth mirrors his antic and constant frustration which soars up the last hill and, motionless in the void, hovers until he himself crests over, whereupon it drops an invisible bridge across the ultimate ebb of night and, still preceding him, leaps visible once more across the swale and touches the copse itself, shortening into the nearing leafy wall, head: shoulders: hips: and then the trotting legs, until at last it stands upright upon the mazy whimple of the windy leaves for one intact inconstant instant before he runs into and through it. (169)

Ike is pursued by the two grim Protestants, Houston and the barn owner who is dedicated to the proposition that man must sweat or have not. It is central to Faulkner's purpose that Ike's love for a cow should be celebrated and not mocked, because it contrasts with the other townsmen who are alienated from sexual instincts and the pastoral rhythms around them, seeing in livestock only a potential profit or exchange. The real grotesquery is not Ike but Lump's sideshow (for profit), even if Ratliff finally persuades the Snopeses to end it by buying the cow (a scene omitted from the British edition of the novel). The corruption of the people is epitomised in the final image of the novel, the farmer Armstid delving in his maddened fury in the grounds of the old Frenchman's Place for a treasure which is not there. The 'Peasants' of the final movement follow a vain commercial god while their farms languish.

Only at the end of *The Hamlet* does one appreciate how beautifully Faulkner has orchestrated these themes of love and commerce, through the thematic chords of 'Flem' to the arabesque and presto of 'Eula', the long, languorous movement of 'The Long Summer' and the lively finale. The one discordant event is Mink's murder of Houston, in that third section. The motivations, I have suggested, are fully in keeping with the theme of sexual desire distorted into commercial greed, but the outcome (Mink's refusal to steal from the body) violates Snopesian principles. A Snopes will gain from every situation, making money even out of his own (as Lump does out of Ike). Mink's crime of passion followed by his lack of commercial instinct outrage Flem, and his refusal to help Mink instigates the rest of the trilogy.

But the people of Frenchman's Bend are also very much victims of their own making. We see their Calvinist background working through the men's assumption that the object of their sexual desire is a fate, or that commercial success will come not through hard work alone but through a lucky break such as buried treasure. But everything is suppressed or projected outwards, preeminently into the myth of Snopes as the snake in an otherwise Edenic garden. In fact, Flem's success in no small measure results from his kinship with the townsfolk, beating them at their own game of suspicion, ruthlessness, mean-spiritedness and commercial calculation.

THE TOWN

The Town (1957) incorporates 'Centaur in Brass' (1932) and 'Mule in the Yard' (1934), and continues the saga of 17 years earlier with the hamlet of Frenchman's Bend replaced by the town of Jefferson. The plot, the rise of Flem Snopes, is now incidental to Faulkner's purpose of social criticism, and that in turn is founded on a portrayal of how and where three men get their stories and ideas about human behaviour. Faulkner uses the device of multiple narration which he used to such powerful effect in *Absalom, Absalom!* but the motivations for the utterances of Ratliff, Gavin Stevens and Charles Mallison are undramatic and unimportant. Faulkner's interest here is in exploring how the more public prejudices are received, perceived and passed on.

Michael Millgate estimates that the narration is divided 54

per cent to Charles, 38 per cent to Gavin and 8 per cent to
Ratliff.[143] Ratliff's relegation to the sideline is cause mainly by
his celibacy, because this is a novel about sex. Ratliff's folk
idiom still inclines us to believe his wry generalisations, chiefly
his evolutionary theory about the Snopeses; the good-hearted
Eck was a sport who had to be eliminated – 'it don't even need
the rest of the pack like wolves to finish him: simple environment
jest watched its chance and taken it' (97). But we are more
suspicious of Ratliff in this volume. He admits himself to be a
taleteller ('between what did happen and what ought to happen,
I don't never have trouble picking ought' [90]), he has a
curious secrecy about his own name Vladimir and a superstition
that the name will bring him luck if it is not uttered (an
admiration for secrecy not reassuring to the tale's listeners),
and he is prepared to help the plot along without getting
involved (like ferrying Flem out to Varner's). Indeed Ratliff
himself knows very well that without emotional involvement a
storyteller cannot get inside any plot, and that such involvement
shifts the listener's focus away from the narrative towards the
personality of the teller. If Stevens were to tell his story, says
Ratliff, 'jest to get some rest from it', then we would find out
about Stevens but not what 'happened', because he would be
saying 'it wouldn't much matter what, to somebody, anybody
listening, it wouldn't much matter who' (89).

As readers, then, we have one ear on the story of Mink
Snopes and one on the unarticulated interrelationship of the
three narrators. Charles hankers for Ratliff's homely view of
things, from his evolutionary 'idea of Snopeses covering Jefferson
like an influx of snakes and varmints from the woods' (100),
which he puts into Charles's mind before he is five years old, to
his idiom. When Charles corrects Ratliff's 'dragged' to 'drug'
Ratliff protests, 'For ten years now, whenever he would stop
talking his-self long enough that is, and for five of them I been
listening to you too, trying to learn – teach myself to say words
right.' (226) If Ratliff admires the learning of Charles and
Stevens, Stevens reluctantly acknowledges Ratliff's elusive guile
('too damned innocent, too damned intelligent' [33]) and his
importance as overseer of the Snopes-Jefferson conflict: 'Jefferson
could do without Ratliff, but not I-we-us; not I nor the whole
damned tribe of Snopes could do without him' (254).

While Stevens sometimes attempts the common touch – 'even

say figgered just like Mr Snopes just said it' (147) – he is
essentially a literate man alone in his office speaking to himself
in a convoluted, late Romantic strain, a mixture of sentiment
and Eliotesque irony: 'the interminable time . . . filled with a
thousand indecisions which each fierce succeeding harassment
would revise' (180). Like Prufrock, he is painfully aware that he
is a gentleman but not a man, relishing the expectation more
than fulfilment; as Eula tells him, 'You spend too much time
expecting' (85). In his own rewriting of history he becomes
McCarron himself, and Snopes becomes an 'hermaphroditic
principle' (121) – a refinement of Ratliff's evolutionary idea in
order to leave Linda untouched by Snopesism. No matter how
conscious his escape from Nothing into Motion, we see that his
non-action, his revelling in 'anguish' and his apparently
ingenuous inability to enter into the plot, is fatal to his two
prized projects: Eula commits suicide, and Linda hands over
her inheritance to Flem. Gavin's idealism, his insistence that
'chastity and virtue in women shall be defended *whether they exist
or not*' (69), contrasts with the cynicism of his twin sister who
claims that women are not interested in morals (45) and whose
husband argues that wives seek revenge for being held 'thralled
all day long day after day with nothing to do' (53). Yet, as the
novel progresses, we see Stevens twisting into convoluted
arguments to protect his precious ideals. While his flirtation
with Linda lasts he can remain in a never-land of nymphet
delight, even when Linda's boyfriend punches him (here he
pompously decides that innocence means being a victim, and
that words like 'reputation' and 'good name' must not even be
uttered or they will be sullied by circumstance). But this
Prufrockian juggling game cannot go on, and Eula pushes him
to the overwhelming question. Faced with contradictory roles,
the romantic and the lawyer, Stevens sees himself splitting into
disparate selves as he reluctantly steps into time, the plot.
Almost inevitably, his halfhearted attempts to help lead to the
shattering of his most treasured ideals, and in this way the
novel comes close to tragedy.

The mood is tempered by Charles's presence. Charles begins
his narrative by saying that he *is* Jefferson and what Jefferson
thought (7). The very first words of the novel are 'I wasn't born
yet', so we are conscious of Charles growing up in an atmosphere
of received stories, listening to 'Uncle Gavin's recalling the

fabulous and legendary time' (16) of Eula and de Spain. Charles starts saying 'I' when Ratliff introduces the Snopes legend, and by the end of the novel he has grown a great deal. From being the cipher of the town's gossip he has developed into an independent, critical spirit. He pinpoints the dynamo of the whole saga in the town's Baptist/Methodist religion, whose very fabric is 'delusion, nothing' (266). His mother could not explain sex to him because she could not acknowledge it herself, and Uncle Gavin could not 'stop talking in time' because talk was also a way of avoiding confrontation with the facts:

> So maybe that was why: not that I wasn't old enough to accept biology, but that everyone should be, deserves to be, must be, defended and protected from the spectators of his own passion save in the most general and unspecific and impersonal terms of the literary and dramatic lay-figures of the protagonists of passion in their bloodless and griefless posturings of triumph and anguish; that no man deserves love since nature did not equip us to bear it but merely to endure and survive it, and so Uncle Gavin's must not be watched where she could help and fend him, while it anguished on his own unarmoured bones. (263–4)

Beneath the endemic Stevens rhetoric we detect a vehement attack on the tyranny of Protestantism and its unnatural divorce of mind and body for the sake of some public morality. For Stevens life 'must be premature, inconclusive, and inconcludable' (274) but even he, at the end, is forced to act and discovers both the ironies of life – lying to Linda frees her to feel, where the truth may have killed her – and the banal stupidities of social pressure – Eula was simply bored with her 'nothing' life, and Stevens cries when he understands this truth. However, Faulkner's larger, more optimistic theme comes through young Charles, who is able to observe both his uncle and the taleteller Ratliff. Life is a confrontation between consciousness (Stevens) and social forces and legends (Ratliff). Eula is trapped by the legend of Eve; as an enlightened Stevens puts it, 'eighteen years ago when Manfred de Spain thought he was just bedding another loose-girdled bucolic Lilith, he was actually creating a piece of buffoon's folklore' (275). Eula herself understands that children should face an open future free from debilitating

conventions and selfconsciousness, so she dies for her daughter –
and, in a sense, for Charles.

What makes this long novel most enjoyable is that both
Ratliff and Stevens have an acute sense of life's absurdity, and
much of the novel borders on black humour. As Ratliff says at
the sad end of Eck Snopes, 'As soon as you set down to laugh at
it, you find out it ain't funny at all.' (223) The bittersweet
humour arises when characters are seen as victims of themselves,
like Eula who was seduced by herself (235), or Will Varner who
was very moral because whatever he decided to do was right
(239). In this wry atmosphere, rigid oppositions in the novel
threaten to collapse also, as when Montgomery Ward Snopes is
described as the necessary hairshirt for Stevens, or Flem
Snopes's embezzling is seen as little different from the behaviour
of Byron Snopes, de Spain and even Colonel Sartoris.
Montgomery Ward's pornography requires the collusion of the
town, while Flem begins to eliminate his own tribe in order to
rise to respectability. What raises *The Town* from the level of
humour of *The Hamlet* is the way Faulkner blurs the formerly
sharp divisions of Jefferson society and morality in this way.

Above all, we feel in this novel the imperatives of Time
driving through the narrative like a nail through a tree. Eighteen
years is not simply an 'ellipsis' in Flem's strategy; during that
time children like Linda and Charles are born and grow up to
challenge society's conventions and myths. Stevens cannot
preserve the old Faulknerian ideal of the sculpted virgin,
because she has married and had children. Ratliff can continue
to tell his stories in the old idiom, but the form of Faulkner's
novel reminds us that different tellers tell different truths, and
that it depends how far away in time the story has drifted, how
well absorbed it can be into the social fabric. The 'immortal
lust' of Eula and de Spain happened a long time ago; since then
several horses, like Byron, have 'come home to roost', and
that's why Faulkner ends with the apparently unconnected
coda of the Indian children: rapacious, anarchic, offspring of
yet another New World which Jefferson's society and stories
will have to absorb.

THE MANSION
The three sections of *The Mansion* (1959) titled Mink, Linda,
Flem, suggest a movement from legend to narrative, as the

almost superhuman vendetta of Mink Snopes modulates through Linda's specific predicament to a new view of Flem not as godfather but as pathetic, lonely old man. Already forced to consider Mink more sympathetically because of the first section devoted to him, the reader is plunged into the heart of subjectivity by the second section, narrated by the three men from *The Town*. But here Charles's three chapters, framing Gavin's climatic interview with Linda, insist even more pointedly on the relativity of all attempts to know or tell. The third and longest section, then, while it tells the end of Flem Snopes and climaxes the centrepiece of the trilogy, is actually preoccupied with the complex motivations for that action and responses to it.

Mink, we see at the outset, is acting within his own narrative. Shattered by the failure of the Snopes story to sustain him (Flem deserted him in his hour of need), Mink has found himself another story. The first two chapters begin identically, reinforcing Mink's isolation from other voices: 'The jury said "Guilty" and the Judge said "Life" but he didn't hear them . . ./ . . . but he wasn't even listening.' Throughout the section Ratliff and Montgomery Ward postulate reasons for the behaviour of Flem and Mink, but get no further than Montgomery's cynical definition of what motivates a Snopes – 'to have the whole world recognise him as THE son of a bitch's son of a bitch' (87). The final, omniscient chapter of the section gives us a tender vignette of Mink shooting a squirrel to help his beaten stepmother, concluding, '*What aches a man to go back to is what he remembers.*' (105) But Mink's life is dominated by another, less liberating memory, the memory of Flem's treachery. By clinging to that memory over forty years Mink shows himself incapable of accepting the flux of time; indeed his one demand of life, 'just not to have anything against him' (105), is part of his impossible desire to be immune from life's vagaries.

Flem Snopes is, of course, the great plotter of the trilogy, but his belief in his own detachment is as presumptuous as Mink's demand. In Linda's section, then, we turn to characters who are trying both to steer their lives and to feel with their hearts. Ratliff introduces the complexities by analysing the other two narrators: he declares Stevens to be too interfering for his own good, trapped into a perpetual adolescence by Eula Varner; he also argues that Charles is jealous of Linda in his uncle's affections. In general, Ratliff inclines to fatalism in human affairs, even though he recognises his own partiality ('I jest simply decline to have it any other way except that one' [122]). Still, there is at least one good side to his belief in Old Moster's doom, and that is his strong sense of humility, the necessity of being aware that 'it might be barely possible it taken a little something more than jest you to get you where you're at' (151).

With Charles Mallison, Faulkner makes explicit the postmodernist concerns which had intrigued him as early as *Sanctuary* and which he was beginning to develop in the Charles of *The Town*. Charles is a less frenetic version of Quentin Compson and his analysis of the place of language in society, while similar in many ways, is less intensely 'Southern' and personal. He is a part of the new generation which fought in the Spanish Civil War: worldly, cynical, and literate. His first words 'Linda Kohl (Snopes that was, as Thackeray would say)...' [171]) show this, yet he envies Linda her silence, because he feels that we who use words are simply blundering about in a game which has no rules – 'trying to find first base at the edge of abyss like one of the old Chaplin films' (199). (At the end of the novel Stevens admits '*he didn't even know he was playing baseball*' [389]). He is aware of how women like Linda and his mother do not need words to communicate, and attributes most of the world's ills to language: 'If there were no such thing as sound. If it only took place in silence, no evil man has invented could really harm him: explosion, treachery, the human voice' (192). He delights, therefore, in the ludicrous scene of Linda and the two Finnish communists, 'one that couldn't speak English and another that couldn't hear any language, trying to communicate through the third one who hadn't yet learned to spell, talking of hope, millennium, dream' (209).

Charles is acutely aware of the power of language to label, divide and stultify. He foregrounds the labels 'KOHL COMMUNIST JEW' outside Linda's house (214) and observes how the war wounded come back 'just like what they were when they left: merely underlined, italicised' (173). He also knows how easy it is to present a version of oneself, as when he says, 'I ... looked not back, I would have liked to say, if it had been true' (192). It is not surprising that, faced with such fierce epistemological uncertainty, Charles is drawn to the slow, wry storytelling of Ratliff. He even begins to sound like him at one point as he describes Stevens's marriage to Ms Backus: 'that pitcher had went to ·that well jest one time too many, as Ratliff said, provided of course he had said it' (238). But he is also drawn to his uncle: partly out of jealousy over his mother and the beautiful girls of Jefferson, partly because he and Stevens are alike in many ways. Although he declares that man stinks, Charles understands his uncle's quest for beauty, even when as a war veteran he is obviously trying to justify his uncle's inactivity, for he declares, 'He is a good man. Maybe I was wrong sometimes to trust and follow him, but I never was wrong to love him' (216–17). Such a declaration would be remarkable in any context, but especially in a novel where expressing love seems so excruciatingly difficult.

We have met Stevens's desire for beauty before in many of Faulkner's novels, but here it is given more sophisticated treatment because it is embedded in a contemporary context of political challenge and change, as well as within the familiar small-town context of legends and gossip which dominate the way men think of women. Stevens wants the camera-caught moment of a girl in a doorway, a sculpture of an Italian boy, an inscription to Eula over her grave, Linda the 'unravish'd bride of quietness'. He admires Helen of Troy above all mythical women because 'the others all talked' (130). In a remarkable discussion between Linda, Stevens, Charles and his mother about literature and its place in the world, Stevens agrees with Linda that 'saying No to people like Hitler' (205) by dying in a war is more eloquent than anything by Shakespeare or Milton; for a moment he is drawn into the sentiment of a plenitude of history where 'Nothing is ever lost' (205). The fact is, as Charles ruthlessly adds, Linda is the one who may be lost: commitment to action threatens both physical beauty and the idea of faithful love.

Charles's fascination with words is, of course, given practical expression in the grotesquely brilliant device of having Linda made deaf by a bomb. The sign is literally foregrounded, and for someone like Stevens is fatal to his idealised notions of love. At first Linda shocks him by her proposal, 'You can   me' (224); then, in his last recorded words, he extends his hands, not to Linda's body but to her writing tablet, in order to inscribe 'I love you'. The sign replaces the thing itself. It is the last gesture of an Old World gentleman, misguided perhaps but sincere; nevertheless, it won't do in the world of post-War Jefferson which has had enough of hiding behind language.

The mood of *The Mansion* is one of change and apprehension. Faulkner borrows from Orwell to describe 'doubleplus the new social-revolution laws' of the new society, where romantic love has been replaced by 'the simple production of children' (323). If he is not fit to be a hero, Stevens at least recognises the role of himself and people like Ratliff to swell a scene or two, to clear space in Jefferson for the men of action like Goodyhay, Devries and McKinley Smith to make their run. Critics have complained that Clarence Snopes is too dangerous a force to be routed by the expedient of a few dogs, but Faulkner's point is that people like Clarence who operate solely on 'plot' level should be eradicated on that same level. Faulkner introduces the issue of racism to show that Clarence, a Klu Klux Klanner, is a far more dangerous force than Flem Snopes because he is spreading a fiction rather than being made the subject of one. Ratliff's victory is only a minor one, and the general tenor of this last section is understanding and forgiveness. Ratliff describes Flem's funeral, which everyone attended, and declares:

> Fate, and destiny, and luck, and hope, and all of us mixed up in it – us and Linda and Flem and that dum little half-starved wildcat down there in Parchman, all mixed up in the same luck and destiny and fate and hope until can't none of us tell where it stops and we begin. Especially the hope. I mind I used to think that hope was about all folks had, only now I'm beginning to believe that that's about all anybody needs – jest hope. (344)

Even Stevens is able to see himself as in the world and so, perhaps, part of someone else's plot – in this case, Linda's, to aid Mink in his revenge.

There is much to do with naming in *The Mansion* – Mink looking at a letterbox and hoping that he will be given the gift of reading; Charles searching for a name for an emotion; Stevens trying out names for himself. At the end of the novel Mink tells Stevens, 'That's my name: M. C.' (397); he, like Linda, Clarence and the other characters, has a middle, and the mansion of fiction is also revealed to have many middles living in it. The Snopes Trilogy plot turns finally not on the

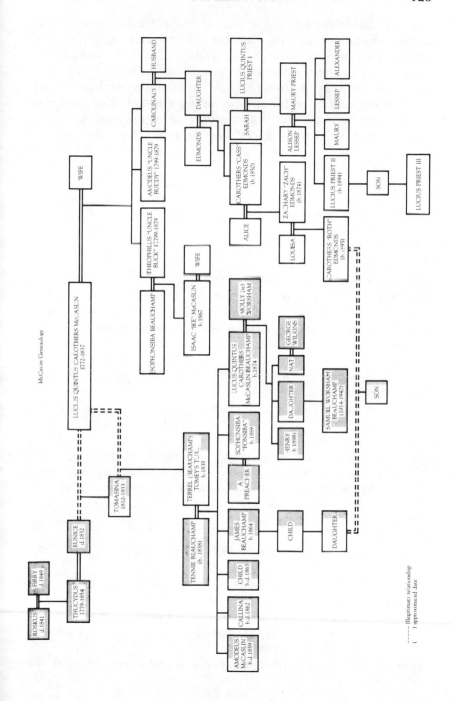

McCaslin Genealogy

----- Illegitimate relationship
(   ) approximated date

mechanical operations of Flem or their transfiguration into town legends, but on almost inscrutable psychological motivations in people like Mink, Eula and Linda. As Faulkner reminds us at the end, all of us poor sons of bitches will share the same ground in the end, yet remain mysteries to each other – even more so for the deceiving and deluding power of words. One might argue that the only person exempt from this ignorance is Faulkner himself, whose novels are pretences of knowing. However, in his preface to *The Mansion* he confesses to contradictions and discrepancies with the earlier novels of the trilogy. Rather than affirming the 'knowability' of his characters and apologising for this failure in omniscience, however, Faulkner endorses change and the endless relativity of perceiver and perceived.

GO DOWN, MOSES

The best example of the new generic form invented by Faulkner, the 'short story composite',[144] is *Go Down, Moses* (1942). A reworking of at least ten earlier stories, five published in the preceding two years, this collection of seven stories has as its centre the two hunting stories 'The Old People' and the more famous 'The Bear'. As one critic wisely noted, 'What *happens* in a Faulkner story is more important than anything else; but it is the last thing we understand . . .'.[145] To follow this collection, one really needs at hand a genealogy of the McCaslins (see p. 123); but, more importantly, an understanding that here Faulkner is treating his central issues – black–white relations, Southern history, greed, marriage, our relationship to nature – in his favourite style: a dialectical, dramatised discussion, where theories are interwoven with plot not to support or cancel each other but to create a rich tapestry of assertion and extenuating circumstance. There are no easy answers, but then there are no easy problems.

The title of the collection recalls the negro spiritual:

When Israel was in Egypt land, let my people go,
Oppressed so hard they could not stand, let my people go;
Go down, Moses, way down in Egypt's land,
Tell old Pharoah, let my people go.

The reference is to enslavement and possible release, and the perspective is assumed omnipotence. But far from endorsing the righteous tone of the Chosen People, Faulkner characteristically undermines moralities and authorities, and finally questions the very medium of print to convey truth. As David Minter says, the text is 'conspicuously fragmentary and cryptic . . . a participatory reader's perfect text'.[146] Faulkner uses the word 'translate' to describe the process whereby settlers turned the Mississippi forests into cash crops, but he also uses it in 'The Bear' to describe what happened to the offerings Ike had left on Sam Fathers' grave: 'not vanished but merely translated into the myriad life which printed the dark mould of these secret and sunless places with delicate fairy tracks, which, breathing and biding and immobile, watched him . . .' (234). This nature, being 'myriad, diffuse, one', is not translatable into words. This truth, to which Ike pledges himself in the central episode of the collection, is not sayable, just as the truth which is in the Old Testament cannot be said. According to Ike,

> There are some things He said in the Book, and some things reported of Him that He did not say. . . . He didn't have His Book written to be read by what must elect or choose, but by the heart, not by the wise of the earth because maybe they dont need it or maybe the wise no longer have any heart, but by the doomed and lowly of the earth who have nothing else to read with but the heart. Because the men who wrote His Book for Him were writing about truth and there is only one truth and it covers all things that touch the heart. (185)

Here is Faulkner's insistent warning that we will not find enunciated 'truths' in his novels, but rather the setting for truths, which must reach the heart by some path other than epistemology.

Despite this radical scepticism, Faulkner is adept at using literary techniques of sequence and juxtaposition and tone to convey the issues. The first story 'Was', for instance, is deliberately nostalgic and comic, washing this tone over the serious subject matter of slavery, black to white and man to woman in marriage. Uncle Buck and Uncle Buddy live contradictory lives, abjuring slavery by living next to the big house but still keeping slaves, locking them in at night but knowing there is a way out the back. While their black slave has run off to be with his girl, the twins themselves want nothing to do with progeny. Yet, given the system where blacks are to be hunted like foxes and women to be feared as vixen, the players at least know where they are. It is only later that Faulkner mocks this opening note of nostalgia by revealing that their slave is in fact their illegitimate nephew, a fact that (as in *Absalom, Absalom!*) shatters both systems, racial supremacy and sexual abstinence.

In the second story 'The Fire and the Hearth' we meet Lucas, the healthiest and most threatful product of old McCaslin's miscegenation. Edmonds himself senses this:

> *He is both heir and prototype simultaneously of all the geography and climate and biology which sired old Carothers and all the rest of us and our kind, myriad, countless, faceless, even nameless now except himself who fathered himself, intact and complete, contemptuous, as old Carothers must have been, of all blood black white yellow or red, including his own.* (88)

Lucas, who had built a fire on his wedding night forty-five years ago which had burned ever since (at least, 'as the tale told' [101]), jeopardises that antebellum-like, nostalgic sense of order and tradition by digging in the ground for gold. His wife Molly's rejection of him reminds us of Moses rejecting the people below Mt Sinai who worshipped the golden calf. But it is a pantheistic god which Lucas has violated; later we are told that the woods would be mistress and wife for Ike (232), and the nostalgia in this story lies in the identification of the land with the woman. We note also that Molly cannot really be possessed, since she goes to the white man Roth Edmonds for a time. In that sub-plot, Lucas clumsily seeks redress, the importance of which is clearly in the attitude of respect rather than in the detail of faithfulness or otherwise. Of course, the other side of that particular moral tenet is the substance of the next story, 'Pantaloon in Black', whose very title suggests its oddity. Rider is an extraneous character to the book, but he stands as the feeling black man whose grief for his dead wife overflows into violence. Nevertheless, Rider's extreme behaviour, almost grotesque as the story's title suggests, also qualifies another looming assertion, that the black is more noble in feeling than the white.

This pattern of enlargement and simultaneous modification continues in the first hunting story 'The Old People'. McCaslin explains the aura of Sam Fathers: 'When he was born, all his blood on both sides, except the little white part, knew things that had been tamed out of our blood so long ago that we have not only forgotten them, we have to live together in herds to protect ourselves from our own sources.' (120) But, he goes on, the primitive blood source was corrupted even in Sam when the Indian and black bloods were mingled. This theory sounds dangerously like Gavin Stevens explaining away Joe Christmas's actions in terms of white and black blood. True, Sam Fathers felt that the black blood was an adulteration, that '*he had had to be a negro*' (152) for too long; but that refers more to a code of behaviour imposed by the dominant white race rather than to anything so biological as 'blood'. More important to Sam is the spiritual wisdom which can be passed on through such experiences as his 'blooding' of young Ike, or of showing him, as he had shown McCaslin, the great deer in the forest. Fathers accepts the alien quality of the forest with humility; he observes the deer and bear rather than shoots them, and it is this attitude which is so potent for the young boys. Moreover, it is a world-view conveyed through the powerful medium of the voice rather than the printed page:

And as he talked about those old times and those dead and vanished men of another race from either that the boy knew, gradually to the boy those old times would cease to be old times and would become a part of the boy's present, not only as if they had happened yesterday but as if they were still happening, the men who walked through them actually walking in breath and air and casting an actual shadow on the earth they had not quitted. And more: as if some of them had not happened yet but would occur tomorrow, until at last it would seem to the boy that he himself had not come into existence yet, that none of his race nor the other subject race which his people had brought with them into the land had come here yet; that although it had been his grandfather's and then his father's and uncle's and was now his cousin's and someday would be his own land which he and Sam hunted over, their hold upon it actually was as trivial and without reality as the now faded and archaic script in the

chancery book in Jefferson which allocated it to them and
that it was he, the boy, who was the guest here and Sam
Fathers's voice the mouthpiece of the host. (122–3)

What Sam Fathers has done is create an imaginative, pre-
lapsarian environment for Ike which makes him reject his own
time and place entirely. The irony, for ironies there always are
in Faulkner, is that despite his name, Sam Fathers has fathered
no one, as if his ideal world of harmony with nature cannot
exist in the human time of generation (that is sexuality, that is
women) at all. No wonder Ike feels that the woods have become
his 'mistress'.

In 'The Bear', justly famous as Faulkner's most elaborate
and impressive short fiction, the author moves closer to the
heart of the dialectic, to the pivot which balances the opposition.
He begins by asserting that the oral tradition is the best,
'forever the best of all listening, the voices quiet and weighty
and deliberate for retrospection and recollection and exacti-
tude . . .' (135). For Ike, in the beginning was the word, and the
word was 'Old Ben'; the tellers support the sense of a 'yearly
pageant-rite of the old bear's furious immortality' (137), while
the men who encroach upon the wilderness are 'myriad and
nameless' (136). The only 'print' he wishes to distinguish is
Old Ben's paw-print. He falls out of the civilised world of print,
using it only to decipher the dark truth of this ancestor in a
section which itself does away with capitals and punctuation, as
if atrophying into the textless world of the heart which Ike
fondly imagines to be epitomised in the Old Testament.

What Ike distrusts about books, even his family's ledgers
which are a 'chronicle which was a whole land in miniature'
(209), is the way they pretend to fix the past 'immutably,
finished, unalterable, harmless' (191). Compared with the
continual 'translation' going on in the forest, and in the
endlessly embroidered stories round the hunting camp fire, the
printed word is unchangeable, sterile. Indeed, while they record
how old McCaslin 'renamed' his slaves, they do not 'spell out'
his real acts of potency, however horrific they may have been.

Nevertheless, moving beyond text only takes Ike deeper into
contradiction. His discussion with McCaslin takes us into the
heart of the Southern paradox; Ike tries to identify the Fall with
possession of the land, and this leads him to repudiate the

Confederate struggle and all his fathers, since the War was undoubtedly fought out of 'love of land and courage' (206). He is adopting not 'the fatherland' (212) but the unenfranchised land itself, his passivity dramatised in his refusal to shoot at Old Ben. But it is at this point that McCaslin introduces his trump card by reading from Keats's 'Ode on a Grecian Urn', that text which lurks behind so many of Faulkner's fictions. McCaslin tries to demonstrate the truth which Ike had witnessed when he pursued Sophonsiba and attempted to hand over his patrimony. There, underfed and freezing, she declared, 'I am free.' Ike echoes her when he tells McCaslin, 'Sam Fathers set me free' (214); but his urn, his ideal is to an outsider as arbitrary as Sophonsiba's love. McCaslin's point is that Ike's ideal does not transcend other things which people have chosen to believe in, but rather takes its place beside them. When Ike watched the awesome trio of Lion the dog, Boon and Old Ben fall in the forest, he was seeing as it were an icon for the Indian (the bear), white settler (Boon) and black (the dog) which make up the inescapable landscape and mindscape of the South. Sam Fathers also fell at that instant as his ideal was destroyed. Nevertheless a narrative drive persisted through that moment, as Boon killed his dog by mistake and had to live on with that knowledge. It is appropriate, then, that 'The Bear' should end with Boon ludicrously trying to fix his gun in order to shoot some terrified squirrels in a tree shouting out, 'They're mine!' (236). Ike may walk away from all this, from the terrible encroachment of the railroad, from environmental pollution, from Boon's bewilderment and agony, but if he does so for a nostalgic, sterile ideal of an American Eden he is being neither original nor responsible. Significantly, the animal which he sees in the forest is not a deer or a bear, but a snake. Moses turned the snake into a staff and went down to lead his people, but Ike, in a rather maudlin gesture, merely salutes it as the new 'Chief . . . Grandfather' (235).

'Delta Autumn' returns to a theme lurking like a timebomb in 'The Bear' and familiar to readers of Faulkner's earlier novels, and that is miscegenation. Old McCaslin's mating with a black slave and then with his own daughter signifies the victory of lust over social discrimination. When Ike, now over seventy, is confronted with evidence of a new generation's miscegenation between Roth and Beauchamp's descendant, he feels a kind of vicious glee that his people are destroying themselves by flouting once again the 'natural' order. We see more clearly what was intimated in the previous story: Ike's nostalgia is a sophisticated form of rigid conservatism, his rejection of the land not so much an endorsement of Sam Fathers' hopeless, sterile ideal as a rejection of his own ancestor's promiscuity. Young Roth Edmonds hasn't observed the rules; he has shot a doe and not a deer. All Ike can think to give the new inheritor is Compson's hunting horn, an obsolete sign from an obsolete system; yet again Faulkner tempers our urge to a sentimental conclusion by pointing out that Ike does not once consider love.

The last story 'Go Down, Moses' has as its suppressed central allusion the tablets inscribed with the Ten Commandments. We have seen that throughout his stories Ike has been looking for some kind of law, and reification of that law as effective as Uncle Buddy's but more grandly inclusive. He thinks he has found it in the land, but we must ask ourselves just what kind of useful imperatives emanate from that source, since it has nothing to say about men and women and families. The other central emotional events of the novel, such as Tomey's Turl's love, Rider's anguish, or Sophonsiba's or young Beauchamp's love, even old McCaslin's passion for Eunice, are not illuminated by Ike's precious 'truth'. Ike says he will not play Isaac to his family's sacrificial wishes, but by opting out of the 'system' he is left in the wilderness awaiting the apocalypse or the revelation of some new laws. In this last story we see that Molly Beauchamp, wife of that Lucas who was 'heir and prototype of all of us', is able to accept her grandson's death (as Rider was unable to accept his wife's) by using not one but two symbolic frameworks. The first is the Biblical one of the title, when she and her friends keen, 'Roth Edmonds sold my Benjamin into Egypt and now he dead.' We do not know the details of Butch's upbringing or crimes, but that is not important. What Faulkner wants us to observe is how Molly and the white Miss Worsham cope with grief. Their blame of the white man and their use of Hebrew mythology are traditional and serve a useful purpose. But Molly is also able to use the white man's technology, that printed page which Ike had so resolutely rejected. 'You put hit in de paper. All of hit', she demands of Gavin Stevens. Illiterate herself, she accepts the medium of her times as an alternative validation of history. It is this flexibility, particularly from a woman who has as strong a sense of the land as has Ike, which makes Molly stand out as a more useful exemplar of how to reconcile the contradictions which shape Faulkner's fiction.

Criticism of Ike comes from another quarter, too. Gavin Stevens's 'serious vocation was a twenty-two-year-old unfinished translation of the Old Testament back into classic Greek' (260). It is his way of trying to find the tablets which will solve our problems. His ludicrous attempt to undo the text, to reveal a metaphysical presence, is a literary analogue of Ike's use of the land. Of course there are valid points in Ike's argument, but his idea that the land belongs to no one fights with his need for a Sam Fathers, a noble savage whose tribe was at the metaphysical centre of things. Faulkner's stories show how inadequate is Ike's solution by the way they coil and turn upon each other, insisting on the variety and uniqueness of human experience and their resistance to the printed word. In the end, the heart's truth must remain a mystery.

Other critics have stressed the theme of black-white relations in *Go Down, Moses*, and some have seen a more positive value in Ike's initiation and discoveries than have I, for example, 'It enacts for us . . . the miracle of moral regeneration; . . . the agony of loss throughout the novel has finally been mastered by its ritualistic expression.'[147] But I feel that Faulkner's love of dialectic once again rules this book, even to its form, that 'The Bear' cannot be extracted and considered as a kind of proto-Greenpeace manifesto without the qualifications and complications of the other stories in the composite. Even within 'The Bear' lies embedded the archetypal Faulknerian scene, a complex bargaining between man and woman, where Ike's nameless wife offers her body in exchange for a promise that he will take up his patrimony. Love and procreation require a habitation, however temporary, however hypocritical (like old McCaslin's), but Ike rejects the challenge and chooses to remain with Old Ben painted on the urn and frozen into immortal immobility.

INTRUDER IN THE DUST

In 1948 Faulkner returned to the territory of the story 'The Fire and the Hearth' from *Go Down, Moses*, and to what Irving Howe calls 'a controlling preoccupation of Faulkner's work: the relationship of the sensitive Southerner to his native myth, as it comforts and corrodes, inspires and repels'.[148] That examination began in earnest with *Light in August*, continued with the historical sweep of *Go Down, Moses* and in *Intruder in the Dust* addresses the here and now. The title itself suggests the importance of space in the novel; the townsfolk of Jefferson live in the dusty desert of history, and Lucas Beauchamp represents a challenge to their tradition. They must put their house in order because of present needs, not out of any obligations to or recoil from the past. As Faulkner himself put it in an earlier draft of the novel, the characters should be seen

> not as the puppet-play of a whodunit but as the protagonist pattern of a belief that not government first but the white man of the South owes a responsibility to the Negro, not because of his past since a man or a race if it be any good can survive his past without having to escape from it (and the fact that the Negro has survived him in the way he has is his proof) but because of his present condition, whether the Negro wishes it or not.[149]

Some critics have dismissed the novel as Faulkner's special pleading for the South; one of them calls it 'a ludicrous novel and a depressing social document'.[150] But this is to confuse Stevens with Faulkner. The speechmaking at the end of the novel is really a debate between the older generation and the new; Charles Mallison's assumptions are different from Stevens's, although he learns a great deal from his uncle, and in his difference he points towards a new future free even from Stevens's guilt.

At first, young Charles is a product of his community. He is angry at Lucas for not being 'a nigger first', for being a host instead of a slave. Like Sutpen he broods on this primal scene of rejection, and his rage becomes sterile, like 'a monstrous heatless disc which hung nightly in the black abyss of rage and impotence' (22). He is like the mass of Jefferson, who have their few simple clichés and a tiny vocabulary to get them through life (48). His uncle's linguistic point impresses Charles, and later on he muses on 'the really almost standardised meagreness not of individual vocabularies but of Vocabulary itself' (80). However, in their earnestness to play the old game of white and black, the mass, ironically, gets things wrong; as wise old Ephraim observes, 'They're too busy with facks.' (71)

Stevens has a contradictory attitude towards language and his society. As much as he berates his countrymen for their illiteracy, he fears a time when 'the very mutual words they used would no longer have the same significance' (152), when the South might lose its homogeneity. So important is the 'fact' of the South to Stevens that he is willing to defend even the Snopes family for the way it stresses homogeneity and gives Jefferson a distinct local colour. While there is much of Faulkner in Stevens's critique of the South, particularly in the way its religion has turned from sustenance to scourge (from Repent or Beware to Burn), we are surely meant to see the strain in Stevens's position, which comes from his sentimental view of history and the South. He yearns nostalgically for a golden time when young girls etched their names on windowpanes and blacks somehow did not exist at all. There is a despair in Stevens which is the natural aftermath of his romanticism, and it compels him to abandon Lucas's case with fatalistic resignation mixed with a dim sense of approval that Southern ways, like lynching, must be allowed to take their course. Stevens has transferred his idealism from the antebellum legend to the far future, in which the South will evolve independently and find its own answers to its own problems. In this novel more than in the Snopes trilogy he is seen as a transitional figure, an impossible combination of conservative and liberal, the joins papered over with rhetoric. A good example of Stevens's love/hate relationship with his community is his description of the mob, which may either be thoughtless or a kind of transcendent group soul:

> Or maybe it's because man having passed into mob passes then into mass which abolishes mob by absorption, then having got too large even for mass becomes man again conceptible of pity and justice and conscience . . . (201)

Charles's mind is far more open than his uncle's, and he thinks while his uncle speechifies. He recognises his father's doubt as being more genuine than his uncle's posturings: 'it was his uncle's abnegant and rhetorical self-lacerating which was the phony one and his father was gnawing the true

bitter irremediable bone of all which was mismatchment with
time . . .' (133). For much of the story Charles is half asleep
and his exhaustion gives him a heightened sense of detachment
and fatalism. When they discover the identity of the new
corpse, Charles concludes,

> you could never really beat them because of their fluidity
> which was not just a capacity for mobility but a willingness
> to abandon with the substanceless promptitude of wind or air
> itself not only position but principle too . . . you believed you
> had captured a citadel and instead you found you had merely
> entered an untenable position and then found the unimpaired
> and even unmarked battle set up again in your unprotected
> and unsuspecting rear . . . (106)

When Charles thinks, the battlelines are not clearly drawn. He
emerges from the 'facks' only by 'quitting abandoning emerging
from scattering with one sweep that confetti-swirl of raging
facetiae' (82).

The last third of the novel has Charles doing his best to
meditate upon recent events, or 'rationalising by reflective' as
Faulkner puts it. He must place his own daring action against
the behaviour of the mob, the 'we', the Face who are also his
people. Under his uncle's tutelage, Charles wants to join the
mob, to merge himself with 'that vast teeming anonymous
solidarity of the world' (207); indeed 'he wanted no more save
to stand with them unalterable and impregnable . . .' (209–10).
But at the same time his own adventure and the behaviour of
the mob are urging Charles to treasure his independence.
Stevens dramatises his problem vividly when he says:

> For every Southern boy fourteen years old, not once but
> whenever he wants it, there is the instant when it's still not
> yet two o'clock on that July afternoon in 1863, the brigades
> are in position behind the rail fence, the guns are laid and
> ready in the woods and the furled flags are already loosened
> . . . it hasn't happened yet, it hasn't even begun yet . . .
> (194)

Charles faces the same problem as Quentin at the end of
Absalom, Absalom!, to endorse or repudiate his tribe. Stevens's

dramatisation is not quite accurate, because the choice has been made on behalf of the new generation, the burden of guilt must be shouldered. After the War, every action will be compromised, any motivation mixed. The choice Charles has he more accurately envisions as lying 'like a hobo trapped between the rails under a speeding train, safe only so long as he did not move' (198). To move is to enter history, just as to speak is to enter a context.

What even Stevens recognises as vital is that one keeps on thinking. His last speech defends the idea that 'a human life is valuable simply because it has a right to keep on breathing no matter what pigment its lungs distend' (244), and that simple wisdom must be kept constantly alive by ratiocination. That is what Stevens means when he tells Charles enigmatically to 'not stop'. Faulkner utilises the car brilliantly in this novel to suggest the Jefferson mob, clogging the square in a mindless traffic jam. Charles's newfound wisdom is his preparedness to cross that line of cars by foot if necessary, in order to uphold the freedom of the individual. While the cars speed in and out of town responding to the winds of rumour and mass hysteria, a lone black man plows his field in a beautiful, Hardyesque epitome of the novel's theme, 'the man and the mule and the wooden plow which coupled them furious and solitary, fixed and without progress in the earth, leaning terrifically against nothing' (148).

Yet, in keeping with the complex dialectic of the novel, Faulkner ends with a deft ironic stroke. Stevens the theoriser receives payment for his services from Lucas, the man who at the beginning of the novel claimed the freedom to judge when an action would be part of the cash-nexus and when it would not. Lucas has been consistently 'free' throughout the novel, refusing even to play the role of either murderer or victim. Charles, as we have seen, has progressed some way towards enlightenment. But Stevens cannot translate words into actions, cannot reconcile his love of the Southern past with the demands of his ethical principles; that he consider all people as individuals.

'Now what?' his uncle said. 'What are you waiting for now?'
'My receipt,' Lucas said. (247)

Intruder in the Dust is a subtle, intelligent dramatisation of the issue of racism, exploring language, custom and different generations. Faulkner resists a rhetorical ending and undercuts Stevens precisely because he understands the fatality of abstraction and ideas which do not move in time. In Stevens he was able to explore what Irving Howe calls 'the relationship of the sensitive Southerner to his native myth, as it comforts and corrodes, inspires and repels.' But through Charles he 'affirms the basic interdependence of the individual and society, of personal ethics and public morality, of the natural world of time and the social world of history'.[151] Another critic pinpoints the value of this novel which, in contrast to the brutal melodrama of *Light in August*, successfully dramatises the theory rather than the practice of racism: 'The South is thus the stage for Faulkner's great human drama, the story of the attempt by human beings to translate these abstract moral values into concrete behaviour.'[152]

A FABLE

The Great War which the young William Faulkner failed to attend only *seemed* to disappear from his work after *Soldiers' Pay* and *Sartoris*. It was a watershed in his life, as it was for any young man born around the turn of this century, even in Mississippi. In his last great novel *A Fable* (1954) he returns to the battlefields of France which he never saw, and tries to get to the heart of the matter. In the middle of the long period of time (from the Second World War to publication) during which he worked on what he came to regard as his *magnum opus*, he delivered his Nobel Prize speech, talking of the human heart and man's capacity to endure. He also published in 1950 the section 'Notes on a Horsethief', and diagrammed the complex plot of his novel over the walls of his writing room at Rowen Oak. Most critics have judged that the heart of the novel is its tortuous philosophical investigation of the enduring human heart, and that the formal problems were merely the result of a declining genius; so Albert Guerard says, 'The ideas and affirmations are from the heart; the obliquities and sudden transitions are of the nerves.'[153] Even a critic sympathetic to Faulkner's narrative inventions sees *A Fable* as descended from *Light in August* and *Absalom, Absalom!* in its philosophical concerns but fatally lacking a narrative drive, as if someone had said, 'Why don't you write something really important, Bill?'[154]

True, Faulkner always fancied himself as a *philosophe*, but fortunately the penchant for storefront wisdom was usually indulged after the event, and carefully framed ironically in a character or narrative situation. I will argue that the case is no different with this novel; indeed, Faulkner's consistent concern with narrative itself is at the heart of his examination, as the title 'a fable' suggests. The 'structural and rhetorical complication' that Guerard complains of is not an overlay but a significant enactment of the ways the human heart seeks stories to model itself on. Although Faulkner himself reluctantly suggested that a 'message' of the novel might be that 'pacifism does not work', he insisted that *A Fable* had no aim or moral, 'I mean deliberately, in its conception, since as far as I knew or intended, it was simply an attempt to show man, human beings, in conflict with their own hearts and compulsions and beliefs and the hard and durable insentient earth-stage on which their griefs and hopes must anguish'.[155]

That sense of stage drama or a Hollywood epic film is apparent from the first scene, a set piece beginning with the empty *Place de Ville*, filling with a cast of thousands which finally dissipates leaving the woman alone, wringing her hands. The vehicles with their loads of prisoners are themselves like the stages of a miracle play, and Faulkner stresses the theatricality of his material whenever possible: the sergeant would 'have been a custodian of wine casks in the Paris Halles if he and the Paris Halles had been cast on some other stage that this' (12) – but his uniform means that he cannot escape a sense of alienation from mankind; while the prisoners move 'like phantoms or apparitions or perhaps figures cut without depth from tin or cardboard and snatched in violent repetition across a stage set for a pantomime of anguish and fatality' (18–19). The generalissimo and the corporal exchange glances 'across the fleeing instant', as Faulkner teases the reader with filmic clichés which belong to the popular genre where individuals change the course of destiny. The actual context, however, is one where a nameless mass, the regiment, is observed by another nameless mass, the crowd. What are the dynamics between the individual and the mass, Faulkner asks?

Do they not hinge on the kinds of fables in which we put our
faith to avoid the inexpressible loneliness, as the runner later
puts it, of breathing?

The next section presents an array of attitudes of the French
military, from Gragnon's existential dismay at the novel silence
and the threatened removal of his role in life, through the corps
commander's contempt ('it is a man who is our enemy' [31]) and
the divisional commander's toying with his aide's belief in
courage and pity (got from a book, *Gil Blas*), to the group
commander's cynical appraisal of the war game:

> Let the whole vast moil and seethe of man confederate in
> stopping wars if they wish, so long as we can prevent them
> from learning that they have done so. . . . It's no abrogation
> of a rule that will destroy us. It's less. The simple effacement
> from man's memory of a single word will be enough . . .
> Fatherland. (53)

In the section 'Tuesday Night' we learn how the runner has
progressed from a similar cynicism about human beings and
their ability to efface themselves and their humanity before an
arbitrary system like the military ('We can't be saved now;
even He doesn't want us any more now' [65]) to excited
proselytising for the rebel regiment. He argues hopelessly with
the sentry that 'they' regard war like 'an unfinished cricket or
rugger match which started according to a set of mutually
acceptable rules . . . and must finish by them' (74) – again,
Faulkner foregrounds the sense of theatricality in the 'theatre of
war'.

Like a ray of light piercing the gloom of military necessity,
the story of the horse reminds the reader of a more liberating
use of the imagination, to create not systems of authority but
stories of freedom:

> the tender legend which was the crowning glory of man's
> own legend beginning when his first paired children lost well
> the world and from which paired prototypes they still
> challenged paradise, still paired and still immortal against
> the chronicle's grimed and bloodstained pages . . . being
> immortal, the story, the legend, was not to be owned by any
> one of the pairs who added to its shining and tragic increment,

but only to be used, passed through, by each in their doomed and homeless turn. (139–40)

But even in Mississippi there are crowds, like the one which assembles to watch justice clip the horsethieves' wings. They prompt the deputy to muse how man is unable 'to cope with his own blind mass and weight' (146), and the lawyer to describe America sarcastically as a place where 'man had had a hundred and forty years in which to become so used to liberty that the simple unchallenged right to attend its ordered and regimented charades sufficed to keep him quiet and content . . .' (157). 'Ordered regiments' exist in peace and in war, and so Faulkner's 'fable' extends beyond the Great War to include Yoknapatawpha and us. If human beings could be inspired by fables of love and freedom alone, all might be well; but they seem to suffer a terrible kind of sloth which congeals them into mindless 'moils' expecting scripted 'charades', and only leaders (often military) can revivify their imaginations or, as Faulkner puts it, get 'some of him in one motion in one direction, by him of him and for him, to disjam the earth, get him for a little while at least out of his own way . . .' (164). Fables of power are, however, most suspect, because they appeal to man's 'mass-value for affirmation or negation' (210) – not only in terms of politics and warfare, but in the world of the multi-national, about which Faulkner also has something to say: Henry Ford may put the world on wheels but that would be peace (robot behaviour, that is) 'and to attain that, the silence must be conquered too: the silence in which man had space to think and in consequence act on what he believed he thought or thought he believed . . .' (170).

It is these silent spaces which Faulkner wishes to explore, the gap between robotlike mass behaviour on the one hand, and exceptional legends of superhuman feats on the other. What fascinates him about the incident of mass rebellion in the trenches of 1917 (based on historical fact) is the way it seems to collapse the two poles of behaviour, just as Jesus the exceptional man, two thousand years ago, was able to 'disjam' and mobilise a crowd. How and why do people come to believe in heroes? Faulkner presents two believers, the quarter-master general and the runner, and examines their tortuous analyses and self-justifications. The quarter-master has the harder time, and his faith is finally lost. His complex argument seems to be based on the idea that the old general deliberately absented himself from Paris affairs to prepare himself for leading man from rapacity to endurance and immortality: "You will save man," he tells him (238). His one apprehension is that the mass will consign the general to 'the dusty lumber room of literature' (237), to become an icon rather than a reality. When the general and his staff contrive to ignore the regiment's attempted ceasefire, the quarter-master is disillusioned; his saviour has joined the 'we', the public stage of conservative expectation, history and legend. In apparent contrast, the runner backs the winner, the corporal, convinced by his activities with the horse that he is a saintly leader. The corporal has served not himself but a sign, the horse which stands for our belief in freedom and excellence. Only as he leads the troops out into no-man's land does the runner realise the lurking danger of the massed 'we' and its ability to play its role to the hilt in the fatal legend of national pride. Even as the runner seeks desperately to counter this mythology with a 'sign', an alternative system of Masonic brotherhood, the bombs begin to fall.

The central section of the novel is really an Aristotelian debate on the sign systems we inhabit and which motivate us. The quarter-master general had hoped his general would be a 'paradox . . . free of human past to be the one out of all earth to be free of the compulsions of fear and weakness and doubt' (294); but he turns out to be rather a quintessence and instrument of those fears. In the great temptation scene with his son the corporal, the old general argues that warfare itself is hermaphroditic, a closed system of victory and defeat endlessly feeding on itself (312), versus imagination or 'unfact'. Even the priest argues that because the human heart is inconstant, the church must be a rock of convention and authority (327). The establishment, we see, argues for an eternal dialectic which simply reinforces the status quo. However the corporal (and the old general also had this potential, in the quarter-master general's view) represents the possibility of escape from that dialectic, a disruption of expectation, that rare kind of imaginative story which, unlike most legends, challenges rather than confirms convention.

Faulkner indicates his fondness for philosophical argument

when he describes the pilot whose own set of rules for glory has been shattered by another set of pragmatic ends:

> Unless of course the sun really failed to rise tomorrow, which as they taught you in that subsection of philosophy they called dialectics which you were trying to swot through in order to try to swot through that section of being educated they called philosophy, was for the sake of argument possible. (289)

Here the very rhythm of the prose expresses, in miniature, the tensions of *A Fable*, where the exception, the 'through line', tries vainly to disrupt the ponderous, closed circle logic which 'they' set up. Whenever possible Faulkner expresses the conflict in terms of language: dialectic, competing stories, legends, orders. The old general keeps insisting to the corporal that he has never 'misread' him, that is, that there is only one reading possible, ending in the youth's inevitable rebellion inevitably quelled. Faulkner, however, as we have found throughout his writing career, was on the side of what a deconstructionist might call 'promiscuous' readings, subversive and always incomplete, open-ended. While the new soldiers arriving at the battlefield 'blood themselves on the old Somme names' (185), there is another kind of language at work that is indomitable; as the negro puts it, 'All you can kill is man's meat. You can't kill his voice.' (182)

The tension between absolutism and contingency is epitomised in the Christ story, where God submits Himself to reality. So Faulkner contrives for the narrative to follow (as did *Light in August*) the events of Christ's life, even to the vanished body. In a brilliantly conceived finale, Faulkner has the corporal's body (after some dealings which read as if the Keystone Cops had performed *As I Lay Dying*) chosen for the tomb of the unknown soldier. It is a fine semiotic paradox: the hero of the trenches, suppressed by official history, is literally exhumed into fame, but a fame dependent precisely on his being unknown. He lies as a sign of military valour, not human protest. It is this paradox of naming which prompts the runner's tears, and the mood in the final lines is a knife-edge between laughter and despair, one of the purest early expressions of the 'black humour' which was to become the staple mood of fiction in the next two decades, particularly in war fiction. Indeed, this story of a 'Milo Minderbinder' sentry whose insurance 'scam' involves soldiers betting that they will die, of a regiment whose crucifixion is 'proof that the world is not worth saving', of a devoted regular army general whose botched execution requires plugging the holes in his head, of a hideously crippled 'runner', takes Faulkner's ironic sense beyond the front steps of the Jefferson general store to metaphysical dimensions of savagery. The old general who 'helped carry the torch of man into that twilight where he shall be no more' (391) ends up killing the soldier whose flame burns forever, his own son. Faulkner's crucial point is this: the reader knows that truth, but no one else does. The moral of the 'fable' comes home to the reader, but not to the inhabitants of that world, the soldiers and people of Paris who still believe in the glories of war and patriotism. At the end the crowd flows on, leaving behind in the gutter the two fabulists, the runner and the quarter-master general, who have come closest to the moral.

Far from being a dislocated failure then, Faulkner's last great novel represents the pinnacle of his achievement, uniting his traditional preoccupations with fathers and sons in a penetrating, wideranging epistemological enquiry. The form of the novel perfectly complements its themes: everywhere people are being told things ('So you tell me . . . tell me then . . . tell them . . . He told me . . . All right, tell me . . . Do as I tell you . . . Tell me why . . . Perhaps you better tell me again . . . I want you to tell me . . . Tell him that', and so on) and then meditating in contorted, painstaking ways upon simple events. The novel itself teeters between historical recreation and stylised invention, from the chapters of days which move beyond us into 'Tomorrow', to the stylised Faulkerian speech which all the characters use. This stylistic flattening creates a kind of silence, a space in which the reader can meditate and into which the violent events irrupt with the meaning or nonsense of a lark's call or a cannon's thud. At the centre of the novel is Magda's account of the general's passion high on a mountaintop, in the midst of his furious meditation. The sexual connection, so often the fraught centre of Faulkner's fiction, here at last finds its proper place in enigmatic silence. Out of that union comes the son whose name 'must be effaced' or his legend will change the world. The locket which Magda flings at the general is echoed in the rejected medal of the runner; Faulkner knows, as he knew early in his career, that fiction is not a matter of inscribing memorable words, but circumscribing the faces of a man and a woman.

5

The Short Stories

Faulkner's veracity and accuracy about the world around keeps the comic thread from ever being lost or fouled, but that's a simple part of the matter. The complicated and intricate thing is that his stories aren't decked out in humour, but the humour is born in them, as much their blood and bones as the passion and poetry. Put one of his stories into a single factual statement and it's pure outrage – so would life be – too terrifying, too probable, and too symbolic too, too funny to bear. There has to be the story, to bear it – wherein that statement, conjured up and implied and demonstrated, not said or the sky would fall on our heads, is yet the living source of his comedy – and a good part of that comedy's adjoining terror, of course.[156]

It was perhaps Faulkner's need to complicate the unbearable facts of life, as Eudora Welty suggests, which made him uneasy with the short story form, and inspired him to transform so many of his shorter pieces into the novels or into short story composites like *Go Down, Moses*. Although he published over seventy short stories (one of the first and most famous being 'A Rose for Emily' in 1930), he did not really explore the genre as he did the novel. Joanne Creighton concludes that he 'works against the autonomous structure and meaning of the short story when he incorporates it into a larger aesthetic whole',[157] and a considerable scholarship is now devoted to the evolution of Faulkner's stories into novels and into short story collections.

For this study I will confine myself to the collections *These Thirteen* (1931), *Dr Martino* (1934), *The Unvanquished* (1938), *Knight's Gambit* (1949) and *Uncle Willy and Other Stories* (from the *Collected Stories* of 1950, and published separately in 1951). The key to Faulkner's anthology technique, particularly in *The Unvanquished* and *Knight's Gambit*, can again be found in Hugh Kenner's reminder that Faulkner's influences included both the taletelling of his Southern neighbours with models like Mark Twain and Sherwood Anderson, and the Symbolist movement of a sophisticated, cosmopolitan Europe. As we have seen in the novels, Faulkner's characteristic method is to contemplate at leisure a fairly brusque, often sensational narrative; these two moods of action and reflection set up an alternating current between the poles, in both the characters and the reader. Kenner puts it this way: 'The Symbolist's ideal timelessness becomes the taleteller's ideal leisure.'[158] Often in individual stories, or throughout collections, the true subject is the psychological resonance between tale and teller, or hero. Where Faulkner carefully assembled collections, the effect of the story sequence is akin to that of James Joyce in *Dubliners*, and there is a similar downplaying of 'endings' in favour of mood. As Faulkner wrote in a letter of 1948, 'Even to a collection of short stories, form, integration, is as important as to a novel.'[159] Understanding these intentions, we might be less inclined than some critics to reject Faulkner's stories as awkward practice exercises for the novels.

Faulkner's first short stories appeared as *New Orleans Sketches* for the *Times-Picayune* newspaper there in 1925. Here he sounds those major themes: a pathetic black slave thinks he is back in Africa as he is pursued and shot ('Dese Af'ikins shoots niggers jes' like white folks does'); in 'The Kid Learns' a boy rescues a girl but her gift to him is more sinister than sexual satisfaction, since she becomes 'Little Sister Death'; in 'Episode' a sketched woman is likened to the eternal feminine mystery of Mona Lisa. There are sympathetic portraits of the mentally retarded ('The Kingdom of God', which looks forward to Benjy) and down-and-outs (in 'Out of Nazareth' a hobo reads *A Shropshire Lad*). Interestingly, 'The Liar' has a character extrapolate the motivations for a murder, to find that he has stumbled on the truth, and, what is more, one of his listeners is the murderer. Here we see Faulkner's love of paradox, and the situation of taletelling becomes literally a matter of life and death; having stumbled on the truth, the liar is shot by the murderer and, Faulkner comments icily, 'his veracity as a liar was gone forever'.

'A Rose for Emily', the first story of *These Thirteen*, is deservedly famous as a tightly written example of the Gothic horror story. Faulkner sets up a narrative point of view which implicates the reader with the 'we' of the town; although at the same time, at a metafictional level, the narrator gives Emily the bouquet for exposing her neighbours. We look on as Miss Grierson plays out the historical drama of the South. First Colonel Sartoris gallantly gets the town to provide for her: 'only a man of Colonel Sartoris's generation and thought could have invented it, and only a woman could have believed it' (10). Then she breaks down at her father's death, but then, 'We remembered all the young men her father had driven away, and we knew that with nothing left, she would have to cling to that which had robbed her, as people will.' (14) Here we see what Judith Fetterley calls the 'violence behind veneration'.[160] But she has also 'vanquished' the townspeople by becoming a role. In the immunity of spinsterhood she can literally get away with murder, although the narrator is awed by her moral absolutism. Only the horrific end with its suggestion of necrophilia shows us at what cost Miss Emily has attempted to reconcile her antebellum Southern values with her own emotional and sexual needs. Poor Homer the Yankee is simultaneously taken and rejected (or consumed) by this Miss Haversham figure whose clock stopped not at a wedding because of men, but at Gettysburg because of history.

The next two stories amplify elements of 'A Rose for Emily'. In the first, Hawkshaw the barber displays a monumental patience similar to Miss Emily's, a displacement of sexual desire which comes close to monomania but has an unusually happy outcome. Not so fortunate is Minnie in 'Dry September', whose repressions encourage her to accuse a black man of rape. After the innocent accused has been lynched, Faulkner takes us back to the ringleader McLendon's house, where we see him beat his wife in a state of excited guilt: 'the cold moon and the lidless stars' (53) watch over this waste land of repressed sexual desire. McLendon, Faulkner implies, acted out of suppressed lust for Minnie rather than in defence of Southern womanhood. 'That Evening Sun' culminates this quartet of studies of extreme passion, the child's point of view contrasting with the earlier Ratliffian voice of nostalgia and misogyny. Nancy's terror at possible sexual violence is no melodrama – *The Sound and the Fury* informs us that she was indeed killed by her husband.

The next two stories show how society rather than the tortured physician can regulate and ritualise desire, from the servant's martyrdom (reluctant though it is) on the Indian chief's funeral pyre, to Doom's Prospero – like manoeuvres to guide a love triangle. Faulkner emphasises the role of 'talking' in establishing and passing on codes of behaviour for the unruly human heart, by using the perspective of an uncomprehending boy in a suspended twilight.

'Ad Astra', the first of a group of war stories, gives us the other side of mythmaking. Although the drunken soldiers attempt to escape their 'inescapable selves' and 'the old verbiaged lusts and the buntinged and panoplied greeds' (131), and although the German prisoner over whom they fight believes in global unity, they are powerless to invent a substitute myth for themselves. Even Monaghan the pacifist is 'inarticulate', and the impotence of the subadar's narrative mirrors the soldiers' inability to break out from their 'terrific stasis'. 'Nothing at home for us now' (171), a comment in 'Victory', epitomises its mood of aimless despair and cynicism. The reluctant war hero Gray ends up selling matches, unillumined, living through 'senseless and unbroken battalions of days' (174). 'Crevasse' continues this anti-war theme by pretending to tell a story of danger and bravery but giving instead a Dantesque topography of living hell, death above and a mortuary below. We have moved from stars to crevasse; the opportunity of war to give shape to our lives in grand tales has proved illusory, and Faulkner's use of present tense and juggled time frames completes a reading experience of chaos.

'All the Dead Pilots' culminates the war stories and is an excellent example of Faulkner's use of 'metafictional' techniques. The narrator is, like the notorious Yossarian of *Catch-22*, a letter censor. Sartoris's love for a French girl combined with a war setting should be the stuff of powerful melodrama, but his jealousy is absurd and emphasised by details like the dog licking his vomit after he crashes. Nevertheless, by speaking for the inarticulate instead of censoring, the narrator has made a story, even its flaws making it the more memorable as literature. Despite the narrator's suspicion of words ('It takes too many

words to make a war' [211]), the inclusion of the letters
themselves and the foregrounding of the narrator's fears about
the status of story set up a sophisticated debate about the
nature and value of reading fiction:

> And so, being momentary, it [the courage, the recklessness]
> can be preserved and prolonged only on paper: a picture, a
> few written words that any match, a minute and harmless
> flame that any child can engender, can obliterate in an
> instant. A one-inch sliver of sulphur-tipped wood is longer
> than memory or grief; a flame no larger than a sixpence is
> fiercer than courage or despair. (213)

By emphasising the fragility of the vehicle of book or paper, the
narrator actually persuades us to internalise the ambiguous
truths of stories: valour and stupidity, mindless action and
anguished reflection.

'Mistral', like 'All the Dead Pilots', also has it both ways.
During a walking tour of Italy the narrator and his friend Don
stumble, Lockwood-like, upon a situation of passion and
murder. The narrator assumes world weariness – 'there's
nothing particularly profound about reality' (231) – because he
sentimentally assigns feeling to the past: 'I cried, because I had
lost myself then and I could never again be hurt by loss.' (241)
He and his friend maintain a distance from the community of
the story, repeatedly telling the tavern folk 'No spika. I love
Italy. I love Mussolini.' They want to create a quiet room of
story 'isolated on the ultimate peak of space, hollowed
murmurous out of chaos and the long dark fury of time' (234)
and couched in florid language like this very quotation. But the
priest's love for his ward (that familiar Faulknerian passion for
the virgin) is like the gust of the mistral which blows through
the story and the observers' wall of detachment, turning Don's
cigarette to 'fiery streamers' at the end. Flames, a motif in this
collection of stories, still flicker, indeed are sustained by the
sheltering frame and contrast of the pair's deflections and
intrusions.

The last two stories in *These Thirteen* are demonstrations of
how form determines content. 'Divorce in Naples' is a comic
treatment of the fraught theme of homosexuality, while in
'Carcassonne' Faulkner poeticises the familiar dualities of light

and dark, male and female, glory and oblivion, body and spirit, life and death. The soaring rider of glory, legend and the spirit courses through the very texture of the prose of this last story, exploding it into fragments and italics, and yet he is 'punily diminishing' while the Earth Mother persists. In artistic terms Faulkner is suggesting that 'life' can be captured in literature only obliquely, by devious frames which set up in the reader states of tension between poetry and prose, oblivion of text and acute awareness of it, a psychological state analogous to those of his characters – the cold yet monumental passions, the flashing yet trivial aberrations which fascinate Faulkner so much.

'Barn Burning', the powerful first story of the collection *Dr Martino* ... introduces the Snopes family and describes the incident which Ratliff reports at the opening of the Snopes Trilogy. Affronted by wealth at de Spain's front door, just as Sutpen was affronted at a front door, Ab believes in the integrity of fire to voice his outrage. 'Bloodless as though cut from tin' (14) he harbours, also like Popeye, a volcano of suppressed emotion, seen in the vivid description of him striking and reining back simultaneously. He treats himself and his family as he treats his horse. Only the point of view of his son suggests an escape from this hermetic fury; the boy realises that to the community his father is as intrusive as a 'buzzing wasp', and the ending suggests that he himself might just escape from his vortex of disappointment. In 'Death Drag' pent up emotions are freed into action and language, first in the daredevil stunts, then in Captain Warren's poetic ecstasy: 'He's got the stick between his knees. . . . Exalted suzerain of mankind; saccharine and sacred symbol of eternal rest.' (49) But all this action and articulation is beyond the 'composite' point of view of the narrating townsfolk, 'we (groundlings, swellers in and backbone of a small town interchangeable with and duplicate of ten thousand little dead clottings of human life about the land)' (45–6).

While the male heroes of Faulkner's stories are generally free to express their outrage at society, his women are usually victims. Like Emily Grierson, 'Elly' is trapped by her grandmother and the past. Even when she tries to break out of tradition with her black lover, she must enact a high drama. In fact she kills her grandmother only so that she won't 'tell

daddy', and she feels robbed of her 'chance to sin' when the
cars pass by her wreck without registering her grand gesture.
Louise in 'Dr Martino' is an unusual Faulkner heroine in that,
although duped by her mother, she does take up the doctor's
challenge, 'to be afraid is to know you are alive' (175). Similarly
Narcissa in 'There was a Queen' upholds her own sense of
honour by sleeping with a blackmailer and then washing in the
river. In this sequence of heroines we see an evolution of the
independent woman making her own code, not trapped like so
many of the male characters (particularly in the war or flying
stories) in social codes of honour. That social code is vividly
present in 'Fox Hunt', where the nouveau riche Blair seeks
ritual in the hunt while his wife becomes victim of an equally
ritualistic sexual game.

In 'Mountain Victory' Faulkner ties social honour to
language. The mountain family want old Weddel to conform to
their notion of a supercilious Southern gentleman but he is far
from being a Sutpen or Sartoris. He has a strong sense of
irony and a close relationship with his black slave, to whom he
muses:

> 'Our lives are summed up in sounds and made significant.
> Victory. Defeat. Peace. Home. That's why we must do so
> much to invent meanings for the sounds, so damned much.
> Especially if you are unfortunate enough to be victorious: so
> damned much. It's nice to be whipped; quiet to be whipped.
> To be whipped and to lie under a broken roof, thinking of
> home.' The Negro snored. 'So damned much'; seeming to
> watch the words shape quietly in the darkness above his
> mouth. (246)

At the climax of the story Weddel is ambushed by the
outraged family, who will sacrifice even their own son to
maintain their pattern of meaning. The slave faces Vatch's rifle
'like a period on a page' (257) – the page of history, or the end
of meaning? In this sophisticated image Faulkner foregrounds
the paradox of his fiction of the South: was the labelling of
black and white by either side worth fighting for? Weren't the
enlightened Weddels of the antebellum South admirable because
they escaped all codes of meaning through humility, scepticism
and endurance?

Faulkner's increasing epistemological and social scepticism lead to the Forsterian stories 'Beyond' and 'Black Music', which suggest another realm where institutions like the law fade into triviality. The only law which Faulkner recognises is that of biological necessity; the judge of the former story tenderly recollects his dead son, who rode 'in the flesh down the long road which his blood and bone had travelled before it became his' (268). The last story of the volume, 'The Leg', dramatises the darker side of this personal compulsion in a superb, Poe-like horror story, the more effective because the narrator and villain is so detached and puzzled. The setting of pre-War England is a perfect guise: two chums, boating on the Thames, 'that peaceful land where in green petrification the old splendid and bloody deeds, the spirits of the blundering courageous men, slumbered in every stone and tree' (306). But the experience of the trenches inspires no such glory, only a revulsion for mankind and no place for women 'weeping for the symbol of your soul'. Davy's amputated leg becomes a symbol for his soul, now petrified and impotent; in his anger and unknown to himself he torments the virgin of pre-War days to death. Davy has been unable to 'kill' his leg, to cure his psychological maiming, because the people around him are still sustained by the language of honour and glory. Davy knows that the 'fine and resounding words men mouthed so glibly were the vampire's teeth with which the vampire fed' (316).

On the whole *Dr Martino* is a grim and disturbing collection, portraying a gallery of victims caught not only in traps of social conditioning, honour and standing, but also in the resulting inner traps of suppressed and warped sensibilities. There is, after all, not much separating Davy from Ab Snopes.

In *The Unvanquished* Faulkner assembled stories from 1934–6 or so into a coherent pattern which interrogates the relationship between history and personal need, in this case the Sartoris legends of the Civil War and the way the war actually impinged on the lives of family members, particularly the children. The boy narrator begins by recalling the 'living map' scraped on the earth behind the smokehouse that summer; the great battlefields of the Civil War are miniaturised into a child's game. The whole volume has a similar effect, concentrating on one family and locality, reducing the war to Faulkner's famous postage-stamp. The war is presented as chaotic and absurd, the opposite of the famous crane shot of Richmond in *Gone With the Wind*. Yet the boys' games are a 'shield between ourselves and reality, us and fact and doom' (2) and so, in Faulkner's world, they are as dangerous and ambiguous as any other sign system. They lead the boys to shoot foolishly at the Union soldiers (fortunately hitting a horse rather than a soldier); they blind the boys to Loosh's insistence that the Confederates are in fact retreating and the battle line is coming closer. Fortunately the boys are saved by the Union commander's willingness to play along with the adult game of noblesse oblige, respecting their grandmother (under whose skirts they are cowering) as a Southern belle who does not tell lies.

'Retreat' signals a retreat from gameplaying. Uncle Buck argues that people belong to the land and insists that the whole idea of the war is folly, that Sartoris is a 'damned confounded selfish coward' (61). He is against the Northerners for simple, immediate reasons: he wants the right to make his own mistakes in his own place, just as Bayard treasures a snuffbox of that smokehouse earth and his grandmother treasures the roses. But our pleasure at Uncle Buck's clear-eyed cynicism is tempered by Loosh's reminder of the inescapable root cause of the war; he prefers 'the man that dug me free' to 'the man that buried me in the black dark' (90).

'Raid' takes us further into that stark reality. It presents an eerie waste land of burnt homesteads, frightened women and children, and black refugees. Faulkner suggests that the reason the Sartorises will remain unvanquished is that they have stories; not apocalyptic dreams like the mass of blacks chanting about Jordan, but sustaining fictions like Drusilla's story of the great race between 'two iron knights' (118) won by the Southern train. While the contest 'proved nothing' the story is a useful incitement – not to Confederacy but to sheer excellence, for its own sake. It is different from the stories of wars on which young Bayard has been raised, because 'wars are wars . . . one tale, one telling, the same as the next one or the one before' (114). Thus the Sartoris family seems to avoid the dangerous precipice of abstraction represented by the Union soldiers. Rosa Millard starts to deal in mules and is vanquished only by one who believes solely in commerce. Bayard's retribution is swift and savage, but he reveals a deeper distrust of commerce (one which also hampers the efforts of Ratliff and Stevens in the trilogy) when he argues that granny was killed by the 'first batch of mules we got for nothing'.

'Skirmish at Sartoris' undermines our confidence in the Sartoris order – indeed, there is total disorder as Sartoris violently imposes his wishes and neglects his domestic responsibilities. Meanwhile a confused Ringo says, 'I done been abolished.' Ultimately there is no way that Bayard can endorse an archaic system that no longer functions. He abandons his childhood map, seeing the crowd as a chorus on a Roman holiday and Drusilla as 'a Greek amphora priestess' (273) in 'a theatre scene' (291). Utterly sceptical of story, seeing an 'immitigable chasm between all life and all print' (284), Bayard goes unarmed to Redmond, not in a romantic gesture of defiance but in a dreamlike resignation. The volume ends with Drusilla, voice of the Old South, offering Bayard verbena in an ambiguous gesture either of defeat or initiation; but Bayard knows that she could pick 'a half-dozen of them and they would be all of a size, almost all of a shape, as if a machine had stamped them out' (319). A prisoner to the past, Drusilla is no longer a Southern belle but a pathetic, mechanical doll, her gestures knee-jerk obeisances to a dead tradition. In the end, the fact that Bayard is unvanquished by the maps and stories of his family is the only true Sartoris victory.

Commenting on the fact that *Knight's Gambit*, like *The Unvanquished*, was formed by adding a final story to a collection of previously published stories (1930–46), Dorothy Tuck laments that it 'remains simply a collection of independent detective stories strung together on the thin thread of Gavin Stevens as the sleuth, and Charles Mallison as his Dr Watson'.[161] What is interesting beyond the ingenious plots is the metafictional debate about language, here dramatised in the relationship between the law and the life it feeds upon. 'Monk' begins:

> I will have to try to tell about Monk. I mean, actually try – a deliberate attempt to bridge the inconsistencies in his brief and sordid and unoriginal history, to make something out of it, not only with the nebulous tools of supposition and inference and invention, but to employ these nebulous tools upon the nebulous and inexplicable material which he left behind him. Because it is only in literature that the paradoxical and even mutually negativing anecdotes in the

history of a human heart can be juxtaposed and annealed by art into verisimilitude and credibility. (40)

Stevens sets up an opposition between the turmoil of life and the clarity of art – not of law, for the story is about a wrong conviction. The law cannot connect with Mink Snopes's preliterate mentality, a man who enjoys feeling his throat buzz but spends twenty-five years learning how to tell his name. Often in these stories the human truth exists beyond the courtroom or slips through the gaps in the law's labyrinthine ritual. In 'Tomorrow', for example, the crucial story concerns not the case before the court but the past of one of the jurors. The passions of Faulkner's characters constantly overflow the urns of law and language, as here: 'But it [the story] wasn't that long. It wasn't long enough for what was in it. But Uncle Gavin says it don't take many words to tell the sum of any human experience; that somebody has already done it in eight: He was born, he suffered and he died.' (88)

'Knight's Gambit' pursues these themes through the familiar novelistic technique of dual narrators, Gavin and Charles. Faulkner sets up a hierarchy of complexity in various media, from the 'magazine instalments' (129) image used by Stevens to describe how the town watched the Harriss marriage, through language to something more complex and loved by the other side of Stevens – 'the garrulous facile voice so garrulous and facile that it seemed to have no connection with reality at all and presently hearing it was like listening not even to fiction but to literature' (123). Stevens enjoys languages, too, possessing 'a certain happy glibness with which to be used by his myriad tongues' (144); and he has taught his nephew the Spanish in which he converses with Gualdres. Stevens insists that literature is one of the best guides to life. When Charles wants to go to Europe to relive his uncle's past, Stevens says, 'You can do that here, in the library. Simply by opening the right page in Conrad . . .' (216). But Charles is obsessed throughout the story with a sense that elsewhere his peers are writing themselves into history. He wonders 'how to assuage the heart's thirst with the dusty chronicle of the past when three thousand miles away in England men not much older than he was were daily writing with their lives his own time's deathless chronicle' (188).

Stevens is similarly dogged by a sense that he is avoiding life.

For him the sense is more acute because the case with which he has to deal involves a past sweetheart, Mrs Harriss. From the plot one might see schematically how Stevens denies his past by rescuing Gualdres, his 'rival' for Mrs Harriss; more deviously one may see Stevens's 'knight's gambit' at work whereby he lets the castle of Mrs Harriss go to Gualdres, while preserving his queen Mrs Harriss. Certainly when Charles returns from the war the two are married, and Charles, by saying to them 'Bless you, my children' (211), symbolically assumes the mantle of storyteller as Stevens drops out of the text and into life.

'Knight's Gambit' is a long, sometimes flaccid story, trying for the kind of epistemological debate generated in the novels by a similar means of multiple tales, tellers, and a suppression of the central fact (in this case the idealised love between Stevens and Melisandre). But the volume as a whole shows Faulkner moving his concern with the place of language into the public domain of the law, as he was shortly to move into the world of the army and politics in *A Fable*.

The stories in *Uncle Willy* . . . were written from 1933 to 1943 and have no general theme. 'Shingles for the Lord' weaves delicately between tall tale and social history, just as the characters themselves veer between a vertical or spiritual sense of events and their own importance, and an intense preoccupation with worldly calculation and barter. The story balances Preacher Whitfield's sense of man's 'indestructibility, endurability' (24) with mean-spirited commerce which threatens, literally, to destroy the church. 'The Tall Men' resumes Faulkner's attack on abstraction. Here, in contrast to 'The Leg', a leg must be buried publically in the family plot as a clear-eyed affirmation of who and where the people are. 'We' modern urban folk, on the other hand, 'done invented ourselves so many alphabets and rules and recipes that we can't see anything else.' (41)

The opening words of 'A Bear Hunt' echo Melville as they emphasise the taleteller: 'Ratliff is telling this.' But even before Ratliff begins, the narrator is using the pronoun 'we', identifying reader and framing narrator as 'descendants of people who read books and who were – or should have been – beyond superstition' (48). Ratliff has the privileged position of being in two worlds, fable and 'realism', half believing in 'a kind of big power laying still somewhere in the dark' (52).

The other stories, apart from those reworked for the Snopes

trilogy, examine various kinds of innocence. The boy who
wants to go to war and loses his brother Pete, tries to cope with
his grief by becoming jingoistic but cannot escape de Spain's
anguished cynicism. In 'That Will be Fine' the boy insists on
payment of his quarter while a story of adultery and murder
rages about him. In 'A Courtship' the innocence is tribal as
Ikkemotubbe and David Hoggenbeck hold up a dying world
like two caryatids, relishing their last moments of innocence
before the 'crying-rope' of the steamboat announces doom. In
'Artist at Home' the innocent Shelleyan poet is used by the
story writer for inspiration, although of course the refiner's fire
transmutes the material: 'live people do not make good copy,
the most interesting copy being gossip, since it mostly is not
true' (238). The sister in 'Pennsylvania Station' is abused by
her swindling son, just as the husband in 'The Brooch' is
victimised by his wife and, more significantly, by his own
mother.

'My Grandmother Millard . . .' is an exhilarating cartoon
version of Faulkner's preoccupations with tradition and naming
in *The Unvanquished*. Melisandre loses words when confronted
first by the Yankees and then by a Confederate suitor whose
derisive surname 'Backhouse' carries unfortunate memories for
her. Only when he is renamed can she forget the past and
marry him. Against this comic mood of the past is set the dark
final story, 'Golden Land', a California where there is no
innocence. Even Mrs Ewing is in danger of being seduced by
the Lotus land of Tinseltown, its dreams based not on language
at all but on 'a few spools' of inflammable substance, and her
own family dessicated and morally bankrupt. Faulkner here
presents the new American innocence which he could foresee as
clearly as he documented the myths of lost innocence from the
past: immaculate of history and all the ambiguities which
tormented Faulkner's Protestant soul, illiterate people 'without
age, beautiful as gods and goddesses, and with the minds of
infants' (315).

Appendix: The History of Yoknapatawpha County

Pages 1-12 of *Crowell's Handbook of Faulkner* by
Dorothy Tuck

Yoknapatawpha County is closely modeled on Lafayette County, Mississippi. Both the real and fictional counties are roughly bounded on the northeast by the Tallahatchie River; in the fictional county the Yocana River to the south is named the Yoknapatawpha. Jefferson, the seat of the imaginary county, corresponds in location and many other aspects to Oxford, the seat of Lafayette County and for many years Faulkner's home town. In Faulkner's saga the city of Oxford is located some forty miles in an unspecified direction from Jefferson, and plays a small part as the seat of the University of Mississippi.

In the discussion that follows, the fictional county, its inhabitants, and the events that take place are treated as if they were real. No attempt has been made to distinguish between purely imaginary incidents and those based on fact, or to suggest parallels between the histories of the real and imaginary counties. The only primary sources available on Yoknapatawpha County are Faulkner's novels, and there are occasional inconsistencies and gaps.

Yoknapatawpha County, William Faulkner's 'mythical kingdom', is situated in northern Mississippi, roughly bounded by the Tallahatchie River on the north of the Yoknapatawpha River on the south, and bisected north and south by John Sartoris's railroad. The face of the land varies from low-lying, fertile and heavily timbered river bottoms to sandy pine hills in the northeast section known as Beat Four. Jefferson, the county

157

seat, is surrounded by gently rolling farmland and is located approximately at the geographical center of the county. Like many Southern towns of the same period, it is built around a columned and porticoed courthouse set in an octagonal park in the center of the Square; at one end of the Square is a monument of a Confederate soldier, shielding his eyes from the sun in the classic searcher's pose and staring boldly south – whether for some lost Yankee regiment heading north for home or for some departing Confederates no one knows. The buildings around the Square are two-storied, most of them with a second-storey gallery reached by an outside staircase. The only other town of any significance is the hamlet of Frenchman's Bend at the southeastern corner of the county. Memphis, the closest large city, is seventy-five miles northwest of Jefferson, and Oxford, the location of the state university, is forty miles away. The county's 2,400 square miles are populated by about 15,000 persons, over half of them Negroes.

The name Yoknapatawpha is derived from that of the Yocana River, sometimes referred to as the Yocanapatafa (or Yocanapatapha) in old records; according to Faulkner, the Chickasaw words *yocana* and *petopha* means 'water runs slow through flat land'. In the old days, the northern part of the county near the Tallahatchie River bottom was a heavily timbered land rife with wildlife – possums, coons, rabbits, squirrels, wild turkeys, deer, and even bears. Then the land was inhabited by the Chickasaw Indians, whose nation was ruled by a great chieftain referred to as David Colbert; the Yoknapatawpha Chickasaws had their own local chief whose title, 'the Man', was passed on from father to son. However, perhaps because the history of the Chickasaws was told to the white settlers of the county many years later, long after 'the People', as the Indians called themselves, had been driven to a reservation in Oklahoma, the various stories about the Indians are not always consistent with one another. The most famous – or notorious – of the chiefs was Ikkemotubbe (sometimes spelled Ikkemoutubbe). He 'had been born merely a subchief, a Mingo, one of three children of the mother's side of the family. He made a journey – he was a young man then and New Orleans was a European city – from north Mississippi to New Orleans by keel boat, where he . . . passed as the chief, the Man, the hereditary owner of that Land which belonged to the male side of the family.' In French-speaking New Orleans he was called *du homme* (or *l'Homme* or *de l'Homme*), from which came Doom, the name he was later called by the People. All the stories agree that Doom returned from New Orleans with, among other things, a wicker basket full of puppies and a small gold box filled with white powder, which, when administered to a puppy, would quickly kill it. Soon afterwards, his uncle the Man, and the Man's son both died suddenly, and the Man's brother refused to accept the chieftainship which was his hereditary right; Doom, as the next in line of succession, became the Man. Beyond this point, however, the legend of Doom has variants. In 'A Justice' Sam Fathers tells young Quentin Compson how Doom came back from New Orleans and, succeeded to the chieftainship. After becoming the Man, Doom took some of the People to drag out a steamboat that had died in the Tallahatchie River twelve miles away and bring it back to the Plantation, where Doom could use the boat as his house. One of the People, Craw-ford (sometimes called Crawfish-ford) stayed at home complaining of a bad back in order to be near one of the black women Doom had brought with him from New Orleans. The woman, although married to a black man, later gave birth to a copper-coloured son; Doom settled the quarrel between Craw-ford and the black man and named the child Had-Two Fathers – the full name of Sam Fathers. In 'The Old People', however, Sam Fathers says that he is the son of Doom and a quadroon slave; in this variant of the legend Doom married the pregnant slave to a black man and named the baby Had-Two-Fathers. In both versions Doom sells the mother and child to a neighbouring white man – in the former story to Lucius Quintus Carothers McCaslin, in the latter to Quentin McLachan Compson II.

The order of succession of the Chickasaw chiefs is not consistent, due to variants of the legend. In 'Red Leaves' Doom is the father of Issetibbeha, who succeeds him as the Man, and the grandfather of Moketubbe. In this variant Issetibbeha became the Man at nineteen. During his chieftainship there arose the problem of what to do with the Negro slaves acquired during his father's lifetime; the question was finally solved by having the Negroes clear the land and plant grain, which the Indians sold. From the sale of grain and slaves Issetibbeha acquired the money to travel to France; he returned with

a gilt bed, a pair of girandoles by whose light it was said that
Pompadour arranged her hair while Louis smirked at his
mirrored face across her powdered shoulder, and a pair of
slippers with red heels. They were too small for him, since he
had not worn shoes at all until he reached New Orleans on
his way abroad.

Issetibbeha's son Moketubbe, a fat, squat, indolent boy,
developed a fondness for the high-heeled slippers that amounted
almost to fetishism. The influence of the white man, direct or
otherwise, had by this time subtly corrupted the Indians: they
had come to own slaves, to sell their produce for money, and to
buy and cherish useless ornaments. Moketubbe, the last of their
chiefs, who succeeded to the chieftainship after Issetibbeha's
death, was nothing more than a sweating mound of flesh, too
lazy even to want to take his traditional place in the manhunt
to capture the escaped slave who, as Issetibbeha's body servant,
was required to be buried with him.

In 'The Old People' a version of the legend is given that
appears to be more reliable in view of later facts. Here Doom is
the son of the sister of old Issetibbeha, the ruling Man. When
Doom returned after his seven-year visit to New Orleans, he
found that Issetibbeha had died and been succeeded by his son,
Moketubbe. The day after Doom's return, Moketubbe's eight-
year-old son died suddenly and Moketubbe himself abdicated,
having been shown by Doom how quickly Doom's white powder
would dispatch a puppy. Doom became the Man in 1807. The
early settlers of the county are reported to have bought or
bartered land from Ikkemotubbe (Doom) between 1810 and
1835 – the years during which Doom would have been the Man
had he succeeded to the chieftainship in 1807.

During the 1830s the Indians were dispossessed and began to
move to Oklahoma. About twenty-five years earlier, the first
white men had arrived in Jefferson, then only a Chickasaw
trading post in the wilderness. The earliest settlers were
Alexander Holston, who accompanied Dr Samuel Habersham
and the latter's eight-year-old motherless son, and Louis
Grenier, a Huguenot 'younger son' who acquired a vast
plantation in the southeastern part of the county and became
the first cotton planter. Holston became the 'first publican,
establishing the tavern still known as the Holston House', and

Dr Habersham 'became the settlement itself . . . for a time, before it was named the settlement was known as Doctor Habersham's then Habersham's, then simply Habersham.' After Holston's death the county remembered his name in the tavern he had owned. When Grenier died, his mansion and his estate fell into ruin and even his name was forgotten; but his property gave the name to the hamlet of Frenchman's Bend, and his house was known as the Old Frenchman place long after Grenier himself had passed from public memory.

Another early settler was Lucius Quintus Carothers McCaslin, who was born in Carolina in 1772 and who arrived in the county in 1813. He brought with him a wife and three children – the twins, Theophilus (Uncle Buck) and Amodeus (Uncle Buddy), and a daughter. McCaslin acquired land from Ikkemotubbe in the northeastern part of the county, seventeen miles from what was to become Jefferson, and began to build a great house which was never completely finished. He had brought some slaves with him from Carolina, but made a special trip to New Orleans and came home with a female slave named Eunice who bore him a daughter, Tomey, in 1810. Some twenty years later Tomey bore her master – and father – a son, Terrel, known as Tomey's Turl. Again from Ikkemotubbe (in exchange for a horse) McCaslin acquired a quadroon slave and her son, the infant Sam Fathers, who was to grow to manhood and live to old age on the McCaslin plantation in the anomalous position of carpenter and hunter, not black and not slave and yet not white and not free. He lived to be the last descendant of Ikkemotubbe remaining in the county and was to become the mentor and guide of young Isaac McCaslin, old McCaslin's only white grandson to bear his name.

A few years later, in 1811, Jason Lycurgus Compson I came down the Natchez Trace toward the Chickasaw agency that was to become Jefferson, owning little besides a pair of pistols and the fine little racing mare he rode. Within a year he was half-owner of the store and trading post; within another year he had traded the mare to Ikkemotubbe, or Doom, for a 'square mile of what was to be the most valuable land in the future town of Jefferson'. He built his house and his slave quarters and his stables, and the property, which came to be known as Compson's Mile or Compson's Domain, housed his successors: Quentin MacLachan Compson II, his son, who was, even if for a short time, a governor of Mississippi; Quentin's son, Jason II, a brigadier general in the Civil War, who put the first mortgage on the property in 1866; and his son in turn, Jason III, a lawyer who sold part of the property in 1909 to pay for his son Quentin III's tuition at Harvard. Of Jason's four children – Quentin III, Candace, Jason IV, and Benjy – only Jason remained long enough to see the final dissolution of the property and house and even the name, which would die with him, that had been illustrious in the county for almost one hundred years.

After Jason I came Dr Peabody, old Dr Habersham's successor, a preacher named Whitfield, and a new post trader named Ratcliffe. There was also a man named Pettigrew, who, though his surname was later forgotten, contributed his first name at the christening of the new town:

> 'We're going to have a town,' Peabody said. 'We already got a church – that's Whitfield's cabin. And we're going to build a school too soon as we get around to it. But we're going to build the courthouse today. ... Then we'll have a town. We've already even named her.'
>
> Now Pettigrew stood up, very slowly. They looked at one another. After a moment Pettigrew said, 'So?'
>
> 'Ratcliffe says your name's Jefferson,' Peabody said.
>
> 'That's right,' Pettigrew said. 'Thomas Jefferson Pettigrew. I'm from old Ferginny.'
>
> [Peabody said] 'We decided to name her Jefferson.' Now Pettigrew didn't seem to breathe even. He just stood there, small, frail, less than boy-size, childless and bachelor, incorrigibly kinless and tieless.

Soon after Jefferson was named, in the early 1830s, a mysterious stranger named Thomas Sutpen arrived in town, causing some local stir because of his silence regarding his antecedents and the wagonload of twenty wild French-speaking Negroes and the dapper little French architect who accompanied him. Sutpen, the son of a West Virginia poor white, had conceived a 'grand design' of becoming a member of the ruling aristocracy, and, in pursuance of his dream, had first married the daughter of a Haitian sugar-plantation owner. When he discovered – too late – that his wife had Negro blood and would thus prevent him from ever taking his desired place in Southern society, he divorced her and left Haiti, taking with him only the slaves and his French architect. Sutpen arrived in Mississippi and bartered or bought from Ikkemotubbe a hundred square miles of fertile bottom land near the Tallahatchie. He spent two years clearing the land and building his plantation house, which was to be, for a time, the grandest in the county. When his house was finished and furnished, Sutpen bargained with Goodhue Coldfield, a Jefferson merchant, for the hand of Ellen, his oldest daughter. She became Sutpen's wife and the mother of two children, Henry and Judith, who, in Sutpen's dream, were to provide him with grandchildren to carry on his name and inhabit his house after his own demise. But Charles Bon, Sutpen's son by his first marriage, met and became an intimate friend of young Henry Sutpen; Henry brought Charles home, where, largely through the machinations of Ellen Sutpen, Charles became engaged to Judith. Henry later discovered that Charles was his half-brother and part Negro, and, horrified at the idea of miscegenation even more than incest, shot Charles at the gate of Sutpen's Hundred to prevent the marriage. Sutpen returned from the Civil War, where he had replaced Colonel Sartoris as head of his regiment, to find his daughter 'confirmed in spinsterhood' and his son a vanished fugitive. He tried to obtain a male heir to carry on his name by seducing the granddaughter of Wash Jones, his poor-white handyman, but the girl gave birth to a daughter; Jones killed Sutpen, the girl, her infant, and himself.

A few years after Sutpen arrived there was another newcomer, a man named John Sartoris, who came from Carolina with slaves and money. He bought land and built his house four miles north of Jefferson; in 1861 he would 'stand in the first Confederate uniform the town had ever seen, while in the Square below the Richmond mustering officer enrolled . . . the regiment which Sartoris as its colonel would take to Virginia'. Intertwined with the saga of the Sartorises, the family most representative of all that was heroic and romantic in the antebellum South, is the beginning of the history of the Snopeses, a numerous clan of mean and avaricious poor whites who swooped down on the county like buzzards in the early years of the twentieth century. Ab Snopes, the first of the line, made his appearance during the Civil War as a horse and mule thief operating on both Yankee and Confederate troops.

Although he began by aiding Colonel Sartoris's mother-in-law, Rosa Millard, in 'requisitioning' animals from both armies, he was at least partially responsible for her death at the hands of a band of lawless poor whites. There were other names linked with that of the Sartoris family through violence, such as the Burdens of New Hampshire, fiery abolitionists who had come to Jefferson during Reconstruction. Two Burdens, grandfather and grandson, were shot in the Square on Election Day by Colonel Sartoris, encouraged by Drusilla Hawk as they were on their way to their wedding. Later Sartoris entered a partnership with Ben Redmond in order to build a railroad that would bisect the county. The two men quarreled, the partnership was dissolved, and Redmond finally shot and killed Sartoris after the latter had run against him – and won – in the election to the state legislature. After Sartoris's death the honorary title of Colonel was bestowed on his son Bayard, who became president of the bank in Jefferson. Bayard's son John (whose history is not recorded) married and fathered twin sons named John and Bayard; John was killed in the First World War, and Bayard was responsible both for the death of his grandfather in an automobile accident and for his own death soon after, when, in Ohio, he tested an airplane that he knew to be unsafe.

Shortly after the end of the Civil War, a young man named Lucius Priest arrived in Mississippi from Carolina. A distant kinsman of old Lucius Quintus Carothers McCaslin, Priest sought out the Yoknapatawpha County branch of his family and found Sarah Edmonds, the great-granddaughter of old McCaslin. The two branches of the family were joined when he and Sarah married in 1869. Lucius came to be a solid and respected townsman; by the turn of the century he was the president of the Bank of Jefferson, the town's first bank, and was known as Boss Priest. His son Maury married Alison Lessup, the daughter of Boss Priest's old friend and schoolmate; Maury and Alison had three children, Lucius, Maury, Jr, and Alexander.

Besides the McCaslins, Compsons, Sutpens, and Sartorises, there were other families of somewhat less distinction and importance. The Beauchamps, brother and sister, intermarried with Yoknapatawpha County people even though they lived in a neighbouring county. Miss Sophonsiba Beauchamp married Uncle Buck McCaslin. The name Beauchamp itself was later borne by the Negro part of the McCaslin family, stemming from Tennie Beauchamp, the slave won from Hubert Beauchamp by Uncle Buddy in a poker game and married to old McCaslin's Negro son, Tomey's Turl. The Coldfields, though their name died with the spinster Miss Rosa Coldfield in 1910, were once respected and relatively prosperous in the early days in Jefferson. The Stevenses were a pioneer family whose line bore its finest fruit after the Civil War in the person of Gavin Stevens, county attorney, Phi Beta Kappa at Harvard and Ph.D. from Heidelberg. There were the Benbow's, whose family included a county judge, a lawyer (the judge's son Horace), and a girl, Narcissa, who married into the Sartoris family and bore a male heir just before her husband, the last male Sartoris, met his rash and untimely end. The De Spains boasted a major in the Civil War, a president of the bank in Jefferson, and Jefferson's most stately mansion.

In the pine hills of the district to the north, known as Beat Four, and in Frenchman's Bend, twenty miles southeast of Jefferson, there sprang up a very different breed of people from the pre-Civil War aristocrats – self-made or otherwise – of Jefferson and its environs. The inhabitants of Frenchman's Bend had come

> from the northeast, through the Tennessee mountains by stages marked by the bearing and raising of a generation of children. They came from the Atlantic seaboard and before that, from England and the Scottish and Welsh Marches. . . . They took up land and built one- and two-room cabins and never painted them, and married one another and produced children . . . and their descendants still planted cotton in the bottom land and corn along the edge of the hills and in the secret coves in the hills made whiskey of the corn and sold what they did not drink . . . there was not one Negro landowner in the entire section. Strange Negroes would absolutely refuse to pass through it after dark.

At about the turn of the twentieth century the old Frenchman place was owned by sixty-year-old Will (Uncle Billy) Varner, who, aside from being the biggest landowner, owned the store, cotton gin and grist mill, and blacksmith shop, and came close to running – if not actually owning – the town itself. The store was managed by Varner's thirty-year-old bachelor son, Jody, and it was to Jody that Ab Snopes applied to rent a farm for the season. This event marked the beginning of the influx of Snopeses into the county. Hearing that Ab Snopes had set fire to Major De Spain's barn some years previously and fearing a similar fate for Varner property, Jody installed Ab's son Flem as a clerk in Varner's store as a kind of peace offering – or perhaps a bribe. Soon Flem began importing and installing various cousins in the county: Eck Snopes, who became the blacksmith; I. O. Snopes, who was for a time the schoolteacher;. Ike Snopes, an idiot and Flem's ward; Mink Snopes, another tenant farmer; and others. Eck married the daughter of the family at whose house he boarded, promptly fathered a son, named Admiral Dewey, and produced another, older son from a previous marriage – Wallstreet Panic. The Snopeses multiplied, to the discomfiture of various members of the local citizenry – Jack Houston, Henry Armstid, Vernon Tull, and others.

In less than five years Flem had risen from a clerkship at Varner's store to become an owner of cattle and a barn, a party to various quick and profitable sales, and a petty usurer – turning his hand, in short, to any reasonably lawful money-getting enterprise. As a kind of climax to his career in Frenchman's Bend, he married Eula, the beautiful and much sought-after daughter of Varner. The marriage, though one of convenience (Eula was pregnant by another man and Flem was impotent), brought Flem the deed to the Old Frenchman Place and a considerable sum of money – both wedding presents, or perhaps bribes, of his new father-in-law – as well as social position as a relative of the most important man in town. Following his wedding and a lengthy Texas honeymoon, Flem moved his family – Eula and her daughter, Linda, who bore the name of Snopes legally if not otherwise – to Jefferson, where Flem became superintendent of the town power plant. Again, as he had done in Frenchman's Bend, Flem quickly moved up to bigger and better positions, and imported more Snopes cousins.

Shortly after the turn of the century – about the time that Flem Snopes arrived in Jefferson – it was beginning to be apparent that the old aristocracy was fighting a losing battle for survival. Their decline was partially due to the difficulty of maintaining plantations without slave labour and to the trying days of Reconstruction. More important, though, was the inability of the once-great planters to come to terms with the post-bellum world. They persisted in trying to live by the economic and moral standards they had known before the war, and they raised their children and grandchildren to believe in these standards, thus rendering them, too, unable to cope with the realities of the twentieth century. It was as if a kind of internal decay, begun in the old aristocracy after the war, was gradually destroying both its strength and its moral fibre. By 1920 not a single member of the greatest prewar families was left who was able to assume a position of leadership in the county.

Thomas Sutpen's family, perhaps the most outrageously unfortunate, had come to an end, as far as most of Jefferson knew, with Sutpen's death in 1869; yet three of Sutpen's descendants, and one of his relatives by marriage, survived forty years more. In 1909 Miss Coldfield, Sutpen's sister-in-law, discovered Sutpen's son Henry ill and hiding in the old plantation house, cared for by his Negro half-sister, Clytie. Miss Rosa summoned an ambulance in an attempt to take Henry to the Jefferson hospital, but Clytie, thinking that the authorities had come to take Henry to prison for the murder of Charles Bon over fifty years before, set fire to the house over her own and Henry's heads. All that was left were the smoking ashes of the once-great house and an idiot Negro named Jim Bond, the great-grandson of Sutpen, who disappeared and was never heard of again.

By 1910 the Compson fortunes had also declined severely. Of the four children of Jason III, Benjy was an idiot, Candace (Caddy) a promiscuous girl who was hastily married to provide a father for the child she carried, Quentin a suicide, and Jason IV a petty, rapacious man whose mind and temperament were more like those of the Snopeses than of the Compsons. Caddy brought her daughter Quentin (named for Caddy's dead brother) back to Jefferson to be raised by the family, and she herself disappeared. Quentin also disappeared, running off with a travelling carnival man at seventeen, and the name of Compson came to an end in Jason IV, a childless bachelor, who sold the property to Flem Snopes during the 1940s.

Although the McCaslin family, particularly as represented by Uncle Buck and Uncle Buddy, had laid no claim to aristocracy, it too – or at least the white branch of it – was beginning to die out. The only male McCaslin to bear the name was Isaac, who, at the end of the First World War, was a childless widower. The McCaslin property, however, was owned by the Edmondses, the descendants of old McCaslin's daughter. Isaac had refused to accept his share, and the property had gone to his cousin McCaslin (Cass) Edmonds, the great-grandson of old Carothers McCaslin, and was passed on to Edmonds' son and grandson in turn. The Edmondses leased it to tenant farmers and set apart a section for Lucas Beauchamp, the Negro grandson of the first McCaslin. The South, and in particular the Old South, still considered descent on the female side to be a lesser strength and importance than lineal descent on the male side – the side which, after all, bore the family name. Thus, although the descendants of McCaslin's Negro son Turl and his wife Tennie Beauchamp bore the family name of Beauchamp, they were in one sense more legitimate heirs of the first McCaslin than were the white descendants of McCaslin's daughter. Furthermore, because Turl's mother was also the daughter of McCaslin, Turl's descendants were two generations closer to McCaslin. Thus Lucas Beauchamp, who was born in 1874, was McCaslin's grandson, while Zack Edmonds, who was born in 1873, was McCaslin's great-great-grandson. The Negro side of the family, which outnumbered the white members three to one, was again joined with the white side in the illicit union of Roth Edmonds and the great-granddaughter of Turl in 1940. Since Roth did not marry the girl, the child remained nameless, and the name of Edmonds came to an end with Roth.

In 1920 only one male Sartoris remained alive: Benbow Sartoris, the infant son of Narcissa Benbow and the late John Sartoris III. Colonel Bayard Sartoris, who died in 1919, had been succeeded as bank president by Manfred de Spain, a descendant of Major de Spain. However, through the machinations of Flem Snopes, De Spain was later driven from town as the result of a scandal over Flem's wife, Eula, and Flem moved into the bank presidency and the De Spain mansion.

There were, however, a few descendants of Jefferson's first settlers who came into prominence in the twentieth century. Among them were V. K. Ratliff, a descendant of the original

Ratcliffe of Jefferson's early history, who became a sewing-
machine salesman in four counties and a more reliable purveyor
of information and local gossip than any newspaper. Gavin
Stevens returned from Heidelberg and began to assist his father,
Judge Lemuel Stevens, before setting up his own law office and
finally becoming county attorney. His second cousin, young
Gowan Stevens, was growing up and would soon boast his
University of Virginia education and his ability (more boast
than fact) to hold his liquor like a man. Gavin's sister,
Margaret, married Charles Mallison and bore a son, Chick,
who grew up to play his part in the unfolding saga of the
county.

The 1930s saw the influx of a number of strangers in
Jefferson, and the town became the scene of some violence and
at least one tragicomic episode, the burial of Addie Bundren.
The Bundrens were poor white farmers who lived just south of
the Yoknapatawpha River, but Addie Bundren had originally
come from Jefferson, and her people were buried there. She had
made her husband, Anse, promise to bury her with her kinsfolk
when she died, and, in accordance with his promise (and a few
ulterior desires of his own), Anse and the rest of the family –
Cash, Darl, Jewel, Dewey Dell, and Vardaman began the
trip with Addie's body, despite the July heat and the flood-
swollen river. After a nine-day journey the family and its
putrescent burden arrived in Jefferson, where Addie was finally
buried, and where Anse promptly acquired a new wife.

Also during the thirties Lena Grove arrived in Jefferson,
having walked from Alabama, far gone in pregnancy and in
search of Lucas Burch, the lover who had deserted her. She
could not find her truant lover, who, under the name of Joe
Brown, was sharing a cabin with another newcomer to the
town, Joe Christmas, on the property of Joanna Burden, the
spinster descendant of the Northern abolitionists killed by
Colonel John Sartoris. Joe and Lucas peddled illicit liquor,
among other things, and were regarded – as was Miss Burden –
with suspicion by the townsfolk. Joe, who appeared to be white
but maintained that he had Negro blood, murdered Miss
Burden after she attempted to convert him and threatened him
with a pistol. He promptly became the object of a manhunt by
the outraged townfolk, who forgot their suspicion of the
Northern woman and accepted her as a symbol of Southern

womanhood violated and murdered by a 'nigger'. Leading the manhunt was a young and belligerent deputy, Percy Grimm, who was descended from a Snopes girl, and who concerned, castrated, and finally killed Joe.

The thirties was a violent era for the county, as well as for Jefferson. During that time an amoral and vicious creature known as Popeye began to do business with Lee Goodwin, a moonshiner living in the old Frenchman Place. There Popeye murdered a simple-minded white man and raped Temple Drake, an irresponsible and provocative college girl from Jackson, who had been brought to Goodwin's place by her drunken escort, Gowan Stevens. In an attempt to pin the murder on Goodwin, Popeye took the unresisting Temple, the only witness, to a brothel in Memphis where he could keep an eye on her. Despite the efforts of Horace Benbow to clear Goodwin, he was tried, convicted, and lynched by the angry townspeople. Temple later married a somewhat reformed and matured Gowan Stevens, all the while maintaining the fiction that she was forcibly detained in the brothel, an innocent victim of a pervert and murderer.

The forties, somewhat quieter than the years between the two wars, saw greater triumphs of Snopesism and of the 'progress' associated with, if not actually related to, Snopes avarice: mechanisation and standardisation, the substitution of mechanical and commercial values for human ones. Jefferson was teeming with Snopeses; Flem Snopes, who had bought the Compson property and had it subdivided, moved into the De Spain mansion and became president of the Merchants and Farmers Bank. Ironically, it was another Snopes – Mink – who, feeling he had been wronged by his cousin forty years before, was responsible for Flem's ultimely end.

A different incident served to spotlight the barrier between Negro and white that had existed since the days of slavery and had grown worse since Reconstruction. Lucas Beauchamp, old Carothers McCaslin's Negro grandson, had long irritated the townsfolk by his independence and his refusal to accept the attitude of servility adopted by the Negroes. When he was accused of murdering one of the Gowries, a fierce hill clan of poor whites living in Beat Four, no one but a boy, Chick Mallison, and an old lady, Miss Eunice Habersham, even thought to question Lucas' guilt, let alone try to prove him innocent.

Thus, over a period of more than a hundred years, a pattern of life in Yoknapatawpha County emerges, a whole small society is seen in terms of struggle and aspiration and development. The vitality and even perhaps the grandeur of pre-Civil War days is contrasted with the impotence and sterility of the present, but it must be remembered that the wrongs committed by the old aristocrats have been, almost literally, visited upon those that came after them. Before the coming of the white man, the Indians had considered the land to be the private property of no one, to be enjoyed in common by all. The settlers brought with them two crucial concepts – that of private property and that of slavery. It is to the outgrowths of these two concepts that almost all the evils of their society can be traced. Antebellum life, built on slavery and property, contained within it the seeds of its own ruin. Unfortunately, the positive aspects of that life – courage, gallantry, and graciousness – were also destroyed, and a residue of evils remained and persisted into the present – artificial social distinctions, greed, and a regard for the appearance, but not the fact, of respectability.

Both the economy and the morality of the Old South were built upon the concepts of private property and slavery, the juncture of which resulted in the formation of a society and a ruling aristocracy. The saga of Yoknapatawpha County suggests that a society built upon a precept that ignores the common humanity of mankind and establishes a morality and an economy that place social and economic codes above human values is doomed to fail. Thus Sutpen, who rejected his part-Negro wife and son in order to conform to a social code that abhorred miscegenation, failed to fulfill his dream of becoming a founder of a great family. Thus Quentin Compson, who placed the abstract idea of honour above the reality of his sister as a human being, was driven to suicide. The end of slavery spelled the end of the plantation economy, but the economy that replaced it was represented by men like Jason Compson and Flem Snopes, whose values were mercenary rather than humanistic, whose morality consisted in adhering to the letter but not the spirit of the law, and to whom other men were tools to be manipulated for profit.

Notes

1. F. L. Gwynn and J. L. Blotner (eds), *Faulkner in the University* (New York: Vintage, 1955) p. 60.
2. Sean O'Faolain, *The Vanishing Hero* (London: Eyre & Spottiswoode, 1956) pp. 101–3.
3. J. B. Meriwether, review of Hoffman and Vickery in *Faulkner Studies* (1952–4) 8.
4. W. Faulkner, preface to *The Sound and the Fury*, 1929, reprinted in *Mississippi Quarterly* 26 (Summer 1973) 412.
5. Allen Tate, 'William Faulkner 1897–1962', *The Sewanee Review* (1963), reprinted in R. P. Warren (ed.), *Faulkner* (Englewood Cliffs, N. J.: Prentice-Hall, 1966) pp. 275–6.
6. Alfred Kazin, *On Native Grounds* (New York: Harcourt, Brace & Co., 1942) pp. 455–63.
7. Olga Vickery, *The Novels of William Faulkner* (1959; Baton Rouge: Louisiana State University Press, 1964) p. 310.
8. J. Pilkington, *The Heart of Yoknapatawpha* (Jackson: University of Mississippi Press, 1981) ix.
9. Leslie Fiedler, *Love and Death in the American Novel* (1967); (London: Paladin, 1970) p. 299.
10. Gail Mortimer, *Faulkner's Rhetoric of Loss* (Austin: University of Texas Press, 1983) p. 124.
11. E. J. Sundquist, *Faulkner: The House Divided* (Baltimore and London: Johns Hopkins University Press, 1983) p. 21.
12. J. Blotner (ed.), *Selected Letters of William Faulkner* (New York: Random House, 1977) p. 32.
13. *Faulkner in the University*, p. 211.
14. R. A. Jelliffe (ed.), *Faulkner at Nagano* (Tokyo: Kenkyusha, 1956) p. 167.
15. V. W. Brooks, *The Yoknapatawpha Country* (1963); (New Haven and London: Yale University Press, 1974) p. 4.
16. Janet Frame, *An Angel at my Table* (New York: Braziller, 1984) p. 158.
17. Flannery O'Connor, *The Habit of Being*, ed. Sally Fitzgerald (New York: Farrar, Straus & Giroux, 1979) p. 292.
18. J. T. Irwin, *Doubling and Incest/Repetition and Revenge* (Baltimore and London: Johns Hopkins University Press, 1975).
19. W. Slatoff, *Quest for Failure* (Ithaca, N.Y.: Cornell University Press, 1960).

20. Mortimer, *op. cit.*, p. 29.
21. Jean-Paul Sartre, *Literary and Philosophical Essays*, tr. Annette Michelson (1955); (London: Hutchinson, 1968) p. 87.
22. *Faulkner in the University*, p. 38.
23. A. I. Bezzerides, *William Faulkner: A Life on Paper* (Jackson: University of Mississippi Press, 1980) pp. 53, 92, 122.
24. D. Fowler and A. J. Abadie (eds), *Faulkner and the Southern Renaissance* (Jackson: University of Mississippi Press, 1982) p. 201.
25. Walter Taylor, *Faulkner's Search for a South* (Urbana: University of Illinois Press, 1983) p. 7.
26. Malcolm Cowley, *The Faulkner-Cowley File* (New York: Viking, 1966) p. 66.
27. J. Blotner, *Faulkner: A Biography* (one volume edition) (New York: Random House, 1984) p. 34.
28. Blotner, *Faulkner . . .* , p. 27.
29. Blotner, *Faulkner . . .* , p. 19.
30. Blotner, *Faulkner . . .* , p. 23.
31. J. Bassett (ed.), *William Faulkner: The Critical Heritage* (London: Routledge & Kegan Paul, 1975) p. 304.
32. W. Blair, *Native American Humour (1800–1900)* (New York: American Book Co., 1937) p. 80.
33. Linda Wagner (ed.), *William Faulkner: Four Decades of Criticism* (Detroit: Michigan State University Press, 1973) p. 82.
34. R. P. Warren, *The Legacy of the Civil War* (New York: Random House, 1961) p. 108.
35. Quoted by Warren and *op. cit.*, p. 63.
36. J. B. Meriwether and M. Millgate (eds), *Lion in the Garden* (New York: Random House, 1968) p. 180.
37. *Lion in the Garden*, p. 101.
38. Michael Millgate, *The Achievement of William Faulkner* (London: Constable, 1966) pp. 280–4.
39. *Lion in the Garden*, p. 255.
40. L. D. Rubin Jr, *The Writer in the South* (Athens: University of Georgia Press, 1972) p. 47.
41. Quoted in Millgate, *op. cit.*, p. 48.
42. Fiedler, *op. cit.*, p. 438.
43. Carvel Collins (ed.), *William Faulkner: The Early Prose and Poetry* (Boston, Mass. Little, Brown & Co, 1962) p. 116.
44. Clifton Fadiman, *The New Yorker* 31 October 1936, quoted in R. P. Warren (ed.), *Faulkner: A Collection of Critical Essays* (Englewood Cliffs, N.J.: Prentice-Hall, 1966) p. 289.
45. E. L. Volpe, *A Reader's Guide to William Faulkner* (London: Thames & Hudson, 1964) p. 38.
46. Wyndham Lewis, *Enemy Salvoes* (London: Vision Press, 1975) p. 148.
47. *Selected Letters . . .* , p. 142.
48. *Selected Letters . . .* , p. 348.
49. *Faulkner in the University*, p. 142.
50. *Lion in the Garden*, p. 141.
51. *Faulkner in the University*, p. 84.

52. *Lion in the Garden*, p. 133.

53. Millgate, *op. cit.*, p. 223.

54. D. M. Kartiganer, *The Fragile Thread: The Meaning of Form in Faulkner's Novels* (Amherst: University of Massachusetts Press, 1979) x.

55. Charlotte Renner, 'Talking and Writing in Faulkner's Snopes Trilogy', *Southern Literary Journal* XV, 1 (Fall, 1982) 63.

56. *Faulkner in the University*, p. 244.

57. Irving Howe, *William Faulkner: A Critical Study* (1952); (Chicago: Chicago University Press, 1975) p. 419.

58. Alfred Kazin, *op. cit.*, pp. 457–9.

59. Sartre, *op. cit.*, p. 73.

60. Kartiganer, *op. cit.*, XV.

61. *Four Decades of Criticism* . . . , p. 136.

62. L. D. Rubin Jr and R. D. Jacobs (eds), *Southern Renascence* (1953); (Baltimore and London: Johns Hopkins University Press, 1966) p. 15.

63. J. T. Matthews, *The Play of Faulkner's Language* (Ithaca and London: Cornell University Press, 1982) p. 9.

64. Hugh Kenner, *A Homemade World* (London: Marion Boyars, 1977) p. 197.

65. Hugh Kenner, 'Faulkner and the Avant Garde' in E. Harrington and A. J. Abadie (eds), *Faulkner, Modernism and Film* (Jackson: University of Mississippi Press, 1979) p. 195.

66. J. E, Bunselmeyer, 'Faulkner's Narrative Styles', *American Literature* 53 (1981–2) 424–42.

67. Wright Morris, *The Territory Ahead* (New York: Harcourt, Brace & Co, 1957) p. 179.

68. *Lion in the Garden*, p. 248.

69. Kazin, *op. cit.*, p. 462.

70. Carvel Collins (ed.), *Early Prose and Poetry* (Boston: Little, Brown & Co., 1962) p. 89.

71. *William Faulkner: The Critical Heritage*, p. 219.

72. John Pikoulis, *The Art of William Faulkner* (London: Macmillan, 1982) p. 47.

73. Lewis Simpson, 'Faulkner and the Legend of the Artist', in G. H. Wolfe (ed.), *Faulkner: Fifty Years After The Marble Faun* (Alabama: University of Alabama Press, 1976).

74. *Mississippi Quarterly* XXXV (Summer 1982) 307.

75. Judith Sensibar, *The Origins of Faulkner's Art* (Austin: University of Texas, 1984) ix.

76. Kenner, *op. cit.*, p. 205.

77. *Early Prose and Poetry*, p. 74.

78. Kenner, *op. cit.*, p. 209.

79. *Early Prose and Poetry*, p. 90.

80. *Mississippi Quarterly* XXVI, 3 (1973) 403.

81. *Early Prose and Poetry*, p. 89.

82. M. Kreiswirth, *William Faulkner: The Making of a Novelist* (Athens: University of Georgia Press, 1984) p. 39.

83. Volpe, *op. cit.*, p. 52.

84. Pikoulis, *op. cit.*, p. 15.

85. A. Bleikasten, *Most Splendid Failure* (Bloomington: Indiana University Press, 1976) p. 84.

86. Millgate, *op. cit.*, p. 72.

87. *Faulkner in the University*, p. 285.

88. Albert Guerard, *The Triumph of the Novel* (New York: Oxford University Press, 1976) p. 220.

89. Matthews, *op. cit.*, p. 50.

90. *Faulkner in the University*, p. 1.

91. Malcolm Cowley (ed.), *The Portable Faulkner* (1946); (New York: Viking, 1963) p. 753.

92. 'An Introduction to *The Sound and the Fury*', *Mississippi Quarterly* XXVI (1973) 415.

93. *Ibid.*, pp. 413–14.

94. Sundquist, *op. cit.*, p. 14.

95. Millgate, *op. cit.*, p. 94.

96. Bleikasten, *op. cit.*, p. 84.

97. *The Portable Faulkner*, p. 743.

98. Cleanth Brooks, 'Man, Time and Eternity', in M. H. Cowan (ed.), *Twentieth Century Interpretations of The Sound and the Fury* (Engelwood Cliffs, N.J.: Prentice-Hall, 1968) p. 67.

99. 'An Introduction . . .', p. 415.

100. Evelyn Scott, in *Twentieth Century Interpretations . . .* , p. 29.

101. *Twentieth Century Interpretations . . .* , p. 20.

102. Joseph Gold, 'Sin, Salvation and Bananas: *As I Lay Dying*', *Mosaic* 7 (1973–4) 60.

103. Calvin Bedient, 'Pride and Nakedness: *As I Lay Dying*', *Modern Language Quarterly* 29 (1968) 62.

104. *Selected Letters . . .* , p. 228.

105. Matthews, *op. cit.*, p. 42.

106. Olga Vickery, 'The Dimensions of Consciousness: *As I Lay Dying*', in F. J. Hoffman and O. W. Vickery (eds), *William Faulkner: Three Decades of Criticism* (New York: Harcourt, Brace and World, 1963) p. 233.

107. Gold, 'Sin, Salvation and Bananas . . .', 62.

108. J. Kawin, *The Mind of the Novel* (Princeton, N.J.: Princeton University Press, 1982) p. 261.

109. Bedient, 'Pride and Nakedness . . .', 75.

110. Faulkner's introduction to the Modern Library Edition, quoted in Millgate, p. 113.

111. Alan Spiegel, *Fiction and the Camera Eye* (Charlottesville: University Press of Virginia, 1976) p. 154.

112. André Malraux, *Yale French Studies* 10 (1953) 92.

113. Fiedler, *op. cit.*, p. 301.

114 J. W. Reed Jr, *Faulkner's Narrative* (New Haven: Yale University Press, 1973) p. 73.

115. Clifton Fadiman, *Party of One* (New York: World, 1955) p. 106.

116. George Toles, 'The Space Between: A Study of Faulkner's *Sanctuary*', in J. D. Canfield (ed.), *Twentieth Century Interpretations of Sanctuary* (Engelwood Cliffs, N.J.: Prentice-Hall, 1982) p. 124.

117. *Ibid.*, p. 126.

118. Sundquist, *op. cit.*, p. 48.
119. *Ibid.*, p. 6.
120. Quoted on the dustjacket of the 1953 Chatto & Windus edition.
121. Dorothy Tuck, *Crowell's Handbook of Faulkner* (New York: Thomas Crowell Co., 1964) p. 119.
122. Ralph Ellison, *Shadow and Act* (London: Secker & Warburg, 1967) p. 147.
123. *Ibid.*, p. 43.
124. Alfred Kazin, 'The Stillness of *Light in August*', in Hoffman and Vickery, pp. 252–3.
125. Blotner, *Faulkner . . .*, p. 763.
126. *Faulkner in the University*, p. 36.
127. Guerard, *op. cit.*, p. 225.
128. *Ibid.*, p. 302.
129. Millgate, *op. cit.*, p. 56.
130. Arthur Kinney, *Faulkner's Narrative Poetics* (Amherst: University of Massachusetts Press, 1978) p. 195.
131 H. B. Henderson, *Versions of the Past* (New York: Oxford University Press, 1974) p. 265.
132. Carolyn Porter, 'Faulkner and his Reader' in G. Carey (ed.), *Faulkner: The Unappeased Imagination* (Troy, N. Y.: Whitston, 1980) p. 255.
133. Conrad Aiken, 'William Faulkner: The Novel as Form', in Hoffman and Vickery, pp. 140–1.
134. Ilse Lind, 'The Design and Meaning of *Absalom, Absalom!*' in Hoffman and Vickery, p. 282.
135. *William Faulkner: The Critical Heritage*, p. 348.
136. *The Evening Standard*, 4 February 1958, 10.
137. Reed, *op. cit.*, p. 288.
138. *Ibid.*, p. 171.
139. Millgate, *op. cit.*, p. 171.
140. *Ibid.*, p. 179.
141. Pikoulis, *op. cit.*, p. 161.
142. Warren Beck, *Man in Motion: Faulkner's Trilogy* (Madison: University of Wisconsin Press, 1963) p. 31.
143. Millgate, *op. cit.*, p. 237.
144. Joanne Creighton, *Faulkner's Craft of Revision* (Detroit: Wayne State University Press, 1977) p. 87.
145. R. W. B. Lewis, 'The Hero in the New World: *The Bear*', in F. L. Utley, L. Z. Bloom, A. F. Kinney (eds), *Bear, Man and God* (New York: Random House, 1964) p. 309.
146. David Minter, *William Faulkner: His Life and Work* (Baltimore and London: Johns Hopkins University Press, 1980) pp. 187–8.
147. Matthews, *op. cit.*, p. 269.
148. Howe, *op. cit.*, p. 33.
149. Typescript quoted by P. Sanway in Carey, p. 84.
150. Sundquist, *op. cit.*, p. 149.
151. Olga Vickery, *op. cit.*, p. 249.
152. L. D. Rubin Jr, *Writers of the Modern South* (Seattle: University of Washington Press, 1966) p. 50.

153. Guerard, *op. cit.*, p. 229.
154. Reed, *op. cit.*, p. 211.
155. William Faulkner, 'A Note on *A Fable*', ed. J. B. Meriwether, *Mississippi Quarterly* XXVI (Summer 1973) 416–17.
156. Eudora Welty, 'In Yoknapatawpha', *Hudson Review* 1, 4 (Winter 1949) 597.
157. Creighton, *op. cit.*, p. 13.
158. Kenner, *op. cit.*, p. 209.
159. Millgate, *op. cit.*, p. 259.
160. Judith Fetterley, *The Resisting Reader* (Bloomington: Indiana University Press, 1978) p. 38.
161. Tuck, *op. cit.*, p. 112.

Select Bibliography

FAULKNER'S WORKS

(Page references in the text are to the following editions, all published in London by Chatto and Windus [the year of publication indicated by square brackets] unless otherwise stated.)

New Orleans Sketches, ed. Carvel Collins (New York: Grove Press, 1961)
Early Prose and Poetry, ed. Carvel Collins (Boston, Mass.: Little, Brown & Co, 1962)
The Marble Faun (1924) and *A Green Bough* (1933) (New York: Random House, 1960)
Vision in Spring (Austin: University of Texas, 1984)
Mayday, ed. Carvel Collins (South Bend, Ind.: University of Notre Dame Press, 1978)
The Marionettes (Charlottesville: University of Virginia Press, 1977)
Soldiers' Pay (1926) [1957]
Mosquitoes (1927) [1964]
Flags in the Dust (1929) (New York: Vintage, 1983)
Sartoris (1929) [1954]
The Sound and the Fury (1929) [1959]
As I Lay Dying (1930) [1958]
Sanctuary (1931) [1966]
These Thirteen (short stories) (1931) [1974]
Light in August (1932) [1960]
Doctor Martino and Other Stories (1934) [1965]
Pylon (1935) [1955]
Absalom, Absalom! (1936) [1960]
The Unvanquished (1938) [1960]
The Wild Palms (1939) [1954]
The Hamlet (1940) [1958]
Go Down, Moses (1942) [1960]
The Portable Faulkner, ed. Malcom Cowley (New York: Viking, 1946)
Intruder in the Dust (1948) [1957]
Knight's Gambit (short stories) (1949) [1951]
Collected Stories (New York: Random House, 1950)

178

Requiem for a Nun (1951) [1953]
A Fable (1954) [1969]
The Faulkner Reader (New York: Random House, 1954)
Big Woods (New York: Random House, 1955)
The Town (1957) [1967]
The Mansion (1959) [1965]
The Reivers (1962) [1962]
The Wishing Tree (New York: Random House, 1964)
Uncle Willy and Other Stories [1967]
Uncollected Stories of William Faulkner (1979) [1980]

William Faulkner's Manuscripts a 44-volume series of all Faulkner's typescripts and manuscripts, is at present being published by Garland Press, New York.

BIOGRAPHICAL, INTERVIEWS ETC.

Blotner, J., *Faulkner: A Biography* (2 vols) (New York: Random House, 1974)
—, (ed.), *William Faulkner: Selected Letters of William Faulkner* (New York: Random House, 1977)
Fant, J. L. and Ashley, R. (eds), *Faulkner at West Point* (New York: Random House, 1964)
Gwynn, F. L. and Blotner, J. L. (eds), *Faulkner in the University* (Charlottesville: University of Virginia Press, 1959)
Jelliffe, R. A. (ed.), *Faulkner at Nagano* (Tokyo: Kenkyusha, 1956)
Meriwether, J. B. (ed.), *William Faulkner: Essays, Speeches and Public Letters* (New York: Random House, 1965)
Meriwether, J. B. and Millgate, M. (eds), *Lion in the Garden: Interviews with William Faulkner 1926–62* (New York: Random House, 1968)
Minter, D., *William Faulkner: His Life and Work* (Baltimore and London: Johns Hopkins University Press, 1980)

SELECTED CRITICISM

GENERAL STUDIES

Adams, R. P., *Faulkner: Myth and Motion* (Princeton, N.J.: Princeton University Press, 1968)
Brooks, Cleanth, *William Faulkner: The Yoknapatawpha Country* (New Haven: Yate University Press, 1963)
—, *William Faulkner: Towards Yoknapatawpha and Beyond* (New Haven: Yale University Press, 1978)
Hoffman, W. J., *William Faulkner* (Boston, Mass.: Twayne, 1961)
Howe, Irving, *William Faulkner: A Critical Study* (New York: Random House, 1952) 2nd ed. 1962
Irwin, J. T., *Doubling and Incest/Repetition and Revenge* (Baltimore and London: Johns Hopkins University Press, 1975)

Kartiganer, D. M., *The Fragile Thread: The Meaning of Form in Faulkner's Novels* (Amherst: University of Massachusetts Press, 1979)
Kawin, B. F., *Faulkner and Film* (New York: Ungar, 1977)
Kinney, A., *Faulkner's Narrative Poetics: Style as Vision* (Amherst: University of Massachusetts Press, 1978)
Matthews, J. T., *The Play of Faulkner's Language* (Ithaca, N.Y.: Cornell University Press, 1982)
Millgate, M., *The Achievement of William Faulkner* (London: Constable, 1966)
O'Connor, W. V., *The Tangled Fire of William Faulkner* (1954) (New York: Gordian, 1968)
Pikoulis, J., *The Art of William Faulkner* (London: Macmillan, 1982)
Pilkington, J., *The Heart of Yoknapatawpha* (Jackson: University of Mississippi Press, 1981)
Reed, J. W., *Faulkner's Narrative* (New Haven: Yale University Press, 1973)
Slatoff, W. J., *Quest for Failure* (Ithaca, N.Y.: Cornell University Press, 1960)
Snead, J. A., *Figures of Division* (London & New York: Methuen, 1986)
Sundquist, E. J., *Faulkner: The House Divided* (Baltimore and London: Johns Hopkins University Press, 1983)
Taylor, W., *Faulkner's Search for a South* (Urbana: University of Illinois Press, 1983)
Vickery, O., *The Novels of William Faulkner* (Baton Rouge: Louisiana State University Press, 1959)

CRITICISM OF PARTICULAR NOVELS

Beck, W., *Man in Motion* (The Snopes Trilogy) (Madison: University of Wisconsin Press, 1961)
Bleikasten, A., *Most Splendid Failure: Faulkner's The Sound and the Fury* (Bloomington: University of Indiana Press, 1976)
—, (ed.), *William Faulkner's The Sound and the Fury* (New York: Garland, 1982)
— *Faulkner's As I Lay Dying* trs. R. Little (Bloomington: Indiana University Press, 1973)
Canfield, J. D., (ed.), *Twentieth Century Interpretations of Sanctuary* (Engelwood Cliffs, N.J.: Prentice-Hall, 1982)
Cowan, M. H., (ed.), *Twentieth Century Interpretations of The Sound and the Fury* (Engelwood Cliffs, N.J.: Prentice-Hall, 1968)
Cox, Dianne, *William Faulkner's As I Lay Dying* (New York: Garland, 1985)
Goldman, A. (ed.), *Twentieth Century Interpretations of Absalom, Absalom!* (Engelwood Cliffs, N.J.: Prentice-Hall, 1971)
Pitavy, F., *Faulkner's Light in August* trs. G. Cook (Bloomington: Indiana University Press, 1973)
Minter, D., (ed.), *Twentieth Century Interpretations of Light in August* (Engelwood Cliffs, N.J.: Prentice-Hall, 1969)
Utley, F. L., Bloom, L. Z. and Kinney, A. F., *Bear, Man and God* (Go Down, Moses) (New York: Random House, 1964)

COLLECTIONS OF CRITICAL ARTICLES

Bassett, J. (ed.), *William Faulkner: The Critical Heritage* (London: Routledge & Kegan Paul, 1975)

Carey, G. O. (ed.), *Faulkner: The Unappeased Imagination* (Troy, N.Y.: Whitston, 1980)

Harrington, E. and Abadie, A. J. (eds), *Faulkner and Yoknapatawpha* (Jackson: University of Mississippi, 1976 and 1978)

Hoffman, F. J. and Vickery, O. W. (eds), *William Faulkner: Three Decades of Criticism* (1960) (New York: Harcourt, Brace & World, 1963)

Wagner, L. W. (ed.), *William Faulkner: Four Decades of Criticism* (East Lansing: Michigan State University Press, 1973)

Warren, R. P. (ed.), *Faulkner: A Collection of Critical Essays* (Engelwood Cliffs, N. J.: Prentice-Hall, 1966)

REFERENCE TOOLS

Bassett, J., *William Faulkner: An Annotated Checklist of Criticism* (New York: David Lewis, 1972)

—, *William Faulkner: An Annotated Checklist of Recent Criticism* (Kent: Kent State University Press, 1983)

Kirk, R. L. and Klotz, M., *Faulkner's People: A Complete Guide and Index to Characters in the Fiction of William Faulkner* (Berkeley: University of California, 1963)

Tuck, Dorothy, *Crowell's Handbook of Faulkner* (New York: Thomas Y. Crowell, 1964)

Volpe, E. L., *A Reader's Guide to William Faulkner* (London: Thames & Hudson, 1964)

Index

REVERSE YOUR VERDICT

REVERSE YOUR VERDICT

A COLLECTION OF PRIVATE PROSECUTIONS

VINCENT BROME

ILLUSTRATED

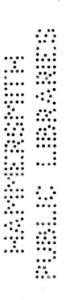

HAMISH HAMILTON

LONDON

Printed in Great Britain
by Ebenezer Baylis and Son Limited
The Trinity Press, Worcester, and London

TO
MRS. AUDREY TESTER
For all her many forms of help

Contents

Illustrations

PREFACE

IN THE COURSE of British legal history there have occurred a number of spectacular—what I will call private—prosecutions carried through by ordinary individuals against the State or the police. Even when the highest courts in the land have issued a verdict on cases as extreme as murder it has sometimes been reversed through the public spirit, zeal and courage of an ordinary private citizen challenging the whole machinery of the law.

It is not generally realized that until 1968 any person could take proceedings—by way of an indictment—for any crime, subject to the proviso that the Crown had the right to intervene where it pleased. Like Habeas Corpus, it was one of the last safeguards against a miscarriage of justice and when invoked has indeed put right such injustices on many occasions. The safeguard was based on a profound principle of English law which until then discriminated between a *conviction* in the courts and *actual guilt*. In fact, in most of the cases which follow a private agitation or prosecution has converted a court conviction into a public admission of innocence.

Almost unnoticed by the newspapers or public at large, one aspect of this absolutely vital safeguard has been struck from our hands by the new Civil Evidence Act of 1968 which makes a number of alterations to the law of evidence and now provides that convictions of certain categories of crime will be admissible as evidence of the commission of those crimes. Contrary to the previous rule in *Hollington v Hewthorn* 1943 A.E.R. 35, it will mean that private prosecutions of the type which Alfred Hinds brought a few years ago will no longer be possible, and at least one of the private prosecutions for libel described in this book would have run into serious difficulties.

To put the case more exactly—the Civil Evidence Act of

1968 had a number of objectives, one of which was to make it possible for convictions in criminal courts to be used as evidence in civil proceedings. Another objective was that in an action for libel, or slander, in which the question whether a person did or did not commit a criminal offence *was* relevant to an issue arising in that action, proof that at the time when this issue fell to be determined that person stood convicted of the offence should be conclusive evidence that he committed that offence.

Why has this happened today? Why have the law officers of the Crown removed this safeguard? Clearly there are cases where the person involved may *in fact* have committed the crime and the reversal of the verdict by a private prosecution creates fresh injustice, but these are very rare. One case also occurs in this book where a private prosecution made life very difficult for an innocent man. It remains true that in most cases 'private prosecutions' have freed innocent men from the burden of guilt and justified the whole principle.

Even in such an extreme case as murder, Henry Negretti succeeded in reversing a State verdict and indicting the real murderer. Two cases are—surprisingly—private prosecutions for murder, another concerns a spectacular gauntlet challenge literally to fight out the issue physically in court, a third the rehabilitation of a boy dismissed by the Royal Navy. A number of private citizens agitated for years on behalf of Adolf Beck, forced a public inquiry into his case and won him a free pardon, and Miss Cass was cleared of the stigma: common prostitute. There remains the prolonged and agonizing story of Oscar Slater.

Author's Note

After prolonged discussion it was decided that the refinement of footnotes was unnecessary to this book.

CHAPTER I

ABRAHAM THORNTON
[1817]

WHEN ABRAHAM THORNTON was charged, one hot August day in 1817, with murdering Mary Ashford, a process began which ended in perhaps *the* most spectacular private prosecution in British legal history.

'By six o'clock in the morning great numbers of persons had assembled before the gates of the County Hall, Warwick, using every endeavour, interest and entreaty to gain admission, and by eight o'clock the time fixed upon for the trial to begin the press at the doors was inconceivably great and it was with the utmost difficulty that way could be made by the javelin men for the entrance of the witnesses and other persons who were subpoenaed.'

A whole hour of struggling confusion went by while the police tried to disentangle witnesses from the crowd and the doors of the court were not thrown open until nine o'clock. When Mr. Justice Holroyd entered every bench and corner was crowded and the ushers had to call for order 'with great vigour'.

Mr. Hilditch, Clerk of the Arraigns, proceeded to call over the names from the jury and when Thornton raised no objection the Officer of the Court read the Indictments. The first charged the prisoner with having 'on the 27th of May last in the Royal Town, Manor and Lordship of Sutton Coldfield in the County of Warwick, not having the fear of God before his eyes but being moved by the instigation of the Devil wilfully murdered Mary Ashford, by throwing her into a pit of water'. The ritual question and answer followed.

'Abraham Thornton, are you guilty of this murder or not guilty?'

'Not guilty.'

'God send you deliverance.'

The Officer then read over the second Count which charged the prisoner with having 'on the morning aforesaid committed a Rape upon the body of the said Mary Ashford'.

Despite his humble origins and appearance—he looked like a lower-class boxer—Thornton's stance in the witness box had all the confidence of an innocent man enlivened by a touch of scornful arrogance. According to the local newspapers of the day he was a stout, fresh-complexioned young man about five feet seven inches high and twenty-six years of age. 'He appeared to evince an unusual degree of firmness' and now he answered 'not guilty' to the second count in ringing tones.

Mr. Nathaniel Gooding Clarke, K.C. opened the case for the prosecution.

'Gentlemen of the jury, you are already acquainted with the nature of the crime with which the prisoner at the bar stands accused, but it is my duty to state you in a more minute and particular manner the precise details of what took place. The deceased was a young woman of engaging manners, handsome in person and of unblemished character. Gentlemen, it will be proved to you that Mary Ashford on the evening of May 26— the night preceding the murder—went in the company with her friend Hannah Cox to a dance at the public house in the neighbourhood of Castle Bromwich called The Three Tuns. The prisoner—when the deceased entered the house—enquired her name and who she was. On being told by one of the company that it was "old Ashford's daughter", he replied: "I have been connected with her sister and I will with her or I'll die by it."

'About twelve o'clock the deceased and the prisoner left the house together—the deceased it appeared, for the purpose of returning home. Hannah Cox, the young woman who accompanied the deceased to The Three Tuns, saw them together and went part of the way with them.

'Now, gentlemen, it will be shown that the deceased left this house between four and five on the morning of the 27th and between that time and the time when the body was found in the pit—which was about half-past six in the morning—the crime must have been perpetrated . . .'

The first witness for the prosecution was Hannah Cox, and Mr. Serjeant Copley examined her.

'Did Mary Ashford come to your master's house, on Monday, the 26th of May last?'

'Yes, she came there about ten o'clock in the morning.'

'Had she anything with her?'

'She had a bundle with her.'

'Did she tell you where she was going?'

'She said she was going to Birmingham market.'

'Did you observe how the deceased was dressed?'

'Yes, she had on a pink cotton frock or gown, a straw bonnet with straw-coloured ribbons, a scarlet spencer, half-boots, and black stockings.'

'You said the deceased had a bundle with her, do you know what it contained?'

'A clean frock, a white spencer, and a pair of white stockings.'

'You saw the things she had in her bundle, did you?'

'Yes, I went with her to Mrs. Butler's, to leave her bundle.'

Hannah Cox described how they arranged for Mary Ashford to return from Mrs. Butler's as soon as possible, to accompany her to the dance at Tyburn House. They set out for the dance between seven and eight o'clock and when they arrived she saw the prisoner Abraham Thornton who was already in the dancing room. The two girls evidently enjoyed a gay evening and continued dancing until somewhere between eleven and twelve o'clock. Hannah Cox then tried to persuade Mary Ashford to go home with her but Mary said she would stay a short while longer and then join her 'on the bridge'.

'On the bridge—how far is that from the house?'

'About 30 yards.'

'Did anyone come to you while you were on the bridge?'

'Yes, Benjamin Carter.'

'Did anyone else come out of the house and join you?'

'Yes, I sent Benjamin Carter back for Mary Ashford, and then they soon came out.'

'How long did you wait on the bridge from the time you first went there, till the prisoner and the deceased came to you?'

'About ten minutes or a quarter of an hour.'

All three then set out to walk home, with Thornton and Mary Ashford leading and Benjamin Carter and Hannah Cox following at a distance. Benjamin Carter presently decided to return to the dance and Hannah joined Thornton and Mary Ashford. She walked with them until they reached a house called The Old Cuckoo a short distance from the road which led off to Erdington. Hannah then left the couple to return to her mother's house. Much later that morning Mary Ashford came knocking on the door and Hannah opened it.

'Do you know what time it was—did you look at the clock?'

'Yes, it was twenty minutes before five.'

'Do you know whether the clock was right—that is, how was your mother's clock by the other clocks in the neighbourhood?'

'The clock was too fast.'

'Did you perceive any agitation or confusion in the person of the deceased?'

'No.'

'Neither her person nor her dress were disordered?'

'Not that I saw.'

'The deceased appeared very calm and in very good spirits?'

'Yes.'

'How long was the deceased in the house altogether?'

'She might be in the house a quarter of an hour, but I cannot exactly say.'

'The deceased then went away, and you saw no more of her?'

'Yes.'

'Did you observe that the deceased's frock was stained?'

'No, but I did not take much notice of it.'

Mr. Reader, representing Thornton, now intervened to cross-examine the witness.

'The deceased, you say, appeared in perfect health, when she came to call you up?'

'Yes.'

'Did you say anything to the deceased, about the prisoner?'

'I asked her how long Mr. Thornton stopped, and she said a good bit.'

'Did you say anything else to her about the prisoner?'

'I asked her what had become of him, and she said he was gone home.'

'Where did the deceased say she was going, when she left you in the morning?'

'She said she was going to her grandfather's.'

The defence had begun to establish, against the line of prosecution, that Mary Ashford suffered no harm although she was alone with Thornton for 'a good bit' and that he had left her —'to go home'. Serjeant Copley resumed the examination of Hannah Cox and she reaffirmed that her mother's clock was fast on the morning Mary Ashford came to the house. Asked to repeat the exact time she said: 'I can't tell exactly but I think it wanted about twenty minutes to five.' Pressed about the condition of Mary Ashford's frock—whether stained or dirty—she would not commit herself and simply said: 'I did not observe anything particular about it.'

Both the question of the precise time and the condition of the victim's clothing were to become very important in what followed. Benjamin Carter, the farmer who went back to the Inn on behalf of Hannah Cox to collect Mary Ashford, was the next prosecution witness examined by Mr. Perkins, also for the Crown. He confirmed Hannah Cox's account of what took place after the dance but with one difference. Apparently he overtook the trio a second time, and walked with them, laughing and joking, until they reached the turn in the road towards Erdington. Hannah Cox then took one road home and he another.

Nathaniel Clarke now began the examination of another witness, John Umpage:

'Do you remember being at Mr. Reynold's house, at Penn's, on Tuesday morning, the 27th of May last?'

'Yes.'

'While you were there, did you hear anybody talking in the road?'

'Yes, I heard somebody talking as I sat in the house.'

'What time was it when you first heard the talking?'

'About two o'clock in the morning—it was after two o'clock. I heard the talking until a few minutes before I started home.'

'What time did you go home?'

'I started home about a quarter before three.'

'When you got out of doors to go home, did you then see anybody?'

'When I came up the lane I saw a man and a woman at the stile.'

'Where did the lane lead to?'

'Into Bell Lane.'

'And where does Bell Lane lead to that way?'

'Towards Erdington.'

'When you got up to the stile, did you discover who the persons were?'

'Yes, I knew the man, it was the prisoner.'

Mr. Reynolds, for Thornton, now rose to cross-examine:

'How long had you seen them before you came up to the stile?'

'I came within about a hundred yards of them before I saw them; the girl was standing and he was leaning against the stile.'

'She evidently appeared to you as though she would not be known, and she held her head down?'

'Yes.'

The cross-examination clearly established that at this point Mary Ashford was completely unharmed and in no fear of Thornton.

Copley now called George Jackson, a labourer, into the witness box:

'At what time did you come out of Birmingham on Tuesday morning, the 27th of May?'

'It was five o'clock when I was at the top of Moor Street, in Birmingham.'

'Later on—when you came near to the pit, did you observe anything?'

'I observed a bonnet, a pair of shoes, and a bundle. They were close by the top of the slope, that leads down into the pit.'

'What did you do then?'

'I looked at them: I saw one of the shoes all *bloody*: then I went towards Penn's Mills to fetch a person to come and look at them; I brought a man from the first house, he was coming out of his own door place, and we went to the pit; his name is Lavell.'

'What did you do then?'

'I told him to stand by these things, while I fetched some more hands from Penn's Mills, as nobody should meddle with them.'

'Going from the pit, had you observed anything?'

'Going down from the pit along the foot-path, I saw some blood about thirty yards from the pit, it might be about a couple of yards round, in a triangle.'

'Do you mean in length?'

'Yes; zig zag, about two yards.'

'Did you perceive any other blood?'

'I went a little farther and saw a lake of blood by the side of a bush.'

'Did you observe anything more?'

'I saw some more to the left, on some grass; then I went forwards to the works at Penn's Mills, to let them know what had happened.'

Jackson was now cross-examined by Mr. Reynolds:

'What is the distance from Birmingham to this pit?'

'It might be about five miles or five miles and a half, as near as I can guess.'

'A public road the whole way?'

'A public road.'

'You left Birmingham at what time?'

'About five.'

'It was, I suppose, between six and seven when you got to the pit?'

'About half-past six.'

'How near to the public road is the pit?'

'Close to the foot-path; the foot-path is close to the carriage road, separated by a hedge.'

'The pit I believe is close to a stile?'

'Yes . . .'

'How far is this stile from the pit?'

'It might be two or three yards to the place where the bundle was.'

'The bundle and things, if I understand you, were on the edge of the pit?'

'Yes.'

'Is not the pit where you saw the bundle very steep?'

'Very steep, in a middling way.'

'You said at first very steep—now you say in a middling way—is it not rather steep than otherwise?'

'It is.'

'How far are Penn's Mills off?'

'About half a mile.'

'Mr. Webster has there a considerable manufactory?'

'Yes.'

'Were the men all collected at work, when you arrived there?'

'I did not see any of them at work, but I saw several about.'

'In point of fact, between four and five in the morning—is not that a very common hour, for labourers in the fields to be up?'

'Yes.'

'How far—exactly—were the bundle and shoes from the top of the slope?'

'About a foot.'

The defence had now introduced by implication two new possibilities into the events presented by the prosecution. First, since a mere twelve inches separated the bundle from the top of the slope to the pit—that slope being very steep and a stile having to be negotiated only three or four yards from the pit—Mary Ashford might have stumbled into the pit and drowned accidentally as she fled in terror from her rapist. Second, many other possible suspects were certainly abroad between four and five in the morning, among them labourers from Penn's Mills. If, as Nathaniel Clarke alleged in his opening address, the crime had been committed sometime between four when she left Mrs. Butler's and six-thirty when her body was found, any one of Mr. Webster's employees at Penn's Mills who was abroad at that time would come under suspicion.

There followed a long examination of William Lavell by Clarke. Lavell was a workman at Penn's Mills and the evidence he gave became damning for Thornton for two reasons.

'Did you go along the foot-path near the pit to see if you could discover any footsteps?'

'Yes. The first steps were a man's, going from the pit towards Erdington.'

'Which way were those footsteps going?'

'Going across the ploughed field to the right hand, as I was going towards Erdington.'

'There is a dry pit at the corner of the field to the right?'

'Yes.'

'Can you tell whether those man's footsteps were coming up towards that dry pit?'

'Yes, they were.'

'Did you go higher up that path towards Erdington?'

'Yes.'

'Did you discover any other footsteps?'

'About eight yards distance, I discovered a woman's footsteps.'

'Which way were those footsteps going from the foot-path?'

'They were going the same way to my right.'

'Did you trace the steps of the man, and the steps of the woman, from these two spots?'

'Yes.'

'Can you tell us whether these two footsteps that you have mentioned appeared to meet together at any time?'

'No, not at all.'

'Did they come up together, so as to run near each other?'

'Yes, they got together about fifteen yards nearer the hedge.'

'Can you form any judgment whether they were running or walking?'

'They were running.'

'How can you tell that?'

'By the stride and sinking into the ground.'

'How far did you trace them to the right hand side of the close?'

'Up to the far corner where the dry pit is.'

'You say, you traced them running together up to the dry pit; what did you observe when you got to that corner?'

'I observed them dodging backwards and forwards.'

'Could you tell whether they appeared to be still running?'

'No, I could not tell; they seemed shorter, as though they had been dodging about.'

'Could you tell which way they went when they got upon the grass?'

'Towards the water pit.'

The witness now described how both sets of footsteps moved on to the grass where, presumably, either intercourse or rape had taken place. He then said that he found another single set of prints going in the opposite direction from the pit. They were the footsteps of a man—alone.

'How did the man whose footsteps they were, appear to be going?'

'Running.'

'Were there any other footsteps, than those of a man going that way, at that time?'

'No.'

'No woman's?'

'No.'

'How far did you trace those steps?'

'About three parts up the piece; it might be rather more; towards the dry pit . . .'

'Can you tell, whether by the way that you traced those steps to the corner of the field, a man would get sooner to Castle Bromwich, than going the regular way?'

'Yes.'

This was a dangerous point for the simple reason that Thornton lived at Castle Bromwich.

Lavell now described how he collected a pair of shoes belonging to Abraham Thornton and proceeded systematically to compare them with the footprints.

'Did they, or did they not appear to be the footsteps of the same man?'

'Yes.'

'With how many footprints did you compare them?'

'I suppose about a dozen.'

'Did the person's shoes fit those footsteps all exactly?'

'Yes.'

'Have you any doubt whether those footsteps were made with those shoes?'

'None; no doubt at all.'

'Did you compare them with those footsteps that turned off the road, about eight yards from where the footsteps of the woman turned off?'

'Yes.'

'Did they fit there?'

'Yes.'

'Did you compare them with those parts where the man and woman appeared to be running together?'

'Yes—and they fitted.'

'Did you compare them where they dodged, as you spoke of?'

'Yes—and they agreed.'

'There were some covered with boards; where were they?'

'At the corner, up by the dry pit.'

'Who covered them?'

'I did.'

'Had those shoes, or either of them, any particular nail?'

'There was a sparrow-bill . . .'

'Were there any marks of this sparrow-nail on those foot-prints that you covered?'

'There was one step trod on a short stick which throwed the foot up, and there were the marks of two nails.'

'You know the slope of the pit where the body was found?'

'Yes.'

'Did you see any footsteps of any sort near the edge of the slope?'

'Yes—just one.'

'Was that a man's or a woman's?'

'It appeared to be a man's.'

'What was the direction of that step?'

'It appeared to be the left foot sideways.'

'Can you tell whether it inclined either from the slope or towards the slope?'

'It inclined towards the slope.'

'I believe you did not compare the shoe with that?'

'No.'

By now the case against Thornton had built up impressively, first because of the identification with his footprints and second because his home was at Castle Bromwich. Immediately, it all seemed fairly damning evidence not only for murder but rape too, and then Mr. Reader went to work once more in cross-examination:

'You have given us an account of the footsteps; had there been much rain that morning?'

'I could not tell.'

'Had there been a thunderstorm, or a hard shower of rain fallen between the time you first saw the steps, and the time you tracked them?'

'It rained while we were going.'

'Had it rained before?'

'I do not know as it did.'

'How many tracks did you cover with the board?'

'Two of the man's and one of the woman's.'

'Was it before the rain began?'

'Yes.'

'In what part of the field did you put the boards?'

'Near the dry pit.'

'There were a great many people collected on the ploughed field, were there not?'

'At one time after another; but not then.'

'Do you think there were more than one thousand footsteps then?'

'Not then.'

'Were there not a great many other footsteps beside the steps you had traced in the morning?'

'Yes, there were a great many.'

'Some thousands perhaps?'

'I won't say thousands.'

'Were there not a great number of footmarks of other persons?'

'Yes.'

'Did you try the shoes of any of those persons, to see if they corresponded with the marks?'

'Yes.'

'And they corresponded too, did they?'

'No.'

'Did you try the marks of the shoes of any other persons there, with what you supposed to be the prisoner's?'

'No.'

Reader now managed to introduce a slight note of ridicule into Lavell's evidence and said that he gave so many details it was almost as if he had *seen* these two people *actually running* that morning. He then proceeded to press home his questioning about the final footprint: 'You saw but one mark on the edge of the pit, how far might that be from the edge of the pit?'

'Close to the slope.'

'You did not measure that?'

'No.'

'How many persons had been near that spot, before you found the marks?'

'There had not been a great many then . . .'

'You have been speaking of seeing a footing going across from the dry pit, crossing the footpath, to the other corner of the close . . . You have been asked whether it would not lead to Castle Bromwich?'

'Yes, it would.'

'Could they not go by another way by Tyburn House?'

'They could if they liked.'

'Which would be the nearest?'

'By trespass, they might have gone a nearer way.'

'Could not anybody have got in less time to Castle Bromwich, if they had gone over the hedge and ditch?'

'Yes, I suppose they could.'

'Near the pit there was only one footstep?'

'Only one.'

'Nor could you tell whether it was a man's or a woman's?'

'I could not.'

Reader had succeeded in riddling Lavell's evidence with doubt on many points. If Thornton had wanted to get to Castle Bromwich in the shortest possible time he would have taken a different course over the hedge and ditch. The footsteps Lavell protected from the rain by boards were near the dry pit and not the pit where Mary's body had been found. Rain and the presence of other people in the field made somewhat suspect any footprint other than those of the protected ones. Far more important, Lavell had admitted that they could not clearly determine whether the crucial footprint beside the water pit was a man's or a woman's. The cross-examination also showed that the footprints of the person—possibly the escaping murderer—running diagonally across the field, were not protected from the rain or trampling feet, and any comparison with Thornton's footprints would be unsatisfactory.

Mr. Serjeant Copley now tried to press home the footprint details by corroborative evidence from Joseph Bird, the man whose assistance Lavell had summoned. He obviously hoped this would remove many of the doubts created in the minds of the jury by Reader's clever cross-examination.

'Did you compare the prisoner's shoes with the tracks down the field?'

'Yes.'

'Did they all exactly correspond?'

'Yes.'

'Did you compare the two footsteps that had been covered by the boards?'

'Yes. . . I kneeled down and blew the dirt out of the right footstep to see if there were any nail-marks. There lay a bit of rotten wood across the footstep, which had turned the outside of the shoe a little up, and the impression on that side of the foot was not so deep as the other; I observed two nail-marks on that side where it was shallowest; the shoes were nailed, and there was a space of about two inches where the nails were out, and they were nailed again.'

'What did you observe about the nails?'

'I marked the first nail on the side of the shoe, and then kneeled down to see if they exactly corresponded, and they did exactly. I could see the second nail-mark at the same time, as well as the shoe, and they fitted in every part exactly.'

Mr. Reynolds, for Thornton, now went to work on this witness too.

'Men walk in many different ways, don't they; some upright —some rather upon their heels—some leaning forwards upon their toes—some take long steps and some short ones?'

'Yes, I believe they do.'

'And some take quite as long strides when they walk, as when they run?'

'I never saw a man take longer steps in walking, than he did in running.'

'Don't you recollect a thunderstorm that morning?'

'It rained sharpish, as I returned from Tyburn House, to measure the footsteps, but I don't recollect any thunderstorm.'

'How long do you think it might rain?'

'It might rain a quarter of an hour.'

'Before you left, there had been many persons walking about?'

'Yes, there had been some.'

'How many, a hundred perhaps?'

'No, not so many.'

'How many then, do you think?'

'There might have been thirty or forty.'

'Thirty or forty persons walking over the ground, and some perhaps where the boards were placed?'

'No, they were ordered to be kept off, by Mr. Bedford.'

'What time did Mr. Bedford come upon the ground?'

'About nine or ten o'clock.'

'How many persons were in the ploughed field at that time?'

'There might be about a score in at that time.'

Once again Reynolds had reactivated doubt about the foot-prints and Serjeant Copley was drawn into a brief re-examination.

'What time in the morning did you first see the footmarks?'

'About seven o'clock.'

'Had there been many persons in the harrowed field then?'

'No.'

Joseph Webster, who owned Penn's Mills, came into the witness box next and was examined by Gooding Clarke:

'What was the information you received on the morning of May 27?'

'I was informed that a woman was drowned in a pit, not far from my house. I ordered the body to be taken to Lavell's house; and I sent the bundle, the bonnet, and the shoes, with it.'

'Did you observe, afterwards, anything near to the pit?'

'I observed, on a spot about forty yards from the pit, a considerable quantity of blood; it lay in a round space, and was as large as I could cover with my extended hand.'

'What else did you observe?'

'There was the impression of a human figure on the grass, on the spot where the blood was. The shoes I had sent with the body, were stained with blood. It appeared that the arms and legs had been extended quite out. The arms had been stretched out their full length. A small quantity of blood lay in the centre of the figure; and a larger quantity of blood lay at the feet. I perceived what appeared to be the marks of the toes of a man's large shoes, at the bottom of the figure, on the same place. The largest quantity of blood at the feet of the figure, was much coagulated. I traced the blood for ten yards, up by the side of the path, towards the pit . . . I then went home to dress, and returned again in about an hour. When I came back, I went into the harrowed field, and there I perceived the traces of a man's and woman's foot; they were pointed out to me by Bird; as I had previously ordered my servants to look over that field. On seeing these footsteps, I sent for the shoes I had before sent with the body to Lavell's; and on comparing those marks with the shoes, they exactly corresponded. There was a spot of blood on the inside of one of the shoes; and on the outside of the same shoe, on the inside of the foot, there was much blood.'

The shoes were called for, and the witness pointed out the spots to the jury. One shoe was handed up to his Lordship, who also examined it very minutely. Mr. Justice Holroyd then questioned the witness:

'Mr. Webster, is it a spot on the inside of the shoe, that you have described?'

'Yes, my Lord; the marks at that time, were plain to be seen; they are not so plain now.'

Clarke proceeded:

'Mr. Webster, after comparing the shoes with the footmarks in the harrowed field, did you go to examine the body?'

'I afterwards went to Lavell's to examine the body. The spencer had been taken off; I observed, on each arm, what appeared to me to be marks from the grasp of a man's hand.'

'Do you know Mrs. Butler's?'

'Yes.'

'Did you examine her clock?'

'I set my watch with Mr. Crompton's, and then went the same morning, to Mrs. Butler's house, at Erdington, to examine her clock. My watch, I believe to be very accurate, and on comparing them, her clock was forty-one minutes faster than my watch.'

Mr. Reader, in cross-examination, now pressed the point of the accuracy of the clocks.

'Mr. Webster, did you examine Mrs. Butler's clock, very accurately?'

'I did.'

'How much was her clock too fast, by your watch?'

'Forty-one minutes.'

'What time does your watch go by?'

'By Birmingham time, by the church clocks.'

The absurd variation in the times given by different witnesses was easily explicable in terms of the total lack in those days of anything resembling Greenwich Mean Time. Publicly, time was frequently kept by uncompensated pendulum clocks—church clocks and grandfather clocks—subject to one minute's variation a day if the average daily temperature altered by only ten per cent. For private individuals, the watch of the period was the silver turnip, which once more suffered from changes in temperature. There was nothing unusual in clocks in the same area varying by as much as forty-one minutes.

Thomas Dale, one of the assistants to the police, at Birmingham, now produced the bundle which he had received from Webster. It contained the clothes worn by Mary Ashford at the time of her death. The pink gown was much stained with blood, and dirty, and the water had caused the blood to spread over the seat of the garment. The white petticoat presented a similar appearance. In the chemise, there was a rent at the bottom, about six inches in length, which was discoloured. The deceased had no flannel petticoat. On the black worsted stockings a spot or two could be perceived, but they were so faint that no one could determine what had caused them.

Daniel Clarke, the licensee of the Inn, Tyburn House, where the dance took place, was next examined by Serjeant Copley:

'In consequence of hearing of the misfortune that had happened to the deceased, did you go anywhere in search of the prisoner?'

'Yes—to Castle Bromwich.'

'Did you meet him in the road?'

'Yes, in the turnpike road, near the Chapel, on a pony. I said to him, "What is become of the young woman that went away with you from my house, last night?" And he made no answer.'

'What did you say then?'

'I said, "She is murdered, and thrown into a pit." And he said, "Murdered!"—I said, "Yes, murdered!" '

'What answer did the prisoner then make?'

'The prisoner said, "I was with her till four o'clock this morning." '

'On his saying that, what more did you say to the prisoner?'

'I then said to him, "You must go along with me, and clear yourself," and he said—"I can soon do that." '

'How far was it to your house, from Castle Bromwich?'

'About a mile.'

'Had you any conversation with the prisoner as you went along?'

'Not about the murder.'

'And yet you went together a mile, at least, and neither of you mentioned another word about the matter at all, did you?'

'No neither of us.'

Clarke was cross-examined by Mr. Reader who took up this strange detail:

'You say that you and the prisoner did not converse about the murder as you went along the road?'

'Yes.'

'Do you think the prisoner had heard of the murder of the deceased, before you told him?'

'No, I don't think he had.'

'And on you telling him, he immediately said, "Murdered! Why, I was with her till four o'clock?"'

'Yes.'

'And he told you so instantly, without any consideration?'

'Yes.'

'You would not have known that the prisoner had been with the deceased till four o'clock in the morning, would you, if he had not told you?'

'No.'

Mr. Justice Holroyd intervened:

'Did the prisoner appear confused when you first told him of the murder?'

'I think he appeared a little confused when I first told him of it.'

Reader proceeded:

'You were greatly affected at the melancholy circumstance, weren't you?'

'Yes, I was.'

'And the prisoner might have been equally affected with yourself, might he not?'

'Yes, he might, I can't say.'

'Persons in general, labouring under any very great distress of mind, are not inclined to talk much, I should think, are they?'

'I should think not.'

'Then, as you say you never said a word of the murder to the prisoner, on the road between Castle Bromwich and your house—there was nothing more remarkable in the prisoner not

mentioning the circumstance to you, than in you not mentioning
it to him—was there?'

'No.'

At this point an interruption occurred while William Lavell
produced the half boots, which he said were those he had taken
out of the bundle beside the pit. His Lordship also examined
the black stockings which the deceased wore. He said they
seemed perfectly clean, except for a spot or two which he could
just perceive on one of them. They were then handed to the
jury. The prisoner's shoes were also produced and minutely
examined by counsel and the jury.

Mr. Freer, a Birmingham surgeon, who had performed a
post-mortem on Mary Ashford, was finally examined by
Gooding Clarke.

'Did you proceed to examine the body of the deceased?'

'I just took a cursory view of the body first. The body was
placed in a very small and dark room; I ordered it to be
removed into another room, which was larger, and more con-
venient for the examination. While they were removing the
body, I went to examine the pit where the body was found.
When I returned, the body had been undressed, and the blood
had been washed from the upper surface of it: between the
thighs and the lower parts of the legs was a good deal of blood;
the parts of generation were lacerated, and a quantity of
coagulated blood was about those parts; but, as it was then
nearly dark, I deferred opening of the body until another day.
On Thursday morning I proceeded to open the body, and
examine it more minutely. There was coagulated blood about
the parts of generation, and she had her *menses* upon her. I
opened the stomach, and found in it a portion of duck-weed,
and about half a pint of fluid, chiefly water.'

'In your judgment, what was the cause of the deceased's
death?'

'In my judgment, she died from drowning. . . '

In answer to a final question about the state of the body
Freer said: 'There were two lacerations of the parts of generation, quite fresh; I was perfectly convinced, that, until those
lacerations, the deceased was a virgin. The *menses* do not
produce such blood as that. I had no doubt but the blood in the
fields, came from the lacerations I saw; those lacerations were

certainly produced by a foreign body passing through the *vagina*; and the natural supposition is, that they proceeded from sexual intercourse. There was nothing in them that could have caused death; there might have been laceration, though the intercourse had taken place by consent. Menstruation, I should think, could not have come on from the act of coition. I think it came on in an unexpected moment; and the exercise of dancing was likely to have accelerated the *menses*; there was an unusual quantity of blood.'

Mr. Freer's evidence concluded the case for the prosecution. In effect, that case attempted to show that Thornton, having failed to seduce Mary Ashford in the fields after the dance, followed her to Mrs. Butler's house where, in the presence of Hannah Cox she changed her clothes. Lying in wait near a stile in Bell Lane, Thornton knew that she would take the short cut across the fields to her home and here was his opportunity.

He revealed himself to her, failed to win her over, chased her (the dodging footmarks), cornered her (where the footmarks vanished on the grass), threw her down, and raped her. Since rape was a hanging matter he then hurled her in a semi- or unconscious condition into the pit and ran off diagonally across the field.

Opening the case for the defence, Mr. Reader was gravely handicapped by being debarred, as the law then stood, from putting Thornton himself in the witness box. Instead, Thornton's deposition had to be read by the Officer of the Court:

'I am by trade a bricklayer and I live with my father at Castle Bromwich. I went to a dance at the Three Tuns Inn on the night of May 26. I danced with the deceased Mary Ashford and came away from the house with her early next morning. Hannah Cox and a young man of the name of Carter went part of the way with us. After we were left alone we walked on by ourselves to a stile and then went over four or five fields. Afterwards we came back to the stile again and talked for about a quarter of an hour. While we sat there a man came by who wished us good-morning. Soon afterwards we went on towards Erdington. I went to the green at Erdington with Mary Ashford and then she went on by herself saying she was going to Mrs. Butler's. I waited on the green some time for the deceased, but as she did not come back I then went towards home. On my road home I saw young Mr. Holden near to his father's house—I also saw a man and a woman there at the same time. After I passed Mr. Holden's house I saw John Haydon taking up some nets at the floodgates. I also saw John Woodcock, Mr. Twamley's miller. When I got home it wanted twenty minutes to five by my father's clock.'

The defence now concentrated on the men mentioned towards the conclusion of this deposition, to give Abraham Thornton a thorough alibi. If they bore out his statement, then the distances and correct times involved in the scene of the murder and the direction in which he was finally said to be walking, made it extremely difficult for him to have committed the crime. The main part of the case for the defence was to rest on this alibi.

William Jennings, a milkman, spoke first:

'Did you see the prisoner at the Bar, that morning?'

'Yes.'

'Where did you see him?'

'I saw him coming down the lane, leading from Erdington to Mr. Holden's house, as if he came from Erdington.'

'What time was this?'

'About half-past four o'clock, as near as I could judge, having no watch.'

'Having no watch, how did you know what o'clock it was?'

'My wife, who was with me, afterwards asked at Mr. Holden's, of Jane Heaton, the servant, what o'clock it was; she looked at the clock and told her.'

'How long was it, after you saw the prisoner, before your wife asked Jane Heaton what time it was?'

'Before she inquired, and after I saw the prisoner, we had milked a cow apiece, in the yard, which might occupy us about ten minutes. The cows were not in the yard then, they were a field's breadth from the house.'

'And you think this time, in all, took up about ten minutes?'

'Yes, about ten minutes altogether.'

'How was the prisoner walking, when you first saw him?'

'Very leisurely.'

'Walking very leisurely along the road, without the least appearance of heat or hurry about him?'

'Yes, walking quite slow; my wife saw him as well as myself.'

Mr. Clarke rose to cross-examine Jennings for the Crown.

2

'Where were you when you first saw Thornton?'

'I was standing in the lane, within about thirty yards of Mr. Holden's house, on the great road.'

'How long had you been standing there?'

'About five minutes.'

'How far was the prisoner from you, when you first saw him?'

'He was within twenty yards of us, coming down the lane. He was between the canal bridge and Mr. Holden's house.'

'Can you tell whether he came down the towing-path of the canal, or down the lane from towards Erdington?'

'No, I can't tell that; I did not see him till he was within twenty yards of me.'

'You say you had been standing there about five minutes before you saw him?'

'Yes.'

Mr. Reader hurried in to re-examine Jennings on a vital point:

'How far could you see down the towing-path, from the place where you stood?'

'Between three and four hundred yards.'

'Then if he had come that way, you would have seen him?'

'If he had come down that way, I think I must have seen him.'

It was important that the witnesses should underline the alibi by showing that Thornton had not come down the towing-path from what was called the Occupation Bridge—the direction of the murder—as the prosecution suggested.

Mr. Reynolds, for Thornton, now called the second witness Martha Jennings, wife of the first witness, to reinforce the details:

'Were you with your husband, at Mr. Holden's, on the morning of May 27 last?'

'Yes.'

'While you were there did you see the prisoner at the Bar pass?'

'Yes.'

'How was he walking?'

'He was coming gently along.'

'What time was this?'

'It was about half-past four o'clock; as I inquired what time of the morning it was, soon afterwards, of Jane Heaton, Mr. Holden's servant.'

'How long do you think it was from the time you saw the prisoner, till you asked Jane Heaton what o'clock it was?'

'Between the time I saw the prisoner, and the time we began to milk, we waited some time for young Mr. Holden, who was gone to fetch up the cows into the yard; and we had each milked a cow apiece, before I asked Jane Heaton the time of the morning. I think it must have been a quarter of an hour at least.'

Mr. Serjeant Copley cross-examined:

'Where exactly were you standing when you first saw the prisoner?'

'In the road, near Mr. Holden's house.'

'Much nearer the house than the canal bridge?'

'Yes.'

'How long had you been in this position?'

'About five minutes. We were looking at a cow that was running at a great rate down the lane; when she had passed us, we turned round to look after her, and then we saw the prisoner.'

'Then as your backs were towards the prisoner, he might have come along the towing-path without your seeing him?'

'Yes.'

Reynolds could not allow this serious qualification to go unchallenged. He re-examined Mrs. Jennings:

'Which way did you and your husband come to Holden's, that morning?'

'Along the towing-path, from Birmingham.'

'How long was this before you saw the prisoner in the road?'

'Not many minutes.'

'You could see some distance along the towing-path, and you saw nobody coming along it then?'

'No, nobody.'

In the end, after further cross-examination, this part of the alibi seemed fairly well established. Now came the question of timing. If Thornton had passed certain well-known points in the district around five o'clock that morning it would have been very difficult for him to crowd in all the events indicated by previous witnesses, including, above all, the murder.

Miss Jane Heaton, a servant of Mr. Holden's, was the next witness for the defence:

'What time did you get up on the morning of May 27 last?'

'About half-past four.'

'From the room of your window, can you see the lane that leads from Erdington to Castle Bromwich?'

'Yes, it is just by my master's house.'

'When you were at the window, did you see a man walking along the road that leads by your master's house, from Erdington to Castle Bromwich?'

'Yes.'

'Do you know who that man was?'

'I think Thornton is the man '

'At what rate was he walking?'

'Quite slow.'

'After you came downstairs, did you see Jennings and his wife?'

'Yes, they came to ask what o'clock it was.'

'And what time was it?'

'I looked at my master's clock to tell them and it wanted seventeen minutes to five.'

'How long was this after you saw the man pass your master's house?'

'About a quarter of an hour.'

John Haydon also reaffirmed the timing of the alibi:

'What time did you leave home, on the morning of May 27 last?'

'I left my own house about ten minutes before five. I went to take up some nets which I had put down the night before, at the flood-gates.'

'How did you know what time it was?'

'As I passed Mr. Zachariah Twamley's stables, at Castle Bromwich, I heard Mr. Rotton's stable clock strike five.'

'How long was it after that, before you saw the prisoner?'

'About five minutes.'

'Where did you see him?'

'He was coming towards Mr. Twamley's mills, in the way from Erdington to Castle Bromwich.'

'Did you know him?'

'Yes, and I asked him where he had been.'

'What answer did he make?'

'He said, "To take a wench home." '

'How long did the prisoner stay with you?'

'He stopped talking with me about ten minutes or a quarter of an hour; and then he went off towards Castle Bromwich, where he lived.'

The Judge intervened: 'What distance is it, from the spot where you first saw the prisoner, to Mr. Holden's?'

'About half a mile, as near as I can guess.'

The last witness for Thornton was John Woodcock, a miller by trade:

'Did you see the prisoner talking with Haydon, Mr. Rotton's game-keeper, at the flood-gates, on the morning of May 27 last?'

'I saw a man talking with the game-keeper, that I took to be him.'

'What time was it?'

'From a calculation I have since made, it must have been about ten minutes past five.'

Mr. Serjeant Copley took him up on two points in cross-examination:

'Do you know the prisoner well?'

'Yes, very well.'

'But you were not sure it was him that you saw with Haydon, at the flood-gates?'

'I thought it was him.'

'You have said that it was ten minutes past five o'clock, by your calculation—pray let us hear how you calculate.'

'I went into the mill the first thing, and when I came out again, I heard Mr. Rotton's stable clock strike five. I then went into a piece of wheat, belonging to Mr. Smallwood, and came back again. It must have been soon after five when I saw the prisoner come up to Haydon, at the flood-gates; for I have walked the ground over since, and it takes me just ten minutes, at a gentle pace.'

Four of Mr. Reader's witnesses eventually agreed that they saw Thornton walking quite slowly past Holden's farm towards Castle Bromwich around 4.30 a.m. by the farm clock. The discrepancy in Woodcock's timing was explained because he took it from the stable clock and, as we have seen, it was common for clocks to register varying times in that area. Two of the witnesses also flatly contradicted the evidence of the Crown that Thornton had come down the tow-path from what was called the Occupation Bridge—the direction of the murder.

It was a peculiarity of law at this time that counsel for the defence were not able to address the jury on the defendant's behalf. They could cross-examine prosecution witnesses—as they had powerfully done—and they could examine witnesses on behalf of Thornton, but no final address to the jury was permissible. Instead, the court briefly adjourned at the conclusion of the evidence for the defence. When, one hour later, Mr. Justice Holroyd gave his summing up, its emphasis was clear:

'Considering the offence to be of a high and very serious nature as it relates to the public as well as the accused, it is your duty as a jury to dismiss entirely from your minds everything you have heard relative to this transaction before you came to court today . . .

'It does seem that these persons, the prisoner and the deceased, were upon the stile about three o'clock so that they had been together during the night about the spot where these transactions took place. It has to be stated that the counsel for the prosecution do not insist that they have produced any direct and conclusive evidence that the prisoner has in fact committed the murder. They have inferred his guilt principally by combining many of the circumstances which provided satisfactory proofs against the prisoner . . .

'One point very material for your consideration is whether connection took place with or without Mary Ashford's consent. If the connection took place against her consent then a rape had been committed and would be a reason why the prisoner —or guilty party—would want to stop her giving any further testimony because this is still a hanging matter. If on the other hand there were no rape and intercourse took place with consent—then this would make it less likely that he should need to commit murder.

'It is very material to determine whether connection took place before the deceased went and changed her dress at Mrs.

Butler's, or afterwards. If connection took place before, then
Mary Ashford arriving at Mrs. Butler's to change her dress and
making no complaint about the prisoner's conduct would show
that she had been a consenting party. The gown and stockings
which the deceased took off at Mrs. Butler's were bloody—yet
her dress—we have heard did not appear disordered and she
was in good spirits.'

Extraordinarily the judge now himself introduced an in-
accuracy into the evidence which weighed in favour of
Thornton.

'It is very material to see at what time the deceased came to
Mrs. Butler's house and what time she left—and therefore what
space of time there was for the transactions to take place between
that time and the time when the prisoner was seen $3\frac{1}{2}$ miles
from that place.'

In fact, the actual distance between Mrs. Butler's house and
Holden's farm was only $1\frac{1}{4}$ miles. The judge continued:

'It seems that the prisoner might have come down by the
canal towing-path through the meadows and it certainly is
possible he might have done so. But then he must have gone a
distance of $3\frac{1}{2}$ miles from a quarter past four and all this pursuit
and the transactions which followed must have taken place
within the period of time within which he was afterwards seen.
If the prisoner had been running, there would have been an
appearance of warmth on his person—but he was also seen
walking slowly and without any appearance of heat or confusion . . .'

Holroyd now concluded: 'The whole of the evidence lies
before you and by that evidence only must you be guided in
your decision. If, members of the jury, on the most careful consideration of all the circumstances of the case you are of the
opinion that no reasonable doubt exists and that the prisoner
was the person who committed the crime then conviction of the
prisoner must follow. But if you have *any* reason to doubt his
guilt—even though you might not consider him entirely blame-
less—then that would be a reasonable ground to acquit the
prisoner. But I would ask you to bear in mind—it is better that
the murderer with all the weight of his crime upon his head
should escape punishment than that an innocent person should
go to his death, wrongfully.'

The implications were clear and not surprisingly the jury consulted for only six minutes without retiring and gave their verdict on the spot:

'Not guilty.'

But this was only the beginning of the spectacular events which presently converted the Old Bailey into a scene reminiscent of jousting medieval knights. The second phase began when the heir at law, the eldest brother of the deceased Mary Ashford—William Ashford—determined to bring a private prosecution for murder against Thornton, convinced that, whatever the courts said, he had brutally done his sister to death.

An ancient and unrepealed Statute 3.D. of Henry VII laid it down that a person acquitted on an indictment of murder, must not be permitted to go free at large if a private prosecution were to be brought against him—within a year and a day— and Ashford's lawyers now decided that this statute might still be invoked. But the judge had not only discharged Thornton —he had not taken bail for his re-appearance as required by the ancient statute. Thus it was necessary for all the papers in the case to be gathered together and sent to a Mr. Constant who gave his opinion on this very technical branch of the law. It consisted in saying that a re-trial would only bring the same verdict—unless fresh and damning evidence could be produced.

But William Ashford, thirsting either for vengeance or justice, remained unsatisfied. His advisers now consulted a second lawyer, Mr. Chitty, who gave the opposite opinion, supporting his view with endless precedents and technicalities:

'In this interesting case I have examined all the books and cases on the subject and made enquiries and searches at the different offices and at the Crown in particular. As Thornton is not in custody the proper course will be to issue a Writ of Appeal directed to the Sheriff of Warwickshire.

'The writ being issued the Sheriff should make his warrant to re-arrest Thornton in the terms of the writ and having apprehended him keep him in custody without bail.'

A moving scene followed. Thornton was sitting in the kitchen of his father's house on the evening of October 9, 1817, with his mother, when two men arrived and told the servant girl that

they wished to see Mr. Thornton. The girl, thinking they meant
Thornton Senior, said he had gone to bed and invited the men
in to talk to Mrs. Thornton. Encountering Abraham Thornton
in the kitchen John Hackney, one of the two men, said:

'How do you do, Mr. Thornton.'

'I suppose you want my father?'

'No, it's you I want to talk to. I have a warrant for your
arrest and I'm afraid I must take you off.'

'Yes I know. Two other gentlemen told me today that
William Ashford was called up on Tuesday evening at twelve
o'clock to go to London and they advised me to escape while
I could but I told them—no. I said I would stay and see it out.
Now don't get upset, Mother.'

But his mother was very upset:

'They can't take you away—that cruel man Ashford. What
does he want with you? Isn't he satisfied? We have him to
thank for this.'

'Yes—what they want is my life and then they will be
satisfied. But not until. Make yourself easy, Mother—I have
made up my mind.'

The Sheriff's men then handcuffed Thornton and took him
away. It was not only William Ashford who had conspired to
bring a private prosecution against Thornton. Many people in
the locality of the murder still believed Thornton guilty and a
wave of popular protest swept the country, encouraged by
spectacular reports in the newspapers. A feeling that perjury
had brought about a miscarriage of justice persisted and
Thornton's rearrest was received with some enthusiasm.

Several days later in the King's Bench Division, Mr. Le
Blanc, for the private prosecution, read the new indictment with
Thornton standing once more at the bar and William Ashford
present:

'Abraham Thornton, you are attached to answer William
Ashford of the death of the said Mary Ashford and thereupon
the said William Ashford in his own person appealeth Abraham
Thornton. For that the said Abraham Thornton not having the
fear of God before his eyes but being moved and seduced by
the instigation of the Devil on the 27th day of May in the 57th
year of the reign of our sovereign Lord George the Third by
the grace of God did feloniously, wilfully and with malice

aforethought make an assault, did take the said Mary Ashford in both hands and cast, throw and push her into a pit of water and so did kill and murder against the peace of our said Lord the King, his Crown and dignity.'

Mr. Clarke once more appeared for the prosecution and Mr. Reader for the defence. When Clarke moved that the appellee, Thornton, be required to plead, Reader at once applied for further time. The whole of the proceedings were something of a shock to Reader who felt that vindictiveness was not absent from the new attempt to indict Thornton. The court granted his request for time and then on Monday, November 16, came a dramatic climax totally unexpected by Clarke or Ashford which revived an almost medieval atmosphere in the court. Mr. Le Blanc first read his statement on behalf of Ashford:

'And if the said Abraham Thornton will deny the felony and murder aforesaid then the said William Ashford who was the eldest brother and is the heir of the said Mary Ashford, deceased, is ready to prove the said murder against him . . .'

Turning to Abraham Thornton, whose demeanour in the dock was one of smiling complacency, he now challenged him.

'Abraham Thornton, are you guilty or not guilty of the said felony and murder?'

Before answering, Thornton slowly produced from his pocket a large pair of gauntlet gloves and clumsily drew one on his left hand. His counsel then handed him a slip of paper from which he read:

'*Not* guilty! And I am ready to defend the same with my body.'

With tremendous panache he then threw the other gauntlet on the floor of the court. A gasp went up from the crowded gallery.

For a moment everything stopped in confusion. What it meant was that Thornton's lawyers had instructed him to invoke the second part of the still extant statute of Henry VII which entitled him, under a Writ of Right, to offer battle to a man bringing a private prosecution against him. It entitled Thornton legally to prove his guilt or innocence by mortal combat between his accuser and himself.

Clarke replied at once for William Ashford:

'I must say I am much surprised by this sort of demand

seeing that Trial by Battle is such an obsolete practice. No civilized court would any longer decide the issues at stake by such a means. It would appear to me extraordinary indeed if the person who has murdered the sister should, as the law exists, in these enlightened times be allowed to prove his innocence by murdering the brother also—or at least by an attempt to do so.'

'It is the law of England, Mr. Clarke,' the judge, Lord Ellenborough, commented, 'and we must not call it murder.' Clarke continued:

'I apologize, my Lord, for using too strong an expression, although I am sure your Lordship will appreciate what moved me to this statement—but I must bring the attention of the court to the very different physique of the two men. It would equally create another injustice to allow right and wrong to be decided because one man by the luck of nature happened to be stronger than the other. The court should—in my opinion—not allow such a combat to take place.'

Reader now intervened forcibly:

'My Lord. I do not think we should continue to waste the court's time by offering such arguments. I think some explanation of our action in reviving this law is called for and it is very simple. I advised my client to *offer battle* in the matter for one powerful reason—it was because of the extraordinary and unprecedented prejudice which has been worked up and disseminated against him throughout the whole country—when a court of English law has already found him innocent of the very grave charges brought against him. Surely—your Lordship—in these circumstances the proper course for my learned friend is to counterplead.'

Clarke hesitated a moment in conference with his assistants, and then said:

'I hereby apply to the court for time.'

'Do you apply for time generally or for time to counterplead?' asked the Judge.

'I apply for time to counterplead.'

'Does the counsel for the appellee consent to that?' Ellenborough asked, and Reader replied:

'I do.'

'Then time is given—until Saturday, November 21.'

The conditions controlling the nature of the trial by battle were now investigated by learned counsel and Reader found that it was still legally valid to stage the combat upon one of the worst plots of ground which could be determined in the limits of the King's Bench providing it did not exceed sixty square feet. The two opponents should, according to ancient precedent, be armed with staves. The combat would continue until either one man killed the other in which case he was cleared of any crime including the killing of his opponent, or, if the accused could continue the fight until sunset, he was cleared of any charge against him. On the other hand if Thornton surrendered or gave in during the battle he was declared 'Craven' and must, as the law then stood, be hanged. One glance at the physique of the two opponents made it quite clear that Thornton would certainly emerge the victor.

William Ashford's lawyers now made powerful efforts to discover fresh and more damning evidence against Thornton. Momentarily it looked as if they might succeed when a certain convict, Omar Hall, on board the prison ship *Justitia* expressed a desire to communicate some information connected with the case of Abraham Thornton. He then signed a statement:

'In the summer of 1817 I shared a cell in Warwick gaol with Thornton, then awaiting trial. He confessed to me that he had chased and outraged Mary Ashford—that she then and there died of shock and that to avoid being hanged for rape and/or murder he had thrown the body into the pit. He added that he was at ease as to the result of the trial for his father had taken care of the evidence.'

The opening sentences of this statement were true—Hall had shared a cell with Thornton. The rest proved to be highly suspect. In any case, Ashford's counsel quickly realized that Hall as a convicted felon would not be allowed to testify. He would first need a free pardon from the Home Secretary and enquiries at the Home Office made it quite clear that such a pardon would not be forthcoming.

Meanwhile, the formulation of the counterplea was inevitably entrusted to the specialist in antiquarian law, Mr. Chitty, but Mr. Le Blanc finally read the document before Lord Ellenborough. Robbed of its more intricate complications, the counterplea for Ashford began:

'William Ashford pleads that Abraham Thornton should not be admitted to wage battle with him because before and at the time of the issuing of the Writ of Appeal there were and still are strong presumptions and proofs that Abraham Thornton was guilty of the rape and murder aforesaid.'

The counterplea continued to reproduce almost all the evidence given in the previous trial. It then stated the legal fact that a man could not offer battle who was taken with *mainou*—in other words caught red-handed. His guilt in such a situation was so clear that any trial by battle became superfluous. As Le Blanc said:

'And surely in the present case the same principle also has application. I submit that the presumption of guilt is so strong that the said Abraham Thornton has no right to trial by battle either.

'Wherefore I pray judgment that Abraham Thornton may not be admitted to wage battle in this appeal against him by William Ashford.'

Reader proceeded to reply to the counterplea with what was known legally as a replication. This re-stated the evidence given in Thornton's defence and concluded:

'Abraham Thornton says that notwithstanding anything said by William Ashford in the counterplea, he ought to be admitted to wage battle with him in this appeal.

'He claims this because there were and still are violent and strong presumptions and proofs that the said Abraham Thornton was *not* and is *not* guilty of the rape and murder.'

Chitty took up the challenge.

'There are two objections to this replication. First it is not right for the appellee Thornton in answer to a counterplea to state circumstances affording a presumption of innocence. Secondly, the circumstances stated in this replication are not sufficient to support the presumption of innocence.'

Chitty now quoted a whole forest of technical precedents, finally coming back to this statement:

'The result of these authorities being that in cases where strong and vehement presumptions of guilt exist the party who was formerly subject to trial by battle is freed from that obligation. The principal circumstances disclosed by the counterplea are these: that Mary Ashford at seven in the morning was found dead in a pit of water—that she had recently been alive and had been thrown into the pit . . .'

Mr. J. Bayley, for Thornton, intervened:

'There is nothing stated in the counterplea from which a necessary inference arises that she was thrown into the pit by anyone. What is there to show that she might not either have thrown herself in or accidentally fallen in?'

'There were marks of blood on some clover grass about a foot and a half from the footpath leading to the pit. Thornton's footsteps were then traced to within forty yards of the pit where the hardness of the ground prevented their being further visible and very near to the edge of the pit there was the mark of the shoe of a man's left foot . . .'

'That was not described as a recent impression. Nor was it shown that it in any way corresponded to Thornton's shoe. It was not even stated that Thornton's shoe was compared with it and found to be different—nor that from the state of the impression comparison was even possible.'

'There is next the question of Thornton's clothing on the morning he returned home. His linen was found stained with blood and he admitted on the preceding night that he had carnal knowledge of Mary Ashford.'

Bayley interposed:

'With her consent.'

'Yes—with her consent.'

Bayley now asked whether Chitty admitted that if the prisoner had been convicted on the first trial that would have *barred* his right to battle. Chitty agreed that it would. Whereupon Bayley asked why—in that case—an *acquittal* in the first trial should not carry as much weight in the opposite direction —namely his *right* to battle. Chitty found this logic faulty and returned to the facts of Thornton's alibi. The whole question, he said, seemed to turn on a very few minutes. Thus at about a quarter past four Mary Ashford left Mrs. Butler's house and *within* fifteen minutes of that time she was last seen by a witness. The precise time was not stated.

'Then,' Chitty said, 'there does in this counterplea come a precise averment that not more than twenty-five minutes before five, the appellee Abraham Thornton was seen at John Holden's house, a distance of a mile and a half from the pit.

Thus the whole issue depends on a very few minutes of difference in timing which are not a sufficient alibi to remove the presumption of guilt.'

Mr. Bayley again intervened:

'You do not state it quite accurately. The fact is this: Mary Ashford left Mrs. Butler, as stated in your counterplea, at about a quarter after four. In about or near a quarter of an hour afterwards she is seen first by one man and then by another in Bell Lane. She has then to go through Bell Lane, she has to cross the harrowed field, to be met by Thornton, then to run away and be overtaken, and then after the criminal intercourse has taken place to be carried thence to the pit and thrown in and then the appellee has to run and be close to John Holden's house at twenty-five minutes before five which by the nearest way is a mile and a half and by the readiest way nearly two miles from the spot. All this must, besides, have happened—according to your evidence—in broad daylight in twenty minutes or so when a good many people appear to have been about. Yet no one saw it.'

An even more learned authority on antiquarian law, Mr. Tyndal, was now called in and analysed the arguments between defence and prosecution. He said:

'The defence is attempting to assert its right to trial by battle, the prosecution to overrule that right and proceed with the private prosecution against Thornton.

'I wish to make four points to clarify the law. First that trial by battle is the undoubted right of the plaintiff in an appeal of this character. Second that the counterplea has not brought the case within the exceptions which the law allows to a wager of battle. The facts brought under this point were too vague and uncertain. Third that even if the counterplea were admissible the answer given to it by the defendant Thornton was a complete and satisfactory answer. Fourth—in my opinion we should no longer argue the rights and wrongs of the outdated trial by battle but should allow the defendant on his evidence to go free.'

But Chitty had not given up hope yet.

'The mode of pleading and the facts pleaded against the trial by battle are in my view quite sufficient. On the other hand my learned friend has isolated only part of the evidence in our counterplea for attack. Let us assume for the moment that he is right and that part of the evidence being invalid we strike it out. That still leaves remaining sufficient evidence to oust the claim of the appellee for trial by battle.'

Once more Chitty plunged into a learned disquisition on precedents and so it went on. Week after week of precedents, technical argument, judge versus counsel, counsel versus antiquarian specialist. It occupied the King's Bench at intervals spread over no less than five months. Even after three months Lord Ellenborough still could not make up his mind.

But by then nobody in the King's Bench wanted to hear any further argument. Even learned counsel seemed bored with the tangle of precedent and counter-precedent. What it finally boiled down to was this: The option of battle lay *as of right* with Thornton and if William Ashford declined it without sufficient reason then Thornton would be discharged—*sine die*, as the law put it—or a free man. It could no longer be contended that *a strong and pregnant suspicion* remained against Thornton because William Ashford's counsel had brought forward no new evidence.

Lord Ellenborough finally gave judgment: 'The general law of the land is in favour of the wager of battle and it is our duty to pronounce the law as it is and not as we may wish it to be. Whatever prejudices, therefore, may exist against this mode of trial, still as it is the law of the land, the court must pronounce judgment for it.'

Counsel for Ashford sought for time to consider this but on Monday, April 20 he had—at long last—to surrender.

Reader immediately asked that his client be discharged 'without a day', or a free man. The Lord Chief Justice at once reminded him that the Crown could take no cognisance of any arrangement which might be made between two private persons. Thornton must, according to law, be charged by the Crown with the crime which the Appellant had laid against him, but it was now very simple to answer that charge with the plead '*autrefois acquit*'. The Attorney General finally admitted the validity of the plea and Thornton left the court a free man.

Public opinion had by now reached fever pitch. Those undercurrents which mysteriously gather their force to reaffirm the worst prejudices had been at work for months to demand

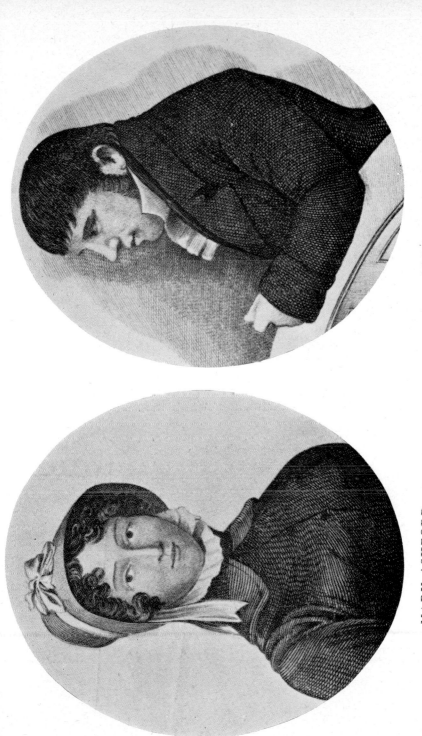

ABRAHAM THORNTON

MARY ASHFORD

ADOLF BECK

WILLIAM THOMAS
ALIAS JOHN SMITH

A PAGE FROM *THE ILLUSTRATED LONDON NEWS*
WITH SKETCHES OF THE PRINCIPAL PARTICI-
PANTS IN THE ADOLF BECK CASE

EDWARD CARSON

RUFUS ISAACS

retribution from Thornton for a crime he had never committed. Such was its intensity that Lord Ellenborough suggested that Thornton should leave by a back entrance 'and thus escape the attentions of a large and ferocious mob which had gathered at the front of the building to give him a warm reception'.

Thornton returned home a chastened man and all his attempts to live down the whole affair failed. In the end he was driven to emigrate to America.

CHAPTER II

SERAFINO PELIZZIONI

[1865]

WALK DOWN HIGH HOLBORN today, from Gray's Inn
Road, and at the far end from Holborn Station turn left into
a network of still narrow streets. There you will come upon a
row of modern buildings standing on the unmarked site of the
Golden Anchor Tavern. Even now, on a dark February night,
the deserted city streets offer sinister possibilities, but step back
a hundred years ago to find gas and oil lamps throwing small
pools of illumination in the otherwise pitch blackness and the
sinister undertones multiply a hundredfold. There, on the night
of February 4, 1865, Serafino Pelizzioni, described as a thirty-
two-year-old Italian glass silverer, was alleged to have wilfully
murdered Michael Harrington, an Englishman. What came
to be known as the Saffron Hill murder case was also one of
the most remarkable and heroic examples of a private individual challenging the verdict of the State.

The first prosecution against Pelizzioni was undertaken at
the State's instance and Mr. Giffard and Mr. Beasley appeared
for the Crown. Sitting in the public gallery, surrounded by
leading members of the Italian community in London, was
Mr. Henry Negretti, director of the famous company of instrument makers, Negretti & Zambra, the man destined to become
the crusading spirit behind what followed. Defending Pelizzioni
were Mr. Ribton and Mr. F. H. Lewis, and as they entered the
Court a burst of clapping came from the Italian section of the
public gallery. The Court Usher quickly called for order and
fifteen minutes later Mr. Beasley began his examination of the
first witness, Mr. Shaw:

'You are the landlord of the Golden Anchor Tavern, Saffron Hill?'

'I am.'

'Do you know the prisoner in the dock?'

'Yes, I do.'

'How long have you known the prisoner?'

'About three months.'

'There could be no doubt whatever about your being able to identify the prisoner in almost any circumstances?'

'No, no doubt.'

'Now perhaps you would give us your account of what took place on Monday evening, December 26, at the Golden Anchor Tavern.'

'Pelizzioni came in about six o'clock in the evening. I and my wife were in the bar and some words developed between the three of us. He suddenly said he could kill any six Englishmen like me, but I took no notice of the remark. He remained a few minutes and then left.'

'Was he alone—or were there others with him?'

'There were five or six others with him—all foreigners.'

'Did they also leave?'

'No, they remained.'

'And what happened afterwards?'

'There was an argument and an Italian I knew as Gregorio all of a sudden struck me in the mouth. That was in a sidebox in the bar leading to the tap room. A short passage divides the tap room from the bagatelle room and . . .'

'Before you give us further details would you please tell the court whether there had been any physical violence in the tap room before the man Gregorio struck you?'

'No—no violence before.'

'And after he had struck you?'

'He went into the tap room and I was about to follow him when some of the customers at the bar dragged me back and pushed me into the bar parlour. Shortly afterwards I saw some of the Italians rushing out of the house and I hurried after them to get a policeman.'

'You were lucky enough to find a policeman?'

'Yes, I found one I knew called Fawell who happened to be passing the door. I brought him in and he went to the tap room. I saw no more until I noticed the prisoner being brought from the bagatelle room by the policeman.'

'And later . . .'

'I saw the deceased, Michael Harrington, brought out into the bar parlour. I heard he had been stabbed and I helped to make him comfortable and arrange his clothes. I saw his bowels protruding.'

Shaw was now cross-examined by Mr. Ribton for the defence:

'I would like to try to clarify precisely what the prisoner is alleged to have said to you when he first quarrelled with you. Can you tell us again what he said?'

'He said he could kill any six such Englishmen as me.'

'Long before coming to this court you were, of course, examined in the Magistrate's Court, were you not?'

'That is so.'

'And in that court—I have your words here . . . you said: "Mr. Pelizzioni said to me he could *settle* six such Englishmen as me." Which of these two very conflicting statements is accurate? Did he use the word *kill*—or the word *settle*?'

'I might have said to the Magistrate that the prisoner used the word *settle*.'

'The question is—which word *did* he use?'

'He either said settle or kill—I don't know which.'

'So your recollection of the actual word used is confused and he could as easily have used the word *settle*?'

'I suppose he could.'

'Now, Mr. Shaw—how clear is your memory on the other *facts* in your evidence? For instance, before the prisoner spoke to you had the other Italians present gone into the tap room or were they still present?'

'I think the other Italians had gone into the tap room before the prisoner spoke to me.'

'But you are not sure?'

'Well—er—yes I am.'

'We must come to a much more important point in the evidence you have given the court, and I want you to think very carefully before answering. Do you still say that the second Italian, Gregorio, not merely quarrelled with you but struck you in the face?'

'Yes, I do.'

'But Mr. Shaw, I have here two depositions of yours, one before the Magistrate and one before the Coroner, in which there is no reference whatever to Gregorio having struck you.'

'But he did strike me. He struck me on the mouth and then rushed into the tap room. I saw no more of him.'

'But is it not very odd that in two previous instances when asked to give evidence you omitted an event which no person could possibly overlook in such circumstances?'

'I persist in my statement.'

Mr. Alfred Rebbeck, a potman at the Golden Anchor, was now examined by Beasley:

'On the evening of December 26,' Rebbeck said, 'I was serving in the bagatelle room. I went into the bar for a pipe. The entrance to the bar is at the end of the bagatelle room and there is a side entrance from the bagatelle room to the tap room. I at first passed through the bar to get to the tap room.' Beasley interrupted:

'That was before you asked for the pipe?'

'Yes.'

'And what happened then?'

'I saw the prisoner and many others in the tap room. The prisoner was at the door. Another Italian spoke to me as I went in, upon which I went back to the bagatelle room and said something to the Englishmen there. I was then asked for a pipe and I went into the bar for one.'

'Were there then any Italians in the bagatelle room?'

'No.'

'Continue please.'

'I took the pipe into the bagatelle room. I then saw one of the Italians knock down a Mrs. King who was in the doorway of the tap room. The prisoner was then going in and I told him I wanted no row, but as I went towards the door he stabbed me.'

'Will you tell the jury where he stabbed you?'

'In my right side.'

'And what happened then?'

'I hit him on the head with a broom-handle and he ran at me again with a knife in his hand, but he did not get me the second time.'

'And when did you first see the deceased, Harrington?'

'It was later. I heard someone shout "Look out" and I turned round and saw the prisoner right on top of Harrington.'

'Were there any other Italians in the room at the time?'

'No, no other Italians.'

'And what action did you take?'

'I could not take any action because I lost my sense and was taken away. I am still a patient in hospital.'

It was quickly becoming clear that the prosecution intended to show that no other Italian beside Pelizzioni had been in the bagatelle room at the time of the murder. Since, to the English clients of the pub, many Italians looked alike, it was important to avoid any confused identity by establishing that Pelizzioni, and Pelizzioni alone, had been in the room. However, cross-examined by Mr. Ribton, Rebbeck began to qualify certain details of his evidence. Ribton asked:

'You struck the prisoner, you say?'

'Yes, I struck the prisoner with a broom-handle.'

'Where did you get the broom-handle?'

'There were two blind rollers, a copper stick and a broom-handle in the bagatelle room.'

'And where did they come from?'

'I had brought them from the kitchen into the room about ten minutes before. One of the English party said: "If they break in here we must defend ourselves, but we have nothing but our hands to do so." They asked if I had nothing to give them, upon which I went downstairs and brought the blind rollers, the copper stick and the broom-handle.'

'And where were you when you thought you saw Mrs. King knocked down?'

'I was going into the bagatelle room with the pipe.'

'And where exactly was she?'

'She was in the passage leading from the tap room to the bagetelle room.'

'And did the prisoner knock her right to the ground?'

'Not right to the ground.'

'Did he knock her down at all?'

'I'm not completely sure.'

'But did you not say before the magistrate that he did *not* knock her down?'

'I am not sure.'

At this point the judge intervened:

'When exactly were you struck with a knife?'

'I was stabbed before I struck the prisoner with a broom-handle.'

Two police constables were now called and both swore that there were no other Italians in the bagatelle room when they arrived on the scene. Pressed by Ribton, one policeman, Richard Fawell, denied that he had been making enquiries after another Italian known as Gregorio. He admitted that in the bad light of the Golden Anchor Inn one Italian might bear some resemblance—especially in English eyes—to another, but he repeatedly denied that anyone else had come under suspicion.

Mr. Peerless, surgeon at St. Bartholomew's Hospital, examined by Beasley, now gave an account of the deceased being brought to the hospital on the night of December 26. 'He was in a state of great collapse and he had an incised wound in the abdomen. The intestines protruded. They were wounded in six places and there was a great deal of haemorrhage. I did the best I could for him. Inspector Potter came in about 9.30. At that time Harrington was still sensible. When he had the conversation with Inspector Potter he was perfectly conscious that he was dying.'

Under cross-examination, the surgeon said that in his opinion the wounds in the intestines were all produced by one stroke of a knife. Inspector Potter of 'G' Division was now called by the prosecution to reveal the macabre situation whereby the dying man in hospital was confronted with his alleged murderer.

'On the night of the murder, after the arrest, I took the prisoner with ten or twelve other persons gathered for the purpose of an identification parade, to St. Bart's Hospital, where the deceased was then lying. I took hold of Harrington's right hand and said to him: "In consequence of what the doctor has told me, I believe you have but a short time to live." The deceased replied: "If I am to die the Lord have mercy on me." I then asked him to look around to see if he could pick out from the twelve men the one who had stabbed him. He looked around his bed and pointed to the prisoner, saying: "That's the man who did it. May God forgive him for what he has done." '

Cross-examined by Ribton the Police Inspector carefully maintained most of the details of his evidence, but one inconsistency emerged.

'I take it,' Ribton said, 'that you had the deceased's statement taken down in writing at the time?'

'That is so, sir.'

'And did the deceased sign it?'

'Well . . . er . . . no, sir.'

'How was that?'

'He did not seem ready to sign.'

'*Ready* to sign. Do you mean he was unwilling to sign?'

'I don't know exactly why he did not want to sign.'

'Do you think it is possible he did not sign at the time because there was some doubt in his mind about the person he had selected as his murderer?'

'No, sir. He was quite firm on that.'

'I believe you have been making enquiries about other Italians who might be involved in the case?'

'That is so.'

'And have any of them been identified as being concerned in this affray in any way?'

'No, sir, none.'

Although the defence had managed to riddle the prosecution's case with minor inconsistencies and some inaccuracies, no less than eight witnesses testified against Pelizzioni and he left the dock at the end of the morning session a desperate man. The evidence against him seemed very black indeed. Ribton opened the case for the defence in the afternoon of the same day.

'Members of the jury. You have heard the evidence for the prosecution and the details given by all the witnesses, but I will put it to you at the outset that the case for the prisoner will rest on the fact that he was not the man who struck the blow which caused the death of the deceased and this I will prove to you by entirely reliable testimony. If one looks first of all at the evidence on which the identification of the prisoner is based, we shall see that it comes from partisan witnesses who have been shown under cross-examination to be unreliable.

We have dealt in considerable detail with the evidence for the prosecution, pointing out various discrepancies and especially the deficiencies of identification, dwelling finally with great force on the non-production of one of two knives. I will show that the second knife—a bloody one—was in fact found next day in the yard of a public house frequented by Italians and that this knife was given to Inspector Potter, who has not said a word about it in this case. That knife I will show you was left at the public house by another Italian who had been very violent in the affray. Even more remarkable, in view of all the evidence accumulating from the eight witnesses for the prosecution, I will show that the prisoner at the bar was in fact absent from the house at the moment when the fatal blow was struck. Under these circumstances I will eventually ask the jury, with the greatest confidence, to acquit the prisoner.'

Ribton now called the first witness for the defence, a woman named Anne Sams.

'I was at the Golden Anchor about five o'clock on the evening in question. First of all I danced with the prisoner and he then left the pub. A row developed between the Italians and the English and got very bad.'

'Was the prisoner present at any time during the actual brawl?'

'I did not see the prisoner present.'

'Were other Italians present?'

'Another Italian who was very like Pelizzioni was there with his brother and I saw one of them strike Mr. Shaw.'

'Will you now tell the jury what you recollect after that?'

'These two men then opened the door of the dancing room and entered the bagatelle room. A moment later the two men rushed out of that room. One had his cap off and he said to a Mr. Wells who was present—"If you come out I will serve you the same".'

Anne Sams was now cross-examined by Beasley.

'You say that the prisoner left the pub after he had danced with you?'

'That is so.'

'So you do not know exactly what happened to him after that?'

'No.'

'He could, in fact, have returned to the pub and entered the bagatelle room later?'

'I don't know.'

'You were not, in fact, in the bagatelle room were you when the stabbing occurred?'

'No, not the actual stabbing.'

'You were sent to get a cab and on your return learnt that Harrington had been stabbed?'

'Yes, sir.'

Giovanni Manzoni, a resident of the nearby parish of Clerkenwell, was the next to enter the witness box.

'On the night in question a man called Gregorio came to my house about ten o'clock. He asked to be allowed to sleep on the shavings in the workshop. I agreed that he could and he then—in great distress—told me what had happened at the Golden Anchor earlier in the evening. He said . . .'

At this point the judge intervened.

'I do not think we can take this alleged statement from the man called Gregorio as evidence.' Ribton hastened to reply:

'My Lord, I would simply say that the effect of the statement would be that Gregorio had committed the fatal deed. I submit with all respect, my Lord, that I am entitled to give this in evidence.'

'If the learned counsel can give me any book or authority in law which would allow such evidence to be admitted I would welcome it.'

'I submit, my Lord, that no authority in favour of the admissibility of this evidence is necessary. I would like to put it to you, my Lord, that although you are probably correct in saying that this point is new it might, nonetheless, be decided at once.'

'The point, in fact, is already decided. There is not the slightest ground for admitting this kind of evidence.'

'In that case, my Lord, I will rest content with asking the witness—did this man Gregorio resemble in any way the prisoner in the dock?' The witness answered:

'Very closely, sir.'

Mrs. Elizabeth Lambert, who had also been at the Golden Anchor on the night in question, was in full flood of giving evidence for the defence, when she also used the dangerous phrase, Mrs. Shaw 'told me', and again the judge intervened:

'Whatever Mrs. Shaw said to you cannot be received as evidence.' Ribton came in quickly on this point.

'But, my Lord, I submit that what Mrs. Shaw said to the witness is receivable and I would like to cite the ruling in the case of the George Gordon riots where noises created by the mob were received as evidence against the prisoner. I ask you to reserve the point for the consideration of the jury.'

'I shall certainly not do anything of the kind and I am surprised that any gentleman of the Bar should raise so untenable a point.'

Two knives were now produced in court, one found near the Golden Anchor with blood on it, the other near the Bordessa pub without blood, but the court did not establish beyond reasonable doubt their respective owners. Later in the afternoon, defending counsel made an impassioned plea to the jury to acquit Pelizzioni and the judge began his summing up:

'This trial is undoubtedly one of great importance because if the prisoner is convicted his life will in all probability have to atone for the offence. It is nonetheless a very old rule that hearsay evidence is never receivable and a wiser rule never existed. This I say in reply to what has fallen from the learned counsel for the defence, who urged me to accept certain hearsay evidence and placed me in the disagreeable position of being obliged to refuse evidence of this description. It appeared to me at one time that this case might be one of manslaughter because the jury is probably aware that the law views with lenity the infirmities of human nature and sometimes reduces a crime of this description from murder to manslaughter, but I am bound to tell you that if you believe the evidence in this case it amounted not to manslaughter but to murder—and so you must find.'

It was a completely damning summing-up.

Less than fifteen minutes after the jury had retired, it returned and gave its verdict—'Guilty'. The judge then passed sentence:

'Seraphino Pelizzioni, the jury have found you guilty of the murder of Michael Harrington and in my judgment it was utterly impossible for them to have come to any other conclusion. The evidence was about the clearest and the most direct that, after a long course of administration in criminal justice, I have ever known. I am also satisfied that the legal character of the offence is murder and not manslaughter.

'It only remains for me to pass sentence upon you, not in my own language, but in the language which the law of this country prescribes: and that sentence is that you be taken hence to the prison from whence you were brought; that you be hanged by the neck until your body be dead—and may the Lord have mercy on your soul!'

Pelizzioni, who had borne himself with dignified fortitude throughout the trial, burst into protestations of innocence, refused to release the handrail of the dock and had to be torn away by two attendants. But now began one of the private prosecutions whereby the final judgment of the highest tribunal in the land was challenged by an ordinary private citizen who refused to believe that all the machinery of police, lawyers and witnesses had arrived at a true verdict.

Mr. Henry Negretti had followed minutely every detail of the evidence and left the court convinced that an innocent man was about to go to the gallows—unless he threw himself into the impossible task of finding the real murderer. But— finding the murderer apart—how could he, a solitary individual, hope to reverse the huge, complex machine of British justice or even seriously challenge it? None the less, within a few hours, Negretti went to work. His friend, Mr. Negroni, had his own bush-telegraph system of communication among the Italian community in London and Negretti now released urgent enquiries along its invisible wires. Two days later Negretti asked for a report and a conversation closely similar to the following took place privately in Negretti's house.

'You have sounded out everyone we know?' Negretti asked.

'Yes.'

'You have been to Gregorio's lodging?'

'He left there the day after the murder.'

'Does anyone know why he left?'

'He had quarrelled with his employer and talked of leaving his job.'

'Doesn't his employer know where he has gone?'

'No, but we have put out an enquiry for Gregorio in all the carpenters' shops we know who employ Italians.'

'You do realise that we haven't a moment to lose?'

'I know as well as you do that Pelizzioni's life depends on this.'

In the next ten days Negretti abandoned his business and threw himself into his crusade. He went to visit Pelizzioni in prison to reassure him that half the Italian community was working for him. He hired a private agent to intensify their efforts to find Gregorio and he gradually put together entirely fresh and damning evidence against Gregorio. Then came his letter to *The Times*:

'Dear Sir,

In reference to the Saffron Hill murder case discussed in your columns recently I must point out that the police were told on the evening of the fatal occurrence by Mr. Worms, who is a close relative of the deceased man, Mr. Harrington, that they had got hold of the wrong man. Mr. Worms told them that Serafino Pelizzioni did not do it but that a man known as Gregorio did. The answer given by the police I will not give you for I can hardly believe it myself. They do not wish to take action to right a wrong in this matter. The police had Gregorio's knife delivered up to them on the morning after the occurrence and all the circumstances connected with it lucidly explained to them from the giving up of the knife by Gregorio to a friend—the friend throwing it away in Bordessa's back yard—and the potboy of Bordessa's picking it up and handing it over to the police.

'The police were told that Harrington and Gregorio had a scuffle in the tap room not ten minutes before the stabbing took place. The police knew that Gregorio and his brother, John (the latter bleeding at the neck), came back after the fight and asked for their hats out of the bagatelle room and that those hats were given to them by Mrs. Shaw, who fetched them from the bagatelle room, clearly showing that Gregorio and his brother John had been in the room. Lastly, the police never seriously attempted to find Gregorio for they knew that the finding of this man would result in the acquittal of Pelizzioni after having charged him with murder.

'I trust you will also give me an opportunity of answering Mr. John William Baddeley's letter that has appeared in your

impression of to-day by stating that if that gentleman has
still the slightest doubt about Pelizzioni's innocence, perhaps
he will procure a copy of all the sworn depositions of the
witnesses that appeared against him at the trial, read and
analyse them carefully as I have done. His doubts will then
be very soon dispelled.'

Mr. John William Baddeley promptly replied to this letter:

'As I heard the depositions constantly referred to by the
Counsel who defended Pelizzioni at the recent trial, and as
I have full notes of the proceedings, it is unnecessary for me
to accept Mr. Negretti's invitation contained in his letter of
your impression today.

'Perhaps he will say whether he can dispose of the evidence
of the four or five witnesses—I say nothing of the dying man's
identification—who swore that they saw Pelizzioni inflict the
fatal wound, either by showing so great a resemblance between
the two men as to make it probable that they one and all were
mistaken, or that there was a conspiracy between them to
give false evidence against the prisoner; or will he produce any
evidence, either a confession of Gregorio Mogni's, or that of
an eye witness to prove that Pelizzioni did not stab Harrington
but that Gregorio did?'

Negretti was quick to answer:

'Dear Sir,
I beg to answer Mr. Baddeley's letter. Charles Bannister,
who was not called as a witness at the Old Bailey, gave this
evidence in the Magistrate's Court: "I was at the Golden
Anchor on Saffron Hill having some refreshment. I was
persuaded, as there was a disturbance, to go into the bagatelle
room and I went. Almost as soon as I got in a number of
Italians, of whom the prisoner was one, rushed in."

'The reason Mr. Bannister was not called at the final trial,
although he was one of the three persons who were wounded,
is this: Had he been called and asked how he had been stabbed
he would have had to contradict the whole of the witnesses
for the prosecution: for these people, in their anxiety to fix the
crime on Pelizzioni made Pelizzioni rush in at the door alone

and stab Harrington *instanter*: Then he was knocked on the head by the witnesses and held over the body of Harrington until taken into custody by the police, leaving Bannister no time to be stabbed, so that Bannister was, for more reasons than one, wisely left out.

'I will now answer Mr. Baddeley's other question as to the dying man's deposition, that solemn mockery enacted by Mr. Inspector Potter. I almost wish for his own sake Mr. Baddeley had abstained from asking it.

'Pelizzioni, an Italian with a strongly marked Italian countenance, wearing a moustache and dressed in the peculiar garb that Italian workmen adopt, was placed nearest the dying man, along with a number of *Englishmen*, none of whom wore a moustache. I ask Mr. Baddeley to put all prejudice aside and tell me what he thinks of this mode of obtaining a dying man's statement. I will not say anything as to the dying man being under the influence of opium, for we have Inspector Potter's own statement that he "roused him with great difficulty".'

Time, meanwhile, was running out. Within a few short days Pelizzioni faced certain death unless they could trace Gregorio, but the police, confronted with all the qualifying evidence, still refused to take further action. A man had been charged with murder, the elaborate machinery of the law had done its work and no less than eight witnesses confirmed the verdict. What was the use at this late stage of dragging up more details about a man who could not be traced? Moreover the police gave no more than cursory help in trying to find the missing man because now very clearly there was a danger that their whole case might be thrown into serious disrepute.

Negretti redoubled his activities. His private enquiry agent followed up new clues in the search for Gregorio and the bush-telegraph of the Italian community sent out reverberations to smaller communities in provincial cities. Battle was now re-joined in the columns of *The Times* between Negretti, slowly elaborating his evidence in greater detail, and the police authorities rebutting him point by point. On March 14, Mr. Richard Mayne wrote from the Metropolitan Police Office in Whitehall Place:

'I request you will have the goodness to insert in *The Times* the enclosed extracts from police reports in contradiction of additional statements made by Mr. Negretti as published in *The Times* of the 13th instant with regard to the evidence and conduct of the police in the cases of Pelizzioni and Gregorio Mogni.

'I am, sir, your obedient servant,

Richard Mayne.

Statement by Mr. Negretti

'Flash Charley [Richard Fawell] was in the tap room at the time of the affray. This fact was stated before the magistrates by one of the witnesses in the first examination of Gregorio. At page 290 of the Sessions Papers will be found evidence stating that Shaw [the publican] went for the police. I know he went out for the policeman. There happened to be a plain clothes policeman there and he fetched another one in uniform.

Statement in Police Report

'Between six and seven o'clock p.m. on the evening of Dec. 26 1864 Constable Richard Fawell 425A (Flash Charley) was passing (in plain clothes) through Saffron Hill having just left No. 9 Greville Street where he had been making an inquiry, when near the Golden Anchor Mr. Shaw the landlord who was standing outside his house called him and said there was a row in the tap room among the Italians. The constable then went in and seeing a number of Italians fighting and breaking up forms he immediately returned into the street for assistance and called the constable on the beat, William Elliott No. 137G who was close to the house at the time. Mr. Shaw and four of the witnesses who were in the house the whole evening assert that neither Mr. Fawell nor any other constable was in the house until called by Mr. Shaw after the affray commenced.

Statement by Mr. Negretti

'The following letter I have received from Mr. Worms . . .

"Sir, I told the police the same evening that the occurrence took place that in my opinion they had got hold of the wrong man and that they should look after the other man: that I did not think Serafino did it but that Gregorio did. This statement I repeated to the Superintendent of Police one evening this week at the Police Station Clerkenwell.

(Signed) Saul Worms."

Police Statement

'On the evening of the 7th instant I saw Mr. Worms at my office at Clerkenwell Station. He then informed me, as in my report, that he had no recollection of speaking to the police on the evening of the occurrence but that he had spoken to Mr. Negretti and given as his opinion from hearsay that Serafino Pelizzioni was not the man. I have seen all the police who went to the Golden Anchor on the night of the affray and also those on duty in the neighbourhood but no one recollected Saul Worms speaking to him.'

Behind the scenes, unknown to the police, Negretti or Gregorio, an English friend of Harrington's, Mr. Cotton, was also hot on the trail of the second suspect. Archie Cotton ran a second-hand clothes business off Ludgate Circus, not very far removed from the scene of the murder, and was an habitué of the Golden Anchor.

For years he had drunk every other weekend with Harrington in the Golden Anchor, and his sudden brutal death not merely upset him but drove him out in search of vengeance. An ex-merchant seaman who had lost one eye from a cargo accident, he was a melodramatic character who always strode into the pub like a swashbuckling pirate making outrageous demands on the bar-tenders. He carried out these entrances with such theatrical extravagance that no one took him seriously. Almost illiterate, he considered all foreigners as 'scum' and automatically represented Italians as the worst dregs in his social barrel.

The happy-go-lucky, ex-merchant seaman was suddenly converted by the murder into a monster thirsty for revenge on almost anyone in the neighbourhood who looked like an Italian, but when he turned up in court and heard the details of the case, some shrewd sixth sense prevailed over his illiteracy and told him that they were sending the wrong man to the

3

gallows. His interest however—unlike Negretti's—was not in saving an innocent man but in making sure that the person who had 'cut up' Harrington should be brought to book. Above all he wanted to set eyes on the 'shit-bastard—just to see 'im in the flesh—and know 'ee was going down the drop'. His second-hand clothes business gave him many contacts in the East Central and West Central areas and he tapped out a message on his own bush telegraph—find a man called Gregorio.

Several second-hand dealers came in from the Midlands to sell goods to Cotton and he repeated his query to every man he met. Every evening too, instead of drinking in the Golden Anchor, he now combed the neighbourhood talking to any person who might have known Gregorio. On one occasion he presented himself, somewhat the worse for liquor, at the Clerkenwell Police Station, demanded to see Inspector Potter and explained very solemnly that he was investigating the death of 'my friend Harrington'. He wanted to see the Inspector, he said. Eventually he was removed by force from the Station and arrived home to find a message from a second-hand dealer saying that he had found Gregorio. Cotton traced the dealer and they spent half the night trying to follow up the clue. Finally Cotton concluded it was all a nasty practical joke, and staggered back home—alone.

Almost simultaneously, Negretti received an anonymous letter giving a new set of whereabouts for Gregorio, in a Birmingham carpenter's shop. Throwing aside everything, he took the first train to Birmingham and there quickly located the shop. Gregorio was out at lunch when he arrived, but he waited patiently and then in the early afternoon they at last met. Negretti gave this account of what took place:

'I shook my fist in his face and said to him: "You rascal, is it possible you could not go in a fight without using a knife?" He seemed rather staggered but in a second or two he said:

' "Mr. Negretti, you would have done the same if you had been there."

' "Do you know Pelizzioni is going to be hung for it?"

' "No, that can't be true."

' "Yes, he is."

' "Is there no means of saving him?"

' "Only by giving yourself up . . ."

'He reflected a little and seemed confused. Then at last he said: "I am ready", and he got up and put his hat on. As he was going along the passage he was crying and said: "He shall not hang for me".'

In great fear, Gregorio at last arrived in London with Henry Negretti, and together they went to King's Cross Police Station. But now the legal complications began to multiply. Throughout the whole search Negretti believed that the police were obstructionist, putting legal difficulties in the way of any action which did not vindicate their behaviour, and now they escaped procedural difficulties by preparing a charge of aiding and abetting. Since Negretti's plain purpose was to show that Pelizzioni had nothing whatever to do with the crime he refused to be satisfied with what he now regarded as a trumped-up substitute charge. Using all the force of his powerful personality, presenting all the new evidence and detailing the discrepancies in the first trial, he succeeded in re-converting the police charge of aiding and abetting into one of murder.

Negretti now sent the names of a number of witnesses to the solicitors Lewis and Lewis, who had conducted the original defence, and they wrote to the Secretary of State (enclosing a copy of the depositions), asking him to take the case in hand so that there should be a full investigation of all the facts. The Secretary of State answered by stating that he declined to interfere in the matter.

Ironically, the new set of depositions was sent to the Treasury Solicitor in case he could be convinced that, having got one man convicted of murder, the State should show their confidence in that issue by defending the new prisoner, Gregorio Mogni. Obviously, in the Treasury Solicitor's view, Gregorio Mogni could not have murdered Harrington and theoretically it was up to them to defend Mogni and prove their own verdict. But the Treasury Solicitor did not, for obvious reasons, follow this course. Further exchanges now took place between the different lawyers involved, and as the second case proceeded rapidly towards the Central Criminal Court, the charge was again revised to one of manslaughter. Simultaneously, something far more important to Negretti was at last conceded. He had fought without ceasing, day and night, to get a stay of execution for Pelizzioni and now dramatically it was granted.

On March 3 the second trial concerning the nature of the death of Michael Harrington began at the Old Bailey but Negretti found himself in something of a dilemma. He must at all costs clear Pelizzioni of any complicity in the original charge of murder but he did not want to ruin the life of Gregorio. In the end he was partly responsible for Mr. Montagu Williams undertaking to defend Gregorio. Mr. Serjeant Ballantine, Mr. Hardinge Giffard and Mr. F. H. Lewis conducted the prosecution. Mr. Serjeant Ballantine opened:

'It would be idle to suppose that the very remarkable circumstances out of which the present enquiry arose have not been brought to the attention of the jury through the medium of the press. The prisoner is about to be tried for an offence of which another person has been convicted and for which he is now under sentence of death. It is, therefore, of paramount importance, both in the interests of the person and also of public justice, that we should on this occasion arrive at the right conclusion. It would be a disgrace to the law of this country if a person might be at liberty to step forward and assume the responsibility of a crime of which another has been guilty and an equally monstrous thing if an innocent man were to suffer a penalty which another has really incurred.'

Giovanni Mogni, the brother of Gregorio Mogni, was one of the early witnesses called and examined by Ballantine. Giovanni said:

'I was in the Golden Anchor pub on Saffron Hill on December 26, from about 6.0 to 6.30. When I first saw my brother, there had been some dispute with the landlord. A disturbance took place and the door of the bagatelle room was opened and I was beaten with sticks. I entered the room and I directly received a blow on the head and some kicks. My face was all covered with blood. I still have a scar on my head. I said to my brother: "Brother, they kill me." I saw him put his hand in his pocket and pull out a knife. They were then beating me and my brother. And then I saw my brother use the knife.'

A knife was now handed to Mogni, and Ballantine asked:

'Can you identify who this knife belongs to?'

'That is my brother's knife.'

'Thank you. I would now like to turn to another matter. Can you tell the jury—was Pelizzioni in the room at the time of the affray?'

'Pelizzioni was not in the bagatelle room when I left. I did not return to the room but up to the time I left Pelizzioni was not in the bagatelle room.'

'And what happened after the affray?'

'I had a hat on when I went into the room as had also my brother. The hats were left in the room. I got mine back about ten minutes afterwards and I saw my brother take his hat at the same time. I afterwards saw him at John Street near the place where we lived. That was about seven or eight. I did not that night know he was going to leave London. I spoke to him in the morning about 8 o'clock as to what happened in the bagatelle room. He told me he had used the knife.'

'And finally, Mr. Mogni, were you examined in the original trial for the murder of Harrington by either side?'

'No, I wasn't.'

Pietro Marazzi, a looking-glass silverer, now came into the witness box and spoke through an interpreter.

'I was there by the bagatelle board and they were beating us with sticks. A few seconds after Gregorio got into the room I saw him with a knife in his hand. I said to him: "For God's sake, Gregorio, put away that knife." Gregorio said: "Let me do it, or we won't get out of this room alive." I met the prisoner the same evening on Cross Street about half an hour after I had seen him with a knife in his hand. He threw his arms round my neck and said: "My dear Marazzi, what have I done?" I said: "You used the knife?" He said: "Yes, I stabbed three or four." '

Ballantine next made a statement to the judge and jury:

'There is one point in connection with this case in respect to which I have had great doubt and still entertain much difficulty—namely, the calling of Pelizzioni, a convicted murderer, to make a statement on the subject. It has seemed to me extremely repugnant to the principles on which our criminal law is conducted to admit such evidence. However, since in the course of the enquiry matters have arisen which still leave a probability of Pelizzioni having committed the crime, I propose calling Pelizzioni himself to clear up the last of these doubts, leaving any further investigation to my learned friend on the other side which he thinks necessary for the ends of justice.'

There was a considerable stir in the court as Pelizzioni walked up the stairs to the dock with great dignity. He gave his evidence calmly and gravely in English, without any of what the judge called 'the expressive action' which characterized some of the other Italian witnesses. Ballantine asked the witness:

'You have been brought here from Newgate Prison?'

'Yes.'

'Where you were under sentence of death?'

'Yes.'

'I fear I must now go back over details of the case in which you have already been examined. You were at the Golden Anchor on the night of December 26?'

'Yes.'

'But you were not there when the trouble began?'

'No.'

'Where were you when the trouble began?'

'I was at Bordessa's house when someone came and told me there was a row at the Anchor among the Italians and the English, and that my cousins were involved.'

'What did you do?'

'I went down to the Anchor with the idea of making things quiet and taking my cousins away.'

'Tell the jury what happened after that.'

'Directly I went into the tap room I heard a woman screaming. It was the landlady of the public house. When she saw me she called me and said: "My God, don't let them make a row." I said: "No, Eliza. Get your husband to keep the English quiet and I will try to keep the Italians quiet." I left her to go to the bagatelle room where I thought the row was, and directly I opened the door just a little way I was knocked down by a blow on the head. My head was inside the room and the other part of my body was outside. Somebody inside the room caught hold of me and dragged me inside. I was kept down there until a policeman came and when the policeman came somebody said: "I will give you in charge." I said: "Give me in charge. What for?"'

'Finally, did you have a weapon with you at the time?'

'No weapon, no. But I had a small white penknife which was taken out of my right hand breeches pocket by the police.'

A close cross-examination failed to shake Pelizzioni on any of the points he had made. Cross-examination of other prosecution witnesses also produced very few telling points. Giovanni Schiena was then examined by Ballantine:

'I used to live in Birmingham and I saw the prisoner there. He told me he had left London because he was in trouble. He also told me he was the man who had killed the Englishman. He told me he wished to have his clothes sent him. I never communicated with the police, but I wrote a note to a man in London.'

And then just when it seemed that Pelizzioni must emerge triumphant and be cleared without the slightest manner of doubt, Williams, the defending counsel, suddenly produced the potboy at the Golden Anchor who had appeared for the prosecution in the first case and now reiterated his story powerfully. Other witnesses followed supporting him.

Peerless, the police surgeon, also repeated that the victim died from wounds which might have been inflicted by such a knife as had been produced in court *at the first trial.*

Pelizzioni was now recalled to the witness box and cross-examined by Williams:

'When I was taken to the police station,' Pelizzioni said, 'the policeman read a paper to me. I did not understand what it was, my head pained me so much. I didn't know that I was charged with stabbing Rebbeck.'

'Did the policeman refer to blood on your hands?'

'Yes, and I said it came from my head.'

'Did you not say that you were protecting yourself?'

'No, I never said I was protecting myself. I did not understand what the phrase meant so I couldn't have used it.'

When it came to the evidence of forty-one-year-old Gregorio Mogni, he spoke no English and an interpreter was called.

At this point, Williams announced that he must make himself more familiar with certain details of the case before he could proceed further. He thought it his duty to the prisoner to ask for a short adjournment. Mr. Justice Wyles asked: 'What do you call a short adjournment, because you know that this jury cannot separate.'

'Three-quarters of an hour will do.'

'Certainly—if you desire it, much longer. In fact I will adjourn the trial until tomorrow morning if necessary. The Court will adjourn for ten minutes now and in that time you can make up your mind.'

After a short interval the trial resumed and then at last Williams addressed the jury:

'You have to answer three questions,' he said. 'Whether Gregorio has actually confessed that he killed Harrington— whether the facts of the case bear out that confession—and whether considering all the circumstances of the affray he acted in self-defence. I contend that all that Gregorio's confession amounts to is that he used the knife and stabbed about him in self-defence. He has not confessed to having killed a man at all and the witnesses called at the last trial prove that Harrington fell not by the hand of Gregorio but by that of Pelizzioni.'

Williams then went at length into the evidence as to the affray, contending that if the prisoner really did strike the fatal blow it was after he and his brother had been brutally beaten and when he thought they were in danger of their lives. The offence—if it had taken place—was thus reduced to justifiable homicide.

Twenty minutes later Mr. Justice Ryles began his summing up. He stressed two points. First the possibility that Gregorio's story was nothing but another example of that pathological reaction well known to the law—a false confession—and second the remarkable part played in the whole affair by Henry Negretti.

'There is another very prominent actor,' the judge continued, 'a gentleman I take to be the prosecutor—namely, Mr. Negretti, and nobody who has heard the evidence can hesitate to believe that he acted in this case with a disinterested and active humanity which was remarkable and which many profess and few so promptly and effectually practise.

'But the annals of crime contain many cases of false confession. There are, in fact, many instances of false confessions where people have surrendered themselves up, until their relatives were safe. You must decide the nature of Gregorio's story. If the prisoner, Pelizzioni, were engaged in an undertaking with a common object to rout the English from the bagatelle room with knives, and Pelizzioni used his, this was his act and his act alone.

'If, on the other hand, members of the jury, you come to the conclusion that the killing of Harrington is clearly brought home to the prisoner you must find him guilty. If you find otherwise you should acquit him. But if you do not know which of the two did it, you must clearly remember in such circumstances that the prisoner must also be acquitted.'

It was a whole long hour before the jury returned to the courtroom, and the foreman spoke:

'We find the prisoner guilty, my Lord, but with a recommendation to mercy on account of the provocation received and the injury done to his brother.'

'I think the jury has well and truly found,' stated the judge. 'In passing sentence I take into account not only your recommendation to mercy but the anxiety which the prisoner has displayed to acquit a person whom he believed, rightly or wrongly, to be innocent. I will say no more except that the sentence of this court under the circumstances, and reprobating as it was meant to do the use of the knife, is to be kept to penal servitude for five years.'

CHAPTER III

THE CASE OF MISS CASS
[1887]

WHEN POLICE CONSTABLE BOWEN ENDACOTT arrested a young woman named Miss Cass one evening in the spring of 1887 on a charge of soliciting for common prostitution, he did not dream what prolonged, agonizing and finally—for him— disastrous consequences would follow. Nor did he bargain for the implacable determination of a certain Madame Bowman in whose house, at No. 19, Southampton Row, Miss Cass was said to work and live.

The first intimation that a straightforward charge of soliciting had gone sadly awry reached the British public in *The Times* for July 11, 1887: 'The Lord Chancellor has commenced an enquiry into the conduct of Mr. Newton, magistrate at Marl- borough Street Police Court, during a hearing of a charge against Miss Cass.'

But it was not Mr. Newton who finally faced the inflexible crusade launched by Madame Bowman: it was the ordinary 'bobby on his beat', P.C. Endacott. Madame Bowman had been summoned to Tottenham Court Road Police Station in order to bail out her twenty-four-year-old employee, Miss Cass, and reacted with such shocked indignation that the Police Inspector in charge realized trouble must inevitably follow.

Confronted with what she regarded as a gross miscarriage of justice, Madame Bowman described the police as criminals, hurried off to see her lawyer, and finally wrote a letter, not to a commonplace Police Inspector or even the Police Com- missioner, but to the Lord Chancellor of England himself.

The steadily growing ferment finally exploded in the face of the police and the public. As *The Times* reported: 'The two ladies, accompanied by their legal adviser, Mr. Bartrum, waited upon the Lord Chancellor at half-past two on Friday afternoon. The interview, which was private, lasted about an hour. Mr. Bartrum stated on Saturday that "the probability was the enquiry would take the form of a prosecution of a police constable for perjury . . ." '

When the enquiry actually began, on July 11, at the Central Police Station, Great Scotland Yard, it was chaired by Sir Charles Warren, the Chief Commissioner of the Metropolitan Police, assisted by the Recorder of Lincoln, Mr. Horace Smith, as Legal Assessor. Mr. Grain and Mr. Abrahams represented Miss Cass and her employer, Madame Bowman, and Mr. St. John Wonter represented Police Constable Endacott. Mr. Staples, the Chief Clerk of the Commissioners, and Superintendent Cutbush, of Great Scotland Yard, were also present.

The enquiry took place in an ordinary room which was part of the normal police offices, and somehow seemed completely out of keeping with the prolonged, solemn and highly significant events which presently unfolded.

Sir Charles Warren opened the proceedings by reading a letter from the Home Secretary, dated the 7th inst., directing an enquiry into the circumstances of the arrest. Sir Charles then asked if the representatives of Miss Cass desired to have the enquiry an open one in the presence of press representatives.

Mr. Grain replied: 'Yes, decidedly.'

Sir Charles now read a second letter from Mrs. Bowman to the Police Commissioner.

'I beg to report a gross case of injustice to a young woman in my employ. On Tuesday night (28th), while passing down Regent Street, she was arrested by Police Constable Endacott, D. R. 42, and was charged at the police station with accosting gentlemen. The police constable said she was in company with a second female, and that they had accosted gentlemen. Both statements are false. Mr. Newton thought fit to "caution" her when discharging her, and thus cast a lasting stigma and shame upon a poor, innocent girl.'

The letter went on to say that the girl's mind had been 'quite unhinged', that she was injured by the charges and the reports of the case, and asked for an enquiry into 'this iniquitous injustice'.

Sir Charles Warren now called for the charge-sheets to see whether, in the case of Miss Cass, any endorsement by the magistrate had been added. One word only appeared in the appropriate column: Discharged. The principal features of the charge-sheet were now read to the court.

Time	Age	Name and address	Charge	Person charging	Degree of education
10 p.m.	23	Elizabeth Cass, 19, Southampton Row, Bloomsbury, prostitute	Being a common prostitute, annoying male passengers for the purpose of prostitution at Regent Street	P.C. Endacott DR42	Imp

Mr. Grain, representing Miss Cass, called Inspector Wylie, of Marlborough Street Police Court, as the first witness. Within a few minutes he put this question to the Inspector: 'Did the magistrate, when he discharged Miss Cass, make any comment on the conduct of Constable Endacott?'

'No, sir.'

'He found no fault with him?'

'No, sir.'

'Do you think that the officer who entered the charge had a right to put "prostitute" and "common prostitute" to the name of a person who gave an address?'

'A constable can so enter a charge if he knows it, or if the woman so describes herself.'

'But if a person is apparently respectable and denies such conduct, is a constable justified in so charging her?'

'The charge should only be made where the constable

knows the woman to be a common street-walker, and he has no right to assume she is such without good evidence.'

'But wouldn't it be the duty of a constable to make an enquiry to prove whether those assertions of an apprently respectable woman were true?'

'If such a person gave her address, the police might send to find out if they had any doubts as to the charge.'

'But this was not done in the case of Miss Cass, who gave her address.'

Grain then pressed Inspector Wylie to give an exact account of what the magistrate did say when discharging the girl. Wylie answered that 'the report in the newspapers is to my mind correct'.

The report was then read: 'If you are a respectable girl, as you say you are, do not walk Regent Street or stop gentlemen at 10 o'clock of a night. If you do, you will be fined or sent to prison. Go away and do not come here again.'

A long wrangle now ensued between Sir Charles Warren, Superintendent Cutbush and Mr. Grain. Sir Charles remarked that if a woman charged a man with an offence, corroborative evidence was required, whereas there were many cases like this one where only one man's evidence was taken as being sufficient against a woman. From the magistrate's answer to a letter of Sir Charles Warren's it appeared to be mandatory for a police constable to arrest any person who, in the view of any constable, was said to be soliciting. The evidence of one constable—and one constable only—would therefore, in such cases, be accepted.

Grain pointed out the dangers involved and then called Sergeant Cumber, the acting inspector who had taken details of the case at the time of Miss Cass's arrest.

'You remember very well the case of Miss Cass?'

'Yes, sir.'

'When she gave you an address, did you send to make enquiries about the truth of her statement?'

'No—I simply sent for assurances of bail.'

'Who went to get bail?'

'Police Constable Endacott.'

'And what did Mrs. Bowman say when he called on her?'

'She did say there was some mistake and she would attend the police court.'

'Did she not also say that the young woman was in her employ?'

'Yes.'

'And that she was perfectly respectable?'

'Yes.'

Asked by Grain whether Mrs. Bowman expressed indignation, Sergeant Cumber at first failed to reply, but when the question was repeated, he said: 'Well, no.'

He then went on to describe how a gaoler had brought Miss Cass from the cell in which she was 'temporarily placed' to see Mrs. Bowman.

Grain returned to the attack:

'Do you recall Mrs. Bowman saying to her, at once: "What is this—what gentleman have you been speaking to?"'

'No, I do not.'

'And you don't recall Miss Cass saying: "I spoke to no one and no one spoke to me until a policeman took me by my arm and brought me here?"'

'No.'

'Are you saying that the words were not used?'

'No—I would not say the words were not used.'

'You admit that she denied the charge?'

'Yes.'

'But you do not remember the words she used?'

'No.'

'But you do remember Mrs. Bowman saying she would bail the girl out?'

'Yes—and I fixed bail at £2.'

'Mrs. Bowman did say, did she not, £20 if you like?'

'Yes, she did.'

'Now, when you finally came to fill up the charge-sheet, why did you put the words "common prostitute" under the heading Occupation?'

'The prisoner made no reply when I asked her what her occupation was.'

'But was she not weeping and too distressed at the time?'

'No, she just appeared sullen to me.'

'Where, then, did you get the idea that she was a common prostitute?'

'I got it from Constable Endacott.'

'Do you make any difference between one person and another—between a young and innocent-looking, respectably dressed young person unknown to you and another who is notorious as one of these characters?'

'She was described as such by Constable Endacott, and in regard to her respectability she was as other prostitutes.'

'Did you ask Endacott what sort of gentleman she stopped?'

'No.'

'By what right did you describe Miss Cass as a prostitute in one part of the charge-sheet and *common* prostitute in another?' (The professional distinction between the two terms meant that a *common* prostitute was well known as a member of that profession, whereas a prostitute was not.)

'Endacott said he had seen her about Regent Street for the last six weeks—he left the impression in my mind that she was a common prostitute.'

'Why, if Constable Endacott had seen her about for six weeks, had he not arrested her before?'

'I don't know.'

'You did not trouble to ask him?'

Cumber remained silent in the face of this question, and Grain tried another approach:

'When Mrs. Bowman arrived at the Police Station she did say, did she not, that she could give evidence that the prisoner was a respectable woman?'

'She did.'

'Did you point this out to the magistrate later, in court?'

'No.'

'Why not?'

'In any case before the magistrate, I do not think it is my duty to tell him there is evidence for the defence unless the magistrate directly asks me.'

'What grounds did you have for describing her education on the charge-sheet as Imp., or Imperfect, when you say she did not even speak?'

'I saw her sign her name in the bail book.'

These early stages of the enquiry were fairly straightforward, but it was quite obvious by now that it must last several days.

On the second day, although the proceedings were still a court of enquiry and not yet a trial, Mr. Wonter—in effect—

put the case for the defence by ironically announcing that he failed to see what exactly they were all gathered here to do.

'I must say that Constable Endacott has made a statement on oath, and for what he has said—if it turned out that his statement is untrue—he is, of course, completely responsible. But I do not see how we can mend matters by examining persons who are not under the obligation of oath, and it is difficult, therefore, to see what we are called here to do. If the constable is to be called upon to give evidence, I shall have to exercise my discretion. But as this enquiry has taken the form of an investigation into the conduct of the constable by his superior officers, the responsibility should be upon the Commissioner rather than upon the constable.

'At the same time, this is not an enquiry into the character of Miss Cass and her employer. At the present moment Miss Cass figures before the public as a young lady who is seriously injured. That may be a very proper light in which to see her, and as I was instructed only yesterday afternoon I am not in a position to say anything to the contrary . . .

'Before I hear any action on the part of this constable, I desire—in order that I shall not involve the constable in any false step—to make further enquiries. I should, I must say, like to know whether the constable is here on any particular charge or whether this is a roving commission to satisfy an angry public.'

The last remark was fully justified since some sections of the press had seized the opportunity to launch a two-faced crusade on behalf of Miss Cass combining salacious details of prostitutes' habits with a demand that respectable women be protected from gratuitous defamation and wrongful arrest.

Sir Charles Warren now explained—as if it were not already self-evident—that the enquiry was the result of a directive by the Home Office, but so far as Constable Endacott was concerned, he did not propose giving him orders as a superior officer, and the constable remained an entirely free agent.

Mr. Grain now took up the argument once more and said that the Government clearly desired all the details of this case to be brought out into the open by the enquiry. He proposed to tender the statements of Miss Cass and Madame Bowman and to call Endacott for questioning, providing the enquiry could first establish what questions were thought to be fit questions in the circumstances under which they operated.

Further discussion followed to determine the precise limits of the enquiry. Mr. Grain then recalled Sergeant Cumber, and asked him:

'When the prisoner was first brought in to Tottenham Court Road Station, do you recall what she said?'

'She said many things and . . .'

'Did she say in particular, "I wish I could convince you that you have made a mistake"?'

'I do not recall that.'

'You are saying that she did not say that?'

'No—I do not say she did not utter those words.'

'Do you, then, remember Miss Cass saying, "The policeman says that I was with another girl, but I was alone"?'

'I heard something of that, but it was later, when Mrs. Bowman came.'

'Did you make a record of what the prisoner said?'

'No.'

'Why was that?'

'There is no rule about taking down what a prisoner says except in serious cases like murder.'

'And who judges whether the case is serious enough to record?'

'The Acting Inspector.'

'Let me try to refresh your memory further since there is no written record. Did you hear Miss Cass say, "I am a stranger in London and tonight is the first I have been out alone"?'

'Yes, she did say something like that, but, again, it was when Mrs. Bowman came.'

'It is also true, is it not, that Miss Cass pleaded with you to fetch Madame Bowman, saying that everything she had said would be found to be correct?'

'Yes, that is so . . .'

'Now I understand Endacott came out to look at the girl in the cell passage?'

'That is correct.'

'And when she said, "I have only been from home six weeks", Endacott replied, "You said three weeks just now"?'

'No, I do not recall that.'

'Did you at any time hear Endacott say, "Don't tell lies"?'
'No, at no time.'

'When Mrs. Bowman eventually arrived, did she not at once bitterly complain about "the mistake, the very cruel mistake, the police [had] made about the girl"?'

'I cannot say whether she said that.'

Mr. Grain indicated that he had come to the end of his questions, and Mr. Wonter for the 'defence' now rose to examine Cumber:

'How long have you known Constable Endacott?'

'Five years.'

'And in all those years he seemed to you entirely trustworthy?'

'Yes, very trustworthy.'

'In fact, he had been placed on this duty in regard to streetwalkers because of his trustworthiness?'

'That is so.'

'Is it not true that some prostitutes are gaudily dressed and some respectably?'

'It is, sir.'

'In fact, there are times when nothing in their garb would mark them out as prostitutes?'

'Yes.'

'Did Miss Cass, when charged, appear to you distressed?'

'No, she took it very quietly and was not crying.'

'Was there anything very different in this case from scores of others which come into your station every night?'

'No, nothing.'

A stir ran through the enquiry room as Miss Cass was now called, and a pleasant-looking young woman who seemed younger than her years entered 'demurely'—as one newspaper put it—and 'quailed before all those searching eyes'. Under examination by Mr. Grain, she said, in a low voice:

'I am 24 years of age, and was born at Grantham. I have been in several employments as a dressmaker, mostly near Scotland. I went into Madame Bowman's service on June 7 as forewoman. In addition to my salary, I had board and lodging. Madame Bowman has a niece, with whom I sleep. My duties end about 8 o'clock as a rule, but often I am in the work-room afterwards. Before going to Madame Bowman I stayed with Mr. and Mrs. Tompkins, at 82, Durham Road, Manor Park, Forest Gate. I had been in Mr. Tompkins' employ at Stockton. I know no one in London except Madame Bowman, Mr. and Mrs. Tompkins, and their families, and a person now at Shoolbred's. I had never lived in London before I came up to Manor Park, and was not in the least acquainted with the streets of London up till June 28.'

Mr. Grain now led her with more specific questions:

'Have you ever been out alone in London before?'

'On one Saturday afternoon only.'

'What did you do then?'

'I went to Liverpool Street to take a train to visit Mr. and Mrs. Tompkins.'

'Did Madame Bowman know where you were going?'

'Yes, she did.'

'Had you ever been alone in Regent Street before June 28?'

'I have never been there but once before, and that was one afternoon with Mrs. Tompkins.'

'Have you ever before been alone near the street at night?'

'No, I have never been anywhere near the street at night.'

'When were you, in fact, there?'

'On Tuesday, June 28, Jubilee Day. After working until after 8.30, I went out with the knowledge of Madame Bowman, who gave me leave.'

'What was the object of your outing?'

'I wanted to purchase some gloves, but I was not going to any particular shop.'

The witness was next asked to give a detailed account of her movements, turning left this way into certain streets, right that way, passing the British Museum and along Oxford Street to Regent Circus. It was obvious to any Londoner, from her description, that anyone out shopping might have followed such a path. And then she said that—afraid of getting lost at Regent Circus—she turned round to walk back again and shrank away as a policeman grabbed her arm.

Grain asked Miss Cass to describe in her own words what happened then, and she launched into a fluent narrative:

'I found someone take my arm and I turned round. It was the policeman Endacott who had so taken my arm, and he said, "I want you." I said, "What?" He said, "I have been watching you for six weeks." I said, "You have made a mistake; I have only been in this part three weeks." He said, "You and that other girl." I replied, "I was alone." He said, "No, you were not; I have been watching you some time." Then he turned down a side street, holding me, and I asked him where he was taking me, and he said, "To Tottenham Court Road Police Station." I asked him how far that was, and he said, "Not far." I asked him what for, and he said that gentlemen had complained about me speaking to them. I said he had made a mistake, for I had spoken to no one. He said I had, for he had been watching me for some weeks. I said I had only come from the country six weeks altogether, and he said, "Why, you said three weeks just now." I asked him to take me to Madame Bowman's, telling him that I was working and living there, at 19, Southampton Row. I pressed him to go there with me, but he said, "No; you must see the inspector first." I asked him to let me walk without his taking hold of my arm, and he said, "No; for then in the morning you will say that I let you go." I said, "In the morning! What?" and he did not answer.'

Grain now turned his examination of Miss Cass to the morning after these events when she was brought before the magistrate, Mr. Newton, at the Marlborough Street Police Court and Constable Endacott repeated verbally the charge of soliciting.

'Did Mr. Newton ask for your own account of the events of the previous night?'

'No.'

'But he did ask you what you had to say.'

'Yes, and I told him it was all untrue. I had not walked the streets, I had not been in the streets at night before, and I worked for Madame Bowman.'

Madame Bowman was now called into the equivalent of the witness box in the enquiry. Examined by Mr. Grain, she gave a spirited, not to say indignant, account of the events which led to the beginning of her crusade. Grain's opening question was:

'You have been in business for some considerable time?'

'Yes,' came the answer. 'I have been in business in London for thirty years.'

'How long have you resided at your present address?'

'For over seven years.'

'Now tell us how you employed Miss Cass, and what transpired.'

'She came to me with the highest references and I employed her on June 7, and she worked every night after that until past 8 at night. She has not been out except to post a letter during the weeks since—she usually stays in to work or write —and sometimes, on Saturday, goes to a friend at Manor Park.'

'She is, I believe, a comparative stranger to London?'

'Yes, she is a stranger.'

'Her behaviour has always been satisfactory to you?'

'Yes. Her conduct is in accordance to her character— exemplary—and she is most diligent in the business.'

'What happened when Police Constable Endacott called on you?'

Madame Bowman had waited a long time for this moment, and now she plunged in with relish to explain just how offensive Constable Endacott had been in stating, and in aggressively repeating, that the girl had walked the streets accosting strange gentlemen. When she came to Mr. Newton, in her account she warmed to her task. His conduct had been 'offensive, overbearing and in every way insulting'.

It now became clear that Madame Bowman was defending not only Miss Cass's reputation, but her own. Why she, a long-established and reputable business woman, should have been dealt with almost as if she, too, were a street-walker was beyond her comprehension, and certainly beyond her tolerance.

Grain continued:

'You were quite willing to give further testimony in the magistrates' court?'

'Yes, but I was brushed aside.'

'If you had known more about police-court procedure . . .'

'I would certainly have given more evidence.'

A break occurred in the proceedings at this point while various messengers were sent to trace another detective sergeant who had also been present in the police station on the night of Miss Cass's arrest.

Meanwhile a huge discrepancy in the proceedings had become apparent to everyone involved in the case. Mr. Wonter, for Police Constable Endacott, had stated at the outset that he did not understand exactly what the court was supposed to do since no one was on oath. He had also admitted that he did not yet know sufficient about the case to carry out any thorough cross-examination of witnesses. Thus, as each witness was examined by Grain, Wonter simply asked leave to reserve any questions, 'for the reasons I have stated'. The result at this stage was an overwhelming superabundance of unquestioned evidence in favour of Miss Cass.

One hour later the court of enquiry resumed once more, with Detective Sergeant Morgan contributing details which told both for and against Constable Endacott.

He said: 'I was reading in the station when the case came in, but, hearing something, I looked round and saw a young woman falling to the ground . . .'

A murmur of surprise went round the enquiry room. This was the first time anyone had mentioned the dramatic collapse of Miss Cass in the police station.

Grain pressed the point:

'Could you tell us the cause of her falling?'

'No, I cannot say what was the cause, but I ordered some water to be brought and two constables picked her up and seated her. She appeared to be giddy or faint.'

'What happened when Sergeant Cumber arrived?'

'Cumber asked Endacott what he knew about the prisoner, and he said he had known the young woman as walking Regent Street for some time.'

'What did Miss Cass say?'

'Sergeant Cumber said, "You have heard the charge", but Miss Cass made no reply.'

Grain paused before speaking very deliberately at this point. 'I want you to consider my last question very carefully,' he said. 'Is it true that since all the events you have narrated took place you have talked them over in some detail with Sergeant Cumber?'

Detective Sergeant Morgan admitted that this was true.

Two fresh witnesses who supported the evidence given by Endacott were now examined, and one, Constable Bareham, repeated that Miss Cass failed to make a reply when asked, on the night of her arrest, what occupation she followed. The second witness, Inspector Wyborn, gave Endacott 'a high character' and bore testimony to the excellent manner in which he had carried out very responsible duties.

But by now the overweighting of witnesses and evidence in favour of Miss Cass had become so blatant that Wonter at last intervened and asked for an adjournment until the 21st, which would give him time to make detailed enquiries into the facts and people involved in the case.

If it seemed extraordinary to the layman that the enquiry should have begun at all without such preliminaries, the point was made without any particular emphasis on these opening exchanges.

Almost a week later the same group of people once more filed into the cold, informal room in Scotland Yard. Sir Charles Warren reopened proceedings.

Wonter, for P.C. Endacott, now led the counter-attack by calling Superintendent Draper, Chief of the Police Division under which Endacott served. In examination, he stated that before questions were asked in the House of Commons about the Cass case, he interrogated Endacott, searching for some independent proof of the statements he had made about Miss Cass. Endacott then named a Mr. James Wheatley, who witnessed the arrest, and Superintendent Draper arranged for this person to call at the police station to be interviewed.

James Wheatley, a carpenter and joiner, of 4, William Street, Manchester Square, now entered the enquiry room. In answer to Wonter, he said that he had known Constable Endacott by sight for some time, but he did not know his name until this case received publicity in the newspapers. Questioned by Grain, he stated that on June 28 he was standing at the corner of Margaret Street—a turning out of Regent Street between Oxford Circus and Langham Place—at about 9.30 or 10 when he saw the girl arrested.

'Did you see the actual arrest?'

'No. I saw the girl in the custody of P.C. Endacott and she was walking as coolly as could be.'

'Had you seen this girl before?'

'Yes, I believe she was the same girl I had seen in the company of a fair woman . . .'

Before pressing home his questions, Grain now called Miss Cass once more. She entered the room and stood facing the witness as Grain said: 'Are you sure this is the young lady you saw with the person you refer to as the fair girl?'

'Almost sure.'

'Would you be prepared to say that on oath?'

'I could almost say so on oath.'

'But you would not go so far as to say you *are absolutely sure*?'

'No.'

'In fact, you might have been mistaken.'

'Yes.'

Wonter took up the examination again and established that the fair woman alleged to have been seen with Miss Cass was —despite her façade as a respectable married woman—known to Wheatley as a prostitute. Grain intervened again and drew the admission from Wheatley that nothing about Miss Cass indicated a practising prostitute . . . 'except that she walked with the policeman as if she was used to it'.

Detective Inspector Robson now came before the court and stated that when sent by his superintendent to interview a Mr. Reeves, manager of a jeweller's shop in Great Portland Street, Reeves had said to him:

'I know Miss Cass to be what she was called and I know, through Mrs. Frampton (the fair lady). I saw Mrs. Frampton last night and she told me that her friend Eliza had been locked up, and I know her friend Eliza was Elizabeth Cass.' Reeves had added that Mrs. Frampton lived in Carlisle Street, but when an officer went with Reeves to Carlisle Street, he failed to point out Mrs. Frampton's house.

Wonter immediately sought to modify this failure by putting two questions to Detective Inspector Robson:

'Are not all the houses in Carlisle Street very much alike?'

'Yes, it is difficult to tell one from another.'

'And what sort of character has Carlisle Street?'

'Not a good one at the hands of the police.'

Robson, continuing his statement, repeated a very damaging phrase from Reeves. 'He declared to me that Elizabeth Cass had accosted him on several occasions.'

The Assessor must, at this point, have become very concerned about the legal validity of the procedures of the enquiry. Hearsay evidence was being bandied about with a cavalier disregard for the rules of evidence.

'Where is Mr. Reeves?' he suddenly demanded. 'He should be here to give evidence.

The Inspector replied: 'He has failed to come, and a constable is waiting to bring him in when he arrives at his shop in Great Portland Street.'

The Assessor clearly felt that Miss Cass should have an opportunity to challenge Detective Inspector Robson's statement, and she was recalled. Examined by Grain, she said: 'I do not know anyone named Frampton, nor do I know where Carlisle Street is. I have never been there.'

'But you have been to Portland Place?'

'Yes—once—on June 28.'

'You had not been there before or since?'

'No, sir.'

'But there is one other part of London you have visited recently?'

'Yes, the house of Mr. and Mrs. Tompkins, at Manor Park.'

This was clearly the point to call Mrs. Tompkins. When she appeared, she stoutly defended the reputation of Elizabeth Cass:

'She was employed in my husband's business at Stockton for two years and she gave every satisfaction. She is a highly moral and well-conducted girl. She also came to us with an excellent character from the predecessors in the business, and she fully sustained that character in every way.'

'Did Miss Cass correspond with you when you came to London?'

'Yes. She wrote this year saying she wanted to come to London, too, and we invited her to stay with us at Manor Park until she found a position.'

'When did she come?'

'In April.'

'And her habits after arriving?'

'She never went out in the evening, but I went to town twice with her, and once we walked down Regent Street.'

'How would you describe her general demeanour?'

'She was particularly quiet; in fact absurdly so—a most retiring girl.'

Surprisingly, Wonter put no questions to this witness. Grain next recalled Mrs. Bowman, but when he attempted to get fresh evidence about a duplicate visiting card belonging to her, the Assessor intervened. Such evidence, he said, could not be taken. 'The court will hear anyone who comes in person, but we cannot have third-person statements. Many anonymous statements have been sent to us, but we cannot go into these.'

At this juncture a messenger arrived from Marlborough Police Court with the sworn deposition of Constable Endacott himself. After careful examination, it was temporarily set aside while a Madame Fernando Pietra, a Frenchwoman of 'some forty years', bustled into the enquiry room elaborately dressed and exuding 'a distinct odour of scent'.

The enquiry now entered upon a new and extraordinary phase. A considerable exchange developed between the ebullient, so-called Madame Pietra and Sir Charles Warren. Madame Pietra passionately declared that her real name must not be given because it would reflect badly on the business in which she held an important position. In the course of considerable wrangling, Sir Charles Warren and the Assessor assured her that if she gave her name and the address of her firm it would be preserved in the highest confidence, and she could, in any case, refuse to answer any questions which she found dangerous to the reputation of her company.

'It will be upon my conscience,' the lady then declared passionately, 'if I do not make a statement.' Finally she chose a second name under which to speak—Botellier—and this was the burden of her evidence.

'I am a dressmaker working in Regent Street, and I was going home, up Regent Street, on June 28, when I saw Miss Cass with a fair girl. They were close together and they took hold of a gentleman's arm. The policeman Endacott pushed the girl Miss Cass and she was saucy to him, and he then took her.' (Endacott's deposition said he ran after Miss Cass and there was no accusation of sauciness.) 'One of the two girls,' Madame Botellier continued, 'was dark with her hair cut like a boy's, and the other was fair.' (Miss Cass had dark, boyishly cut hair.) 'I have seen Miss Cass often during the last two months in the same area with another woman. And I know the fair lady is certainly a fast woman. I have seen many such arrests.'

Grain came in to cross-examine her. 'Why in particular

should you notice the arrest of Miss Cass when you had seen so many other similar arrests?'

'I don't know.'

'And how, at 9.30 at night, could you so clearly see the arrest across the broad thoroughfare of Regent Street?'

'I just saw it.'

'What evidence do you have for saying Miss Cass was—on the streets?'

'Because of the way she acted in going quietly with the policeman after being saucy.'

The reports in the press of the enquiry were already widespread and constantly carped at a public enquiry being converted into a public trial with none of the safeguards normally surrounding proceedings in the Law Courts. The next step in the enquiry crystallized such complaints. To the astonishment of the Law Officers of the Crown, a half-hearted, miniature and very amateur identity parade was held, when Mrs. Bowman, Miss Cass, Mrs. Tompkins and two other ladies were brought into 'court' and asked to form a line. When requested to pick out among them the 'dark girl of Regent Street', Madame Botellier, alias Pietra, pointed an unerring finger at Miss Cass.

Ebullient, passionate and not easily controlled, Madame Botellier then burst into a long account of the habits of 'working girls' until Sir Charles Warren intervened sharply and put a stop to her outpourings. Grain took the opportunity to examine some of her statements more closely:

'Whose was the arm you allege Miss Cass held when Endacott arrested her?'

'It was an American who frequently walked up that way and went with bad women.'

'Can you describe him?'

'He is about 40 years of age, and the fast women about there know him by a nickname.'

'You appear to be well acquainted with the lives and habits of this class of woman, madam?'

The witness laughed, and replied:

'I have been 20 years in England.' (Laughter in court.) 'It is quite a common thing to see these arrests in Regent Street at night.'

'What were you doing when you saw this arrest?'

'Waiting for a friend, a dressmaker.'

'Is not 9.30 a late hour for a lady friend to be waiting alone in Regent Street?'

'I don't think so.'

'Can you give us her name?'

'No. I decline to do that.'

'But you were quite happy for your friend to be kept waiting among prostitutes.'

Wonter intervened acidly: 'Miss Cass was there, and she is highly respectable.'

Grain quietly rejoined: 'Yes, she is highly respectable, and was *not waiting there.*'

Sir Charles Warren declared testily: 'There must be no imputations because persons are in Regent Street. The street is open to all.'

Wonter now drove home the crucial part of Madame Botellier's evidence with the question: 'You are quite sure that the girl who was arrested was the one you saw soliciting the American gentleman?'

'Yes, I am.'

Sir Charles Warren said there were a number of questions he desired to ask the witness, but he must ask her to give simple, straightforward answers. Madame Botellier was then drawn into the admission that her own account of the arrest differed materially from that given by Constable Endacott.

By now several people in the enquiry room looked tired and tempers were showing signs of strain. At the end of a prickly interrogation of Madame Pietra by Sir Charles, the enquiry adjourned until the following Monday.

Meanwhile the case re-echoed powerfully in the House of Commons. Mr. H. Vincent asked the Secretary of State for the Home Department 'why the unfortunate circumstances of the arrest of Miss Cass were not referred—according to the usual practice of the Home Office in cases of police misconduct possibly forming the subject of further prosecution—to the Solicitor to the Treasury to investigate the facts.'

Despite further protests in the press and the House of Commons, the enquiry went ahead on July 25 and quickly brought dramatic scenes. The irrepressible Madame Pietra came bustling into court, clouded in finery, with the air of an opera singer responding to applause, but her manner changed abruptly when Mr. Grain's first question was blunt and to the point: 'What is your *real* name?'

Madame Pietra responded to this with what *The Times* described as 'a volume of angry words in which she exclaimed vehemently against her name having been mentioned'. Sir Charles Warren tried to check her outburst, but she rushed on to denounce Grain as a man who broke his word and sent 'men to make enquiries about me'. He had 'done her wrong' —'she was outraged'—she would bring not one action for defamation—but several!

When at last Sir Charles succeeded in silencing her, Grain put a second question: 'Do you know a police sergeant of the name of Scott?'

'I will not answer.'

Grain repeated his question, stonily, whereupon Madame Pietra said she knew many police sergeants in the Marlborough Street Police Court area. Grain then pressed for more precise information about her relationship with the police, but Sir Charles Warren—possibly to avoid another flood of embarrassing abuse—intervened: 'Mr. Grain, will you please bring out what you want to bring out.'

Grain stated that he possessed information of a serious character about the witness, and immediately put a third question to Madame Pietra.

'Did you—when you took your present lodgings—state that you were the wife of a police detective?'

Disentangled from another burst of angry volubility, the answer was: 'No: no references were necessary because the landlady expressed complete satisfaction with my appearance.'

What followed is best represented by a quotation from *The Times* for July 26, 1887:

'There then arose a passage of arms between the witness, the Assessor and Mr. Grain. The Assessor told the witness to simply answer a question or refuse to answer it, and when she proceeded to run on with assertions, protestations and threats instead of replying, the Assessor sharply told her to be silent after each answer . . . Mr. Grain then put, once more, the question whether she had not told her landlady, when she took lodgings, that she was the wife of a detective officer, and the witness at once passionately inveighed against Mr. Grain for daring to ask such questions.'

The Assessor once more intervened and demanded that Grain should receive a short answer and pass to another point. 'You *must* answer *simply*, without adding a multitude of irrelevant words,' he snapped at Madame Pietra.

By now the atmosphere in the court was highly charged and even learned counsel found it difficult to contain themselves in the face of Madame Pietra, who seemed determined to reduce the proceedings to a brawl.

The climax came when Grain almost demanded to know what business she followed when she charged a woman called Glass with robbing her. Again *The Times* reported:

'At once the witness burst out in what the Assessor called "a flood of language", declaring that she would not answer "that man", pointing an accusing finger at Mr. Grain. The Assessor strove once more to calm the witness and Mr. Grain pressed home his questions: "Is your name not Picard? Did you charge Mrs. Glass under that name? Are you not a Belgian?" The witness now rose from her seat and continued to talk so much and so loudly that the Assessor declared that it was dreadful to have this flood of angry speech, but the witness continued to ply Mr. Grain with angry reproaches and at last the Assessor abruptly ordered her to leave the court.'

It was as if a storm had blown itself through the court room, leaving everyone tense and apprehensive.

When Madame Pietra had at last vanished from the scene, the Assessor addressed Grain in the sharpest terms: 'What is it you have to press the witness so much about?'

A brief interval followed in which unrecorded details were exchanged privately between Grain and the Assessor. When the court resumed, the Assessor asked Wonter whether there was anything more he wished to ask Madame Pietra.

Wonter replied that he *certainly did not*. He then added, with considerable emphasis: 'I desire it to be known that we who represent Constable Endacott did not bring this woman here.'

Later, on the same day, Constable Endacott was called, and stated, under questioning, that he had arrested Miss Cass on the north-east side of Regent Street.

The Assessor remarked at this point that it would be invaluable to the work of the enquiry if some respectable person who had independently witnessed the arrest would come forward to corroborate the facts. Two witnesses had given identical evidence as to the place of the arrest, which was totally different from that named by Madame Pietra and Constable Endacott.

Grain then asked Endacott: 'Have you been able to trace the fair woman much mentioned in the evidence we have heard?'

'No, I have not.'

'A search has been made?'

'Yes.'

'Do you expect to trace her in due course?'

'I am not sure that we will.'

Superintendent Draper, when recalled, confirmed Endacott's statements. Every effort had been made to trace the fair woman, without success, and now, at this late stage, without hope of success.

The proceedings for yet another day—the third—then closed. When they reopened again on July 26, the atmosphere in the court was distinctly acrimonious. Detailed evidence from police witnesses about the precise time or place of the arrest ran on interminably, and then, finally, the Assessor turned to Grain and said:

'Is there anything more you desire to ask on this point?'

Grain acidly replied:

'No, I do not feel inclined to do so after the manner in which I was treated yesterday.'

Sir Charles Warren then, at last, terminated the enquiry with the words: 'As there is no more evidence to be put forward, the enquiry is now concluded unless, before I make my report to the Secretary of State for the Home Department . . . some new evidence is brought to my notice . . .'

From all these tortured and very unorthodox proceedings it seemed highly probable that Miss Cass's name would be cleared, but such a resolution was not sufficient for Madame Bowman. Dramatically, on August 16, through her legal representatives, she carried her crusade into a quite different arena. She charged Constable Endacott with wilful and corrupt perjury before Mr. Vaughan at Bow Street Police Station.

Grain opened the preliminary proceedings with the statement

that he thought it right to put Mr. Vaughan in possession of the facts, which crystallized around a letter he had received from the Director of Public Prosecutions dated August 10:

He then gave a very precise and lucid recapitulation of the events and evidence which had brought them into the Bow Street Magistrates' Court.

There followed another prolonged series of encounters between the two counsel, the magistrate and witnesses, and then Wonter, who once again represented Endacott, said that he desired to put in the whole of the proceedings of the previous enquiry. Vaughan promptly refused permission on the grounds that they had been unsworn statements. Wonter pressed his point, saying that he wished to put one particular question to Miss Cass as to an answer she gave to a certain question at that enquiry, but the magistrate remained adamant.

He then turned to Endacott, told him that he was charged with perjury committed in his evidence given at Marlborough Street Police Court against Miss Cass, and administered the usual caution. Wonter replied that Endacott reserved his defence.

Vaughan enquired whether there were any witnesses to be called and after Wonter had answered, 'not here', committed Endacott to take his trial at the next Sessions of the Central Criminal Court.

This extraordinary case had gathered impetus as it progressed from a small protest to a solicitor, followed by a letter to the Lord Chancellor, through a prolonged public enquiry which had filled the newspapers with the names of Miss Cass and Constable Endacott. Now at last came a grandiose charge of perjury in the Central Criminal Court. A private individual seeking to redress the reputation of an innocent woman had fought her case through every barrier to place it before no less a person than a High Court judge.

The Solicitor General opened the case for the prosecution in a court crowded with reporters waiting, as one put it, to see 'the final kill'. Half England watched fascinated, through the newspapers, the last stages of this David and Goliath battle. However, Goliath, in this case, was symbolized by a sadly diminutive British bobby whose situation had become to him deeply worrying and very painful.

The Solicitor General proceeded to recapitulate once again

the history and details of the case. Almost at the outset Mr. Justice Stephen interposed and he did not appear to have over much sympathy with Miss Cass.

One of the first new witnesses called was Mr. Crowe, Second Clerk at the Marlborough Street Police Court, who produced a note of the evidence given by Endacott. Mr. Besley cross-examined him for the defence:

'A large number of charges of this description are heard at Marlborough Street?'

'Yes, sir.'

'In some of which Endacott has given evidence?'

'Yes, sir.'

'Has his evidence ever been challenged in any case before?'

'Not so far as I know.'

'Isn't it quite customary for a magistrate to discharge a woman the first time she is brought up on such a charge?'

'Yes, sir.'

'Did the prosecutrix put any questions to Endacott on his evidence in the police station?'

'No, sir.'

A changed and suddenly more mature Miss Cass—she had married since the case began—was now called, but her first composure began to give way to uneasiness. Examined by the Solicitor General, she said:

'My maiden name was Cass. I have been married since the commencement of these proceedings and am now Mrs. Langley. I am 24 years of age . . .'

Marriage being a respectable activity, it at once created the correct impression with the jury which the Solicitor General did not fail, subtly and quietly, to exploit.

The new Mrs. Langley was then taken through a labyrinth of details to show that she had led a very cloistered and highly respectable life during the short time she had lived in London, hardly venturing out alone into the streets.

Her account was very convincing in all its array of minute detail and a fully drawn portrait of a completely innocent young woman emerged.

Mr. Besley then cross-examined her, and for the first time succeeded in seriously qualifying the romantic picture of Miss Cass, the innocent provincial maid:

4

'On the night of June 28, did you not tell Madame Bowman that you were going out to meet a young man?'

'I did not tell her why I was going out.'

'Did you not make enquiries at Shoolbred's for a Mr. Settle?'

'No, I did not.'

'And you have never before in public made any statement about walking with Mr. Settle to Trinity Square?'

'No . . .'

'Do you know Bridget Costellos, a barmaid from Stockton?'

'Yes, I do.'

'When did you last see her?'

'I saw her on the Wednesday morning when I left Stockton.'

'Was there anyone else with you when you left Stockton?'

'A friend of mine, Mr. Bryan, was with me . . . He joined the train at Eagescliffe to go to York . . .'

'What happened when you arrived at York?'

'We had luncheon . . .'

'Did you know he was married?'

'Yes, I knew he was married.'

'Was your meeting accidental?'

'No, it was by a verbal appointment made the Monday before.'

'How often had you met this gentleman before?'

'I had seen Bryan about twice a week for some time '

'Did he give you a satchel?'

'No, he did not give me a satchel.'

'Something else?'

'A pair of gloves.'

'Anything else?'

'A glove-box and a diamond ring.'

'Did Bryan ever tell you that he had been forbidden his wife's brother's house because of his acquaintance with you?'

'No, he did not.'

'Have you been with him in any house?'

'No.'

'Have you been driving with him?'

'Yes, Bryan took me for a drive in a dog cart.'

'Was anyone else in the dog cart?'

'No, no one else.'

'Where exactly did you go when you reached Castle Eden?'

'We went to an hotel.'

'Why was that?'

'Because the horse needed a rest.'

'Did you enter a private room in the hotel?'

'Yes, we did.'

'How long were you at Castle Eden?'

'About an hour.'

Besley now elicited from Mrs. Langley that there had been many meetings—always alone—with Bryan for one or two hours, and then he gave another turn to the inquisitorial screw:

'Have you ever been to his house while his wife was away?'

'No, never.'

'Have you ever walked the lanes near Stockton with him?'

'Yes.'

'At what hours?'

'Between eight and nine o'clock.'

'In the winter?'

'Yes.'

'So it would be dark?'

'Yes.'

'Do you recall a man called Mr. Bevan?'

'Yes.'

'Did he not see you at Darlington Station as late as 11 p.m.?'

'Yes.'

'Was he kissing you?'

'No.' (This was said with some emphasis.)

'What had you been doing in Darlington?'

'Some work for Mrs. Costellos.'

'On passing an hotel with Mrs. Costellos, did you make a sign to anyone?'

'No, I did not.'

'Did you not say, "See how I will take him on"?'

'No, certainly not.'

'But you did meet a man?'

'Yes, I met a young man I knew in business named Turner, and went with him to the station.'

'Did you miss the train home?'

'Yes, but it was by accident . . .'

'Do you remember being introduced to a Mr. Simmons by Bridget Costellos?'

'Yes, I do.'

'What happened then?'

'I did not meet him afterwards. I have never spoken to him since the introduction.'

'Did you not make an appointment to go to his house one Sunday afternoon?'

'No, that is not true.'

'You have never been to his house?'

'No.'

The cross-examination was long, detailed and sustained, and as it ended the jury were obviously impressed. The Solicitor General hastily summoned the next witness, Madame Bowman, who firmly repeated her statements about her relations with, and opinion of, Miss Cass. Mr. Besley rose once more to cross-examine, and was equally successful in throwing some doubt on Madame Bowman's character. *The Times* duly noted: 'In cross-examination certain questions were put to the witness with respect to the manner in which her house was conducted, to the suggestions in which the witness indignantly and emphatically gave a denial, and Mr. Justice Stephen observed that such questions ought not to have been put without good ground, in which opinion the jury expressed their concurrence.'

The impression left on the jury by Besley's clever cross-examinations of both witnesses was rescued from a dangerous ambivalence by the examination of three more women witnesses, each of whom testified to the accuracy of Miss Cass's statements, her good character and retiring nature.

When the court resumed on November 1, the Solicitor General called Mrs. Elizabeth Tompkins, Miss Cass's employer for two years. Her evidence did not materially add to what had gone before, but it reaffirmed again the good character of Miss Cass.

When, at last, Mr. Besley opened the case for the defence, he made it quite clear that he would rely mainly on witnesses as to character. Besley, like the Solicitor General, then called a number of witnesses who reaffirmed the honesty, integrity and sense of responsibility of Constable Endacott. The evidence was less detailed but in substance it suggested that when Constable Endacott had uttered—or written—such words as were complained of, they were either true or he had made a genuine mistake. It was on this last question—of a possible misunder-standing—that Mr. Justice Stephen later seized. Turning to the Solicitor General, he said bluntly: 'Where is the corroboration necessary to support the assignment of perjury?'

The Solicitor General not unnaturally submitted that there was corroboration:

'I contend that the witness Walford corroborated the evidence of Miss Cass. One of the statements of Endacott on which perjury is assigned is that he saw Miss Cass catch hold of two gentlemen, one of whom said: "It is very hard that I should be stopped." I submit that there is evidence to go to the jury.'

Further exchanges took place until the Solicitor General sharpened his argument with the words: 'Endacott stated that he had seen Miss Cass in Regent Street three times before—and that is in the statement upon which perjury is alleged.'

Finally Mr. Justice Stephen ruled: 'You must confine yourself to one point—namely, whether or not he committed perjury in saying that he had seen her three times in Regent Street. I would just remark on the great difficulty of asking the jury to say that a man committed wilful perjury in saying that he had seen a person, whom he did not know, three times before; especially when she says she was there once and walked down the street. The suggestion of mistake is so very obvious that I think you had better consider the matter.'

The Solicitor General, after consultation with Mr. Grain, said: 'I think, having regard to the intimation from your Lordship, that I will not address the jury upon the residue of the charge. Of course, if the whole case had been in your Lordship's judgment sufficiently supported to have gone before the jury, I should have gone to the jury upon it; but if it is to be limited under your Lordship's direction to the question whether Endacott did or did not see her three times in Regent Street, I do not think I can pursue the matter further. I quite feel the force of the observation that it may have been a matter of mistaken belief on his part; and while I regret to some extent this course, I do not think it would be consistent, after your Lordship's observations, for me to ask for a verdict on the question left.'

Mr. Justice Stephen had the final words: 'You have taken

the proper course, and one which I should have expected from you in the circumstances. Therefore nothing remains for me but to direct the jury that the man must be acquitted upon the whole charge. In doing so, I must make some observations in explanation of the position in which we are placed.

'In the first place, there is considerable room for mistake on the part of the constable; and what would have to be proved in order to convict of perjury is not merely the mistaken apprehension, but wilful perjury. It occurs to me as a possible thing that a man walking along the streets where there were many passers-by might very well take the wrong woman, especially as she passed through a small crowd of people at the time. If there was a mistake of that kind, it would be a cruel injustice to convict a man of perjury. Let us suppose that he made a mistake about it. It must not be forgotten that his evidence was given in such a summary way and so shortly that he was not cross-examined . . . He had no opportunity of qualifying or setting himself right upon the statement with respect to which the perjury is assigned. If he had been cross-examined he might have had fair play. I do not say that there has been any want of fair play in the conduct of the case, for it has been tried with perfect fairness. If Elizabeth Cass had been treated in this manner in consequence of the evidence she has given here, perjury might have been assigned against her, as she made one or two mistakes, but I am bound to say that she has given her evidence with extreme frankness and there was no perjury as far as I can see.

'But still she showed some want of candour in not admitting at once the receipt of the diamond ring from Bryan, but it would have been a cruel thing to snap a verdict of perjury against her in consequence, and it would be hard to convict this man because he said something which might have been a mistake. Your duty will be to acquit the prisoner. I will just say this—that the course of holding a private enquiry, or an enquiry by a public authority, into the conduct of a man who is afterwards to be accused of crime, such enquiry not being authorized by any statute, is greatly to be avoided. According to the law of this country there is a marked division between three different departments of Government.'

Thus it came about that both parties emerged to some extent

satisfied and dissatisfied. Endacott had, according to the verdict, been the victim of making a serious mistake, and if he had made a mistake Miss Cass was cleared of any charge of prostitution. But Madame Bowman and Miss Cass had failed in their avowed aim to convict Endacott of perjury.

Outside the court Endacott was received by his fellow police officers with enthusiasm, and was quickly reinstated in the force. Miss Cass, for some unknown reason, lingered about the court with her husband and friends for nearly an hour before she disappeared in the direction of Holborn.

CHAPTER IV

ADOLF BECK

[1904]

IN ONE OF HIS prosperous periods, Adolf Beck presented the image of a dandified man wearing all the regalia of a 'gentleman of means'. The silk top hat was offset by a morning coat, the starched butterfly collar by a silk tie, the flawlessly rolled umbrella by a gold watch chain. In periods of poverty, when harried by creditors, he sometimes relapsed into a shabby, nondescript person whose sadness quickly conveyed itself to anyone who met him.

Thus, even within the same person, two images could easily arise to confuse the eye of any observer. The contradiction became especially relevant with Adolf Beck since he served eleven long and terrible years in prison partly because a number of women wrongly identified him.

It all began one raw November day when a certain Mme Meissonier was accosted by a stranger in Victoria Street, London. 'Oh—pardon me,' he said gracefully lifting his hat, 'are you Lady Everton—or would it be Ellington?'

What Mme Meissonier did not, at this stage, know was that the cheap flattery of his remark had brought a quick response from many earlier victims. He next asked her where she was going and when she said to a flower show, he replied that he kept ten gardeners at his country home in Lincolnshire where he had a display of flowers far better than anything she would see at such a show. Convinced, by now, that she was talking to a 'perfect gentleman', Mme Meissonier revealed that she had that very morning received a box of very beautiful chrysanthemums. At once the stranger expressed great interest and asked if he could call on her sometime at her convenience to see them. Whether a combination of flattery and conceit confused Mme Meissonier's normal intelligence is not clear, but at this stage she does not seem to have seen anything suspicious in his behaviour. A self-evident ruse became for her a commonplace response. Although the man spoke in English she detected an accent but when she asked if he came from abroad he at once replied with some emphasis: 'Oh no, I am an Englishman.'

Promptly, on the following day, the stranger called on Mme Meissonier and built up the image of a very rich man with an estate covering half of West Brompton, claiming none other than Lord Salisbury as his cousin. By now the stranger had himself discovered that he was dealing with no mean person. Mme Mcissonier spoke three languages, had a wide knowledge of music and the arts and employed her own servant.

Quickly consolidating his relationship with her, in no time 'Lord Willoughby', as he called himself, was persuading Mme Meissonier to part with two watches and several rings, giving her a fraudulent cheque. Gullible though she seemed, throughout this farrago of lies, some small suspicion dawned at last when the stranger left her flat. It drove her to hurry to the Union Bank, St. James's Street, on which the cheque was drawn. There, the manager shook his head. The cheque was forged.

Three weeks later Mme Meissonier walked down the south side of Victoria Street one day and there, standing in the shadow of No. 135, she saw someone closely resembling the man she referred to as 'her deceiver'. She went up to him at once and spoke to him. By now she had taken a decision which was to ruin a large part of Adolf Beck's life. 'Sir, I know you,' she said. Immediately he tried to brush past her saying, 'What do you want with me?' She at once retorted passionately, 'I want my two watches and rings.'

Any man with a clear conscience might have stopped and challenged her. But Adolf Beck had been living on his wits for years, had many pressing creditors and enough guilt of a minor kind to make him decide to run for it. According to the evidence she later gave, he now did a very foolish thing. He swore at her and ran across Victoria Street dodging between the buses

and cabs. Mme Meissonier went after him. She had great
difficulty in keeping up with him and he constantly brushed
her off with the words, 'Leave me alone!' Simultaneously, they
both sighted a policeman standing at the junction of Victoria
Street and Vauxhall Bridge Road. What followed should have
appeared hopelessly illogical to any jury trying to convict this
man of obtaining goods under false pretences, because instead
of fleeing from a representative of the law, Adolf Beck went
straight up to the policeman and complained that this woman
had accosted him and would not leave him alone. His complete
honesty proved to be another element in his downfall. The
policeman scrutinized Mme Meissonier, decided that she was
a perfectly respectable lady and accepted her story about the
missing property. Both parties were now escorted by P.C.
Edwards to Rochester Row Police Station and there, once
again, Mme Meissonier's charge was accepted, but Adolf
Beck's—to his horror—was rejected by the officer on duty.

Later the same evening another alleged victim of Beck's
activities, Daisy Grant, appeared at the police station to
identify him. At first she said: 'I believe he is the man but I
should know him better if he took his hat off.' The Police
Inspector quickly arranged a rough and ready identity parade
with seven other men and when Adolf Beck removed his hat
Daisy Grant said, 'Yes, that is the man.'

Now formally charged with stealing property, Adolf Beck at
once answered forcefully: 'It's a great mistake. I have never
seen these ladies before in my life.'

Within a few days chance once again intervened to damn
Adolf Beck even more certainly. A complete stranger wrote to
Scotland Yard pointing out a remarkable similarity between
the frauds described by Mme Meissonier and those perpetrated
by a man called John Smith many years before in 1877. The
stranger suggested that the two men must really be one and the
same man operating under aliases, so closely did the details of
the different crimes resemble one another. Whereupon Scotland
Yard summoned out of retirement the two police officers,
Inspector Redstone and Constable Elliss Spurrell, who had
handled the earlier case of John Smith in 1877. Confronted by
Adolf Beck, Spurrell then stated:

'In 1877 I was in the Metropolitan Police Reserve. On May

7, 1877 I was present at the Central Criminal Court where the prisoner in the name of John Smith was convicted of feloniously stealing ear-rings and a ring and eleven shillings of Louisa Leonard and was sentenced to five years' penal servitude. I produce the certificate of that conviction. The prisoner is the man.'

Carefully cross-examined by the magistrate, Elliss Spurrell added: 'There is no doubt whatever—I know quite well what is at stake on my answer and I say without doubt he is the man.'

Thus it came about that Adolf Beck was committed for trial at the Central Criminal Court on three charges of obtaining by false pretences, larceny, and conversion as a bailee, the charges involving no less than ten different women.

At the outset, the Central Criminal Court that March day of 1896 had nothing very special to mark it out except perhaps the bearing of the prisoner who had dressed himself very carefully and gave every appearance of pride. As he later admitted, his belief that an innocent man would not be condemned by a British Court of Law reinforced the confidence in his bearing. Presided over by the Common Serjeant Sir Forrest Fulton, Counsel for the Crown were Mr. Horace Avory and Mr. Guy Stephenson and for the prisoner Mr. C. F. Gill and Mr. E. Percival Clarke.

Mr. Avory made his opening speech:

'My Lord and Gentlemen of the jury, the allegations in this case are that the prisoner has systematically got himself up in swell clothing and with a certain amount of discrimination, accosted women of various ages in the street flattering them by mistaking them for Lady—so and so. Upon the said ladies denying their alleged identity he—nonetheless—had sufficiently established the conversation to be able to obtain the address of his victim and to arrange a meeting at her home the following day. His method there on would sometimes vary. Perhaps it was a letter which arrived on the notepaper of the Carlton Club or the Grand Hotel confirming the meeting or in some cases a telegram.'

Another form his approach sometimes took, Mr. Avory continued, was to represent himself as owning a large property in St. John's Wood for which he was desirous of finding a housekeeper. Having talked about the new clothing the housekeeper would require for the job he then wrote out a large cheque to cover the cost.

'Next he would enquire what jewellery the woman possessed and then under various pretexts take whatever he could away with him when he left. In one case the value of such jewellery was £150. As the various victims later discovered the cheques he left with them were all fictitious . . .

'It is not to be expected that any of the stolen property would be found in the prisoner's possession. He would of course get rid of it at once. You would hardly expect a thief to go about with a pair of elephant tusks under his arm or a row of rings around his neck . . .

'I understand there will be no dispute as to facts, the defence being that it was a case of mistaken identity . . .'

Avory now called as witnesses for the prosecution one woman after another, all telling closely similar stories. The first was a widow, Mrs. Fanny Nutt:

'Tell the jury what happened in December of 1894.'

'I was living in Delaney Street, Regent's Park and my husband had passed away about a year before. I was in Bond Street . . .'

'Which day would that be?'

'It was Monday evening, December 2.'

'And the time?'

'About 6 p.m. . . . I was in Bond Street dressed in widow's weeds when this gentleman came up to me and said: "You must be a very young widow," and I told him I was twenty-one. He said, "Tell me all about your husband and how he died . . ." He eventually asked me whether he might call on me. I said I was not in the habit of receiving gentlemen but he might call as he said he would be such a friend . . .'

A letter was now produced in court, and Avory continued:

'On the following morning you received a letter?'

'Yes. It had a printed heading—Grand Hotel. It said— Please expect me tomorrow, Tuesday, between one and two o'clock. He arrived the next day in a cab . . . He said he had a nice house in St. John's Wood—but he had to send his house-keeper away to Coventry—would I like to be his new house-keeper . . . he would give me £5 a week to begin with, to be increased to £10 if everything went well . . . He said he would make out a list of dresses I should get because I must leave off my mourning. He gave me a cheque for £15 15s. He put it into an envelope addressed to the Union Bank, Belgravia . . .'

'Did he at any point discuss your jewellery with you?'

'Yes, he said he must have a ring for the size of my finger. He wanted one to take away for size and he would buy me a more massive wedding ring . . . He took my wedding ring for the size and another one . . .'

Mr. Gill cross-examined the next witness, Mme Meissonier. Some of the key questions and answers were as follows:

'How long did you speak to the stranger the first time you met him?'

'About four or five minutes.'

'You had never met him before?'

'He was a perfect stranger to me.'

'You say his moustache was waxed then?'

'Yes—it is altered now.'

'There was another identifying mark?'

'Yes. I'm sure about the scar or something I spoke of on the right side.'

'You say—or something?'

'It might be from a drawn tooth—it was something I could notice. I see the mark on the prisoner now.'

'When you charged him was he dressed as he is now?'

'I think so—At my place he wore a necktie with a pearl pin.'

'Did he have patent leather boots?'

'I cannot say . . .'

'Did you speak rudely to him when you accosted him in the street?'

'No—quite calmly.'

'What exactly did you say?'

'I said I would follow him wherever he went . . .'

'What did he say to the policeman?'

'He said I was a common prostitute who accosted men.'

'Was that the first thing he said?'

'No. He said—"I never did see this woman before. I don't know why she follows me."'

'Did he not say—"What am I to do with this woman who keeps following and annoying me?"'

'No, he did not say that.'

'At the police station did you see what boots he had on?'

'No—I was so upset.'

'Or whether he wore a watch chain?'

'No. I was so much upset and excited at the police station I did not notice small details.'

Gill had succeeded in emphasizing a quite different although improbable reason for Mme Meissonier accosting Mr. Beck and had thrown in doubt some of her descriptive details.

Mary Harvey, Mme Meissonier's servant, followed her into the box and confirmed certain points of her evidence. John Watts, the police constable who was on duty when they brought in Adolf Beck and Mme Meissonier at Rochester Row Police Station, now described what took place there:

'I told him he answered the description of a man giving the name of Earl Wilton who was wanted for stealing jewellery and he replied, "It's a mistake".' As we have seen, the Inspector on duty then collected eight men from adjoining streets and shops to form an identification parade and Miss Daisy Grant picked out Beck.

Cross-examining, Mr. Gill asked Constable Watts whether he had searched Mr. Beck's apartment, and whether he had found any papers.

Watts agreed that he had, and Gill pursued the point:

'What exactly were you looking for?'

'I was looking for some cheques.'

'But you did not find any?'

'No.'

'Did you find any paper with the name and address of any of these women?'

'No.'

'There are, I believe, ten women who have lodged complaints. Did you trace any single article belonging to any one of the ten women?'

'No.'

Several more women witnesses for the prosecution followed, some agreeing that the man who accosted them had worn a gold watch chain, a pearl tie pin and spats.

Mr. Marcus Browne, proprietor of the Covent Garden Hotel, then gave evidence of large debts owing to him from Beck. 'The prisoner lived at my house about six years—he left because he had not paid his bills and I said I could not keep him any longer.'

This—inevitably—left a bad impression with the jury. There followed further evidence which showed that Beck was a needy person willing to borrow five shillings at the time of the offences and thus having a strong motive. Detective Inspector Frank Froest next described how he searched the prisoner's apartment at Covent Garden and found a number of pairs of spats, a wedding ring and a 'few photographs of ladies'.

Then came the crucial witness, Thomas Henry Gurrin, a handwriting expert: 'I have examined the cheques and promissory note forms produced—also this manuscript book . . . I have also examined the three letters . . . sworn to be in the prisoner's writing. They are all in the same writing . . . It is true the prisoner's writing is in different hands. I prepared the report produced, giving my reasons and with facsimiles showing similarities. The cheques and lists are not written in the prisoner's ordinary hand. Two forms of disguise have been adopted. One is a back-handed or vertical scribble . . . The other disguise is an ordinary hand more resembling the writing in the books but written large and more distorted . . .'

In cross-examination, Gill referred back to the handwriting of a man called John Smith who had been charged with similar offences in 1877, and now began the first of a number of fatal legal technicalities. In the final event far more sinister terms were applied to what came to be seen by at least one man as corruption of judicial procedure.

Mr. Avory for the prosecution strongly resisted the introduction of the handwriting of a man called Smith and his 1877 conviction. Cross-examination to establish whether the present prisoner was the same person, he said, could not legally be justified. The 1877 case formed a collateral issue not to be brought up until the jury had returned their verdict on the present case. Otherwise 'it might be suggested that the prisoner had been improperly convicted' because of past events not directly concerned with this case.

Gill—knowing that John Smith was a different person from Beck—now fought hard to bring that fact out in court. It was, he said, directly in issue. He had every legal right to raise the question because the key to his defence rested on the fact that the man convicted in 1877 was the same man who had today committed these frauds, and a totally different person from the prisoner in court. He could demonstrate that the writing in the exhibits brought before the present court was the writing of the man convicted in 1877 and not that of the prisoner.

Gurrin, recalled to the box, now stated that he had seen the exhibits in the case of Smith back in 1877 and there was a reference in his Police Court Report on the matter. Gill immediately replied that he was entitled to have produced all the documents on which Gurrin based his opinion. Clearly, Gill at this point wanted to ask Gurrin whether the exhibits from the 1877 case were identical in style with the documents in the present case, but Avory once again strongly objected to such questions being put.

The Common Serjeant now gave a ruling which completely damned Beck's chances of acquittal. Whether that ruling arose because Avory and the Common Serjeant wanted to protect Beck from guilt by association with an earlier series of crimes or whether much more sinister motives lay deeply hidden under the conflicting web of communications between the police, the Treasury and the judiciary may presently appear.

On the afternoon of Wednesday, March 4, Mr. Gill made his statement for the defence. The main burden of the opening paragraphs concerned the question of unreliable identification. Describing the emotional state of the prosecution witnesses, Gill said: 'They were evidently a little off their heads and had imagined that the hour had at length arrived when their charms would be appreciated.' Could it be conceived that in such an emotional state, either in the first instance—one of glowing response to flattery—or in the second—blind anger at their deception—they represented *fit* witnesses to identify any-one? There were too many inconsistencies in the descriptions they gave. After all, 'the tigress in the jungle pursuit of her prey' was the only fit symbol of their feelings when they discovered that all this flattery was a trap leading to bare-faced deception.

Gill now called seven witnesses on two main points, one of which would have undermined the whole prosecution case if the Common Serjeant had admitted the evidence from 1877.

Annie Smith, a chambermaid at the Buckingham Hotel,

Strand, said that Beck had stayed there in February 1894. She never saw any jewellery in his room, he did not in her knowledge possess a gold watch and he never wore a white waistcoat or white spats. She smiled as she responded to one of Gill's comments: 'No—I never saw anything like a mandolin or elephant tusks there.' Her evidence put in question certain details of identification and denied any dealing in stolen jewellery.

Charles George Kistner, a solicitor's clerk, now gave evidence that Beck had called at the offices of Messrs. Jenkins, Baker & Co. almost every day from the middle of January 1895 for several months. In professional business jargon, Beck at this time was engaged, he said, in 'introducing a mine' and several large cheques were paid to him for sums varying between £100 and £300. One cheque in September amounted to £285, another in October £100 and 3,500 shares were allotted to him.

Although there was no strict coincidence between the time of the frauds and these payments it did make slightly ridiculous the idea of a man accustomed to business deals of this kind going to such trouble to procure a few pounds on stolen jewellery. As to identification, once again Kistner said that he had never seen Beck wearing a massive gold watch chain, gold watch or pearl tic-pin such as several of his accusers described.

One of the last witnesses Gill produced was a Colonel Harris who stated—irritably—that he had been brought to the court by subpoena. Yes, he had known Mr. Beck in Peru from 1875 to 1882 and he had seen him with a very good class of persons. Re-examining him later Gill pin-pointed the fact that Colonel Harris had met Beck frequently from 1875–82 in the streets of Lima.

This was reinforced by a Gentleman of the Chamber of the King of Denmark, Major Hans Rudolph Sofas Lindholm. 'I knew Beck several years at Lima. I first knew Beck in June or July 1880 and from then until 1883–4. He was a good friend and an honourable man.' These two witnesses pressed home what had unfortunately become a superfluous point. If John Smith who committed the frauds in 1877 was the same person committing them in 1895 he could not be Adolf Beck because in 1877 Beck, on the evidence of Colonel Harris and Major Lindholm, lived at that time thousands of miles away in Peru.

On Major Lindholm's evidence, while Smith was in prison in England, Lindholm met Beck in Lima. None of this could take its full impact upon the jury because the Common Serjeant, under pressure from Avory, had ruled out any consideration of the 1877 case.

On the last day of the trial Gill opened the proceedings with the words:

'My Lord—several witnesses have spoken of the prisoner speaking with a foreign accent. May I ask permission for him to speak to the jury?'

When permission was granted the prisoner said: 'From the beginning to the end of these horrible charges I have nothing to do with them. I am absolutely innocent.' Only the slightest trace of a foreign accent could be detected.

Despite considerable doubt about the efficiency of the identification parades and some other aspects of the case—especially the relevance of John Smith—the jury retired and in a very short time returned a verdict of Guilty.

Avory then addressed the court again: 'The police are in possession of certain information about the prisoner, my Lord.'

The Common Serjeant replied that he would not be influenced by this information, whereupon Gill spoke again with some force: 'There are four indictments charging the prisoner with having been previously convicted of felony and I submit I am entitled to have them tried or discharged. It is part of the prisoner's defence that the man convicted in 1877 and sentenced to five years was the same man as has carried out these frauds. This man was in prison from April 28. 1877 until April 1881 and the witnesses from South America spoke of frequently seeing the prisoner during that time in South America. This, in my submission, has become a case of a grave miscarriage of justice.'

Avory quickly replied: 'I ask that the prisoner be sentenced on the indictment on which he has been convicted and that the other indictments shall be postponed until the next session when I shall consider the necessity of applying to the Attorney General for a *nolle prosequi*. My learned friend almost admits that his object is to show that the verdict of the jury is wrong. I can be no party to that.'

Gill replied with considerable emphasis that there was no

precedent he knew of for an indictment remaining on the files against the will of the accused.

The Common Serjeant now summed up the situation. He said that if he acceded to Mr. Gill's application it would be a clear violation of practice in this and all other Criminal Courts. The question whether the prisoner was or was not the man convicted in 1877 could not be admissible upon the ground that it concerned another and distinct issue and one calculated to mislead the jury. Therefore he could not do what Mr. Gill required but he would 'postpone the other indictments until next session and sentence the prisoner only on the charges of which he has been convicted'.

He next claimed that the evidence as to identity had been 'absolutely overwhelming' and implied that the prisoner had been—rightly—found guilty of 'a most base and wicked crime'.

There followed a series of separate sentences on different counts which totalled seven years of penal servitude. Four other indictments on the file charging Beck with larceny were not dealt with despite Gill's protests. It seemed to those concerned in Beck's defence a savage sentence, as indeed it did to an onlooker, G. R. Sims, who had sat in the Press Gallery throughout the trial. Before he left the court Sims saw the face of Adolf Beck momentarily crumple and then Beck pulled himself together again, drew himself up and said, 'I am absolutely innocent.'

Sims was a man steeped in criminology whose gift for simple exposition had made him not only the *Daily Mail*'s crime correspondent but one of the leading popular criminologists of the day. Moreover he already knew Beck and because he had had no reason to suspect him he left the court a saddened and confused man.

A number of petitions were quickly launched on Beck's behalf but the most persistent attempts to clear his name came from his solicitor, T. Duerdin Dutton. He was the first of three private citizens who slowly developed a powerful campaign. These early attempts took as much patience as time since the official defences remained implacable for the whole of the first year. Very few details remain of Beck's reaction to prison life but despite a terrible despair he behaved, as the Governor of Portland Prison said, 'like a good prisoner'.

The first petition presented by Duerdin Dutton on behalf of Beck on May 20, 1896 claimed that the case was one of mistaken identity as a result of which there had been a mis-trial. It did not have the slightest effect. Beck himself made a second petition on June 9, again without any result. On July 22, G. R. Sims wrote his first article denouncing Beck's conviction. He claimed to have circulated it to Scotland Yard, the Home Office and the Treasury, but Scotland Yard later denied receiving it. 'The only thing,' he wrote, pinpointing at the outset the key to the case, 'is to find John Smith and then the Home Secretary will grant Adolf Beck Her Majesty's gracious pardon for a crime he never committed.'

On May 10, 1898 Dutton finally addressed a letter to the Principal Secretary of State for the Home Department, stating that: 'Circumstances connected with the case which were not admitted as evidence on the trial . . . point strongly to the fact that notwithstanding the evidence of identity produced on behalf of the Crown, the prisoner was and is innocent.'

A correspondence developed between Dutton and the Under-Secretary of State which slowly reached stalemate with the Home Office refusing to admit the grounds of the petition. Sims now came into the picture again and here, in a sense, was a much more formidable campaigner. He had long ago come to the conclusion that a serious miscarriage of justice had taken place and, as he later wrote: 'during the period of [Beck's] penal servitude I made every endeavour to induce the authorities to see their terrible mistake—but failed to obtain the slightest recognition . . .' At this stage he believed that nothing more sinister than a very bad mistake had been made.

Sims now wrote the second mild article in a series which was later to reach fiery heights of invective. For the moment his words amounted to nothing more than reasonable protest. His article simply pointed out 'clearly and logically the impossibility, on the evidence given at the Old Bailey, of Beck being John Smith alias Lord Willoughby'.

When, at last, five years later, Beck was released from prison one of the first men he sought out was G. R. Sims. Beck then became a frequent visitor to Sims' home and together they planned a new campaign to clear his name. Week after week he arrived with what he thought to be powerful new evidence, and time after time it proved useless. Inspired by Sims, Major Beasley of the Salvation Army's International Investigation Department took up Beck's case but according to Sims 'was unable to carry the matter through owing to difficulties constantly encountered'.

Beck's initial optimism slowly collapsed into deep depression. As Sims wrote in his colourful prose: 'When he had met with disappointments, when after spending hundreds of pounds with solicitors, inquiry agents and others he still found himself faced by an impenetrable darkness, he would come to me with tears in his eyes to tell me of his failure . . .'

One day, Beck brought to Sims an article published in a well-known daily which said that its representative had carefully checked the facts of the conviction with Sergeant Spurrell and a police Inspector at Scotland Yard. Both gave categorical assurances to the paper that there had been no case of mistaken identity and stated that Beck was undoubtedly Smith.

Sims wrote: 'I saw the man who had been so villainously wronged a prey to a storm of despair. I . . . heard him, with trembling lips and a voice choked by grief, cry aloud to God to be merciful and not let him carry to the grave the black stain his enemies had put upon him.'

Another article now appeared praising the police for exposing one of the most contemptible scoundrels of modern times. It was too much for Sims. He made a long pilgrimage to those newspaper offices which were printing what he considered to be—inspired—attacks on Beck. In two of the most malicious cases, he laid before the editors a number of new facts about the case and they suddenly realized that if and when Beck's innocence was proved they might be open to a very costly suit for libel. They tried to strike a bargain with Sims. Would Beck indemnify them against such action if they wrote articles in favour of an enquiry into his case? Once again the motive had a strong machiavellian element, but all was grist to Sims' mill, and the articles were printed.

In the next few months Sims exhausted himself, Beck spent over a thousand pounds, the Salvation Army found its enquiries still bogged down by bureaucratic evasions, two more newspapers clamoured for an enquiry, and still the Home Office remained unmoved.

One day in March 1904 Beck said to Sims, 'God will answer my prayer. I will not abandon hope while I live.'

And then, unbelievably, the second blow—in a nightmare of such proportions that it finally shattered Beck—fell. On April 15 Inspector Ward arrested him once more on a complaint lodged by a Miss Pauline Scott that he had fraudulently obtained jewellery from her. Beck could not believe his ears. Sims was stunned. When the magistrate's court finally committed Beck for trial once more at the Old Bailey he lifted his arms as if appealing to the Christian God in whom he believed and cried in a voice which rang through the court: 'Before God, my maker, I am absolutely innocent of every charge brought against me! I have not spoken to one of these women before. They were set against me by the detectives. I ask the Press to get all evidence in my support from my solicitor.' It was useless. A Kafkaesque machine—ruthless once it had begun to turn—had trapped him all over again.

There followed an almost farcical duplication of the earlier trial in 1896 with four women repeating closely similar charges. According to their evidence, 'this man' had carried out his ritual almost word-perfect from the model practised by John Smith. He claimed to have encountered the women previously, he suggested calling upon them the following day, he professed to have a house in St. John's Wood which needed a housekeeper, he issued a cheque on the Union Bank, he collected rings for the correct size, and he wrote on the notepaper of a well-known hotel.

It could be argued that in the eyes of the Home Office Adolf Beck had been driven to repeat his earlier crimes despite the terrible sentence which they had brought down on his head—but for one fact. Sims was later to disclose that the Home Office by now had admitted in their confidential records that Adolf Beck was not the same man as John Smith. Moreover Sims' agitation and the facts he had publicized could not have gone unnoticed. 'And yet,' Sims wrote, 'they permitted the monstrous iniquity of criminal proceedings against this unhappy man to be carried out *again* to the bitter and inhuman end.'

In one sense incredible—in another it was understandable. Someone had to be indicted with four fresh women bringing new accusations and it was better to reaffirm the guilt of Beck than to allow an enquiry which might uncover a whole chain of suppression, deceit, and—could it be—conspiracy by silence.

The conclusion was foregone. Once again Beck heard the verdict—Guilty—with what he later described as 'an icy heart', but now Sims' fury knew no bounds. This could no longer be tolerated. Something dramatic and final must be done, and at once. It took the form of a series of articles launched in the *Daily Mail* on August 15, 1904, which were, in effect, a private prosecution of the official prosecution of Adolf Beck.

Sims' opening sentences struck dramatically to the heart of the matter: 'I want in plain words to tell the story of a foul wrong done to an innocent man. The case of Mr. Adolf Beck has been described as one of "mistaken identity". I propose to show that it was nothing of the sort. It was a case of *wilfully "mis-represented identity"*, and the story forms one of the blackest pages in the annals of our courts of justice.'

Sims went further when he proclaimed that the use of the word 'justice' in connection with this trial was a total mockery of such a term. 'From first to last this unhappy man has been the victim of proceedings which are nothing short of a conspiracy to procure the conviction of a prisoner by suppressing facts which would have ensured his acquittal.'

Sims next paid a visit to Beck in Portland Prison and revealed to him the crusade he had launched. He found Beck, as he expected, deeply depressed, but he was quickly fired by Sims' eloquent indignation to resolve to join forces with him in an effort to clear his name at any cost. Very few details of this prison interview survive, but Sims came away more determined than ever.

His *Daily Mail* articles now set out to draw comparisons between the case of John Smith charged at the Old Bailey in 1877 with stealing a pair of ear-rings, a ring and eleven shillings from Louisa Leonard, and the crimes which Beck was alleged to have committed in 1898.

Miss Leonard's evidence recorded a pattern of lies with which the reader is by now very familiar: the suggestion that she should become his new housekeeper, the criticism of her jewellery, the borrowing of rings to check their size—all this unfolded in the expected order. As in some other instances he also made out a list of new clothing and gave her a cheque on the Union Bank.

In 1877 no less than seventeen similar charges were brought against Smith and he was sentenced to five years' penal servitude. Now came a crucial piece of information about the lawyers concerned in that trial. None other than that *Mr. Forrest Fulton—the judge who presided over Beck's trial—had represented the prosecution in Smith's trial.* This fact echoed like a thunderclap down Fleet Street, and many other newspapers pricked up their ears. A chance to expose a scandal was always a circulation-winning device not to be missed, but combined with a miscarriage of justice and a possible conspiracy it provided the elements of a real headline story *with a moral basis.*

Still more sensational disclosures flew from Sims' angry pen, running dangerously close to the elaborate libel minefields which surrounded most official reputations. He now made public what had, until then, remained a secret on the confidential files of the Home Office.

John Smith, it seemed, had been stripped of his clothing and every mark of identification recorded—including the fact that he was a circumcised Jew. Sims merely stated that he was a Jew, circumcision being too indelicate a matter to include in a popular pamphlet. The question at once arose—did Mr. Forrest Fulton who prosecuted him in 1877 know that Smith was a Jew and did he, when he came to preside over the court trying Adolf Beck, know that *he* was *not*?

Sim's object in his early articles was to stress the persistent repetition of the claim to aristocracy, the house in St. John's Wood, the need of a housekeeper, the borrowing of rings, and the forged cheques drawn on—always the same—Union Bank. Clearly, on this persistent parallel alone, these frauds were perpetrated by one and the same man—John Smith.

Sims next turned his attention to the evidence given by ex-Police Constable Elliss Spurrell at the preliminary proceedings against Beck in the Westminster Police Court. As we have seen Spurrell made two categorical statements. First: 'I was present at the Central Criminal Court on May 7, 1877 where the prisoner in the name of John Smith was convicted of feloniously stealing ear-rings'; and second, under cross-examination: 'I say without doubt he [Beck] is the man.'

Sims now said he would prove that at the time Elliss Spurrell gave evidence, the authorities—he did not specify which authorities—had in their possession identification marks of Adolf Beck and John Smith which were totally different. One set showed that Smith was a Jew, the other that Beck was not.

Now came Sims' fourth vital point driven home with italics: 'Elliss Spurrell did *not* appear as a witness for the prosecution at Beck's trial at the Old Bailey. Since he had given vital evidence that Smith and Beck were one and the same man in the Police Court why was he not called at the Old Bailey?'

Here is Sims' explanation: 'Let us see how this ingenious method of "planting" the evidence of Spurrell just where they wanted it benefited a prosecution conducted by the leading Counsel for the Treasury.

'If Spurrell had gone into the box . . . as he did at the police court and sworn that Beck was Smith . . . the case for the prosecution would have been hopelessly discredited . . .'

This was based on the fact that the defence had called two witnesses who swore that while Smith was imprisoned in 1877 they often met Beck in Peru thousands of miles away. Why, Sims asked, did the prosecution, or was it the police, resort to what seemed to be a piece of very dangerous legal chicanery? 'By putting Spurrell in the box in the police court,' he wrote, 'his evidence that Beck was Smith formed part of the deposition, and so in the Old Bailey calendar Adolf Beck's name appeared with a previous conviction against him in the margin—that of John Smith.'

Sims made no bones about describing this as a conspiracy and commented: 'We shall see how deadly to the unhappy prisoner was the result of this clever move.'

He next dealt with a sixth piece of suppression, concerning the handwriting expert, Mr. Gurrin, who had stated, at the Old Bailey trial of Beck, that the exhibits in the case of Smith alias Willoughby in 1877 and the exhibits in Beck's case were all in the same handwriting. 'The disguise then adopted is the same as that now adopted and the exhibits in that case must, in my opinion, have been written by the person who has written the bills and cheques in this case.' As we have seen, when Gill tried to bring out this point as evidence, Avory claimed that the 1877 offence was a collateral issue which should not be enquired into until the jury had returned their verdict. He went further. He objected to the witness being asked whether those exhibits were in the same writing as in the present case. Far worse—the Common Serjeant Sir Forrest Fulton upheld him.

Now came this unanswerable passage in Sims' pamphlet: 'Sir Forrest Fulton, Common Serjeant of the City of London, had, as Mr. Fulton, prosecuted the man Smith for the Treasury. Surely he must have remembered the fact . . . and would see the importance of Beck being able to show that the writing of Smith was the writing now before the jury? It ought to have struck him that he was listening again to the story of John Smith—word for word . . . Yet he refused Mr. Gill's request to correlate the two sets of offences.'

Sims wrote his pamphlet at a time when Sir Forrest Fulton was still very much alive and the law of libel forced him to qualify what he really wanted to say.

'A judge presides over a trial to assist both prosecution and defence in bringing out the truth, but by his most unfortunate decision Sir Forrest Fulton assisted—unintentionally of course —the Treasury in obtaining the conviction of an innocent man.'

The real effect of Sir Forrest's decision was to misconstrue the true implications of Beck's alibi for the 1877 crimes.

The Common Serjeant had ruled that the question of different identity was not admissible and Sims exclaimed: 'Not admissible! Great Heaven. It was the whole case.'

Sims had also dug out yet another piece of evidence which convincingly showed that Beck had in fact been convicted as Smith. In prison Beck was forced to wear a lettered number which read D.W. 523. Sims discovered that the 'D' meant convicted in 1877 and the 'W', convicted in 1896.

Sims finally formulated his attack in bolder terms: 'Who deceived the Public Prosecutor so shamefully?—What subordinate or subordinates took part in this unholy plot against an innocent man and hoodwinked the Public Prosecutor . . . and the high officials at Scotland Yard?'

Full of pious reverence for distinguished lawyers Sims could not quite countenance the idea that anyone above the rank of a police sergeant or clerk had 'perpetrated this abominable outrage on justice', deliberately overlooking the very ambiguous position of the judge himself. Could a lapse of nearly twenty years have wiped from Forrest Fulton's memory the countenance of John Smith so effectively that he saw no contradiction in the quite different features of Adolf Beck? It is possible.

Many daily newspapers had, by now, followed Sims' lead and an uproar arose in the press, some newspapers clamouring for an enquiry, others appalled at the suggestion of conspiracy. So powerfully did he present the case, with such colourful invective, that the *Daily Telegraph* invited a distinguished lawyer to examine his evidence and publish a report. An article appeared on August 16 called 'The Case of Adolf Beck: Its Legal Aspects'.

With considerable cunning the *Daily Telegraph* had dug out another article (March 8, 1896) in the *Sunday Referee* by Sims where he appeared far less sympathetic to Beck. He had written: 'I have known Adolf Beck the sham Earl for over ten years. During that time there was never the slightest suspicion in my mind that he was anything but a cultured . . . Scandinavian gentleman . . . He might I suppose have passed as a German, a Swede . . . or a Norwegian but no one would talk to him . . . and say he was an Englishman. Yet most of the duped women seem to have accepted him as an English nobleman . . .'

Quoting these words the *Daily Telegraph*'s lawyer proceeded to demolish the case for a conspiracy. Nonetheless, he did think it possible that an enquiry was justified and suggested that it should be carried out by—of all people—the Home Office. So an organization suspected of complicity was to investigate itself!

Sims plainly and boldly stated that such a course was no less a mockery of justice than the actual trial. He fully acknowledged his early doubts about the case but claimed a change of mind on the evidence which he had laboriously uncovered.

Fought out in the public prints, these battles brought the case constantly into the headlines, the precise objective of Sims' campaign. Presently, even the *Daily Telegraph* began to feel the rising pressure of public opinion and now it said: 'People are no longer talking about mistaken identity . . . the ugly word conspiracy has arisen . . . whether wisely or not . . . and definite charges are being levelled against the authorities . . .'

This was based on an article in the *Daily Chronicle* said to have been inspired by Sims once more, which announced: 'To any clear-sighted analyst the facts of this case are becoming so disturbing that nothing short of a public enquiry will satisfy the public conscience . . . There remains one way of testing the veracity of Mr. Sims' devastating analysis of the facts, and this is to trace the second person involved in these crimes, the ubiquitous but vanished John Smith. Why does not Scotland Yard send out his description to all police stations . . .'

Why not indeed, but Sims thought he knew the answer. Too much—duplicity?—carelessness?—corruption?—would be uncovered if ever John Smith gave his own account of what had taken place. However, by now, such was the mounting hue and cry and such the doubts of Mr. Justice Grantham who presided over the second trial, that he decided to postpone sentencing Beck. In the interval, Mr. Harold Furniss, a fellow campaigner with Sims, wrote to Grantham recapitulating the proofs of Beck's innocence of the earlier crimes. From the Royal Courts of Justice on July 1, 1904 came this reply:

Adolf Beck

'Dear Sir,

I have already made special inquiries into this case and have no doubts whatever of the correctness of the verdict and cannot therefore direct or allow any other investigation to be made.

Faithfully yours,

William Grantham.'

Sims' wrath ran over. Who dared to keep from the knowledge of a judge making *special inquiries* that Adolf Beck had been wrongfully committed in 1896, who dared to deny the Home Office admission of a mistake? Who dared to keep from him the fact that the handwriting expert Gurrin had reported to the Treasury in 1896 that *all* the documents in the Beck case were in the handwriting of Smith of 1877, which was also the handwriting of 1904?

Some person, or group of persons, Sims exploded, were prolonging this appalling conspiracy—and for what purpose?—

their own protection—to mask corruption—or simply to conceal
incompetence?

Meanwhile, in a state of near collapse, Adolf Beck waited in
gaol for a sentence which could have been as much as ten more
years. And then came the third amazing twist in this long
painful story . . . A certain Inspector John Kane was present
at both of Beck's trials, and Sims' campaign convinced him
that tracing the ubiquitous John Smith alone could clear up
the whole issue. He therefore kept his ears pricked for any
hint of Smith's whereabouts. Hearing that a man had been
charged at Tottenham Court Road Police Station one day,
with crimes closely resembling those alleged against Beck, he
hurried down to the cells and scrutinized the prisoner with
Beck's case in mind. He saw at once on the man's jaw the scar
for which so many witnesses had looked in vain when identifying Beck. He quickly realized that this man, calling himself
William Thomas, was none other than the by now notorious
John Smith alias the Earl of Willoughby.

He hurried at once to Scotland Yard and wrote a detailed
report. Within forty-eight hours, Adolf Beck was released from
prison and every newspaper in the country headlined the story.

Inevitably, pressures from private and newspaper sources
for an enquiry into the whole terrible saga now aroused widespread public support. Waves of indignation swept the press
and it slowly became clear that not all the complacency of
legal bureaucracy or the stalling devices of interested parties
could stop what, in effect, converted a private prosecution into
a public enquiry.

Meanwhile a splendid document with a magnificent seal,
entitled 'The King's Pardon', arrived for Adolf Beck, but the
joke to him was more hollow in proportion to the magisterial
trappings surrounding the document. Why all this pomp and
ceremony to extend 'Our Grace and Mercy to Grant Him
Our Free Pardon' when what he needed was some much more
concrete redress for a terrible crime committed against him
by the State? In fact, he received two engraved and embossed
documents—two free pardons, one for each charge—the very
duplication of which made more apparent their flimsy
inadequacy.

But the State could no longer hold out against the enquiry

and in due course the names of the members of the Committee were announced: Sir Richard Henn Collins, Master of the Rolls, Sir John Edge, ex-Chief Justice from India, and Sir Spencer Walpole, K.C.B.

Meanwhile, Sir Forrest Fulton felt driven to write a very long explanatory letter to *The Times* on August 29, 1904. He attempted to justify his ruling which refused Mr. Gill permission to bring in the case of John Smith, and recalled the repeated identifications of Beck by many women; he pin-pointed Mme Meissonier's claim that she had described the mark on the right side of Beck's neck which the jury examined and found to be a mole; he suggested that if Mr. Gurrin was wrong about Beck's handwriting then he might just as easily be wrong about Smith's handwriting which made his evidence worthless to Mr. Gill for the defence; and he claimed that the Crown had described Beck at the time of the offence as a needy person glad to borrow five shillings which showed clear motive.

Nearly two months later, the Committee of Enquiry began to take evidence on October 18. Extracts from the Report, when finally delivered to the Rt. Hon. A. Akers Douglas, M.P., emphasized what appeared, at first sight, to be nothing worse than inner bureaucratic negligence. Confusingly, a civil servant whose name was identical with the journalist crusader Sims, but with different initials (F.J.), Clerk to the Director of Public Prosecutions, seems to have tied the first knot which suppressed certain vital information in the Home Office Records. But to see this in perspective let us examine the correspondence between the solicitor T. Duerdin Dutton, acting on Beck's behalf, the Commissioner of Police and, later, the Home Office.

On March 26, 1898, after the first trial of Beck, Dutton had written to the Commissioner of Police stating that since there was good evidence—which the judge ruled inadmissible—that Beck and John Smith could not possibly be one and the same man: 'Will you under the circumstances allow me to inspect the papers of John Smith and Adolf Beck so that I may have an opportunity of comparing them?'

Three days later the answer came back that these papers were confidential and could not be examined by Mr. Dutton. Whereupon Dutton wrote to the Under Secretary of State at the Home Office. He pointed out that as long ago as May 1896 he had presented a petition to the Secretary of State on Beck's behalf giving all the evidence to prove his innocence.

On May 25 he wrote again saying that John Smith, alias Ivan Weisenfells, was of Jewish persuasion and would, therefore, have been circumcised in accordance with the customs of his race. 'I do not know whether this appears on the records of John Smith but it can of course be easily proved that Beck has not been circumcised.'

The Prison Commissioners now found themselves forced to write to the Governor of Portland Prison saying that they wished to examine the Penal Records for convict D.W. 523 Adolf Beck.

The record was sent and returned with a Minute which said: 'Please have this prisoner's description carefully revised.' A Minute dated 19/5/98 from B. Partridge, Governor of Portland Prison to the Commissioners, now admitted the full truth. John Smith had been circumcised and Beck, after fresh examination by the medical officer, showed no signs of circumcision.

In the Home Office Minutes for May 23 there occurred a document which said: 'I believe Mr. Dutton is so far right that Beck and Smith are different persons which is shown by the marks on them which I have compared and which differ widely and which curiously have never been referred to before . . . but this does not prove that Beck was not guilty of the many offences of the same kind of which he was convicted, he having been satisfactorily identified by numerous women whom he had defrauded . . .' Numerous women? Yes, but there were several qualifications. Alice Sinclair said: 'That is as much like the man as any of them. I believe he is the man.' Miss Vincent said: 'I feel almost sure he is the man.' Miss Johnson: 'That is as much like the man as any but I should not like to swear he is the man.'

A second Minute dated June 27 said: 'It is a very curious case but the evidence of Beck's identity by the numerous women he had defrauded was positive.'

A very curious case! Did no one see fit to follow up all these doubts? Well—yes, someone signing himself with the initials C.M., aroused by the various documents steadily accumulating more and more evidence in Beck's favour, at last commented in a Home Office Minute dated June 27, 1898: 'Though the present conviction is not affected by the representations made by Mr. Dutton I think the papers should go to the Common Serjeant for his opinion and observation.'

Thus we are back once more with Sir Forrest Fulton, the man who prosecuted Smith and presided over the trial of Beck. The vital question remained: did these minutes and the new evidence ever reach Sir Forrest Fulton? Before we attempt to answer that question, consider a number of other details which lead up to it.

The Report of the Committee of Enquiry dealt with the evidence of the second Mr. Sims, the Civil Servant who seems to have choked the proper flow of information half-way through its very sluggish channels. From December 26, 1895 Sims managed the documents in the case under the super-vision of the Public Prosecutor, Lord Desart. Shortly after Beck's arrest the police were told that the prisoner was really the ex-convict Smith under another name. The police informed Sims who took the preliminary steps required for confirmation by applying—'in the proper quarter'—for the identification marks of both men.

The Report continued: 'The marks of Smith were received in due course but Mr. Sims states *that his recollection was that he did not receive those of Mr. Beck*' (author's italics).

None the less, Inspector Froest did himself receive Beck's identification marks on January 15, 1896 from the deputy governor of Holloway Prison and 'was under the impression that they had been sent on'.

So two men, the Civil Servant Mr. Sims and the policeman Inspector Froest, both behaved in what seemed to be a very lax way. One did not press for the identity marks he had requested and claimed he never received them, and the other was not completely certain that the marks had been forwarded to Sims. The report said:

'Mr. Sims' . . . explanation of his inaction is that about the time when he ought to have received them a witness was found who could identify Mr. Beck as Mr. Smith in the person of Spurrell an ex-constable who had charge of the case against Smith.'

But Spurrell had not seen Smith for nineteen years and yet

Sims was prepared, it seems, to accept his evidence as so conclusive that all the suspicions by now aroused were swept aside.

The report certainly mentioned this fact as a mild reproof but proceeded to whitewash another and far more remarkable detail, which the enquiry had brought to light.

Inspector Waldock, the man who organized the early proceedings in the case, happened to know Beck and now admitted to the enquiry that he could not believe him guilty until after his conviction. When he received information that Beck and Smith were one and the same person he asked Beck to strip to check the identification marks quoted on the police document. 'This document,' the report said, 'which had attached to it a photograph of Smith did not, as above stated, record the fact of circumcision.' But since Waldock could see no likeness between Beck and the photograph 'for his own satisfaction, without any order from his superiors he made the examination with the result that he could not find on Mr. Beck the corresponding marks'.

The report now stated that since the examination was unauthorized no written statement was made by Waldock to his police superiors.

The incredulity which that statement arouses is modified somewhat by Waldock's claim that he did report the discrepancies verbally to Mr. Sims. Then followed this savagely funny contradiction in the report: 'Mr. Sims though he threw no doubt upon Waldock's veracity was quite positive that no such communication had been made to him.'

So Waldock remains truthful when Sims denies the communication on which that truthfulness rests! Even this very establishment-minded court of enquiry had to attempt some justification for this paradox and now—in a mild way—its wrath fell on that lesser scapegoat of a minor civil servant: Sims.

In the view of the Court's findings there was only one plausible allegation of unfair conduct on the part of Beck's prosecutors, and that centred on this failure of communication between Inspector Waldock and Sims. 'If Mr. Sims' recollection is right, the charge of course falls to the ground. If his recollection is wrong, and we must confess that we incline

5

to the latter view, his conduct was, nevertheless, in our view (to put it at its worst), quite consistent with a perfectly honest intention to bring together the necessary materials on which the prosecution was to be based.' So—once again here was a culprit who turned out to have perfectly honest intentions.

There followed, in the report, a desperately strained attempt to justify Sims' suppression of Waldock's verbal information which the members of the enquiry assumed did reach him. The burden of the accusation against Sims was that having received information early in the case, which must lead any intelligent man to understand that Smith was not Beck, he nonetheless allowed the case to be conducted as if they were identical persons. 'The facts,' the report said, 'are susceptible of another explanation. With his greater experience of the untrustworthy character of these "descriptions" he might well suppose that no weight could be attached to the fact that Waldock had failed to find on Mr. Beck all the marks specified in Smith's description.'

'*All*' the marks! He did not find *any* of the marks. And was no weight to be attached to that?

We turn now to what the report regarded as the kernel of the whole series of terrible injustices. Following his conviction in 1877, no one examined John Smith for signs of circumcision, first because such a special detail did not commonly concern the police and second because he had anyway declared himself a Protestant. When, in 1879, Smith applied to correct his description in the prison records to that of a Jew, the prison doctor did at last establish that he had been circumcised. We quote the report once more: 'Owing—apparently—to the negligence or omission of the governor of the prison, who has since died, the fact that Smith was circumcised was not entered in his record of marks. The doctor's report was, however, placed on the file with other papers relating to the prisoner.'

When released in 1881 no mention appeared on Smith's record of circumcision, and when the Public Prosecutor in January 1896 asked for his identification marks, he received a report which excluded this fact.

'This omission,' the report said, 'whether due to a defect of system or to negligence on the part of an individual was in our opinion the primary cause of the miscarriage of justice.'

A representative of the Prison Commissioners told the court of enquiry that there was no set regulation which made it obligatory for prison governors to add details such as circumcision to their records.

What the report gently refers to as another 'defect in the process of review by the Home Office' concerned Beck's first petition on June 9, 1896 to that august body. 'From what I have heard,' Beck wrote in his petition, 'there can be no doubt that this person [John Smith] whoever he is, is the same man who has committed the crime for which I am accused by this woman. Your lordship will find that in examining that man's trial of 1877 there will be found the same story as told by this woman against me, the same cheques, the same handwriting and signature.'

By now the Home Office knew that one man was circumcised and the other not, but did 'they' proceed to investigate the contention in Beck's petition and compare the records of the two men? No.

Who failed to compare them? The report does not say. Certainly not Sir Matthew White Ridley, then Secretary of State, because—'none of the documents in the case bear his initials'. Was it the Public Prosecutor's responsibility, or that of the Police? No answer. Sims could not be invoked at this late stage because he was a small cog in a much earlier part of the legal confusions.

We turn, finally, to the role of Sir Forrest Fulton, the man who not only prosecuted John Smith but presided over Beck's first trial. On this very vital issue he told the court of enquiry: 'I had not the faintest recollection either of the case or the man.' He then added a curious extension to his reply: 'I cannot lay my hands on my fee book for that year, but I expect I only held the brief which was probably a court prosecution for a friend.'

Chairman: '. . . What I should like to know is, were the documents which disclosed the non-identity of Smith with Beck by reason of the fact of circumcision, included in the documents that were sent to you [by the Home Office]?'

Here, instead of a direct negative, Sir Forrest replied: 'I think not.'

Later the Chairman put the same question in a different

form: 'Then I understand your recollection is that it was not brought home to you by the official evidence that it was the fact that these distinguishing physical circumstances existed?'

On this occasion Sir Forrest gave a definite answer: 'No—certainly not.'

Doubt occurred in the first answer and none in the second.

On another vital question his answers once more became cloudy. The Chairman reminded Sir Forrest that the Home Office claimed 'to have instituted that investigation (into circumcision) at their own instance before they communicated with you—I mean the investigation whether Smith was a Jew.'

'I do not know anything about that,' came the answer, 'but I thought that the investigation was the result of my letter but I do not know.'

Sir Spencer Walpole now took up the cross-examination:

'Have you seen by any chance this paper which the Home Office circulated among us which contains the distinctive marks?'

'No.'

'Would you mind looking at that. It contains the distinctive marks of Smith and Beck.'

'No—I have not seen it.'

'You will see that paper was prepared for the Home Office in May of 1898. You will observe that at the bottom of these facts there is the fact that one man is circumcised, and the other is uncircumcised.'

'Yes.'

'If you will kindly look at Mr. Murdoch's letter to you of July 1898, two months afterwards, it purports at the end of it to forward to you a note of the distinctive marks found upon Smith and Beck . . .'

'Yes.'

'What I want to ask you is, if you can recollect whether that note of the distinctive marks on the previous page was the document enclosed to you in that letter and if so whether there was anything on it to show that it was an official document and not a document furnished to the Home Office by Mr. Dutton.'

The point was vital. If it came from Dutton it was suspect as part of his campaign to clear Beck's name, but if it came from the Home Office . . .

The witness withdrew and later was recalled. Sir Forrest Fulton now stated that he had examined the document sent to him by the Home Office. 'There is nothing on it which would indicate that it is an official document.'

'Except,' Sir Spencer Walpole said, 'the stamp on the paper.'

'Yes—copied by the Home Office but I cannot say that I thought it was an official document from that . . . It is on their paper of course.'

The reader is invited to make his own interpretation of these answers.

In its final report the enquiry also censured Sir Forrest Fulton for his ruling that Gill could not bring in the issue of John Smith. 'It seems to us that the learned judge did not fully appreciate the ground on which Mr. Gill claimed the right to put the question and treated the sound rule as to evidence on collateral issues as applicable to the special circumstances of this case which, with the greatest deference to the learned judge, for the reasons . . . given we venture to think it was not.' As a result of this wrong ruling, the report said, a mis-trial took place.

None the less, the report continued, it was a failure in the Home Office which prevented Beck's petitions being properly understood by Sir Forrest Fulton. When they referred the new evidence of circumcision to him 'they did not explain to the learned judge with sufficient clearness that this information was derived from official sources, nor did they ascertain the indisputable fact that the incriminating documents of 1896 were in the same handwriting as those of 1877'. The report concluded that Sir Forrest Fulton would clearly have seen a miscarriage of justice if he had been in possession of these facts.

One other man came under the closest scrutiny by the Enquiry, Horace Avory the prosecuting counsel in the 1896 trial.

The Chairman posed one particularly salient question: 'You said at the end of your speech for the prosecution—"And should not be enquired into until after the jury had returned their verdict lest it should afterwards be said the person had been improperly convicted"?'

'Certainly,' answered Avory. 'My feeling at that time was that it might be said that the evidence had been improperly admitted, contrary to the statute of a previous conviction against this man. Now it has been further said at the conclusion of the trial after the jury had convicted, I improperly refused to allow one of the "indictments upon the file of the Court for felony which contained the charge of a previous conviction to be tried".'

The answer to that, Avory said, was self-evident to anyone familiar with the criminal law. 'The statute provides that a man who is tried for obtaining goods by false pretences may nevertheless be convicted. He is not to be acquitted if it turns out to be larceny and to suggest that he should afterwards be tried for larceny on the same facts is, of course, ridiculous to a lawyer . . . So that there I had an express provision of a statute which absolutely prevented me from trying a second indictment for larceny upon those same facts.'

Inspector Waldock, Elliss Spurrell, Sims, Sir Forrest Fulton and Avory all, like Beck, had their 'alibis', but unlike Beck they were given the full benefit of whatever doubt arose. In the intricacies of the enquiry the smoke-screen of professional protections made it very difficult to isolate any one fact which indicted, without equivocation, any one of the witnesses.

But at long last, towards the end of the enquiry, Beck himself was *almost* allowed to put a question, and he chose to try to put it to Mr. Gurrin the handwriting expert. It is necessary to say *almost* because when he rose and said to the Chairman: 'May I put a question to Mr. Gurrin?' the Chairman brusquely said: 'Let me know what the question is.'

Some rapid consultation took place and Sir George Lewis spoke on Beck's behalf. Even now, after all these appalling evasions and deceptions had been exposed, the poor victim was not allowed to present his own question. Sir George Lewis' question was: 'Does Mr. Gurrin think that if he had been allowed to give evidence at the trial and was not stopped from doing so, his evidence would have made Beck's innocence apparent at the trial?'

The Chairman's answer was: 'He said so.'

Anyone interested enough to analyse the forest of technical complexities in this case, which can only be summarized here, should read Eric R. Watson's definitive book, *The Trial of Adolf Beck*. Any shorter account must remain unsatisfactory.

In the introduction to his book, Mr. Watson built up a number of circumstances which could only be said to exonerate the police and lawyers. The luck, for instance, was continually against Beck. John Smith frequently operated in the very area where Beck lived, as was testified by Nellic Cawston who met him within a hundred yards of Beck's apartment. When he came out of prison after his first sentence, Beck moved to rooms in Oxford Street, and Smith promptly shifted the scene of his operations to Oxford Street. They both used the Grand Hotel, Charing Cross, they both pawned jewellery and both men were of foreign origin. Mr. Watson omitted from his account the worst piece of bad luck—that a completely anonymous stranger should set moving the whole horrible nightmare by not only recalling the resemblance between the crimes of John Smith and Adolf Beck, but taking the trouble to write to the police.

The committee of enquiry drew one important moral from their work: 'That evidence as to identity based upon personal impressions is, unless supported by other facts, an unsafe basis for the verdict of a jury.'

Mr. Watson drew another and far more important moral: that grave dangers of injustice may arise if a judge, swayed by the arguments of the prosecution, allows a technical objection upon which the whole defence may depend, to be sustained. As for Gill's failure to press home the real issue with much more vigour, elaborate justifications within the requirements of legal etiquette were not really convincing.

It was left to a private individual again—Mr. George R. Sims, an ordinary citizen, but an eloquent journalist—to challenge the machinations of the State.

CHAPTER V

GEORGE ARCHER-SHEE
[1908]

MR. MARTIN ARCHER-SHEE was an agent for no less a financial institution than the Bank of England and the story of his fight against the august powers of the Admiralty really began one day in October 1908. On that day he was astonished and totally dismayed to receive a letter from the Admiralty marked 'Confidential'.

'I am commanded by my Lord Commissioners of the Admiralty to inform you that they have received a letter from the Commanding Officer of the Royal Naval College at Osborne, reporting the theft of a postal order at the College on the 7th instant, which was afterwards cashed at the post office. Investigation of the circumstances of the case leaves no other conclusion possible than that the postal order was taken by your son, Cadet George Archer-Shee, and we must accordingly, with great regret, request that your son be withdrawn from the College.'

It came as a terrible shock to Martin Archer-Shee. His son dismissed—which is what the letter really meant—his career blighted, if not ruined, at the very outset. Worse still, the stigma might easily remain for the rest of his life. It was too much for Mr. Archer-Shee. In a burst of moral indignation he consulted several friends who warned him that challenging such a remote and powerful body as the Admiralty might prove to be a foolhardy business, but Martin Archer-Shee was a very determined man when roused.

His elder son by an earlier marriage had become an M.P.

and he now sought his advice. 'Get a good lawyer's opinion before you go any further,' his son said. 'There's only one man,' he added, 'who can really take on the Admiralty, and that's Edward Carson.'

It seemed absurd. A five-shilling postal order stolen and the greatest advocate in the land called upon for an opinion. The colossal expense, the sense of invoking a steam hammer to crack a nut, made Martin Archer-Shee hesitate, but such was his by now steadily mounting indignation that he determined if necessary to ruin himself financially to clear his son.

Sir Edward Carson, when approached, read the relevant documents, found the case fascinating, and gave a long opinion which said:

'I arrived at the conclusion that the postmistress *may have* been mistaken in her evidence and I am *led* to the belief that at least there is reasonable doubt in this case. I am therefore of the opinion that any legal tribunal would come to the same conclusion. Under the circumstances how is it possible with any justice to brand as a thief and a forger a boy of thirteen of the antecedents and character I have already described? It means disaster to him at the threshold of his life.'

But now the bureaucratic machine began to introduce difficulties. After all, George Archer-Shee had been condemned by the officers of the Admiralty—men of high integrity and great perspicacity—and their verdict could not be questioned lightly. Mysterious obstacles arose one after another to block the path of Mr. Archer-Shee. He was told that since his son had not yet become a fully fledged naval officer he could not be tried by court martial. The Director of Public Prosecutions also refused to take criminal proceedings. One by one the normal procedures of the law rejected every approach made by Martin Archer-Shee and his lawyers. Sir Edward Carson now decided to invoke a very little known process which enabled a private individual to challenge the legal maxim—then held inviolate—that the King could do no wrong. It was known as a Petition of Rights under which any one of the King's subjects could bring an action in the Courts, the writ of claim being recognized by the ancient words— Let Right be Done.

It was first necessary, nonetheless, to establish a contract between George Archer-Shee and the Admiralty, and Sir Edward Carson contended on behalf of the suppliant that a contract had been entered into between the plaintiff and the Commissioners of the Admiralty representing the King. The Solicitor General now rejected this:

'The question is whether the suppliant had any course of action to enable him to maintain a petition of right against the Crown. I submit that there is no contract between the suppliant and the Crown in a legal sense and as the foundation of a petition of right is a breach of contract there is no right to present a petition in the present case.'

More than eighteen months dragged away. And then at last Carson managed to get a preliminary hearing in the King's Bench Division of the High Court on July 12, 1910. Sir Rufus Isaacs, the Solicitor General, persisted in arguing a point of law:

'The Crown, as everyone knows, has immunity from legal proceedings and has the absolute right to dismiss anyone who has entered its service. Therefore this petition of right will not lie.'

Rufus Isaacs in support of his demurrer contended that the suggested contract was one between the suppliant and the Admiralty to train the plaintiff's son as a cadet. He submitted that on becoming a naval cadet the latter had entered into the service of the King and was therefore liable to dismissal at pleasure. The contract as set out in the petition showed that it was made with the Admiralty on behalf of the King and that it was subject to regulations. The first regulation was that all naval cadets entered the Service under identical conditions and were trained together until they attained the rank of lieutenant. The period of training was a period of probation and at the request of the Admiralty parents were understood to be ready to withdraw their sons. He then referred at length to *Dunn v Regina*, and *Mitchell v Regina*.

Carson received these statements equably enough and at once replied: 'The only question in my view is whether the petition discloses any cause of action—that is any contract. Of course this is not a claim by a gentleman in His Majesty's service but by a gentleman who entered into a contract for training his son. The contract would be to train the boy for four years, the parent undertaking certain payments and also undertaking that his son should follow a naval career. It is impossible to contend that the Crown cannot sue the plaintiff for failure to pay the amounts he has agreed to pay. Surely there must be a reciprocal obligation—subject only to the Crown's immunity from liability to have an action against it which the Sovereign had waived when he endorsed the writ— Let Right be Done.'

Mr. Justice Ridley intervened:

'I am in favour of the Crown, but would it not be better to go into the facts as there would no doubt be an appeal on the point of law.' The Solicitor General was quick to rejoin:

'My Lord, I am entitled to your judgment.' But Carson persisted:

'My Lord, I hope you will hear the facts. We have been persisting for two years under the most aggravating circumstances that ever occurred. I must say it does seem to me that this point of contract should have been taken before and decided in one way or another. The plaintiff has gone to great expense in getting up the facts of the case and I am surprised that the Crown should have taken this very unusual course.'

Mr. Justice Ridley: 'The plaintiff might himself have applied to have the point argued first.'

'Why should we?' Carson asked. 'We want to have the facts tried.'

'I know it may seem a hardship on the plaintiff remembering the expense to which he has been put, but I think the Crown must have the point of law decided first.'

'The Crown is shirking the issue of fact,' Carson insisted. 'It is a public scandal. The Crown can, I suppose, be high handed out of court but in open court it is not to be tolerated.'

'I submit,' said the Solicitor General, 'that I am entitled to judgment.'

Mr. Justice Ridley finally ruled in Rufus Isaacs' favour:

'The plaintiff's son is in the service of the Crown and naval cadets are so treated all the way through. No fresh document is given when they obtain a commission and take up duty on board ships. The words "naval cadets enter the Service" are used. They are appointed not elected. Their time as cadets is no doubt on probation but it is probation in the *King's*

Service. It is difficult to distinguish this case from others relating to officers in the service of His Majesty. Even if there were a contract it has been held in several cases that a condition was imported into it that the Crown should have the power of dismissal. I must therefore give judgment to the Crown.'

Sir Edward Carson was furious: 'This is the case of the grossest oppression without remedy that I have known since I have been at the Bar.' The Solicitor General calmly commented:

'All I can say is we have made all the necessary enquiries.'

'Only a hole in the corner enquiry in which the boy was not represented.'

'That is not so,' Isaacs retorted. 'Mr. George Elliott, K.C. went down.'

'Yes—that was *our* enquiry.'

'Assisted by the Admiralty.'

'It's a gross outrage by the Admiralty.'

Mr. Justice Ridley intervened again: 'I do not think you should say that. I know nothing of the facts. I have merely decided the point of law.'

Carson glared round the court, slowly gathered together his papers and stalked furiously away. Martin Archer-Shee was now beginning to wonder whether he had not been mistaken to challenge one august institution of Britain—the Admiralty—when other institutions would become involved and close their ranks against him.

However, encouraged by Carson's determination, he next agreed to take the issue to the Court of Appeal. There Carson brought to bear his eloquence, force of personality and legal knowledge to try to reverse Mr. Justice Ridley's ruling:

'Your Lordships may be interested to know that the charge against the boy is that he stole a postal order and forged the payee's name. The charge is totally devoid of foundation. It is admitted that the boy's conduct was entirely satisfactory until the date of the letter calling on the plaintiff to withdraw his son from the College. The trumping up of such a charge cannot render his conduct unsatisfactory. It raises a serious question of fact which ought to be tried.'

'Yes indeed,' said Lord Justice Vaughan Williams, one of the Appeal Court Judges, who had begun to take a warm interest in the case. 'Where are the facts?' The Solicitor

General now fought back with his claim that legal objections must be satisfied first, but the Lords Justices unanimously agreed on a re-hearing before the Lord Chief Justice. Carson appeared personally before his Lordship and as a direct result of this, a trial was at last arranged within less than two weeks.

Very little is known in detail about the life of the boy Archer-Shee, but Sir Edward Carson's is of course fully documented. Born on February 9, 1854 from the marriage of Edward Henry Carson and Isabella Lambert, he was destined to become, as his biographer H. Montgomery Hyde put it, a giant amongst men. At one period of his life he was described by a writer under the pen-name of Jehu Junior: 'Having more knowledge of Ireland than most Members of Parliament he contrives though he has not yet made a great name *as a statesman* to say even more distasteful things about the oppressed nationalists than the most brutal of the Saxons. He is a bold and sinuous person who pays no heed at all to the persuasions of the Nationalists who so prettily chide him for his want of patriotism. He seems to like the disgrace of being stigmatized as Mr. Balfour's Crown Prosecutor . . . He is a hard-working, painstaking, lynx-eyed practitioner of the law who can speak strongly. A lean, pale-faced Irishman who has as much wit and as much ability as Irishmen often have, he has not fattened even on robust Unionism . . .'

By the time Carson became involved in the Archer-Shee case he had reached legal and political heights beyond any possibility envisaged by Mr. Jehu Junior. In fact no silk gown had ever before been given to a barrister within so short a time of being called to the bar, and few politicians left their impress so rapidly on the House.

In the early 1900s the combined strain of his parliamentary and legal life were beginning to tell on a man now knighted for his services to the country, and by the time the Archer-Shee case came into court—1910—there were those among his friends who wondered how much longer he could bear the double burden, and those enemies who gleefully anticipated the first symptoms of a breakdown. His wife's health had begun to worry him, other domestic troubles were threatening, and as the newly elected Leader of the Irish Unionists they constantly sought his advice.

But he opened the case with his usual confidence. The morning of July 26, 1910, when the trial began, was a flawless summer day but the temperature quickly rose to heat wave proportions.

'This is a case of an unusual nature because as we know it is a time honoured tradition and legal fact that the King cannot be sued in the ordinary way in his own courts, but where there has been an alleged breach of contract by the Crown the King may endorse in special cases the writ which says—Let Right be Done—and this has been carried out in the case before the court. In 1908 the suppliant, Martin Archer-Shee, entered into an agreement with the Admiralty establishing his son at the Royal Naval College, Osborne. The suppliant paid certain fees and entered into certain engagements—for example to withdraw the boy if his conduct was unsatisfactory. The little boy from his birth in 1895 until 1905 was brought up at home and during that time he did not give his parents one moment's anxiety, nor was anything suggested against his character so far as character could be said to be formed at that early age.

'On October 18 the suppliant received a letter from the Admiralty, and by that letter this little boy of thirteen was branded as a thief and a forger, labelled and ticketed as such for the rest of his life.

'In the investigation which led to this disastrous result neither the father nor any friend of the boy was present to hear what was said. I protest most strongly against the boy being branded in this way as a thief and a forger. The little boy from that day up to the present moment, whether when called before his Commander, or under the softer ordeal of the enquiry by his loving parents, has never faltered in his declaration of innocence. Two years have elapsed since then. We have pressed again and again for a judicial enquiry into the matter—not a departmental enquiry—but a judicial enquiry—but we have pressed in vain until we were driven at last to bring this petition of right—and even that has been most strongly opposed until we got an order of the courts. If the boy's character is to be cleared it will not, therefore, be by any action of the State but the verdict of twelve of his fellow citizens. The suppliant asks only for that which every street Arab obtains. Indeed he does not ask so much. The Admiralty, having taken up a certain attitude, will never go back. They have fought and are fighting to the bitter end. One of the weapons used in their fight is Mr. Gurrin, the handwriting expert. I shall have an opportunity of asking Mr. Gurrin questions as to the evidence given by him on other occasions . . .'

Suddenly the judge, Mr. Justice Phillimore, intervened:

'That observation is unworthy of you, Sir Edward. Everybody knows Mr. Gurrin.'

'I resent that observation, My Lord. I hope you will withdraw it.'

'I cannot, Sir Edward.'

'Well then, I don't mind it.'

It quickly became evident that the judge was either beginning to sympathize with the case for the Crown or showing his dislike for Carson's forceful personality in court. Several unpleasant clashes occurred between them as the case proceeded. Sir Edward continued:

'I shall try not to become upset in this case and simply do my duty. I must therefore point out at once that the boy's financial position at the time he is alleged to have stolen and forged the five shilling postal order is as follows: He had £2 3s. in the school bank and £4 3s. 11d. in the Post Office Savings Bank. The boy also had a shilling a week pocket money. I appeal to the jury's experience to say whether, whatever a boy might do under the stress of want, he would steal and forge when he had plenty of money from other sources.

'On October 7 the boy wanted to buy a model steam engine for 15s. 6d., as the other boys knew. He applied for a chit to the lieutenant of the term entitling him to withdraw 16s. from the school bank, which he did, after one o'clock, and put it in his locker. After changing into flannels he went to see the boys roller skating and then asked a boy named Scholes to go with him to the Post Office. The latter refused as he had to meet friends. The suppliant's son obtained from a petty officer leave to go to the Post Office as it was out of bounds. Is this the way a thief would have acted without any attempt whatever at secrecy?'

Sir Edward Carson now roundly criticized in turn the Admiralty, the Commander who conducted the enquiry into the theft and even the Lieutenant involved in interviewing the boy:

'The Admiralty argued that the enquiry was not one in which representation in any sense of the word was appropriate, but Lieutenant Wilson was supposed to represent the boy.' Mr. Justice Phillimore again intervened:

'I am not quite clear what you are saying.'

'It seems to me I am being censured by the learned Judge as to the meaning of what I had supposed I was saying.'

'That is all well and good, Sir Edward, but you are censuring everybody and I suppose it is my turn now.'

'Now Your Lordship is censuring me again. To proceed— the day has at last come when the whole of this most unfortunate matter can be sifted and tried in open court and I need not remind the jury of the vital issue which depends on their verdict.'

Carson's first witness was, of course, Martin Archer-Shee, the boy's father:

'I have never at any time had reason to suspect my son's honesty. He is conspicuously open and straightforward. There is nothing secret about him. Whoever forged the signature on the postal order used a feigned hand but that person was not my son.'

George Archer-Shee himself was called next and gave his answers to Sir Edward's questions with a quiet confidence.

'You joined the Naval College in the same term as another boy?'

'Yes.'

'What was that boy's name?'

'Terence Back.'

'You knew him quite well?'

'Yes, he was in the next bed to me.'

'You each had lockers and sea chests?'

'Yes.'

'What was the nature of these sea chests?'

'Each boy had a sea chest and in it was a till with a separate lock but the lockers had no locks.'

'Did anyone have master keys to the sea chests?'

'Yes, all three servants.'

'When you went to the post office on the day in question what did you do?'

'I bought a 15s. 6d. postal order and sent it in payment for the engine I wanted to buy.'

'Did you know the technicalities of signing a postal order?'

'No. I signed the 15s. 6d. postal order as if I had received the money.'

'Tell the Court who was in the post office at the time of your visit and what happened between yourself and the postmistress.'

'There was a telegraph boy sitting on a chair, as well as the postmistress. I asked for a 15s. 6d. postal order and a penny stamp, handing her 16s. She gave me the order and the stamp and 3½d. change. I thought that all postal orders cost 1d. and asked why she had not give me a ½d. more. She said the order cost 1½d.'

'At no time did you cash a 5s. postal order?'

'No, sir.'

'Now that you know such an order was cashed and signed by someone, what is your comment on the signature?'

'It was not mine, sir.'

'And when you returned to the College?'

'I saw Back and another boy.'

'What did Back say?'

'He said: "Isn't it rot. I've had my postal order stolen and this is how I found my writing desk." '

'Were you aware up to that time that Back had a postal order?'

'No, sir.'

'And what happened the following morning?'

'I was called before Commander Cotton.'

'Was there anyone present who could be said to represent your interests?'

'No, sir.'

'What did Commander Cotton say?'

'He asked me whether I was at the post office yesterday and I said I was. He asked me whether I cashed an order and I said: "No, I bought one." '

'Did he press the question about cashing the order?'

'Yes, he said: "Are you sure you did not cash the order?" and I said—Yes, I was sure.'

'And then he asked you to write something?'

'Yes, he asked me to write my name and Back's name.'

'When you had written these names what did the Commander say?'

'He said: "It's funny you know Back's christian name." '

'Yet you had entered the College together, your lockers were together and you were class fellows from morning to night?'

'Yes.'

'Finally, I must ask you—is there any truth in the charge made against you?'

'No, certainly not.'

The Solicitor General now cross-examined the boy:

'There is a rule, I believe, that boys must not go into the Reading Room between two and three?'

'Yes.'

'When was it you put your money in the locker in the Reading Room?'

'I put the money there about two o'clock.'

'A second or two before the banned hour, in fact.'

'Er—yes.'

'You said nothing about putting the money in your locker until the enquiry took place before Mr. Acland?'

'No.'

'Was anyone present when you put the money in the locker?'

'I cannot say.'

'You did not put the money in your trouser pockets as would seem normal?'

'We have no pockets in our trousers.'

'But were you not accustomed, say, to put the money in an inner coat pocket?'

'No.'

'Were there no pockets outside the coat?'

'No.'

'Let me put it to you that there is in fact a pocket in the trousers.'

'I made a mistake—there is a pocket in the trousers.'

'Then why was it necessary to go to the Reading Room?'

'I don't remember why.'

'On the question of the signature. Have you ever at any time written Back's name for practice?'

'No.'

'Commander Cotton asked you how you knew Back's christian name.'

'Yes.'

'And did you not tell him that you and Back had been practising writing each other's signatures?'

'No. I do not see any reason why I should have done so.'

'Am I right in saying that when before Mr. Acland you wrote out the sentence—Working the Territorial Force would make Mr. Brown's back ache?'

'Yes.'

'The object of the sentence, of course, was to get certain letters written without drawing attention to them.'

Sir Edward Carson intervened at this point to re-examine the boy:

'You have seen Back's signature in other forms without copying it?'

'Yes, I have seen Back's signature in his exercise books.'

'And did the signature on the postal order resemble it?'

'It was decidedly unlike it.'

The judge now commented: 'I understand that the suggestion is that it was strange the boy before Commander Cotton should have written Terence H. Back, Back's signature, instead of Terence or T, or T. H. Back. It is not suggested that he practised the signature with a view to imitating it.'

'I certainly so understood it,' Carson said, 'and I think the jury did.'

The Solicitor General resumed his cross-examination:

'You say you cannot recollect whether anyone was there when you put the money in the locker?'

'Yes.'

'But you went to the post office with your friend, the boy Scholes?'

'Yes.'

'Did you inform the officials at Osborne that you had thrice asked Scholes to accompany you to the post office?'

'I am not sure: but I told my solicitors and Mr. Acland.'

'Did you not say in your first account to Commander Cotton that you went to the post office between 3 and 4 o'clock?'

'Yes, I think I did at first say that but I corrected myself at the time.'

'I suggest to you that it was not until Messrs. Lewis & Lewis came upon the scene that you altered the time to half-past two.'

'I cannot recollect when I altered it.'

'And did you not say to Captain Christian at the first enquiry that you knew on the morning of October 7 that Back had received a postal order?'

'No, I did not.'

'When did you know that Back had received a postal order?'

'I did not know until Back told me he had lost it.'

'But surely at the enquiry you did in fact tell the Captain that you knew on the Wednesday.'

'If I told the Captain that, then I misunderstood the question.'

The boy stood up remarkably well to a clever cross-examination and the details of his account were borne out by his close friend and fellow cadet, 15-year-old Patrick Scholes. Sir Edward Carson examined him:

'Can you recollect whether you were asked to accompany your friend Archer-Shee to the post office?'

'Yes, he asked me to go with him to get a postal order.'

'At what time was that?'

'About a quarter past two.'

'Why was it you did not go?'

'Because I was expecting some friends about 2.30.'

'Did he ask you to go a second time?'

'I cannot remember that.'

The Solicitor General cross-examined Scholes:

'How is it you remembered so exactly the time you were to go to the post office?'

'I kept looking at the clock to see when my friends would arrive.'

'Did you say at one time that Archer-Shee said he was going to *cash* an order?'

'I have never said that Archer-Shee was going to *cash* an order.'

Carson did not like the way the Solicitor General framed these questions and he immediately re-examined Scholes himself:

'What were the actual words you used?'

'I said—Archer-Shee said he was going to *get* an order.'

'Get and not *cash*?'

'Yes.'

'Was any suggestion ever made to you until yesterday that you had said *cash* and not *get*?'

'No.'

'Was it made to you yesterday by the Treasury Solicitor?'

'Yes.'

Carson directed a long look at the jury. He had succeeded in putting the Solicitor General in an embarrassing position, as the Solicitor General's next words indicated:

'The enquiry was made to settle a doubt in my mind.'

'I do not suggest anything improper on the part of the Treasury Solicitor,' Carson replied ironically.

But that was part of the complicated impact this exchange had on the jury. The expression on their faces clearly indicated that they, in turn, disliked the way in which the Treasury Solicitor had made his enquiry from one of the plaintiff's witnesses.

The next man in the box was J. G. Arbuthnot who had been a fellow cadet of Archer-Shee's at Osborne. Mr. Leslie Scott, K.C. examined him. Arbuthnot said that he was given leave on October 7 to go to the post office to cash one order, buy a second for himself and a third for a friend. 'The order to be cashed was for 10s., my own for 2s. 6d. and the third one for my friend Barton 12s. 3d.' When he arrived at the post office he saw a telegraph boy inside. Arbuthnot first cashed the 10s. order, then with the money bought a 2s. 6d. order and finally bought Barton's order for 12s. 3d. An interval followed the cashing of the first order when the postmistress went to another room to telegraph and telephone for about a quarter of an hour. When Arbuthnot finally left the post office he met one of the cadets' servants in uniform going in, but he did not know him by name or sight.

The effect of this evidence was to suggest that one of the cadets' servants had been seen entering the post office at the crucial time when the stolen postal order was cashed and might easily be a concealed culprit. The prosecution did not allow it to go unchallenged. Mr. Horace Avory cross-examined Arbuthnot:

'It is not your belief that a cadet's servant could be mistaken for a cadet?'

'I don't think so.'

'Do you remember having signed your order wrongly?'

'No. I do not remember.'

'Did not the postmistress draw your attention to this discrepancy?'

'I do not remember.'

'When Barton gave you the money where did you put it?'

'I put it in my pocket.'

'You have seen other cadets put money in their pockets?'

'Yes.'

'Which pocket?'

'The outside breast pocket.'

'Did you meet anyone else in the post office?'

'No.'

'You did not meet Archer-Shee?'

'No, I did not.'

The telegraph boy, Frederick Charles Langley, was now called for the defence and examined by Mr. Leslie Scott:

'You were on duty at the post office at what times?' Scott asked the boy.

'I was on duty from 9 to 1, from 2 to 4, and from 5.30 to 8.'

'Do you remember a cadet coming in?'

'Yes, a cadet came in about ten past two and remained there for over five minutes.'

'Did any other cadet enter around this time?'

'Yes, a second cadet came in a few minutes after the first one left.'

'And when did the second cadet leave?'

'About 2.30.'

The Solicitor General found this evidence too important to leave to his junior counsel, Horace Avory, and broke into cross-examine:

'How do you know the time was 2.30?'

'I glanced at the clock.'

'Can you tell us—how long after October 8 did you make this statement?'

'Some weeks. Someone came to see me and asked questions about it.'

'What did he ask you?'

'How many cadets came in that day, or anybody else, and the times.'

'You paid no particular attention to those cadets?'

'No. I often saw cadets coming in.'

'Could you say how many cadets came on the day before or after?'

'No. I could not say.'

'What work are you doing now?'

'Nothing.'

'Do you remember the day of the week it was?'

'Wednesday.'

'But at one time you thought it was on a Tuesday.'

'Yes.'

'And at one time you said the first cadet came in just after three.'

'I do not remember saying that.'

In the first instance the evidence of the telegraph boy had clearly brought a second—unidentified—cadet under suspicion and introduced confusions into the evidence against George Archer Shee, but confidence in his statements was shaken by the Solicitor General's cross-examination. If he could not say how many cadets entered the post office the day before or after October 7, why should the boy so clearly remember that particular day, and if he had once thought it happened on Tuesday instead of Wednesday, what reliability could be placed on any detailed evidence he might give? To counter these bad impressions, Carson intervened once more and proposed to read a statement made by the witness, but His Lordship upheld the Solicitor General's objection to this.

Carson next called Major Martin Archer-Shee, half-brother of George, who said he was originally in the Navy and had served in the South African war.

'You now have the misfortune to be a Member of Parliament?'

'Yes.'

'You have associated closely with your half-brother?'

'Yes and I have found him honourable and truthful. I

corresponded with my brother and I am convinced that the signature on the postal order was not George Archer-Shee's.'

Major Martin Archer-Shee concluded the evidence for the suppliant.

Opening the case for the Crown, Rufus Isaacs submitted that legally there was no case for the Admiralty to answer but he would argue this issue later. For the moment he would accept the *form* the case had taken:

'The first issue is clearly whether or not the suppliant's son took the order and as to this Miss Tucker, the postmistress, is the most important witness. I do not propose giving her evidence in detail at this stage because she will give it herself. She was called to give evidence on the morning following the theft and her statement was—and it is the crucial fact—that the boy who bought the 15s. 6d. order was the boy who cashed the stolen order. If the jury believe that, then the suppliant's son is necessarily guilty. I will not speculate on the motive actuating the boy's mind. I will have an opportunity of addressing you on that later.

'Cadet Back will tell the jury that the postal order was the subject of conversation at table and that he had laid it on the reading room table where it could be seen by everyone. When questioned in the first place, the boy Archer-Shee said he went to the post office between 3 and 4 o'clock. This is of importance in determining on which side the truth lies.'

The Solicitor General now dealt forcibly with Carson's attack on the Admiralty, and said he was there to justify their actions because questions of great importance were involved:

'It is not suggested that the Admiralty was actuated by any ulterior motive or malice or spite. I am most anxious that this should be made clear. The question is—had they reasonable grounds for their belief, for if he was guilty, it was plain he could not continue with other cadets. The officers were bound to act on their honest belief. Archer-Shee has been asked as to his signature of Back's name and he replied that he and Back had been practising each other's signatures. This explanation was untrue because Back was sent for the same day and he denied that they had done this. They also submitted the postal order to a handwriting expert—at any rate the most accredited among them. Handwriting experts, like other experts, no doubt make mistakes and this might be suggested against Mr. Gurrin, but this is the only means of testing handwriting. Even the suppliant has had to rely on it. Mr. Gurrin reported that the handwriting on the postal order was by the same hand as that of Archer-Shee. On that the Admiralty took the course which has led to this case. There may be some difference of opinion on the question of the right to a legal enquiry, but putting that aside for the moment, what we now have to determine is whether the boy or the postmistress is telling the truth.'

Miss Tucker, the postmistress, came into the witness box, and was examined by Mr. Avory:

'You keep a record of the postal orders issued each day from your post office?'

'Yes.'

'On the day in question, October 7, what orders did you issue?'

'Between 1.30 and 5 o'clock I issued the following orders: One for 2s. 6d., one for 3s., two for 5s., one of 12s. and one of 15s. 6d.'

'You have another record of the total amount paid in exchange for postal orders?'

'Yes. On that afternoon it amounted to 15s. in two orders.'

'How many cadets came in during the course of the afternoon?'

'Two—the first cashed an order for 10s. and bought one for 12s. and another for 2s. 6d. That was about seven minutes past two.'

'Do you remember the name of the 10s. order?'

'Yes. It was Arbuthnot. I kept him rather a long time because I was sending a telegram.'

'How did you know the precise time of Arbuthnot's visit?'

'By the time of those telegrams.'

'When did the other cadet appear?'

'He came in about an hour later with a 5s. postal order to cash.'

'You saw that something was wrong with this postal order?'

'Yes. It had Royal Naval College erased. I said to the cadet: "That ought not to have been erased." He said: "It was so when I got it." '

'And what happened then?'

'I gave him a half-crown and as I put the cashed order into a drawer the cadet asked me for a 15s. 6d. postal order and one penny stamp. He gave me half a sovereign and three florins.'

'Are you sure it was the same cadet who cashed the 5s. order as bought the 15s. 6d. one?'

'Perfectly.'

A very delicate moment in the whole trial had now arisen for Carson. Miss Tucker gave every appearance of being an honest and reliable woman who had recorded her evidence to the best of her recollection. In order to justify Carson's written opinion of the case he had now to show—without antagonizing either the witness or the jury—that not only *could* she have been mistaken in that recollection but that she probably *was* mistaken. He began his cross-examination:

'I believe you signed a statement giving a correct reproduction of your evidence?'

'Yes.'

But you only *signed* the document *after* you told Commander Cotton that you could not identify the boy?'

'Yes.'

'All you said was that the voice of the cadet in the office was gruffer than any of those you were given an opportunity of hearing.'

'Yes.'

'Do you know in whose handwriting on the signed document the pencilled words—but she could not identify him—were written?'

'No.'

'Is there anything in your books to show the *order* in which postal orders are dealt with or the times?'

'No.'

'So on the question of whether the same person cashed the 5s. order as bought the 15s. 6d. we must rely on your memory?'

'Yes.'

'Are all these cadets very much alike?'

'Yes.'

'All smart, good-looking boys about the same age?'

'Yes.'

'When Petty Officer Paul first came to see you about the stolen postal order what did he say?'

'He asked me if a cadet had cashed the 5s. order.'

'He first suggested it was a cadet?'

'Yes.'

'Did he say he had only given leave to two cadets to visit the post office?'

'I am not sure.'

'But he did say such people were not wanted in the Navy?'

'Yes.'

'Was he in a very excited condition?'

'I thought so, but I never seen him before. I would have said he was almost raving.'

'You knew that a charge of theft was being made?'

'No.'

'Did you say a word to anyone that evening about it being the same boy who bought the 15s 6d. order who had cashed the 5s. order?'

'I did not say it.'

'But there was another person who was present when the naval authorities first rang you up in the evening?'

'Yes.'

'Who was that?'

'A lady clerk from the Cowes office named Miss Paul.'

'Did you tell Miss Paul that the same boy who cashed the 15s. 6d. order cashed the 5s.?'

'I will not swear I said it.'

'Did you ever say it was a cadet who cashed the order before you saw Commander Cotton?'

'If I told Mr. Elliott I had not, it must be correct.'

'You said nothing about the dispute with the second cadet as to the change—to Mr. Elliott?'

'Perhaps I was not asked.'

'Can you remember anyone else having a transaction or conversation with you that day?'

'No.'

'Do you remember if any of the cadets' servants came?'

'No.'

'Were you never asked about the cadets' servants by the Commander or Paul or the Captain?'

'No. I do not remember being asked as to any body else.'

'So you paid no attention to anyone else that day?'

'No.'

'And no one attempted to test your memory on that point?'

'No.'

It was a remarkable feat of cross-examination carried out with such delicacy and charm that the witness had been drawn into a completely honest attempt to re-assess the reliability of her own evidence. Neither the jury nor the witness were antagonized, but the key points in Miss Tucker's evidence were now shown to be open to serious doubt. At the conclusion of Miss Tucker's evidence the court adjourned.

On the third day of the trial—July 28—Carson said he might have to ask for a further adjournment as he did not feel well, but perhaps he might get better as the case proceeded. By now the whole of London was talking about the boy Archer-Shee and hundreds of people were turned away from the court. Nonetheless, too many were left standing in the passages of the court and Mr. Justice Phillimore ordered them to be cleared. Cadet Back, the boy whose postal order had been stolen, was at last examined by Mr. Avory:

'Did you mention receiving the postal order for 5s. to any other cadets?'

'It is very likely I did.'

'Could you be a little more precise?'

'I mentioned it to Burrows.'

'And to anyone else?'

'As I went to the dormitory I met Archer-Shee and told him I had lost the order.'

'How do you usually sign your name?'

'I sign it "T. H. Back" if writing to strangers and "Terence Back" if writing to people I know.'

'Is it true that you and Archer-Shee practised each other's signatures?'

'No, it is not true.'

Sir Edward Carson rose to cross-examine:

'How many cadets were present at breakfast on the morning you received the postal order?'

'There were about sixty present.'

'And cadets' servants?'

'Yes, there were many present.'

'Did you show the postal order to Archer-Shee?'

'No, I did not. But he, with others, was at the table.'

'Did Archer-Shee see you put it in your locker?'

'No, as far as 1 know, he did not.'

'Was it Petty Officer Paul who brought in Archer-Shee's name?'

'I think it was.'

'Was he excited—even raving?'

'Excited, but not raving.'

'Did he cast suspicion on Archer-Shee?'

'I do not think so.'

'Have you seen Archer-Shee sign his name and has he seen you sign yours?'

'Yes.'

'When did you know that Archer-Shee had been to the post office?'

'Chief Petty Officer Paul told me.'

Chief Petty Officer Paul was now examined by the Solicitor General:

'When did Archer-Shee ask leave to go to the post office?'

'He asked for leave while he was on duty at the flagstaff.'

'At what time did this occur?'

'It must have been three o'clock, or after, because another cadet, Arbuthnot, had been there previously and reported himself as having returned. That was about 2.30 or after.'

'How long after did Archer-Shee apply?'

'Not less than half an hour later.'

'Were these the only cadets who had leave to go to the post office on that day?'

'To my knowledge Archer-Shee and Arbuthnot were the only cadets.'

'When you rang the postmistress and asked who had cashed the postal order, what did she say?'

'She said: "A cadet." '

'Can you give us the gist of the conversation that followed?'

'I asked how many cadets had been there and she said—two. I asked her who cashed it, the first or the second and she said—the second.'

Sir Edward Carson rose to cross-examine: 'Are you quite

sure the postmistress told you a cadet had cashed the postal order *before* you went to the post office?'

'Yes.'

'But the postmistress says she did not speak about a cadet until the following day before Commander Cotton.'

'That is inaccurate.'

'Did you not ask the postmistress when you went to see her if a cadet had cashed the order?'

'No—I already knew it.'

'Do you suggest that the postmistress is telling an untruth?'

Mr. Justice Phillimore once more intervened:

'I think you are going to the very verge of what you may ask, Sir Edward. Judges have again and again said that to ask a witness—"If 'A' says so and so, is he telling a lie?"—is most unwise.'

'Your Lordship seriously rules that I cannot do so?'

'No, I do not do so.'

Carson—still in devastating form and quite untroubled by the obvious hostility of the judge—pressed on to establish another point with Chief Petty Officer Paul:

'Have you formed a very strong opinion about Archer-Shee?'

'Nothing whatever.'

'Did you suggest that he had broken into his own sea chest?'

'No.'

'But I have here notes of answers given at the Naval enquiry to Mr. Elliott where you said: "I can only think that he broke into the chest himself." Let us anyway turn back to the time of Archer-Shee's visit to the post office. Had you any precise means of fixing that time?'

'No.'

'It might have been 2.30 when Arbuthnot reported himself.'

'It might have been.'

A number of lesser witnesses for the Crown were examined and cross-examined, beginning with Russell Gordon, a gunner on H.M.S. *Cornwall* who had originally been a cadet at Osborne. Russell Gordon said that Chief Petty Officer Paul reported the theft of the postal order to him and ordered him to go to the post office to make enquiries. He went personally rather than telephone because it was a confidential matter.

Under cross-examination he stated that Archer-Shee seemed to be quite an average cadet, but he would not like to say that he was favourably impressed with the boy's demeanour at the enquiry before Commander Cotton.

'Was he self-possessed?' Carson asked.

'Yes, very self-possessed.'

'Why were you not favourably impressed?'

'It was my experience.'

Mr. Justice Phillimore intervened: 'There was an indefinable something which, according to your experience, did not favourably impress you?'

'Yes.'

'But you were not unfavourably impressed?'

'No.'

Mr. Leslie Scott now read the evidence taken on commission from Russell Gordon at the time of the inquiry. In this document he admitted that there had been losses before this affair and even more after Archer-Shee left Osborne. He also stated, that he had no reason whatever to suspect any of the cadets' servants because great care was taken in their selection.

William Pritchard, a pensioner in the Marines, followed Gordon. He described himself as a cadets' servant at Osborne during October 1908 working in Mr. Archer-Shee's dormitory as a personal servant to Mr. Back. He first heard of the loss of the postal order when it was put before him at the enquiry after Archer-Shee had left Osborne. He admitted buying a postal order for Cadet Startin about a month before Archer-Shee came under suspicion.

Cross-examined by Mr. Scott, the witness was shown a postal order for 2s. 6d. issued at Osborne on October 7 and said that he had bought a postal order for Mr. Startin about that time.

W. H. Hopgood, another cadets' servant, followed Pritchard and said that he had never seen the 5s. postal order before the enquiry by Mr. Elliott and on no occasion did he go to the post office on October 7. Pressed on this point he repeated that he was sure he did not go.

Whereupon, Gunner Gordon was recalled by Carson and said: 'Hopgood told me that he did go to the post office on October 7 to purchase postal orders.'

The number of possible suspects in the case had certainly begun to widen under pressure from the prosecution.

Commander Cotton of H.M.S. *Terrible*, formerly in command at Osborne, now came into the witness box and under examination by the Solicitor General detailed the steps he had taken to set up the Osborne enquiry. Cross-examined by Scott. he admitted that Arbuthnot had told him that he had seen a man coming out of the post office, 'a squint-eyed chap dressed like a cadets' servant,' on the vital day. When, later, Cotton said to Archer-Shee that things looked black against him, Archer-Shee had replied: 'I swear by Almighty God I am innocent.' He remembered that because on a similar occasion another cadet had used the same expression.

The witness then stated that he had made a report to Captain Christian and Sir Edward Carson at once asked to see the report. The Solicitor General protested that the report was a privileged document and he did not propose arguing the point because he could not waive the privilege.

Surprisingly Mr. Justice Phillimore held that the document was admissible since the respondents had raised the plea to which it was relevant.

Mr. R. D. Acland, K.C. was now examined by the Solicitor General and said he was Recorder of the City of Oxford and Judge Advocate of the Fleet. He did not appear as Counsel for the Admiralty but had simply held an enquiry at Osborne before he had seen Cadet Archer-Shee in London.

Sir Edward Carson was quick to intervene:

'My Lord, I strongly object to evidence of anything that was done at an enquiry in which the boy was not represented. We asked that the boy should be represented and were refused.'

'Mr. Acland may show that he went there unassisted by either side,' commented Mr. Justice Phillimore.

The witness said he was sent down to form an independent opinion, and proceeded to give details of what he had found. Once again Sir Edward appealed to Mr Justice Phillimore:

'My Lord, I strongly object. All this was done behind the boy's back.'

'Once and for all,' Mr. Justice Phillimore said, 'I do not take the view that this was done any more behind your back than behind that of the Crown.'

'But that is nothing to me,' Carson replied. 'The Crown is not being tried. But I will put it in any way Your Lordship likes.'

Mr. Justice Phillimore proceeded to overrule the objection on the grounds that the evidence was directed to the point raised. Sir Edward Carson then put one crucial question to Acland in cross-examination:

'When you try a prisoner as a Recorder, do you not hear *both* sides?'

Acland was forced to admit that he did, whereas in this case he had heard only one side.

As they approached the end of the third day and the climax of the case it still seemed to at least one legal observer that the odds were equally divided. Before the adjournment on that day Carson said ironically:

'I do not suppose, remembering what has passed in this court, that the Solicitor General will claim the privilege of the Crown to have the last word with the jury. I have never known it claimed in a civil case and I was a Law Officer for six years.' Mr. Justice Phillimore again disagreed with Carson:

'I am sorry to have to tell you my experience is longer than that and I have known it so claimed.'

'It seems to me the law is getting out of date,' Carson retorted.

Despite Carson's protest it was arranged that the Solicitor General should have the last word on the following day, and with the verdict hanging finely in the balance that last word came as a shock.

After hurried consultation with Carson on the morning of the fourth day, the Solicitor General rose to make a special statement:

'As to the issues of fact, the court and the jury will not be further troubled. I say now on behalf of the Admiralty, as a result of the investigation which has taken place, that I accept the declaration of Cadet George Archer-Shee that he did not write the name on the postal order, and that consequently he is innocent of the charge which has been brought against him. I make that statement without any reservation of any description, intending it to be a complete acceptance of the boy's statements. The other issues of fact which are before the court

6

for decision arising out of the pleas set up by the Admiralty raise questions of great public interest as to the discipline and administration of the College.

'My learned friend, Sir Edward Carson, with reference to these questions of fact, accepts the statements of the Admiralty as to their action and agrees that those responsible for all that has happened were acting under a reasonable and *bona fide* belief in the truth of the statements which have been made to them. In justice to the postmistress, Miss Tucker, upon whose evidence so much reliance has been placed, it is right to say it has never been suggested that there was any want of *bona fides* on her part, and indeed the cross-examination of Sir Edward Carson had only been directed to show that she has been mistaken.'

As Carson rose to make his final reply there were tears in his eyes, so deeply had he become involved in the case:

'The complete vindication of his son, George Archer-Shee, was the object of the suppliant in bringing this action. That object has been entirely achieved. That is the first issue of fact. With regard to the other two issues, I agree that those responsible acted *bona fide* and under a reasonable belief in the statements put before them.'

But where, on this last day at the climax of a trial which could make or break his future, was the boy whose fate had become a matter of national moment, filling the newspapers with long reports? Lawyers, jurors, spectators all crowded round Carson to congratulate him but the boy did not join them. A quick search of the court failed to reveal him.

It was then at last discovered that having been to the theatre the night before the boy had overslept and was still at home. When, later in the morning, he went to see Sir Edward Carson in his chambers to thank him, a last conversation took place,

'What a strange boy you are,' exclaimed Carson. 'Didn't you feel too nervous to go out to the theatre?'

'Nervous, sir? I never had the slightest nervousness when I got into a court of law. I knew I'd be all right. Why, I never did this thing.'

'Well, after all,' Sir Edward replied, 'that's a very good way of looking at it.'

Lady Londonderry sent Sir Edward a telegram of congratulation. As Montgomery Hyde has recorded in his brilliant biography of Carson, he replied: 'You know how I appreciate it. It has been a great victory and I feel quite tearful over it— I was always convinced of the boy's innocence and I know it all arose from the blundering suggestion of the officers in charge. You should have seen the boy when he came to thank me. He was so frank and honest. My regret is that the Navy will have lost so promising a boy.'

Martin Archer-Shee celebrated his son's victory with a champagne supper and his mother read to the assembled company a letter from Sir Edward: 'You are quite right as to my belief in George. Will you please tell him I hope he will always look on me as a friend and I sincerely hope that the whole incident will in the long run turn out to his advantage. He will, I am sure, do well at whatever profession he adopts, and has the good wishes of everyone.'

Several M.P.'s finally brought the whole matter up in the House of Commons, and over the next few days indignation against the victimization of the boy mounted to the point where Mr. Reginald McKenna, First Lord of the Admiralty, agreed to appoint a tribunal composed of Lord Mersey, the Admiralty lawyer, Sir Rufus Isaacs and Sir Edward Carson to determine whether compensation should be made to Martin Archer-Shee for the big expense involved in proving his son's innocence. At the end of a long wrangle no offer came from the Admiralty to reinstate the boy, but his father was awarded £7,120 for compensation and costs.

Sadly, the remainder of George Archer-Shee's life was short and tragic. Four years later he volunteered for the Army at the beginning of World War I, accepted a commission in the South Staffordshire Regiment and almost at the outset vanished one day in the first battle of Ypres. The official communiqué posted him 'Wounded and missing' and he probably died of wounds. One record remains of his brief life. His name is inscribed along with many other heroes on the Menin Gate.

CHAPTER VI

OSCAR SLATER
[1908]

ON MONDAY, DECEMBER 21, 1908, a handsome old lady named Marion Gilchrist was found murdered in the most brutal manner in her Glasgow flat. The discovery set off a hue and cry which brought out the worst kind of vengeful reactions.

Marion Gilchrist was a well-to-do middle-class woman with her own servant, and the first obvious motive seemed to be a small hoard of jewellery concealed in her wardrobe valued at £3,000—equivalent today of possibly £15,000. But the sheer savagery of the murder—both eyes had been driven into her head and the bones of the face smashed almost to a pulp, with the brains seeping out—suggested a special kind of fury.

Mrs. Gilchrist's young servant-girl, Helen Lambie, had left the flat to carry out an errand on the evening of the murder and was away hardly ten minutes. When she returned, she found Mr. Adams, the brother of two sisters who lived below Mrs. Gilchrist in the same house, ringing the front door bell. It was known that for some mysterious reasons Mrs. Gilchrist had considerable fear of robbery with violence—witness the double locks on the doors—and she had arranged with Mr. Adams that she would knock a signal on the floor if she found herself in any kind of trouble. Before Helen Lambie returned that evening the two Adams sisters suddenly heard unusual noises coming from the flat above and Mr. Adams immediately ran upstairs to ring the bell. There was no reply but he heard a noise resembling someone chopping firewood. Instead of pressing home his enquiries he returned downstairs again only to have his worried sisters send him back, post haste.

With his hand on the bell the second time, he heard footsteps behind him, turned and saw Helen Lambie returning from her errand. He at once described the suspicious noises, she swiftly opened the two locks on the front door and hurried towards the kitchen. Suddenly—sheer audacity could go no farther—what must have been the murderer came out of the bedroom behind Helen Lambie and walked past Adams looking, as he later described him, 'quite pleasant'. Once outside the flat, the man's attitude changed and he dashed down the stairs 'like greased lightning'.

Not until Helen Lambie entered the dining-room did she stumble on the gruesome scene of the body with the head brutally smashed. She screamed 'Come here!' Mr. Adams rushed in. Everything near the fireplace was spattered with blood. Immediately they both turned and tore down the stairs in the hope of catching a fresh glimpse of the murderer, but the street was empty, dark, brooding, with only the old-fashioned gas lamps throwing limited pools of light through bursts of rain.

Almost at the outset, something peculiar emerged in a divergence between the accounts given by the two witnesses. Lambie later swore that after opening the door she stood beside Adams on the mat. Adams said she went straight on into the hall, and possibly the bedroom. If Adams' evidence was true, Helen Lambie must have seen the man leaving and since she raised no alarm, must have known him as in some way connected with Mrs. Gilchrist. This fact later assumed fresh significance.

Now, in the middle of his horrific discovery, Adams summoned the police and a doctor, who turned out to have the same name—Dr. Adams. The doctor examined Mrs. Gilchrist just before she died but she was quite incapable of uttering a word. Surveying the room for any further details of assault, Dr. Adams noticed a heavy, old-fashioned chair near Mrs. Gilchrist, one leg of which was drenched in blood. There and then on the spot he swiftly reconstructed the method of murder. The assailant had grabbed up the chair, thrust it downwards at his victim, crushing the bones, and driving one leg through the eyes into the head. As Mrs. Gilchrist struggled to rise, he had thrust his foot powerfully on her chest thus fracturing the ribs of the chest. The use of the chair and its downward thrust explained one astonishing characteristic of the man Mr. Adams and Helen Lambie had seen leaving the flat—a complete lack of any bloodstains on his clothing. In its downward thrust the seat of the chair would act as a shield to prevent the spurting blood reaching him. Once again, in view of the subsequent prosecution case involving a quite different weapon and technique for the murder, these facts must be borne closely in mind.

The police now issued to the Glasgow force a somewhat misleading statement which read: 'Robbery appears to have been the object of the murderer as a number of boxes in a bedroom were opened and left lying on the floor. A large-sized crescent brooch set with diamonds, large diamonds in the centre graduating towards points, is missing. No trace of the murderer has been got. Constables will please warn booking clerks at railway stations as the murderer will have bloodstains on his clothing . . .'

In view of the evidence already available, the last statement was calculated to guarantee the murderer a perfect alibi since there were no bloodstains on his clothes.

Presently the police issued two further descriptions of the wanted man. The first came from Helen Lambie and Mr. Adams: 'Man—between 25–30, 5 feet 8 or 9 inches in height, slim build, dark hair, clean shaven, dressed in light grey overcoat and dark cloth cap.'

The second description came from Mary Barrowman, a girl who happened to be passing the house when the murderer rushed out, and claimed that he had collided with her.

'About 28 or 30, tall and thin with his face shaved clear of all hair, while a distinctive feature is that his nose is slightly turned to one side. The witness thinks the twist is to the right side. He wore one of the popular round tweed hats known as Donegal hats and a fawn-coloured overcoat which might have been a waterproof, also dark trousers and brown boots.'

So many points of difference emerged in these descriptions that the police assumed at the outset there must be two men involved and the search proceeded on these lines. In the next few days not only Glasgow but a large part of the civilized world became aware of a brutal crime brazenly committed in the heart of a big Scottish city at a time when scores of people were normally abroad, and the police, driven by the public outcry, found themselves under heavy pressure to get results quickly.

Four days later, on Christmas Day, a bicycle salesman called McLean reported to the police that a 'German-Jew' whose Christian name was Oscar had tried to sell to the members of the Sloper Club a pawn-ticket covering a diamond crescent brooch. It never seemed to occur to the police as they closed in on their victim that since the newspapers had blazoned details of the brooch throughout the whole country, the last thing a guilty man would do was to try to auction—publicly—the pawn ticket for such a brooch. Moreover, the early conclusion that the wanted man might be a friend of or known to the victim—since he had entered the flat without breaking in—was conveniently forgotten as they fastened on this suspect. The public wanted results and they were determined to get them even at the cost of hasty and unscrupulous behaviour.

Friends of McLean, who knew Slater better, not only spelt out his full name but revealed that he lived under the alias Anderson—in police eyes another highly suspicious detail—at No. 69 St. George's Road. Every trick of luck and accident coincided to incriminate Slater. When the police arrived in force at his address a young German maid, Catherine Schmalz, informed them that her master and mistress had left that very night for Liverpool heavily loaded with baggage. The Liverpool police took up the trail and discovered that Oscar Slater had already sailed on board the *Lusitania* for New York. This, in the eyes of the police, was easily converted into headlong flight from the scene of the murder and even when they discovered that the brooch for his pawn ticket had been continuously in pawn from November 18, long before the murder, it could not stop an impetuous demand for Slater's extradition from the States.

When these proceedings ran into difficulties the police were relieved instead of bewildered to find that Slater himself was only too willing to return to Scotland of his own accord, simultaneously proclaiming his complete innocence of the crime.

Glasgow prepared to give him what was locally described as a 'hot welcome' since the public were already convinced that one of the most brutal murderers of the century would step ashore. Feelings ran so high and the threat of mob violence became so powerful, that the police decided to take Slater off at Renfrew to the west of Glasgow and avoid the thousands of spectators who lined the banks of the Clyde.

Even when it was discovered that Oscar Slater, a one-time bank clerk in Hamburg, had been born in Oppelin, Germany, and bore a markedly 'foreign cast of countenance', the omission of this major distinguishing characteristic from either of the police descriptions still could not stop the law from gathering its force to destroy him.

The trial opened on Monday, May 3, 1909 at ten o'clock in the High Court of Judiciary, Edinburgh, with the Lord Advocate Mr. Alexander Ure, K.C., Mr. T. B. Morison, K.C. and Mr. W. Lyon Mackenzie (Advocate's Deputy) presenting the prosecution's case for the Crown, and Mr. A. L. M'Clure, K.C., and Mr. John Mair, Advocate, appearing for the defence.

Slater pleaded not guilty in ringing tones to the charge that he 'did on December 21 . . . assault the said Marion Gilchrist and did beat her with a hammer or other blunt instrument and fracture her skull and did murder her'. The weapon had been introduced as the result of finding a hammer among Slater's possession, against all the evidence of Dr. Adams that a heavy chair had caused her death.

One of the early witnesses for the prosecution, William Sorley, a partner in a Glasgow jewellery business, was presently examined by the Lord Advocate. Sorley said:

'I knew Mrs. Gilchrist quite well. She had been one of our clients for over twenty years. Sometime in early January a detective called on us and asked me to give him a sketch of a diamond crescent brooch which belonged to Mrs. Gilchrist.'

'Would Exhibit No. 24 be that sketch?'

'Yes. I simply cut out of our catalogue the print of a similar brooch.'

'When did you last see the brooch?'

'We had it for cleaning in March 1908.'

'Did she have any other diamond crescent brooch?'

'No, that was the only diamond crescent she had.'

Slater watched these opening proceedings with considerable composure. A good-looking man with a Roman nose and neat moustache, he was well dressed and dignified. He leant forward and concentrated his attention as Mr. M'Clure rose to cross-examine the jeweller:

'Can you remember the precise date when the police first made enquiries regarding brooches?'

'Not the precise date, no.'

'Would it be the middle of January?'

'No, early in January.'

'Long after the 21st of December, the date of the murder?'

'Fairly long.'

'And was a diamond brooch shown to you by the police for identification?'

'Yes.'

'How many rows of diamonds did the police brooch have?'

'Three.'

'Did the police tell you that this was the brooch which had been pawned by Slater?'

'I think they did.'

'Only think?'

'Yes.'

'Were you aware of the date when Slater pawned it?'

'No.'

'In fact you were unaware that the brooch—which was not Mrs. Gilchrist's brooch—had been lodged with the pawn-broker two months before her death.'

'I was unaware.'

That seemed to dispose entirely of any suspicion attaching to the pawn ticket.

The prosecution now examined Constable Francis Briern, the policeman called to the scene of the murder, and he explained how his beat included the south side of West Princes Street which embraced Green's Terrace where Miss Gilchrist lived. Briern was asked:

'Are there very many people about in West Princes Street?'

'No, not very many.'

'And at night—about seven o'clock?'

'It is particularly quiet at that time.'

The Judge Advocate now indicated the prisoner:

'Do you know this man?'

'By sight, yes.'

'Where have you seen him?'

'I saw him one night standing a few yards from the corner of West Princes Street and St. George's Road.'

'How far from Mrs. Gilchrist's home?'

'About seventy-five or eighty yards. I saw him there the week before the murder.'

'Could you give us a date?'

'No. I cannot give a date.'

'Tell us what you saw.'

'He was standing there alone. I thought he was a drunk man. I took a good look at him when passing . . .'

'Had you seen the prisoner before that?'

'Yes, several times.'

'In what locality?'

'On St. George's Road . . . He was always alone. The first time was about seven weeks before the murder so far as I can remember. I saw him occasionally in or about St. George's Road between that and the week before the murder.'

Briern's evidence steadily became more damning until he described how on February 22 he picked out Slater from a number of men in an identification parade.

Once again Mr. M'Clure for Slater went to work and cleverly undermined any real precision in his evidence:

'Perhaps you could tell us what number of persons were in the police station where you identified the prisoner?'

'Three—or rather four.'

'All Scottish?'

'Yes.'

'With no foreign-looking gentleman among them?'

'No.'

'Were you asked to look at him especially?'

'Yes.'

'By whom?'

'Superintendent Douglas.'

'Did I understand you to say that the only time you saw the prisoner about West Princes Street was in the week which preceded the murder?'

'Yes . . .'

'How was he dressed?'

'He had on a hat and coat.'

'What manner of hat would that be?'

'I cannot describe the hat . . .'

'Did you talk to him?'

'No. I passed on.'

'You thought he was drunk?'

'Yes.'

'But later changed your mind. What made you change your mind?'

'I took a good look at him.'

'You walked up and looked into his face?'

'Yes.'

'And he never said a word?'

'No.'

'And you cannot say what clothes he wore?'

'No.'

M'Clure proceeded to ask for a description of his trousers, boots and hat and failed to get any details whatever. It had already become clear that Briern's identification of Slater was based on the most flimsy pretexts for any real observation.

Another witness for the prosecution, Mrs. Margaret Dickson, who associated a loitering stranger outside Mrs. Gilchrist's house with Slater, came under equally penetrating cross-examination. She lived at No. 16 West Princes Street and when pressed for details was equally vague until M'Clure drove her into a corner:

'Is it not true that you were not completely certain of the man and only felt that he resembled him?'

'He is the man who was loitering about West Princes Street.'

'The picture in the newspapers was something like him?'

'Yes, they were like him.'

'When you went to the police station you also saw a man *like* him?'

'Yes.'

'Was there present any other foreign-looking person?'

'None but himself.'

In the light of what followed years later, one of the most

important figures in the whole trial was Detective Lieutenant Trench and his evidence became crucial. Mr. Morison examined him for the prosecution:

'What arrangements were there for making the identification parade fair?'

'The prisoner was placed in the office along with eleven other men.'

'Who were these other men?'

'They were mostly police officials and were all in plain clothes—but two railway officials were also there—and two of them had peculiar noses.'

'How was the prisoner placed in line?'

'He was allowed to take up any position he pleased in the row.'

'And every precaution was taken to avoid the witnesses seeing Slater alone before they saw him with the others?'

'Yes—every precaution. Slater was taken to the doctor's room—where he got his tea—during the time the witnesses were collecting in the office.'

It is interesting that throughout the trial Trench supported the prosecution without very much qualification, and it was years later before he became conscience-stricken about certain aspects of the case and entirely reversed his attitude. For the moment M'Clure once more went to work on him in cross-examination:

'You picked up the prisoner at Renfrew, did you not, and motored him to Glasgow?'

'I did.'

'Can you tell me whether his arrival in the motor-car could be observed by any of the witnesses?'

'None of them was present when he arrived . . .'

'Is there a glass door in the witnesses' room which looks on the lobby?'

'There is.'

'And if the witnesses had been in their room they would have seen him?'

'Yes.'

'You still say they were not there?'

'Not to my knowledge. He arrived at two and they were not there until four.'

'Do you say—precisely—that when Slater arrived none of the witnesses was there?'

'Not so far as I know . . .'

This spread an aura of doubt which M'Clure developed around the identity parade itself.

'Were there any foreign-looking men in the identification parade?'

'No. They were all Scotsmen, I think.'

'No person of foreign appearance or dark complexion?'

'Some of dark complexion.'

'And foreign appearance?'

'No—not foreign.'

'If somebody were warned that the person they were looking for was a foreigner, they would go straight to the prisoner would they not?'

'Possibly.'

'Isn't that a very odd way of conducting an identity parade?'

'No—I don't think so.'

'Am I right in assuming that when you want to identify a possible criminal he is placed in line with people roughly of similar appearance?'

'No, you are not.'

'Is this common practice in Glasgow?'

'No—it isn't.'

'But as a matter of common fairness, would not that be the best practice?'

'It might—but we do not do it in Glasgow.'

Trench now admitted that since Slater's photograph had been published in the Glasgow evening paper before the parade any witness might automatically have selected him. If three witnesses, Lambie, Adams and Barrowman, had no difficulty in identifying Slater it was not surprising in the circumstances.

The medical evidence against Slater came shortly afterwards and rested on the opinion of Professor John Glaister, Professor of Forensic Medicine in Glasgow University:

'From my experience, my view is that the assailant knelt on the woman's chest . . . and struck violently at the head with the implement that he employed . . .'

He was then shown the hammer found among Slater's possessions, and stated:

'This hammer could, in my opinion, in the hands of a strong man and forcibly wielded have produced the injuries found on the body . . .'

Glaister spoke for some time, his medical reports were produced and read and then M'Clure began his cross-examination:

'I gather that you cannot positively affirm that the hammer was used?'

'No—I cannot.'

'There is no trace of blood on it?'

'We found certain corpuscular bodies which looked as if they belonged to blood, but I cannot absolutely say they were blood.'

'You cannot, in fact, say there was blood on the hammer?'

'No—not positively.'

'Supposing,' M'Clure said, 'that the hammer had been washed, would the dirt have been washed up into the head of the hammer?'

'It depends how it was washed.'

'Yet,' M'Clure persisted, 'there was coal dust remaining at the point where the handle met the head.'

'Dirt,' Glaister corrected him, 'not coal dust.'

'We are still in the realms of hypothesis,' M'Clure said, and Glaister replied, 'Speculation.'

The evidence for the prosecution was so long and complicated that it occupied nearly 150 very closely printed papers and cannot adequately be summarized here, but as the examination of witnesses drew to a close Slater still remained confident that his innocence would be proved.

On the afternoon of Wednesday, May 5, M'Clure opened the case for the defence. The first witness was Mr. James Dow, an accountant from the post office of Edinburgh who read a letter which Slater had addressed to the Comptroller of the Post Office Savings Bank, West Kensington, London, under the name of Adolph Anderson. This letter dated November 11, 1908 did not in fact arrive until December 22 and carried the Glasgow postmark December 21. It said:

'Dear Sir,

Enclosed you will find my savings book. Be kind enough to send me the money at once as I have an urgent call to America because my wife is ill. If possible wire the money and I will pay all expenses here.'

M'Clure elicited from Dow that the letter had, in fact, caught the 5 o'clock post on December 21, two hours *before* the murder was committed.

Hugh Cameron the next witness, a bookmaker's clerk, also made it quite clear that Slater's trip to the United States was no sudden decision of a murderer wanting to escape justice:

'It would be at least a fortnight before December 21 that Slater told me of his intention of going abroad. He spoke about it very openly among his friends . . . I especially remember it because of a letter he received from San Francisco.'

'You actually saw Slater two or three times between the day of the murder, December 21, and December 25. Did he look in any way not his usual self?'

'No.'

'He didn't show anxiety of any kind or try to hide himself?'

'In fact it was the opposite.'

'You moved around with him in several public places where he could clearly be seen?'

'Yes.'

'And he gave no sign in any way that he might be a fugitive from justice?'

'No.'

In cross-examination, the Lord Advocate was now allowed to bring out antecedents from Slater's history which were very damaging in the eyes of the jury:

'After you became acquainted with him, did you become aware what he was?'

'Yes—he was a gambler.'

'Was there anything more?'

'Well—yes—he lived on the proceeds of women—like many others who came to Glasgow.'

Catherine Schmalz, the German maid employed by Slater, reaffirmed his alibi of eating dinner at home at 7 o'clock on December 21.

'Did he always take dinner at 7 o'clock, or was it sometimes a little before or after?' M'Clure asked.

'It all depended on whether I had the dinner ready—but usually it was seven.'

'Was he ever away on any occasion at that time?'

'No, I cannot remember him being away.'

'And did he mention that he must go to America?'

'Yes. That was three weeks or a month before December 21.'

'Now, specifically, did he come home for dinner on the 21st?'

'Yes.'

In the phrase of the *Glasgow Citizen* which reported the trial, the Lord Advocate now 'proceeded to make mincemeat of these statements' in cross-examination:

'Did he usually come home to dinner?'

'Yes, always.'

'Was the dinner sometimes early, sometimes late?'

'7 o'clock usually.'

'But sometimes it might be eight?'

Miss Schmalz saw the obvious trap and when she first replied, hastily, 'It was my fault,' she immediately corrected it with, 'Mr. Slater was already in.'

'But because you were late, it was about eight before dinner was served?'

'No. Mr. Slater was in after seven and already waiting.'

'How late had dinner sometimes been served?'

'Sometimes half past seven to eight.'

By the fourth day of the trial, half the country was reading every detail and every other newspaper carried headlines on the proceedings. Hundreds of people were turned away from the court and it was well after 10 o'clock on May 6 before the atmosphere inside became calm enough to continue the case for the defence.

The second witness, on the fourth day, was Dr. W. G. A. Robertson, a doctor of medicine and science and a Fellow of the Royal Society of Edinburgh.

He said that examining the multiple injuries inflicted on Mrs. Gilchrist, it seemed to him that some kind of blunt instrument had been used but . . . 'the hammer produced does not strike me in the least as being a likely one because the wounds and their extent are out of all proportion to the size of the hammer'.

'Did you examine the hammer for bloodstains?' M'Clure asked the witness.

MRS GILCHRIST'S HOUSE IN QUEENS TERRACE

THE DINING-ROOM WHERE MRS GILCHRIST'S
BODY WAS FOUND

MRS GILCHRIST

OSCAR SLATER

OSCAR SLATER IN THE DOCK

ARTHUR CONAN DOYLE

'I did and there are no bloodstains on it.'

'Did you see any signs that the upper part of the handle or top of the hammer has been washed—or even scraped?'

'No appearance whatever of washing or scraping.'

Asked in closer detail whether he had examined the hammer microscopically for the presence of any blood or corpuscles, he said no, he had not but 'there are no clots of blood at all, even in the crevices . . .'

The afternoon of the fourth day brought brilliant sunshine and the blinds screening the huge windows of the courtroom were half drawn, but as the Lord Advocate rose to make his address to the jury, shafts of sunlight illumined his craggily austere face. At first hearing the address was devastating:

'May it please Your Lordship—Gentlemen of the jury—On the evening of December 21 last a lady upwards of eighty-three years of age . . . was found murdered . . . under circumstances of such savage ferocity as to beggar all description . . .

'I say, gentlemen, that the hand which dealt these blows was the hand of the prisoner and I hope to be able to satisfy you that he and he alone was the perpetrator of an act of savagery which finds few if any parallels in the annals of crime . . .'

There followed a vivid reconstruction of Slater's character and record which should strictly have had no bearing whatever on his innocence or guilt, but which clearly carried enormous weight with the jury. The Lord Advocate continued:

'. . . We heard from the lips of one who knew the prisoner better than anyone else . . . that he had followed a life which descends to the very lowest depths of human degradation . . . a man who lives upon the proceeds of prostitution has sunk to the lowest depths . . . I say without hesitation that the man in the dock is capable of having committed this dastardly out-rage . . .'

The Lord Advocate then repeated a detailed description of the murder and drew from it seven 'priceless inferences':

(1) The murder was carefully and coolly planned not by some amateur but by an expert.
(2) The murderer knew the locality in detail.
(3) He had taken great trouble to become familiar with the

character of the residents in the house and their daily habits.

(4) His plan had included careful observation of the movements of the sole policeman whose beat included Mrs. Gilchrist's street.

(5) He carried a weapon into the house and carefully removed it afterwards.

(6) The murderer was a man looking for jewels—not money —who knew how to negotiate the sale of jewellery.

(7) He did not know the inner lay-out of the house or precisely where the jewels were kept, but simply knew of their existence.

The Lord Advocate now had the audacity to indicate that if these vague generalities fitted, with equal vagueness, Slater's character and movements, then the jury were well on the way towards a verdict of guilty.

Step by step he recapitulated the evidence, slanting every detail against Slater, and now his case emerged much more powerfully. Finally he did make a gesture towards a more balanced view of the evidence and then immediately withdrew it again:

'Gentlemen, I have done. I cannot prove more in this case ... On your verdict undoubtedly depends a man's life ... If you ... entertain any reasonable doubt as to the evidence bringing home guilt to this man, then you are bound to give him the benefit of that doubt ...

'My submission to you is that his guilt has been brought fairly home to him, that no shadow of doubt exists, that there is no reasonable doubt that he was the perpetrator of this foul murder ...'

How any man trained in the extrapolation of truth from a mass of conflicting evidence could have come to this conclusion with such certainty remains a mystery—but too often such cases revealed the law courts as arenas where battles of wits were joined between professionally trained legal adversaries, with disastrous consequences to the truth.

It has to be stressed that there were several gross errors of fact in the Lord Advocate's Address which later remained uncorrected by the Judge, the Hon. Lord Guthrie, in his summing up. The Lord Advocate stated that Slater hastened his departure to America because his name and the description from Barrowman were printed in newspapers dated December 25. It was not, in fact, until January 2 that the *Glasgow Herald* first mentioned his name. The Lord Advocate also promised to show how Slater came to know that Mrs. Gilchrist possessed jewels, without fulfilling that promise. Slater not only did not know about her jewellery; he did not even know Mrs. Gilchrist.

Slater's defending counsel, M'Clure, was reckoned, professionally, not to be in the same class as the Lord Advocate, and he now faced the formidable task of undermining the details of the prosecution's case and—still more important—dispelling the hostile atmosphere which Ure's powerful address to the jury had created. His opening words were impressive:

'Gentlemen of the jury, I must confess to a feeling of great responsibility in rising to address you now on behalf of the accused . . . Not only has he got, with slight resources and the assistance of a few friends, to fight his case single-handed against the forces of the Crown and the power of the Lord Advocate, but I think he has also to fight a most unfair fight against public prejudice roused with a fury I do not remember to have seen in any other case . . . Certainly the newspaper campaign which has been conducted against this man Slater is without parallel for its absolutely irresponsible character, for the rumours it has set afloat and for the prejudice created . . .'

The prisoner—M'Clure continued—had been convicted by public opinion before he was tried in a court of law, a manoeuvre so machiavellian as to endanger the whole course of justice.

'Let me now go into the details of the case . . .' He proceeded to dismiss the idea that the brooch pawned by Slater had any connection whatever with the brooch stolen from Mrs. Gilchrist and was equally scornful of any suggestion that Slater's trip to America—a perfectly normal, previously broadcast trip—had anything whatever to do with a flight from justice. The jury must remember that while the hue and cry was at its height, Slater openly exposed himself in public places without any attempt at disguise or any sign of anxiety.

As for Miss Barrowman's identification of him: 'It is said that the man had on a Donegal hat. A Donegal hat is a tweed hat with a rim all round it. It is also said that he had brown boots. Gentlemen, they have been through all the prisoner's baggage—they have produced everything that would assist them—but there are no brown boots and no Donegal hat!'

Having exposed the flimsy nature of all the identification evidence given by Lambie, Adams, Barrowman and the policeman Briern, M'Clure turned to the hammer allegedly used in the murder:

'The doctors are uncertain as to the hammer being a likely instrument to cause the injuries that resulted in death but even if it were—hammer and coat alike are absolutely free of blood. Do you see any plausibility in the suggestion that the hammer has been scraped and washed to remove traces of blood? Our doctors tell you that they would have great difficulty in removing traces of blood in that way.'

M'Clure's speech reached a climax with a dramatic reference to the Adolf Beck case where ten women and two policemen all swore that Beck was the wanted man, but long after his sentence of seven years' penal servitude, it transpired that they had convicted an innocent man. M'Clure continued:

'In that case there was the sworn testimony of ten concurring witnesses who had ample opportunity of knowing him. Was that class of evidence not better than the stuff you have got here—self contradictory, inconclusive, given by witnesses who had no personal acquaintance with the accused? . . .

'I will not ask that you give this man the benefit of the doubt—but the benefit of the evidence which has been led. I think it is proved that he was not out of his house on the 20th and there is only a blank of fifteen minutes unaccounted for on the 21st—that might happen to any of us and are you on that account to sacrifice a human life? I do not believe it for a moment—the sum total of the evidence in this case warrants nothing other than an acquittal . . .'

After the colourful rhetoric of the Lord Advocate's address, Mr. M'Clure's fell rather heavily on the jury's ears, but his cool insistence on factual matters left the final impression that no unprejudiced jury could unequivocally convict this man.

There followed the judge's charge to the jury, the bias of which quickly became clear. Lord Guthrie claimed that the evidence on Slater's bad character was amply proved and the

Lord Advocate should be entitled to 'found' on such evidence; he implied that variations in dress were of no great moment in the evidence; he tended to discredit some witnesses for the defence because of their way of life; and he even went so far as to suggest that the prisoner had not the presumption of innocence in his favour. From the legal point of view completely confusing innocence with character he said: 'A man of that kind has not the presumption of innocence in his favour which is a form in the case of every man, but a reality in the case of the ordinary man.' The words were pernicious. If he managed to find several points in Slater's favour before the end of his charge, that did not reduce the ironic ring of his final words:

'Gentlemen—I suppose you all think that the prisoner is possibly the murderer: you may very likely all think that he *is* the murderer. That, however, will not entitle you to convict him. The Crown have undertaken to prove not that he is possibly or probably the murderer but that he *is* the murderer. That is the question you have to consider. If you think there is no reasonable doubt about it, you will do your duty and convict him. If you think there is, you will acquit him.'

The jury retired at 4.55 p.m. and Slater confidently expected a rapid reappearance. So confident was he that he remained waiting in the dock. When a whole hour slipped away and still they were absent, he became agitated.

And then, at five minutes past six, they filed back into court and a stunned silence followed the verdict. 'The jury by a majority find the prisoner "guilty as libelled".'

'By a majority . . .' It was a clear-cut difference between English and Scottish law that, for such a verdict in a murder case, England required a unanimous vote whereas in this case the verdict was carried by a majority of three only on a jury of fifteen. Three votes . . . It showed how wide and deep the divisions within the jury must have been.

Slater came to his feet at once and called across the court: 'My Lord, may I say one word. Will you allow me to speak?'

Guthrie, extraordinarily, appeared in an attitude of prayer, his face flushed, his eyes troubled, and he said quietly to Slater: 'Sit down a moment please.'

Pens scratched in the deep silence, while Guthrie remained with his head bowed, and then Slater broke out with:

'My Lord, my father and mother are poor and old. I came on my own account to this country. I came over to defend my right. I know nothing of this affair. You are convicting an innocent man.'

It was useless. With the accustomed deliberation Lord Guthrie donned the black cap and sentenced Oscar Slater to death—on Thursday, May 27.

The majority of newspapers almost gloated over the verdict, but the *Edinburgh Evening Dispatch* was one exception: 'It is notorious that the verdict in the Slater trial came as an intense surprise to the public.'

There were those in legal circles equally disturbed and now began the first ripples of a campaign to save Slater from the gallows which quickly widened and deepened. In the end it led to a counter-prosecution which involved some of the most distinguished men in the country including none other than Sir Arthur Conan Doyle.

First a petition was organized by Rabbi E. P. Phillips whose belief in Slater's innocence led to a door-to-door canvass for signatures supporting a commutation of the death sentence. Against all expectations and the scorn of *The Scotsman* no less than 20,000 people signed the petition and now Slater's law agents prepared a document—Memorial on Behalf of Oscar Slater—which they sent to the Secretary of State for Scotland, barely ten days before the execution date.

Perhaps the most extraordinary part of this document quoted the deposition of Agnes Brown, a witness originally named for the *prosecution*. She stated: 'On Monday 21st December, 1908 about 7.8 p.m., I left [my] house to attend evening classes in Dunard Street School. I went west along Grant Street to West Cumberland Street and turned along the north-east side of that street until I came to West Princes Street. I was in the act of stepping off the foot pavement there to cross West Princes Street . . . *when two men came running past me* . . .'

Since the deposition introduced two men into the scene of the crime it was obvious why the prosecution did not call this witness, but the defence, too, were equally deterred by the second part of her statement in which she claimed to recognize Slater as one of the two men.

The pamphlet simultaneously analysed at least half a dozen

flaws in the evidence which convicted Slater and the law agents sent a copy to Lord Pentland, Secretary of State for Scotland, Lord Guthrie the judge, the Lord Chancellor and the Minister of War, Mr. Haldane.

Public opinion in Glasgow was disgusted by these attempts to 'interfere with the wheels of justice which have turned so accurately'. A letter in the *Weekly Mail* opened: 'Just as expected, an unseemly and nauseating campaign of sentiment has been started on behalf of Slater—or whatever be the name of the condemned man . . .'

But many forces were already at work behind the scenes to challenge the verdict, and suddenly—against all public expectation—two days before Slater was due to die the Lord Provost of Glasgow received a telegram from the Under Secretary for Scotland:

'Case Oscar Slater. Execution of death is respited until further signification of His Majesty's pleasure.'

Later, in the *Empire News* of November 20, 1927, Slater described his reception of the news:

'My cell door opened. It was evening. As the warder un-locked the cell and swung the door open I saw several men. One wore a tall hat. He did not come in. To me he appeared like the judge who had sentenced me . . .

'I was informed by one of the party who did enter my cell, that there was good news for me. They had come especially from Edinburgh to inform me that His Majesty the King had granted a reprieve.'

The police, through a high-ranking officer, expressed them-selves as utterly dismayed. There followed an interview with the same officer in the *Weekly Mail* which contained this statement: 'From first to last every man who was placed on the Slater case worked only with one object—the securing of the guilty person. And it was a difficult case to tackle.'

In the House of Commons a brief exchange between two M.P.s and the Secretary of State for Scotland proved most unsatisfactory. One member asked the Secretary of State:

'Why is Slater still detained in custody?'

'Because he has been convicted of murder,' was the reply.

'On what grounds was the prerogative of mercy extended?'

'It is not accepted practice to reveal the grounds.'

'Do we then understand that the view of the Government is that Slater is guilty of this brutal crime?'

To this last question—ominously—there was no answer. As private forces slowly gathered in power and numbers on Slater's behalf, the appearance of William Roughhead's new volume in the Notable Scottish Trials series published by William Hodge in April 1910 caused further disquiet.

Roughhead had, in fact, been present at Slater's trial and came away convinced that he was about to see an innocent man go to the gallows. He managed to convey his dissatisfaction with the evidence of a number of witnesses for the prosecution with considerable delicacy and he obliquely drew attention to the failure of the Lord Advocate to correct his statement that Slater fled on the day his name was first printed in the newspapers. Several other points were subtly questioned.

Since all the people concerned in the trial were still alive, it was difficult for him to do more without the threat of libel, but *The Times*, reviewing the book, said bluntly: 'We are constrained to speculate whether Slater is not another victim of false impression . . .' Far more important, the book first brought Sir Arthur Conan Doyle's attention to the case and left him feeling very uneasy about the treatment of a foreigner in the English law courts. A man who specialized in lost causes, he had already fought for a wrongly imprisoned Parsee solicitor named Edalzi and now his sense of justice was freshly outraged by the details of Slater's case.

'I went into the matter most reluctantly, but when I glanced at the facts I saw that it was an even worse case than the Edalzi one and that this unhappy man had in all probability no more to do with the murder for which he had been condemned than I had . . .' Conan Doyle commented.

Doyle collaborated with Roughhead to carry out new enquiries into the case and then he wrote, in the summer of 1912, a powerfully precise pamphlet *The Case of Oscar Slater*. It was widely circulated and reviewed, but *The Times* received it sceptically, the *Glasgow Herald* was scornful and the *Evening Times* said: 'Perusal of this booklet leaves the impression that on the whole Oscar Slater was not a bad sort but . . . facts that "winna ding" reveal a slimy blackguard of whom the community is well rid.' Nonetheless, a big correspondence developed around the pamphlet until Sir Herbert Stephens wrote to *The Times* on September 19, 1912:

'I think it highly probable that Oscar Slater had nothing to do with the murder of Mrs. Marion Gilchrist for which he was sentenced to death . . . I think the evidence manifestly failed to establish his guilt and that his conviction was a miscarriage of justice . . . and I prophesy that a Court of Criminal Appeal for Scotland will be in working order before the year 1970.'

This referred to the appalling fact that at that date Scotland had no final appeal court before which dubious convictions could be reviewed and 'the year 1970' was an ironical comment on the interminable delays which met every attempt to create one.

There followed a series of exchanges in the House of Commons between the famous lawyer Marshall Hall and the then Secretary of State for Scotland, T. McKinnon Wood, which showed just how stubborn the Scottish police and lawyers were in refusing to concede any point in Slater's favour.

Marshall Hall asked whether the Secretary for Scotland 'is aware that the verdict has been secured by a majority of *three only* in a jury of fifteen, that the prosecution speech for the Crown contained inaccurate statements of fact, and that there is general uneasiness as to the justice of the verdict?'

When McKinnon Wood said he was aware of all this, Marshall Hall asked: 'And what is going to be done?'

McKinnon Wood replied: 'No new considerations have in my opinion emerged such as would justify me in reopening the case.'

That might easily have been the end of it and then, out of the blue, Sir Conan Doyle received a remarkable letter, on March 30, 1914, from a Glasgow solicitor named David Cook: 'Dear Sir,

You will be good enough to treat this letter meantime as confidential. In view of the interest which you have taken in the above case, it is proper that I should give you an indication of the position.

'It is generally admitted in Glasgow that Detective Lieutenant Trench of the Central Division is an officer of ability and integrity. From the time that Slater's name was mentioned in connection with the murder of Mrs. Gilchrist until today

Trench has been of the opinion that Slater was an innocent man. I have never had any other view.

'Trench is my intimate friend and I have frequently spoken to him regarding the case. He has time and again told me that he was not satisfied with the action of the police in the matter.

'Mr. McKinnon Wood is in possession of a signed statement by Trench. This statement was prepared by me from the facts obtained by Trench and also from documentary evidence—to be accurate, copies of documents. The copies were made by Trench from the originals and I warned him to take the numbers of the various books with the page in each case. He followed my advice.

'I may tell you that the original statement of the girl Barrowman as copied from the police books, bears no relation to the evidence which she gave at the trial. I venture to say that had the original statement been produced at the trial, Slater would not have been convicted.

'There is no mention in the original statement of the girl having knocked against a man who came out of the close . . . Frankly, I am of the opinion that Mary Barrowman was not in West Prince Street at or near 7 o'clock. Very probably she was in West Prince Street some hours afterwards when the public had obtained information that the murder had taken place . . .

'As for the message she was said to be carrying on the night of the murder which took her past Mrs. Gilchrist's house, the records of Barrowman's employers showed that it was delivered on the 18th and not the 21st of December. When they showed a detective the office record book and insisted on the incorrect date he simply replied that the girl herself persisted in her story.'

As to the evidence of Lambie—Cook's letter continued— Trench was prepared to swear that she once more gave him quite different details on January 3, 1909. Within fifteen minutes of the murder she told him that another person 'whose name I need not mention here—was the man whom she saw leave the house'. The police knew of this statement but 'purposely concealed the information from the defence and from the court'.

The letter quoted further devastating contradictions of

evidence given in court, and concluded with the suppression by the police of facts which distorted their case out of all recognition.

David Cook also had in his possession yet another document which implied that the name of the real murderer was already known to certain friends of Mrs. Gilchrist. Trench had been briefed by Chief Superintendent Orr to interview Miss Birrell —one of Mrs. Gilchrist's friends—about a person referred to as 'A.B.' and to press for the details of what Lambie had said when she first visited Miss Birrell on the night of the murder.

Trench had carefully copied all the relevant documents from the police records and one of these gave a verbatim account of Miss Birrell's replies, part of which said:

'I can never forget the night of the murder. Mrs. Gilchrist's servant, Nellie Lambie, came to my door about 7.15. She was excited. She pulled the bell violently. On the door being opened she rushed into the house and exclaimed: "Oh, Miss Birrell, Miss Birrell, Mrs. Gilchrist has been murdered, she is lying dead in the dining-room and oh, Miss Birrell, I saw the man who did it."

'I replied, "My God, Nellie, this is awful. Who was it—do you know him?" She replied, "Oh, Miss Birrell, I think it was A.B. I am sure that it was A.B." I said to her: "My God, Nellie, don't say that. Unless you are very sure of it, Nellie, don't say that." She again repeated to me that she was sure it was A.B.'

Miss Birrell, it now appeared, had repeated this conversation to a number of friends, including a member of the Glasgow Corporation, and he it was who informed Chief Superintendent Orr and asked for further enquiries to be made.

Trench had carefully recorded in his personal diary—now made available—the date and nature of his interview with Miss Birrell and he also recounted a second interview conducted jointly by Detective Keith and himself with Helen Lambie: '. . . in the course of the talk . . . I brought the subject round to A.B. and asked if she really thought he was the man she saw, and her answer was: "It's gey funny if it was not him I saw." '

Back at the police station, Trench repeated this to Superintendent Orr who replied that another police officer had investigated the matter and 'cleared that all up'. Finally Trench admitted contributing to what amounted to a conspiracy to suppress the evidence by once more visiting Miss Birrell—this time with Detective Cameron—and warning her not to say anything to anyone about the story of A.B.

Five long years had intervened between Slater's conviction and David Cook's letter to Sir Arthur Conan Doyle, during which Slater suffered the hardships of a penal system far more rigorous than anything we know today. Why had Trench waited so long to reveal these shattering documents? First, he would be forced to break the professional secrecy of police evidence and second, it took time for his conscience to reach the point where he was prepared to risk dismissal from the police.

There was one other important reason. The year 1912 had also brought him into touch with Charles Warner, a vagrant, charged with the murder of a Miss Milne who was also found battered to death. Over one hundred witnesses had incriminated Warner as the murderer and yet Trench had eventually shown that on the actual day of the murder Warner pawned a waistcoat in Antwerp—hundreds of miles away across the North Sea! If Warner could be so easily mistaken as a murderer, why not Slater?

Simultaneously with revealing his new documentary evidence, Detective Trench had taken into his confidence a tall, powerfully built Glasgow journalist whose drunken habits did not blunt a mind attuned to good music and a refined sense of justice. The journalist, William Park, became so fascinated by Trench's revelations that he devoted all his spare time to following up the evidence for many months.

By now three private individuals, Sir Arthur Conan Doyle, William Park and David Cook, were slowly building up the details of a private challenge to the State verdict with unprecedented persistence. Conan Doyle had first been shocked and then delighted to receive Cook's letter and at once offered him every possible assistance.

All unaware that their work was destined to drag on for years, they plunged in enthusiastically but rather than freeing Slater their campaign first, amazingly, resulted in Trench's dismissal from the police force.

Many steps led to this early climax in the long crusade.

Trench, Cook and Park had decided that any approach to the police would inevitably meet a hostile reception, since the evidence was no less damning of them than it was of the witnesses in the trial.

Instead, persuaded by the now dedicated Park, they agreed to release the material to a newspaper, brazenly print the contents of the documents and force a public enquiry. Presented with the broad outline of the new evidence, one of the leading Scottish newspapers wanted nothing whatever to do with it. Since the editor personally knew many of the officials concerned in the trial that was not unexpected.

The three crusaders went into conference once more and this time it was agreed that Cook should reveal the facts to a local member of the Prison Commission. Unable to overlook such powerful evidence, the Commissioner decided that it must be brought to the attention of the Secretary for Scotland, but not until February 13 did the Secretary reply asking for a written statement from Trench.

In the light of what followed, it is astonishing that McKinnon Wood made no attempt to protect Lieutenant Trench from the consequences of his actions. Certainly Trench regarded his invitation to present the evidence as sufficient protection for breaking the rules of police secrecy, and went to work preparing his dossier.

On March 10, Cook received a brief letter from McKinnon Wood acknowledging the completed document and saying that on such evidence an enquiry would be held, led by the Procurator-Fiscal, Mr. Hart. Delighted with the news of the enquiry, the trio were dismayed at the choice of Chairman. The Procurator-Fiscal had himself been deeply concerned in the police investigation of Slater and was an interested party. Under heavy pressure, the Secretary of State agreed to reconsider the selection of a chairman and finally settled on a substitute, James H. Millar, K.C., the Sheriff of Lanarkshire. This, at first sight, was more satisfactory to Cook, but when he learnt the limitations to be imposed on Millar he again protested to the Secretary of State. The official letter from McKinnon Wood laid down that '. . . the enquiry should be conducted in private, should be limited to questions of fact, and should in no way relate to the conduct of the trial . . . but subject to these limitations it is his [the Secretary for Scotland] desire that you should exercise your own discretion as to the conduct of the enquiry . . .'

William Park, like David Cook, exploded with indignation: no questions about the conduct of the trial—in private—and no mention of calling Slater as a witness! What sort of enquiry was this? Park now wrote once more to Conan Doyle who gave an interview to the *Empire News*: 'What we fear,' he said, 'is not so much that the Sheriff will give a decision contrary to the evidence—he is a man of the highest integrity—but that he will limit the enquiry to such an extent that much of the vital evidence will be ruled out of the case . . .' *The Times* reinforced Conan Doyle's view: 'We can hardly believe it will be to the satisfaction of the Scottish people that the enquiry should be held in private . . .'

What later came to be regarded as a whitewashing operation began—despite these protests—in April 1914 and completely fulfilled the aims of such a farce. Within a few hours it became evident that corroborative evidence for the documents copied by Lieutenant Trench would not be forthcoming. Indeed, exactly the opposite impression rapidly built up from witness after witness.

When Miss Birrell's statement to Trench was read out to Helen Lambie, she flatly denied ever having uttered such words. Nor had she ever made, she said, any references whatever to A.B. Confronted with the details of the interview between Keith, Trench and herself, she again had no recollection of using the words, 'It's gey funny if it wasn't him I saw.'

Miss Birrell, called before the 'court', reaffirmed Miss Lambie's denials. When Trench's account of the interview was read to her she vehemently denied the words imputed to herself or Miss Lambie.

Much more damaging to the crusade was the evidence of Detective Inspector Keith who accompanied Trench on the second interview. His recollections were somewhat hazy but he certainly did not remember Miss Lambie using the phrase, 'It's gey funny if it wasn't him.' Most of the details in the document read to him he said he was hearing for the first time.

So it went on until no less than ten witnesses had denied one statement after another made by Detective Trench. One

major inconsistency in the police evidence—that they had
satisfied themselves as to the movements of A.B.—was lightly
skated over, but so far as one can trace, no one was able under
the rulings of the enquiry to press home the question: if Miss
Lambie had never mentioned A.B.'s name to the police, where
was the need to trace his movements?

And then, at last, one small piece of corroborative evidence
came from Detective Inspector Cameron, only to be quickly
qualified.

'. . . I remember that on 23rd December Lieutenant Trench
was sent on a mission by Superintendent Orr. Afterwards we
talked over it and he told me that it was to go and see Miss
Birrell and that the girl Lambie had said to her on the night
of the murder that the man who passed her in the lobby was
A.B. . . . My visit to Miss Birrell had nothing to do with the
story I heard from Lieutenant Trench . . .'

Two possible interpretations could be read into all this.
Either Trench, Cook and Park were conspiring to discredit
the police with a carefully prepared tissue of lies, or the
majority of the witnesses were determined at any cost to protect
their own interests and those of whoever A.B. might be. Either
case seemed plausible. Certainly the accumulation of witnesses
who denied Trench's story was impressive, but Trench had a
very distinguished record in the police and no obvious reason
for wanting to be vindictive towards anyone involved in the
Slater case. Quite the contrary. He had every reason to clear
his name.

Fresh anomalies and confusions arose before the enquiry
drew to a close. No one questioned the discrepancy between
the two statements which Mary Barrowman had given, one
to the police and the other at the trial. In her original deposition she said: 'After leaving our shop at 8 p.m. I went to my
brother's shop at 480 St. Vincent Street and saw a crowd
opposite No. 49. I learnt of the murder and I then thought of
the man I had seen running out of the close there . . .' Her
evidence at the trial read: 'I had gone with my message and
then back to my employer's shop and then to a Band of Hope
meeting . . . there I heard of the murder and went back to
West Princes Street because of hearing of the murder.' Mary
Barrowman's employer, Mr. MacCullum, declared to Mr.

Millar that he had never told Trench that Miss Barrowman delivered her message on a night *other* than that of the murder . . .

Surprisingly, as the enquiry concluded, no 'verdict' was given but Mr. Millar and the Secretary of State for Scotland indicated that, in view of the widespread agitation, the details would be published first as a White Paper.

Cook felt that a remarkably clever operation intended to whitewash the police had been conducted by Superintendent Orr, and on April 24, 1914, he wrote again to Conan Doyle. Describing Lieutenant Trench's upright bearing under examination, he stressed the point that he did not withdraw one detail of the story he had elaborated.

'. . . In the first place the Sheriff went for him like a pickpocket: told him that Miss Birrell and Lambie had denied the A.B. matter, and would he dare insist. He replied that he insisted, and produced his diary which has been kept in first class order showing that he made visits.

'Latterly Trench had to turn upon the Sheriff and object to be catechized on the question of why he passed over his superiors and consulted me. Trench's reply was apt. He said that he held a letter from the Secretary of State for Scotland stating that he [the Secretary] would be glad to have Trench's statements along with a copy of the documents . . .'

Clearly, far too many reputations were liable to be lost if Trench came anywhere near establishing his case and it could easily be true that protecting A.B. was a minor part of an elaborate defence mechanism which involved lawyers and police.

Cook remained undismayed. He thought the result of the enquiry a foregone conclusion and in due course another theatrical gesture was made in the House of Commons. On June 17, McKinnon Wood said: 'The Sheriff of Lanarkshire has reported to me the result of the enquiry which was held recently at my request. Certain statements relative to the case have been laid before me and after very careful consideration of the matter I am satisfied that *no* case is established that would justify me in advising any interference with the sentence.'

It was an extraordinary statement in view of what later transpired, but hidden behind a forest of personal motives lay

an even deeper one. Not only private and professional reputations were at stake, but the whole standing of the Scottish
judicial system which differed in several respects from that of
the English. As we have seen, to the dismay of English lawyers
there was no Court of Appeal in Scotland at that time.

Once more David Cook and William Park went into fresh
consultation and now Cook proposed that they should deliberately publish copies of the documents in the case, stressing
those points which the police had concealed. This—in their
view—would achieve two ends: discredit the enquiry's con-
clusions and add fresh fuel to the still growing flames of
agitation. By now, too, they had a new and hidden ally even
if he was in no position actively to help them. Both Cook
and Trench left the enquiry convinced that the Sheriff, Mr.
Millar, no longer believed in the guilt of Slater.

When the White Paper appeared it received a mixed
reception but something far more devastating quickly super-
vened. On July 14, 1914, the Chief Constable suspended
Trench from duty and placed all the details of the enquiry in
the hands of the Glasgow magistrates. It was, of course,
inevitable. Once Trench's case against the police had, to all
intents and purposes, collapsed, the Chief Constable was forced
to act under the ruling that any officer communicating information acquired while on duty to any persons outside the police
force had broken a long established principle of police practice.

Cook and Park were horrified when on September 14 the
Glasgow magistrates—after a brief examination of the evidence
—summarily dismissed Trench from the police force. It is
impossible to measure the chaotic reactions of the public to
this second catastrophe in the trio's crusade, but one note ran
persistently through the confusion. Why on earth would a police
officer with a distinguished record, a man recently decorated
by King George with the King's police medal, who had
personally arrested four of the most dangerous murderers of
our time, risk his reputation, career and pension by inventing
a series of documents and statements incriminating witnesses
and fellow police officers? Either the man had gone mad or—
as Cook and Park believed—in telling the truth he had become
a new victim to an appalling web of conspiracy and injustice.
Worse was to follow.

7

Penniless and unemployed, Trench, deprived of his pension rights, decided he must join the Army and enlisted in November 1914 as a drill instructor in the Royal Scots Fusiliers. And then, six months later, on the eve of his departure for the Dardanelles two policemen—one of them a Glasgow detective—arrived with a warrant for his arrest on a charge of receiving stolen jewellery. Simultaneously another pair of policemen descended on Cook with a similar warrant.

It was almost unbelievable. The curious smell of conspiracy still pervaded the whole police case against Trench but now—as if to finally pin their accusers mercilessly to the wall—this trumped up charge brought Cook and Trench before Lord Justice Clerk Charles Scott Dickson. The coincidence of Cook's written intention to publish the documents and his arrest on the incredible charge of receiving stolen goods did not escape the attention of the still growing number of people in high and low places who were freshly outraged by each new turn of events. Even the Lord Justice Clerk found the charge faintly absurd: 'I confess on these facts to my mind it would be exceedingly difficult to find these two [men] are criminals . . .' A great wave of applause swept through the court when the jury returned a unanimous verdict of Not Guilty.

But the dismissal of Trench and the persecution of Cook took their toll. After this trial both, at last, with great reluctance, abandoned any further attempts to prove Slater's innocence. Trench became a quartermaster sergeant, retired in 1918 and died in 1919 at the early age of fifty. Cook followed him to the grave within two years. Both men were said to have aged as a result of the appalling conflicts set up by their struggles. Convinced that they were crusading against a conspiracy to sustain a gross miscarriage of justice, they had themselves become its victims.

There remained in the field the determined quixotic journalist William Park, who throughout all these years had continued to investigate details of the case, and, for the moment a shadowy background figure, Sir Arthur Conan Doyle. The police were totally unaware that Park had gradually been manufacturing yet another bombshell which would burst on the public with volcanic force. His fanaticism by now knew no bounds and he had become convinced that everyone concerned with the prosecution and conviction of Slater was hopelessly corrupt. Privately, he announced his avowed intention to 'disembowel the police'. Drinking more and more heavily he rushed from one newspaper officer to the next, digging out every minute scrap of news, comment and evidence. His interviews with possible witnesses went far beyond the range involved in the police records. His determination—even after all these years of crushing bureaucratic victories—to force the police to release Slater involved him in quarrels with lawyers, editors, clergymen. Nothing was too much trouble for him; no detail too insignificant to investigate.

Meanwhile, no one quite knew what psychological tortures Slater was forced to endure, imprisoned year after long drawn out year—he had now served sixteen years—for a crime which he had never committed. That he did not become deranged is remarkable tribute to the toughness of his psychological constitution. Many a man torn out of the rational context of justice has found himself slowly driven into a self-destructive pit where yet another shattering and undeserved blow will finally break what remains of his world in pieces.

Not so Slater. Hardly an ideal prisoner, he remained, it seemed, balanced enough to crack an occasional joke with his guards. But sixteen years   for total innocence!

And then in 1925, a fellow prisoner about to be released concealed a message from Slater to Sir Arthur Conan Doyle in a tooth cavity, and once more the distinguished writer's interest in the case flared up. The smuggled message simply appealed to Conan Doyle not to forget Slater still mouldering in prison, and to renew—at any cost—his efforts to prove his innocence. Conan Doyle, who had followed every detail of the case and expressed total dismay at the fate of Trench and Cook, realized that he and Park were alone together now in the field. Immediately on receipt of Slater's message, he injected fresh life into the campaign with a letter to the new Secretary of State for Scotland, Sir John Gilmour:

'. . . I must say . . . that after a careful analysis of the case I am personally convinced that Slater never knew that such a woman as [Mrs. Gilchrist] ever existed until he was accused of her murder . . .

'. . . the man has now served sixteen years which is . . . the usual limit of a life sentence in Scotland . . . I would earnestly entreat your kind personal attention to this case which is likely to live in the annals of criminology.'

Against the horrifying drama which had already wrecked two, if not three, peoples' lives, these were mild words indeed. One would have expected something much more powerful from the pen of a distinguished writer. Nonetheless, Park now reinforced Conan Doyle's determination to get Slater released, with a letter which said: 'Slater will never be allowed out—he is too dangerous a man.' Park then disclosed that he was determined 'to publish at some later date a new book on the case'.

On February 28 a brief reply came to Conan Doyle not from the Secretary of State but from the Scottish Office:

'. . . I am directed by the Secretary for Scotland to say that he has considered your representations but does not feel justified in advising any interference with Slater's sentence.'

This news redoubled Park's efforts to complete and publish his book. When at last it did appear in 1927, it caused a sensation. Step by step, fragment by fragment, Park dissected the details of the long, painful story until the case for the prosecution collapsed in confusion.

The official enquiry conducted by the Sheriff of Lanarkshire, Mr. Millar, was subjected to withering scorn. What strange satire, Park asked venomously, was this avowed desire to elucidate the truth which deliberately prohibited any enquiry into the conduct of the trial itself: what sense of farce insisted that the whole enquiry should be held *in private*: what deliberate evasion of any quotable record enabled the Secretary for Scotland to proscribe the presence of even a shorthand writer: and what sense of fresh conspiracy denied not only the presence of the prisoner Slater, but anyone who represented him?

As to the witnesses for identification, in the original trial Lambie's evidence showed obvious signs of fabrication, and Adams was reasonably fair but failed clearly to identify. Miss Brown spoke of two men running in a direction opposite from that given by another key witness, Barrowman, and all five contradicted one another when describing Slater's clothing. Evidence? Identification? The terms were sadly abused for such a farrago of conflicting nonsense.

Mary Barrowman admitted having been shown a photograph of Oscar Slater in the office of Mr. Fox, agent for the Glasgow authorities, before she identified him. Asked whether when she went to the court she was looking for a man like that in the photograph, she said yes, which made a travesty of any independent identification. It was the photograph which selected Slater for her, not her memory of the events of the night of December 21.

Turning to the evidence of Adams, Park began to expose the appalling misrepresentations presented to the jury by 'The Highest Crown Official in Scotland', during the trial. Adams' actual evidence said: 'I pointed out Slater, but I did not say he *was* the man. I said he closely resembled the man.'

And here, Park declared triumphantly, is what the Lord Advocate made of that in court: 'And Mr. Adams says the prisoner *was the man.*

'The distinction between a witness affirming that a prisoner *is the man* and the reservation "*like the man*" is the difference between a verdict of guilty by the jury with the death sentence from the Judge and . . . a verdict of acquittal.'

The passion in Park's attack gathered fresh force: 'A motley collection of stuff of this sort dignified with the label "evidence" was accepted by the authorities and used at the trial to support their preconceived theory that Slater for nearly two months preceding the trial had watched the house of Mrs. Gilchrist.'

A devastating section headed 'The Contradictions of Mary Barrowman' next claimed that 'this little message girl was the solitary witness at the trial who was positive in her identification of Slater as "*the man*". Yet she produced two contradictory depositions—one in New York and one in London. Here was a serious problem for the officials. Their principal witness was now disclosing to them a vital departure from an earlier declaration on oath.' And did this bother them either at the trial or the enquiry?—*No!* When the evidence was placed before the Commissioner in 1914 for his investigation, the solicitor acting for Trench carefully stressed the discrepancies in the two statements. He also 'declared that this witness had either lied at the trial or lied in her first statement'.

Park comments: 'And what transpired when this challenged

witness was before the Commissioner? Nothing! Absolutely
nothing.'

Chapter by chapter the book, journalistic though it was,
mounted in power until it reached the details of evidence
which, Park claimed, were deliberately suppressed in court.
The evidence submitted to the court covered only part of the
actually known circumstances of the crime and the relation to
it of the person in the dock.

Now came the climax of the suppressed witness, Duncan
McBrayne. The Lord Advocate had said at the trial: 'There
is no man so destitute of friends and circumstances that he
cannot establish his identity and show who he is and what he
is and what his movements were and where he was at the time
the crime was committed and laid at his door.'

Duncan McBrayne could in fact do precisely that. Indeed
he did so to the Central Police Office in Glasgow, but he
never appeared in court because the prosecution failed to disclose his evidence to the defence. Park hammered home this
point.

Finally came his reconstruction of what really happened on
that terrible night of December 21. Since he had no need to
break into the flat, the man who visited Mrs. Gilchrist that
night must have been, according to Park, well known to her
and pursuing some kind of vendetta. A relative did, in fact,
declare before the 1914 Enquiry that Mrs. Gilchrist was on
unfriendly terms with certain people. 'His object in coming to
the house,' wrote Park, 'was to force her to yield up some
document she possessed in which he was interested.' He argued
with her, a quarrel ensued, he struck her and she fell, her head
hitting the coal box. (The coal box did show signs of blood.)

Swiftly examining her, he came to the conclusion that there
might be fatal consequences, and in order to obliterate any
possibility of identification if she did survive, he grabbed up
the chair and smashed it down time and again on her head
and face until there was no doubt of death. Carried away in a
moment of extreme panic, the assailant yet remained sane
enough to search for the paper he desperately needed and
remove it from the box. Other reasons apart, that paper had
to be removed because it would identify him as the murderer.
And then the doorbell rang as Mr. Adams pressed it . . .

The book was widely reviewed, the press made extensive quotations, and another wave of public anxiety, if not indignation, grew. The *Morning Post* ran a strong leading article in Slater's favour and in the same issue (August 1, 1927) Edgar Wallace, the famous crime novelist, reviewed the book. 'Nothing,' he wrote, 'was said of the bloodstained chair because it did not fit in with the case which had been manufactured against Slater. And no questions were asked of Lambie that were in any way inconvenient to the prosecution . . .'

Did all this tremendous outcry and mountain of evidence shift the Secretary of State for Scotland? Not a bit of it. A copy of the book was sent personally to him but when on July 29 the new Lord Advocate, the Rt. Hon. W. Watson, K.C., was asked in the House of Commons once again whether yet another enquiry would be granted, he replied that 'if it were I would be very much suprised'.

Lawyers, journalists and M.P.s now coincided in the view that this simply was not good enough. Once more Conan Doyle took up the cudgels, this time writing a strong note to Ramsay MacDonald who, to his eternal credit, quickly recognized the possibility of a terrible injustice. He proceeded to read Park's book, wrote to the Lord Advocate and addressed a letter to Conan Doyle on September 26: 'I have been going into the case and am quite convinced that this man has received a most horrible injustice and that the matter must be wound up, not only by releasing him but by clearing him.'

The *Daily News* did not wait for the official mill to grind out its slow legal grist. The editor appointed E. Clepham Palmer as a special correspondent to write a daily article on the case, selecting a new aspect to attack every day for a whole month.

So it was that half of England fell once again to talking about the case and the wave of public protest continued to mount. On October 23 came a dramatic interview in the *Sunday Empire News* with the identification witness, Lambie, which brought the last pillar of the case for the prosecution crashing down. Lambie was reported as saying:

'When I told the police the name of the man I thought I recognized, they replied "Nonsense—you don't think he could have murdered and robbed your mistress!" They scoffed so much at the notion of this man being the one I had seen that

I allowed myself to be persuaded, that I had been mistaken . . .

'I had my reasons for not looking too closely. The man I thought I saw coming out of the flat had been visiting Mrs. Gilchrist on another occasion and I happened to mention his name to my mistress afterwards.

'She flew into a temper with me and told me that if I ever displayed the slightest curiosity again about any of her visitors she would discharge me without a character . . .'

At least one Scottish paper immediately implied that these words had been put into Lambie's mouth by one of 'those' who had fought to clear Slater's name.

Whatever doubts arose around Lambie's confession, there was no questioning a similar act of penitence from the other key Crown witness, which finally appeared in the *Daily News* for November 5, 1927. Since the 1914 enquiry, Miss Barrowman had vanished from the scene but now it was not the police, or any agent of the law, who broke through a mass of confusing trails to trace her: it was an intense collaboration between Clepham Palmer, Park and—of all people—an ex-convict. Once again a group of private citizens banded together and ruthlessly pursued their quest to finally crush the verdict of the State.

This time Miss Barrowman's confession was exact, unequivocal and vouched for as authentic by her own signature.

'. . . I only thought at the time that [Slater] was very like the man I had seen, and I did not say in my identification that he positively was the man . . .

'It was when I was returned to Glasgow that the question of Slater being positively the man was brought before my notice. This was done by Mr. Hart, the Fiscal.

'This gentleman was most severe in his treatment of me as a witness. He made me appear at his office day after day to have a meeting with him.

'I should say that I was in attendance at his office for the purpose of going over my evidence on at least fifteen occasions . . .

'It was the same routine every day. He went over my evidence himself doing all the talking and I for the most part listening. He was so much the director of things that were to be said that I had no opportunity, or very little, to have my say.

'It was Mr. Hart who got me to change my statement from being "very like the man" to the emphatic declaration that Slater "was the man" . . .

'I was just a girl of fifteen then and did not fully appreciate the difference . . .

By now the case for another enquiry into the Slater case not only seemed overwhelming, but morally imperative. And what was the Scottish Secretary's reply to a tenth repeated question in the House? 'Oscar Slater has now completed more than eighteen and a half years of his life sentence and I have felt justified in deciding to authorize his release on licence as soon as suitable arrangements can be made.'

Outrageous! That was the word which sprang to the lips of Sir Arthur Conan Doyle, and the *Morning Post* in its mandarin English prose echoed a similar reaction.

At three o'clock on Monday afternoon, November 14, 1927, the great gates of Peterhead Prison opened and Rabbi Phillips collected a man very different from the person who had entered the prison all those years ago. He wore the same clothes which they had taken from him, but he looked like an old-fashioned farm labourer. 'I am tired,' he said. 'I have not slept for the last five nights since I heard I was coming back again. I want rest. I want rest.' But the newspaper reporters and photographers had to have their story. A milling crowd literally pursued him from the prison for the next twenty-four hours.

As the national press blazoned its interviews and photographs across the front pages, Conan Doyle struck his last powerful blow. He circularized Members of the House of Commons with a letter vividly exploiting his writer's skill to recapitulate the incredible facts of the case and demand a really impartial enquiry. At last, on November 15, the Secretary of State for Scotland had to give way. It was useless trying to protect certain officials in the case any longer. Providing the House would pass a brief Act giving retrospective effect to Section 16 of the Criminal Appeal (Scotland) Act of 1926 he would, he said, 'remit all questions concerning the case to that Court'.

It was not until June 8, 1928, that the words, 'Call the appeal of Oscar Slater against His Majesty's Advocate', echoed round

7*

the crowded benches of the High Court of Edinburgh. The scene was the same as twenty years before, but the cast for the drama which followed very different. Instead of one fallible judge, Lord Guthrie, there were five judges of Appeal, Lord Clyde the Lord Justice General, Lord Alness the Lord Justice Clerk, Lord Sands, Lord Blackburn and Lord Fleming . . . For the former prisoner Slater appeared Mr. Craigie Aitchison, K.C., Mr. Watson and Mr. Clyde, with the Crown represented by the Lord Advocate and Mr. Alexander Maitland, senior advocate deputy. In what the Scottish court called 'the free seats' among the ordinary public sat a quite new Oscar Slater —'bronzed, stalward and well-groomed'—his eye moving round the crowded court with just a hint of sarcasm. All this panoply of judges, robes and wigs, all these deliberately old-fashioned ceremonials, had once brought him, utterly falsely, within a step of the gallows. What did he think of it all as he sat in exactly the same court a second time? No one precisely knows. Not far from him sat a second famous figure, that of Sir Arthur Conan Doyle who had come far north to spend a whole week watching the final scene of a drama for the initiation of which he was in considerable part responsible.

To cut the whole long tortured story short, Mr. Aitchison, for Slater, now appealed for leave to lead on further evidence and the 'recovery of certain documents'. The case he built up brought together Helen Lambie's recantation, the deposition of Duncan McBrayne now dead, nine witnesses who had never been called as to the so-called 'flight from justice', the absurd anomalies of identification, medical evidence to dispute the hammer as the weapon which caused death, misdirection of the presiding judge, and many other points of detail.

Equally vital was Aitchison's statement that he wished to recall Helen Lambie—if she could be made forthcoming.

'According to our information, a week before the crime, Helen Lambie who was a maid in the service of Mrs. Gilchrist, went to her former mistress who is still alive, without . . . any explanation whatever of why she had come. She had not seen that lady for three and a half years. She told her former mistress that there were strange goings-on in the house of Mrs. Gilchrist . . . and that Mrs. Gilchrist said she was going to be murdered. The most significant thing of all that Helen Lambie said was in answer to a question by her former mistress whether anyone could obtain access to the house in the maid's absence. She replied that no one could gain access to the house unless a pre-arranged signal was given. A week after the crime, Helen Lambie returned to the same lady: and on that occasion being asked how the man who committed the crime could have got access to the house, she did not answer the question but volunteered the information with very great emphasis that she would not know the man again: and on being pressed as to how the man got in and being reminded of her former statement that he could only get in in accordance with a pre-arranged signal, she became agitated and denied that she had ever made any such statement . . .'

Their Lordships listened to all this with suitable detachment, but to Slater there was something farcical in their solemn retirement to consider what parts of the new evidence would be legally admissible. His fury knew no bounds when he, as the appellant, heard their spokesman finally declare that 'it would be quite unreasonable to spend time over [Slater's] examination now and the Court, therefore, is not prepared to allow his evidence to be received'. This was partly the result of Aitchison stating that Slater had nothing new to say and 'that his evidence would amount to nothing more than a repetition of his plea of "not guilty" '. For the rest, most of the remaining counts of new evidence were admissible, but this did not stop Slater—now convinced that the long conspiracy against him had begun anew—rushing off to attempt to with-draw his appeal altogether. Once again the dramatic news hit the headlines the following morning: '*Slater Wants to Drop Appeal*'. Many people now combined to persuade him to change his mind once more, including Conan Doyle, and at last Slater agreed to allow the appeal to continue.

For four long days Aitchison proceeded to riddle, detail by detail, the greater part of the case against Slater and when on Thursday, July 12 the Lord Advocate rose to reply for the Crown, he faced not only a formidable, but a highly embar-rassing task.

William Roughhead, the great criminal historian, who was present at the Appeal wrote:

'As regards the Crown conduct of the case, he held that the

Lord Advocate at the trial was entitled from the evidence to draw the inference that the appellant knew the murdered woman was possessed of jewels and that he dealt dishonestly in jewels. As to the attack upon the accused's character, no objection was taken when questions regarding his mode of life were put. That was equally the case with regard to the Judge's charge . . .

'On the conclusion of his address which occupied over two hours and was marked throughout by dignity and moderation in the discharge of a necessary duty—judgment was reserved and the court adjourned.'

'Dignity and moderation . . .' What a sham those words were to Oscar Slater. Perhaps a little more dignity and moderation and a little less browbeating and duplicity in the first place would have made 'a necessary duty' completely unnecessary.

Worse was to follow. On Friday, July 20, the day of the final scene, the Lord Justice General read the written findings of the Court. There were four points on which the appeal could succeed or fail:

(1) Whether the jury's verdict was unreasonable or unsupported by evidence. Answer—the appeal failed.

(2) Whether any new facts had been disclosed material to the issue. Answer—amazingly—failed.

(3) Whether the appellant had suffered prejudice by nondisclosure of the evidence to the Crown. Answer—against every conceivable use of the faculty of reason—failed.

As he heard one count after another dismissed, Slater 'leaning forward in his place with his hand behind his ear strained every nerve in his anxiety to follow the low, rapid reading of the judgment'.

It could not be. It simply could not be. Failed on the first three counts and he must be lost, condemned to public execration for the rest of his days. And then—how grudging could these gentlemen of the law be in their concern to mask the terrible record of the first prosecutors—on the fourth count (misdirection of the presiding judge) the Court held that Slater's conviction must be quashed.

So, after all the multiplicity of damning details which riddled the conspiracy against him, Slater had been saved on

one miserable count alone. It was not only a vindication of
Slater; it was an attempt to vindicate the law too.

As Peter Hunt concluded in his excellent and, in some
senses, definitive account of the case:

'Nineteen and a half years did not alter [the] misdirection:
it was no more or less wrong in 1928 than it was in 1909.

'This was pointed out in the Memorial which Slater's agents
submitted to Lord Pentland after his conviction. Nothing was
done about it . . .

'Lord Guthrie had made material alterations to his charge
to the jury in the *published* report. Nothing was done about that
either.

'Lord Clyde had been Lord Advocate from 1916–20. In
1920 he had been appointed Lord Justice General and Lord
President of the Court of Session. What did he ever do to right
the misdirections and mis-statements of his learned friends?'

Behind all this there stands the biggest criminal of all, a
ghost figure who could conceivably have been sitting among the
public at the very last scene in the Court of Appeal—the
actual murderer. He continues to haunt the scene. He may still
be alive today, although that is unlikely. But Helen Lambie
never came forward to identify him.

There remains a depressing postscript. Amazingly, the
Secretary of State for Scotland, when questioned about compensation said: 'I think it proper that the person concerned
ought to have a reasonable opportunity of putting forward any
claim he may wish to make.'

The words 'proper' and 'reasonable' seemed hopelessly
inadequate to the occasion. Not unexpectedly Slater refused
—himself—to put in any such claim. Clearly it was up to the
Secretary of State to make not only an offer but a very generous
one indeed. When it came, for the once more inadequate sum
of £6,000, no mention was made of costs. It then transpired
that Sir Arthur Conan Doyle had generously agreed to under-
write these before the trial. A defence fund had raised by
public subscription £700 of the £1,500 involved, but no
further offer came from the Government and sadly, the man
who had fought so long and so courageously, Sir Arthur Conan
Doyle, found himself forced to meet the remaining £800.

POSTSCRIPT

ONE SOFT SUMMER day in July 1954 the *Jaroslav Dabrowski* was lying alongside Mark Brown's wharf in London's dockland, flying the flag of Communist Poland. Two English dockers from Bermondsey, James Walsh and Sidney Palmer, were unloading huge bales of wood wool from No. 5 hold when a long thin arm reached out and a weak voice cried: 'English police! Water . . . please . . . water!' The dockers rushed over to the boxes and found a man lying there too weak to stand. They swiftly carried him to the 'scale-board' by which the crane lifted cargo out of the holds, but as the crane driver engaged the clutch and saw a man instead of cargo coming up from the hold, he stopped the engine at once. This was fatal. Members of the crew rushed forward, seized the man swinging in mid-air and carried him off to lock him away in a cabin.

The two dockers went on with their unloading, but they were troubled by a surly sense of having witnessed an injustice. Later they agreed that they must deliberately spread the story abroad when they went ashore and try to stimulate interest in the stowaway's plight. In the pub that night the story was repeated endlessly and half a dozen dockers decided that more drastic action should be taken. A man was being held against his will aboard a ship in a British port—and that was no way to behave. They reported the matter first to the immigration authorities and the following day a British officer went aboard the ship and asked to interrogate the man. The captain acted as interpreter and the immigration officer concluded that he was dealing with an ordinary stowaway named Klimowicz whose fate—legally—must lie in the hands of the master of the ship. He therefore refused him permission to land.

But he had reckoned without the tenacity of purpose which possessed the two dockers, Walsh and Palmer, and the fury which their story aroused among London's Polish community. The Poles knew from the dockers that Klimowicz had asked for the English police, in what was obviously a carefully rehearsed phrase, and to them that meant only one thing: he wanted political asylum.

The ship had docked on Wednesday night but Klimowicz was not discovered until Thursday afternoon, July 29. By Friday a big demonstration developed at the quayside, consisting of dockers and Polish refugees. Daily and evening papers had been tipped off and scores of reporters and photographers appeared on the scene. What the dockers did not realize was that the reporters were there mainly to cover the departure of two American citizens, Dr. Joseph Cort and his wife, both long-term residents in Britain. When Dr. Cort received his call-up papers from the American Consulate he publicly announced that he would not return to his native United States to face 'terror and persecution' for his pro-Communist views, but would travel to Czechoslovakia to 'live in a free country'.

The coincidence of one person claiming political asylum and the others fleeing from American persecution was ironic enough to give the reporters and photographers a field day. It simultaneously added numbers to the demonstration for Klimowicz and confused the issue. All the chanting of 'We want Klimowicz' and the threats of 'No more unloading' had no effect on the Polish ship's captain.

Something more powerful was required. How could they arouse not only public opinion, but the law, on Klimowicz's behalf? As it then stood, international law regarded him as a stowaway under the captain's jurisdiction, but supposing, one Pole argued, some trumped up charge could be brought against Klimowicz to answer which he must appear in a British law court. It is now possible to reveal that the Pole was the distinguished lawyer Jan Jaxa and he came up with what seemed the obvious solution.

A special police squad was guarding the ship as a result of Dr. Cort's departure and now Jan Jaxa rushed over to the inspector in charge and said: 'That man Klimowicz stole my wallet. I want him arrested before he leaves British jurisdiction.'

The inspector saw through the ruse at once and replied: 'I'm sorry, I can't arrest him.'

The argument which followed in the middle of a threatening crowd became angry, but the police inspector was adamant. At this stage the average citizen would have abandoned the cause and regretfully retired from the scene, but the spontaneous combustion of moral indignation reached a new pitch when the crowd heard that the captain had arranged to hurry the departure of the *Jaroslav Dabrowski*.

One last line of appeal to English justice remained open and Jan Jaxa knew how to use it. As he later wrote in an unpublished document: 'A dramatic race against time and tide now started. It was then about 11.30 and there was roughly an hour before the ship sailed. With screeching tyres I raced through the now empty streets of London . . . Having reached the private house of a magistrate I made a deposition to the effect that Klimowicz stole my wallet during one of his previous visits to London. The magistrate, in his pyjamas and dressing gown, signed my deposition.'

He rushed back to Mark Brown's Wharf and presented a signed document to the police inspector, who remained unimpressed: 'I'm sorry, sir. Your information is inaccurate.'

Another crowd had gathered and another demonstration took place. At its height, Jan Jaxa turned to the crowd and called: 'Gentlemen, you have just witnessed murder. No action will be taken.'

Still the police inspector refused. By now the Thames pilot had gone aboard the *Jaroslav Dabrowski* and it looked as though all was lost. But what had begun as a small-scale demonstration was now converted by four or five ordinary citizens into a public outcry and newspaper reporters once more flocked around the ship.

By Saturday morning the story had become a headline story and—unknown to the agitators—Winston Churchill himself began to take a personal interest. He asked to be kept informed of every new move in the situation and remarked to the Prime Minister, Harold Macmillan, that one law and one law only could fit such 'a dastardly conspiracy—Habeas Corpus'.

As everyone knows, this lays it down that no man must be held under arrest in Britain by the police for more than twenty-four hours without a charge being brought against him.

By Saturday morning, Jan Jaxa too had decided to invoke Habeas Corpus on behalf of Klimowicz, but this was the Saturday of an English August Bank Holiday and he knew too well what that meant—the wheels of commerce, shipping, business and, above all, justice simply ground to a halt.

No less determined than the dockers, he managed to contact the Registrar of the High Court of Justice and presented his case so vigorously that this gentleman broke all legal precedents and agreed to stand by with his staff ready for action.

By now matters had taken a far more decisive turn. The *Jaroslav Dabrowski* had set sail and was heading down the Thames towards the open sea. Speed became of paramount importance. Jaxa did not hesitate to take a taxi and break into the sacrosanct privacy of a High Court judge on a Bank Holiday weekend. His reception by the Hon. Mr. Justice Davies nonetheless staggered him. No questions of niceties of etiquette arose but instead came a blunt statement: 'It is already under control . . .'

The high wind of rumour and agitation had anticipated the request and Jaxa found that Lord Goddard, the Lord Chief Justice of England, had just informed Mr. Justice Davies that leave was granted to take out a writ of Habeas Corpus.

The Home Office now issued its first official communiqué: 'The Lord Chief Justice has given leave to issue a writ requiring the master of the ship *Jaroslav Dabrowski* to produce A. Klimowicz at the Law Courts on Tuesday next. The matter is, therefore, *sub judice* and no further statement can be made at present.'

The Polish Ambassador had already been consulted and asked to give instructions to Captain Glowacki, the master of the ship, 'to make Klimowicz available'. He replied that the man was a stowaway and he had no power to intervene. Jan Jaxa, the Home Office and Foreign Office were all busy telephoning one another over the next hour, Jaxa stressing the critical urgency of taking action before the *Jaroslav Dabrowski* escaped from the Thames.

The Home Office said that they must give the Polish Ambassador time to consult his government in Warsaw and Jaxa said the delay might prove fatal. At 7.15 p.m. the Polish Ambassador telephoned the Home Office and said that he had communicated with his Government who completely endorsed his ruling on the matter. Nothing more could be done.

Still the writ of Habeas Corpus remained unserved and now despair overtook many of those engaged in this private prosecution. Niceties of diplomatic etiquette and bureaucratic discretion threatened to allow the ship to escape.

Two more hours went by with the telephone lines between private prosecutors and public bodies exchanging on one side urgent and the other blandly reassuring messages.

At 4 p.m. on Saturday, the Polish Ambassador was invited to call at the Home Office and there Sir John Nott-Bower, Commissioner of the Metropolitan Police, showed him a copy of the writ of Habeas Corpus. It left the Ambassador completely unimpressed. Once more he was asked to communicate with the ship's master and have him deliver up the person of Klimowicz. The Ambassador said he could do no such thing.

By now action seemed inevitable—but did not follow. The crusaders learnt to their total dismay that Home Office procedure required time to be given the Ambassador to contact the ship's master once more. It seemed to them complete madness. It was an empty formula and could only waste the last precious hours when the ship could be stopped.

Meanwhile the *Jaroslav Dabrowski* steamed full speed ahead towards the sea. And then at last, at Erith River Police Station, urgent orders went out for every available police launch to go in pursuit. The destroyer *Obdurate* proceeded to the scene late on Saturday night, July 31, from the Pool of London and a second destroyer stood by in readiness at Chatham. Simultaneously 120 river police accompanied by the Commissioner of the Metropolitan Police himself boarded police launches and joined the chase.

Aboard the *Jaroslav Dabrowski*—as he later related—Klimowicz, locked in a small cabin without a light, kept his ears pricked to detect the first murmur of the ship's engines, a sound fatally indicating that they were free of the pilot and almost clear of the Thames. Instead came the confusing noises of many smaller engines with one big monster in the background and, simultaneously, he felt the *Jaroslav Dabrowski* lose speed and begin to wallow to a halt. The police launches had surrounded the ship and with the threat of the destroyer in the background forced her to stop.

But this was only the beginning of more dramatic developments. The ship had been brought to a halt in Woolwich Reach and was now ordered by the Port of London Authority to moor at Rainham Buoys. The first man aboard was a representative from the Polish Embassy but immediately afterwards nearly a hundred policemen, led by Sir John Nott-Bower, clambered up her ladders. While the ten launches continued to circle the ship, Nott-Bower solemnly delivered to Captain Glowacki that time-honoured document—a writ of Habeas Corpus. The captain stood firm, shook his head and simply refused to co-operate. When told that a search would be made for Klimowicz, he shrugged his shoulders. The police then began the search and nearly an hour went by with a new posse of police taking up positions on the jetty at Erith in case they were needed.

Finally the river police narrowed their search to the locked door of Klimowicz's cabin and the captain was requested to open it. He refused and the police hacked open the door with fire axes. The first to greet the pale, staggering Klimowicz was a Polish-speaking immigration officer. His opening words were classic: 'You are free.'

By now several members of the crew had become threatening, scuffles broke out, a truncheon rose and fell and then a Greek seaman leapt at Klimowicz and tried to knife him. A policeman jumped on him and before he could use the knife knocked him down.

Later an official Home Office communiqué said that 80 not 120 police were used, someone incited the crew to attack, and when an ugly situation arose 'it became necessary for the police to take prompt measures to prevent it developing'.

Klimowicz was hurried off the ship at 11.30 in the evening and spent the night in Erith Police Station. Clearance papers were then granted the *Jaroslav Dabrowski* and she caught the tide at 4 a.m. the next morning.

Two more campaigners cannot be overlooked in this account
—Mr. S. Soboniewski, Chairman of the Polish Ex-Combatants'
Association and Mr. S. Lis, Chairman of the Federation of
Poles in Great Britain. They visited the Home Office and urged
the Home Secretary to grant Klimowicz political asylum,
simultaneously offering him legal aid. The Home Office then
issued another bland statement which said that (1) 'arrangements had been made to ensure compliance with the direction
of the Lord Chief Justice'; (2) 'Klimowicz was no longer considered as under detention'; and (3) 'it was not the practice
of the Home Office to reveal the whereabouts of individual
aliens'. At this point in the story Jan Jaxa took over as
Klimowicz's legal representative and briefed Mr. Glanville
Brown to appear on his behalf.

Three days later, Klimowicz with his lawyers appeared
before Lord Goddard in his private room at the Law Courts.
In order to avoid any further publicity or the dangers of an
attempted kidnap, Klimowicz entered and left the Law Courts
by a private gate at the rear. Once more came a bland communiqué: 'All further proceedings over the writ of Habeas
Corpus have been stayed. Mr. Klimowicz's future is a matter
for the Home Secretary under the Aliens Order of 1953 but he
has already been granted leave to land for a week.'

The Polish Ex-Combatants' Association busied itself applying
to the Home Office for a work permit and sent a special letter
of thanks to the dockers who had initiated the whole fantastic
affair.

By now the Polish equivalent of the British Home Office had
addressed a note to the British Embassy in Warsaw strongly
protesting against the course events had taken and claiming that
Klimowicz was a criminal who had been discharged from the
Polish Merchant Navy.

When, at last, the Home Office granted him political asylum
he revealed many of the missing details from his side of the
story. It was quite true, he said, that he had been discharged
as a deck hand from the *Jaroslav Dabrowski* in 1951 but not for
criminal reasons. He had refused to act as an informer in
collaboration with the *Jaroslav Dabrowski*'s political officer. It
was then that he had first thought of escaping from Poland,
but after his discharge he had been quickly conscripted into

the Polish Army where he served for two years as a private. When he tried once more to go to sea he was told that his political record precluded the Merchant Navy and he must take a shore-based job. Thoroughly disillusioned, he made his first real attempt to escape in February but he lacked sufficiently convincing papers to pass the guards at the gangway of the *Jaroslav Dabrowski*. For the second attempt he decided to use his old merchant seaman papers merely faking new dates. He managed to brazen his way past the two soldiers on the ship's gangway, and quickly hid himself in the hold but, to his total dismay, mechanical troubles delayed the ship from sailing for forty-eight hours. When at last he heard the engines beginning to stir, he was already suffering from hunger and thirst and now he became very alarmed to think of the days which lay ahead before they reached London. His anxieties grew every hour. Time and again he thought that he could not stand the hunger, discomfort and smell any longer and must give himself up—but he stiffened his resolution and remained in hiding. Nearly seven unbelievably long, tormenting days he remained, cramped, hungry and sometimes afraid of suffocation in the hold of the ship. He was without food or drink from 8 p.m. on July 22 until 4 p.m. on Tuesday afternoon, July 29. No wonder the man eventually discovered by the dockers at Mark Brown's wharf resembled a ghost.

Almost from that first hour of discovery sustained efforts were made by representatives of the Polish Embassy to persuade him to return to Poland. They boarded the ship, asked him to sign a statement saying he desired to return to Poland and when he refused offered him a better job in Warsaw and a free pardon. Still he refused and now the threats began. 'They called me a traitor, a swine and a dog and did everything in their power to stop England taking me.'

Questioned about his alleged criminal record he said he had been punished by the British authorities for trying to smuggle a camera ashore . . . because seamen were very poorly paid and he wanted to exchange it for nylons or razor blades. But he was never convicted of anything in Poland.

Klimowicz finally went to live in the United States where he first lectured on his experiences and then joined the staff of a cosmetic factory.

SELECT
BIBLIOGRAPHY

S. AKEMAN, *Thornton's Trial-Wager of Battle* (1818)

AN ATTORNEY AT LAW, *An Investigation of the Case of Abraham Thornton* (1818)

JOHN DICKSON CARR, *Life of Sir Arthur Conan Doyle*

J. COOPER, *Report of the Proceedings Against Abraham Thornton* (1818)

SIR ARTHUR CONAN DOYLE, *The Case of Oscar Slater* (1912)
Memories and Adventures (1930)

J. FAIRBURN, *Thornton's Second Trial* (1818)

W. J. FOWLER, *Remarks in Reference to the Murder of Mary Ashford* (1879)

R. T. GOULD, *Enigmas* (1946)

SIR JOHN HALL, *The Trial of Abraham Thornton* (1926)

P. HUNT, *Oscar Slater* (1951)

H. MONTGOMERY HYDE, *Sir Edward Carson* (1953)

W. PARK, *The Truth About Oscar Slater* (1927)

W. ROUGHHEAD, *The Trial of Oscar Slater*—1st ed. (1910)
The Trial of Oscar Slater—2nd ed. (1915)
The Trial of Oscar Slater—3rd ed. (1929)
The Trial of Oscar Slater—4th ed. (1950)
Knaves' Looking Glass (1951)

G. R. SIMS, *Two King's Pardons* (1904)

E. R. WATSON, *The Trial of Adolf Beck* (1924)

G. W. WILTON, *Fingerprints* (1938)

Other Sources

1. Seventy unpublished letters supplied by Anthony Negretti on the Pelizzioni case.
2. Jan Jaxa's unpublished dossier on the Klimowicz case.
3. Unpublished interview material on the George Archer-Shee case.
4. Scores of reports from a wide range of national and local newspapers.
5. Official report of Slater's extradition proceedings in New York.

INDEX